PARTITIONED BORGU

State, Society and Politics in a West African Border Region

Adonis & Abbey Publishers Ltd

St James House
13 Kensington Square,
London, W8 5HD
United Kingdom

Website: http://www.adonis-abbey.com
E-mail Address: editor@adonis-abbey.com

Nigeria:
Suites C4 – C6 J-Plus Plaza
Asokoro, Abuja, Nigeria
Tel: +234 (0) 7058078841/08052035034

Copyright 2019 © Hussaini Abdu

British Library Cataloguing-in-Publication Data
A catalogue record for this book is available from the British Library

ISBN: 978-1-906704-21-6(PB)
      978-1-906704-20-9(HB)

The moral right of the author has been asserted

All rights reserved. No part of this book may be reproduced, stored in a retrieval system or transmitted at any time or by any means without the prior permission of the publisher

PARTITIONED BORGU

State, Society and Politics in a West African Border Region

Hussaini Abdu

Table of Contents

Dedication xi
Acknowledgement xii
Foreword xv

INTRODUCTION 21
    Sources and Analytical Framework 27
    Geography and People 30
    Problem of Etymology 31
    Ethnogenesis and Pluri-ethnic Formation 32

PRE-COLONIAL BORGU

CHAPTER ONE
Early States and Societies 45
    State and Political Formation 48
    Kisra Myth and Politics 51
    Pre-dynastic Political Organisation 61
    Settlement Pattern 67
    Occupational Groups 68
    Kinship and Lineage Groups 71
    Religion and Society 77
    Trade and Islam 81

CHAPTER TWO
Political Centralisation and Dynastic Politics 85
    Political and Governance Structure 90
    Territorial Organisation 97
    Fiscal System 101

 Defence and Military Organisation 102

 Confederacy and Inter-State Relations 105

 Dynastic Politics and Succession 111

 Women and Dynastic politics 118

CHAPTER THREE
Pre-Colonial State and Economy 121

 Agriculture and Peasantry 122

 Local Industry 124

 Means of Exchange 126

 Slavery and Slave Trade 128

 Long Distance Commodity Trade 134

 Aristocracy, Banditry and Economy 143

CHAPTER FOUR
Pre-Colonial Borgu and its Neighbours 147

 Songhai in Borgu History and Politics 148

 Borgu and Hausa Relations 152

 Borgu Factor in Oyo (Yoruba) Political History 155

BORGU UNDER COLONIAL RULE

CHAPTER FIVE
European Scramble and Partitioning of Borgu 169

 The Scramble for Borgu 172

 Steeplechase for Nikki 176

 Anglo-French Military Occupation and Hostilities 181

 Final Negotiation and Partitioning of Borgu 186

CHAPTER SIX
Colonial Administration in Borgu 191

 Colonial Administration in British Borgu 192

    Native Authority Structure and System 198

    Native Authority and Borgu Aristocracy 209

    Colonial Administration in French Borgu 215

CHAPTER SEVEN
Anti-Colonial Revolt in Borgu 223

    Revolt in British Borgu 224

    Revolt in French Borgu 234

CHAPTER EIGHT
Amalgamation of Kaiama and Bussa Emirates 243

    Abdication of Emir of Kaiama 245

    Emergence of Borgu Emirate 251

    From Emir to District Head: Kaiama in a New Era 254

CHAPTER NINE
Politics and Development under Colonial Rule 261

    Forced Migration and Depopulation of Borgu 266

    Economic Stagnation and Social Services 270

    Colonial Education 272

    Colonial Control and Water Crisis 276

CHAPTER TEN
Colonialism, Identity Politics and Intergroup Relations 277

    Colonial Cartography and Social Differentiation 279

    Invented Identities 280

    Intergroup Relations in French Borgu 293

POST-COLONIAL BORGU

CHAPTER ELEVEN
Continuity and Change in Post-Colonial Borgu 301

    Colonial Partition and Post-Colonial Identity 303

Dynamics of Post-Colonial Development 306
Dilemma of Urban Preference and Rural Exclusion 312
Dilemma of Geography, Population and Political Structure .. 315
Dilemma of Roads, Poverty and Exclusion 319
Dilemma of informal Institutions, Networks and State Capture 324
Dilemma of Weak State and Weak Society 331

CONCLUSION 337
Reversing the Trend: Agenda for Development 337
Compensatory and Strategic State investment 338
Transport and communication infrastructure 339
Trans-frontier Regional Integration 342
Small Towns and Urban connectivity 343
Civil Society and Participatory Governance 346
Conclusion 348

REFERENCES 351
INDEX 393

List of Tables

Names According to Hierarchy of birth 74

Common Princely Names of Nikki and Kaiama 75

Cowries to Mithqal with days of Journey 127

Bussa Native Administration tax 1940 – 1941 207

Jangani Tax, Kaiama Emirate 1941 – 1946 208

Tax and representation 253

Population Distribution of Borgu 1933 – 1934 269

Tax Revenue 1928 – 1938 270

Population of Borgu (Nigeria) 317

Kaiama NA Administration, Proposed Works Budget 1941–1941 .. 322

Maps and Illustrations

Precolonial Borgu xxi
Kisra Map.. 60
Trade Routes to the Volta Basin 142
The Partioned Borgu 187
Borgu in Nigeria: Districts Lost by Nikki 1898.................................. 189
Provinces of Northern Nigeria 1906 195
Dilemma of Development in Borgu.. 312
Patron-Client Structure 328

Abbreviations

ADP	Agricultural Development Programme
AG	Action Group
AR	Annual Report
ASR	Annual Assessment Report
AU	African Union
BORGUDIST	Borgu District
BORGUDIV	Borgu Division
CSO	Civil Society Organisation
DO	District Officer
DOB	Borgu Division
DFFRI	Directorate of Food, Roads and Rural Infrastructure
ECOWAS	Economic Community of West African States
EU	European Union
FAO	Food and Agriculture Organisation
FERMA	Federal Road Maintanace Agency
FGN	Federal Government of Nigeria
GDP	Gross Domestic Product
NA	Native Authority
NAK	National Archive Kaduna
NAI	National Archives Ibadan
NEPU	Northern Element Progressive Union
NPN	National Party of Nigeria
IBRD	International Bank for Reconstruction and Development
ILORPROF	Ilorin Province File
ITP	Ilorin Talaka Parapo (a political Party)
OAU	Organisation of African Unity
PRP	Peoples Redemption Party
PRPB	*Parti de la Révolution Popualaire du Bénin*
RWAFF	Royal West African Frontier Force
SAP	Structural Adjustment Programme
WB	World Bank
UNDP	United Nations Development Programme
UNESCO	United Nations Educational, Scientific and Cultural Organisation

Dedication

In memory of
Fatima Manu Abdullahi-Maikano,
my loving mother who died in August 2017.

Acknowledgement

This book was long in coming. I contemplated something like it for a while and made feeble attempts that went nowhere. However, when the notion came to my mind to push on with the project in memory of my mother, Fatima Abdullahi Maikano, things changed; the book in your hands started to become concrete. Leads to pursue and a structure to hang them on came in quick succession. She was my teacher and mentor. My initial account of the history and social structure of Borgu was from her and her father (my grandfather), Sulaiman Yerima Kura (*Akuto*) and her older cousin, Musa Zume Yerima (*Baa Giya Kpandu*). I still relish the stories: a combination of fables, myths and realities all presented as history.

Completing this work in a timely manner has been the result of the contributions, support, encouragement and help I received from a diverse set of people, amongst them family, friends, colleagues, research partners, mentors and respondents.

I take this privilege to unconventionally start with my immediate family. In most cases, this comes last. I am particularly grateful to my wife, Rahina, my Number 1 critic, adviser and fan. She would always question my style, "Note that not everyone who reads you is an academic." I am certain that her comments and criticism have helped in improving the "readability" and lucidity of this work. I am equally grateful to my children for believing in me. They were always excited each time I told them a little bit about this book. I thank them all for tolerating my frequent travels, and for accepting my responses to their queries: Salim, himself an author (*Bionic Evolution*, a science fiction novel), Bilkisu, Abdallah and Amin-Adam. Having them around me and thoughts about their future, the future of our country and Africa made this work all the more compelling. I particularly appreciate the encouragement of my extended family in Gwangwazo, Kano. The colonial expiriences of our late patriarch, Alhaji Abubakar Kaiama (*Galadiman Tsafta* and *Wazirin* Kaiama) inspired the present effort.

In researching this work, I benefitted substantially from conversations with a lot of people within and outside Borgu. I appreciate the insights of M. T. Omar (*Ciroman* Kaiama), Mohammed Idris, Hussaini Lafia, Senator Sadiq Umar Suleiman, Zakari Musa,

Tijani Yari Ahmed, Saifudeen Aliyu, Shero Boni, Bio Adamou Mako, Adamu Bawa Isa, Ahmed Musa (Abass), Tanimudari Zakari, Mohammed Baba Jibrin, Mohammed Ladan, Ahmed Baba Jibrin, and Abubakar Bani Usman, just to mention a few. Combing the National Archives at Kaduna and Ibadan would have been an uphill task without the support of Abdullahi Bawa, a staff of the National Archives, Kaduna and native of Borgu who diligently supported my research effort, sometimes photocopying and sending archival materials when I was unable to be physically present.

I have been very fortunate to have mentors, teachers, friends and colleagues whose years of engagement have contributed to developing my personality and intellectual capacity. Professor Attahiru Jega, Professor Jibrin Ibrahim, Dr. Kole Shettima, Muazu Yusif, Ibrahim Muazzam, Y. Z. Ya'u, Salihu Lukman, Naseer Kura, Auwalu Ibrahim Musa (Rafsanjani), Dr. Otive Igbuzor, Professor Dung Pam Sha, Professor Sam Egwu, Dr. Aliyu Dadan Garba, Professor Abdullahi Ashafa, Dr. Sanusi Abdullahi, Dr. Adedeji Ebo, Innocent Chukwuma, Sandeep Chachra, Hong Pong Thao and Umar Tabari Yero. The years of interaction, those passionate side discussions, advice, encouragement and queries have brought out the best in me.

I also benefitted a great deal from critical reviews and comments by scholars and friends particularly Professor Kyari Mohammad, Professor Mahmood Yakubu, Professor Etannibi Alemika, Professor Anthony Asiwaju and Professor Farooq Kperogi. I am particularly grateful to Professor Kperogi, a native of Borgu, for the incisive comments and queries on the manuscript. This significantly contributed to strengthening the quality of the book. I want to especially thank Professor Asiwaju, Professor Emeritus at the University of Lagos and a pioneer border and borderland scholar in Africa. He is one of the few Nigerian scholars to have written on Borgu. Professor Asiwaju did not only provide valuable comments on the manuscript, but he also volunteered to write the fascinating foreword to this book. I would also like to recognise and appreciate Professor Moreas Farias of Birmingham University, UK, who I met through self-introduction by email. One of the most prominent Borgu scholars, he provided interesting and invaluable literature on pre-colonial Borgu.

I cannot thank my editor, Richard Ali, enough. Richard worked seamlessly with the copy editor, Nkechi Usani, to produce what we have. They made invaluable comments and suggestions on practically every page and advised on the general organisation of the book. Finally, I want to thank my publishers for accepting the work with limited hassles and doing a fantastic job with the production.

Foreword

This is an evidently fascinating study of Borgu, arguably the most adversely impacted, colonially fragmented, single culture area in the Nigeria region, if not in the wider Africa. It is far more significant for a purpose not stated by the author than the one so specifically articulated by him: Whereas the stated objective is to make *Partitioned Borgu* an insightful contribution to the interdisciplinary field of political economy and development studies, the more distinguished purpose served has been to showcase the equally critical and, indeed, closely interconnected, interdisciplinary field of border and borderlands studies.

Whether as a scholarly interest, dwelling on the strictly empirical and theoretical essentials, or at the overlapping strategic level, more explicitly concerned with matters of practical outcomes and public policy making, both intrinsically interconnected, the interdiscipline of Borderlands Studies (i.e. research focusing on affected localities and populations whose social and economic lives are significantly impacted by their proximity to an international boundary or border) has mushroomed since the initial definition and scientific articulation in the mid-1970s by scholars, Americans and also Mexicans, engaged in research in respect of the globally spectacular US-Mexico border and borderlands 'where North meets South.'

The phenomenal world-wide expansion of the specialism is based on adaptation of the research perspective by experts working on similarly challenged localities in Europe and erstwhile Europe-impacted wider-world of the nation-state territorial structure and border problematics. This is evidenced in the radical growth in membership of the now renowned world apex learned society, the Association of Borderlands Studies, which began in 1976 as the Association of Borderlands Scholars that initially embraced pioneer members of admirably mixed disciplinary backgrounds in History, Geography, Anthropology, Political Science, Economics, Public Health, and Environmental Engineering, to name the leading ones. In the late 1980s, the learned society changed the name in recognition, first, of the increasing enrolment of members, even in relation to the US-Mexico borderlands, who were from outside mainstream academia. Secondly, the ever-increasing interest shown in membership by experts from other regions of the world, notably Europe, Africa, South America, and Asia.

The interests outside the initial catchment area of the U.S.-Mexico border and borderlands, hitherto erroneously and narrowly conceived as 'the' border or borderlands, was driven by the demonstrable pertinence to endeavours in these other continents for the widening and deepening of ongoing regional integration processes, primarily to achieve peace, resolve and prevent ubiquitous territorial and boundary conflicts and attain sustainable development through the initiation and systematic promotion of cross-border cooperation and even development with special reference to the demarginalisation of structurally neglected adjoining border regions everywhere in the world of the nation-state territorial structure, especially in regions where the inherited boundaries initially functioned as barriers rather than as bridges between the integrating national economies. In this regard, post-1945 Europe's success story held and, even now, still holds itself out as a model, in spite of the recent trumping up of ultra-nationalist setbacks such that has produced a problematic BREXIT.

Nigeria leads Africa in the insertion into 'modern border studies,' an alternative analytical reference to 'borderlands studies' in which research is focused on international boundaries in the context of the localities that they functionally and significantly impact, as distinct from the 'traditional' or diplomatic category in which borders are viewed strictly as markers of sovereign state territories and hitherto available for study largely, if not solely, by experts in international relations for whom only the sovereign states are the legitimate subjects of enquiry, not the localities and local communities that are victims of sovereign state boundary-making and theoretically only mere objects of study in International Law, for example.

There exists an impressive range of illustrative policy research literature, which has been generated by the Nigerian National Boundary Commission since its establishment in the late 1980s, incidentally, largely as a result of research impact by academic experts in Nigerian universities, related specialised research institutions, and antecedent scholarly publications. Many of these have been diligently researched and honestly acknowledged by the author in his illuminating case of Borgu, include our own more humble pioneer case study of western Yorubaland astride the Nigerian southwestern border with the Republic of Benin, formerly French Dahomey, in 1976 and Bill Miles' magnificent *Hausaland Divided* between northern Nigeria and southern Niger, both of which ostensibly influenced the design and execution of Paul Nugent's highly distinguished book on Togo-Ghana borderlands, published in 2002.

Wider African and global contextualization were effectively driven, not only by our well known edited volume, *Partitioned Africans: Ethnic Relations Across Africa's International Boundaries, 1884-1984* (1985) and the more recent *Borders in Africa: An Anthology of the Policy History* (2015), there has also been John Igue's (2010) *Frontieres, Espace de Development Partagé* (Paris; Karthala) and his older *Le Territoire et L'Etat en Afrique* (Karthala,1995), as well as Miles' gorgeous *Scars of Partition: Postcolonial Legacies in French and British Borderlands*(2014) and the just-published West African showpiece, *Boundaries, Communities and State-Making in West Africa: The Centrality of Margins* (June, 2019) by Paul Nugent, amongst ever-increasing pertinent scholarly and policy research publications.

In 2007, 13th June to be more precise, at Edinburgh, the U.K. African and Africanist borderlands research community felt sufficiently strong to justify pooling into a distinct professional organisation, the African Borderlands Research Network (ABORNE), especially in due celebration of the widely acknowledged decisive contributions key protagonists among them had made to the planning and launching of the truly innovative African Union Border Programme (AUBP) in Addis Ababa, just a week earlier, on the 7th of June 2007. ABORNE quickly won international recognition. It secured a five-year grant of five million euros (€5,000,000) from the prestigious European Science Foundation and executed an exciting Memorandum of Understanding (MOU) for mutual sustenance with the AUBP in Addis Ababa. In 2010, its members also succeeded in publishing a heralding special issue of the ABS' reputed *Journal of Borderlands Studies* (JBS), Vol. 25, No 2, *From Empiricism to Theory in African Borderlands Studies,* guest-edited by David Couplan, a renowned Professor of Social Anthropology at Witwatersrand in Johannesburg, South Africa.

It is against this fascinating background of a rapidly expanding interest and attendant *avanlanché* of scholarly and policy research literature on African Borderland Studies, with particular reference to Nigeria being strategically located between West and Central Africa sub-regions, that one must warmly welcome Hussaini Abdu's extensively researched and elegantly written *Partitioned Borgu: State, Society and Politics in a West African Border Region*. As a north-central Nigerian case history, it is long overdue. Though presented within an admittedly refreshing perspective of the author's well-known disciplinary bias for political economy and development studies, a sub-field as inter-disciplinary and policy-sensitive as the borderlands research perspective, the core originality of the contribution has been in the demonstration of the interconnections more explicitly.

Dr. Abdu's *Partitioned Borgu* has contributed to knowledge in at least two broad directions: national and international historiography that has combined extensive desk or library and archival research with an uncommonly insightful fieldwork based on the rare advantage of an insider, a long-standing 'participant observer.' Abdu has skilfully harnessed massive secondary data from a wide spectrum of published works, mostly by historians but also anthropologists, Nigerians and foreigners, who, over the decades, have held in fascination this historically and culturally complex region, a typical 'African frontier', and complemented these with primary data from colonial archives, mainly at the National Archives in Kaduna, and local oral traditions. The result is, first and foremost, a comprehensive and, indeed, authoritative historical account, long-awaited by the local community in Nigeria as well as limitrophe localities in the Republic of Benin, who have evidently longed for a scientific explanation about why they have come to be as they are: a seemingly hopeless, structurally marginalised population in a deplorable, infrastructurally deficit region, largely on both sides but more especially so on the Nigerian side of the border with the Republic of Benin.

Apart from a highly predictable embrace by the bi-national local community, *Partitioned Borgu* is also eagerly awaited by readers in a wider world of interest in the still relatively little known local and yet vital dimension of the big-time European diplomacy that occasionally came close to outbreaks of conventional war between hotly competing European powers, notably France and Britain, dangerously hustling for shares of African territories in the infamous era of the so-called

Scramble and Partition. Here lies the capital importance of the history of partitioned Borgu on the Niger, paralleled only with the Fashoda Episode on the Nile in the area of the present-day Republic of Sudan, formerly the Anglo-Egyptian Condominium, where the experience of the Anglo-French 'Steeple Chase to Nikki' was nearly neatly replicated. Thus, although the focus is on the implications for the ethnically diverse affected local community. *Partitioned Borgu* is a brilliantly written local history that is strongly inclusive of an analytically rigorous account of the incidental, even if decisive, European imperialist intervention involving military manoeuvres that brought France and Britain extremely close to the brink of war over an African territory.

With regards to the argument about the interconnectedness of perspectives between political economy and development studies, understandably more explicitly espoused by the author on the one hand and, on the other, the Border and Borderlands Studies standpoint, not so explicitly articulated by him, there is a clear merger of vision in the 'Conclusion, Reversing the Trend: Agenda for Development' in the closing pages of this epochal publication. There is, not too surprisingly, a coincidence in the brilliantly articulated list of policy recommendations and those already proffered in so many existing scholarly and policy research publications on border and borderlands studies, particularly those focused on Nigeria and proximate neighbours in ECOWAS and ECCAS (Economic Community of Central African States). Notably, the edited proceedings of national workshops, such as those of 1989 under the auspices of the National Boundary Commission, and in 2006 at the then African University Institute, later incorporated as African Regional Institute, Imeko, Ogun State, southwestern Nigeria.

In fact, as could be easily shown in the history at the National Boundary Commission [of Nigeria] and subsequently, the more focused Border Communities Development Agency, one created by a decree of December 1987 and the other by an Act of 2003 (amended in 2005), both Presidency-level parastatals statutorily presided over by Nigeria's Vice-President, to say nothing about ECOWAS Cross-Border Initiatives Programme (CIP) of 2005 and the aforementioned AUBPC (African Union Border Programme) of 2007, many of the well-meant recommendations in *Partitioned Borgu* have been anticipated in actual developments in actual policy articulation and even seen some measure of implementation. It is just that, for most of the time, as is usual everywhere, especially in Nigeria, policy implementation has painfully lagged behind policy articulation. This is true in Nigeria vis-à-vis limitrophe or proximate neighbours in West and Central Africa, and, in the particular case of Borgu that is not only partitioned between Nigeria and Benin but also more mindlessly scattered across the internal boundaries of no less than three of Nigeria's thirty-six federated States. The 'weighty silence' in Hussaini Abdu's excellent book is in the strongly implied clarion call for a strategic coalition between those in 'development' and existing borderlands perspective studies to mount a reinvigorated pressure on government and inter-related international development agencies, including Plan International Nigeria, where Dr. Abdu, author of *Partitioned Borgu,* is the current and highly influential Country Director, to do the needful to reverse the gory trend of neglect and prevent the danger of a widespread degeneration into the kind of generalised insecurity that we have witnessed and are still witnessing in the coastal border region of the Niger Delta and the Nigerian northeast around the Lake Chad Basin, to say nothing about the fast-emerging scenario in Nigeria's northwest in and around Zamfara State.

I share Dr. Abdu's overall incisive conclusion that only an aggressive affirmative action programme, capable of bringing about a planned and accelerated development of border regions in Africa, is the way out of the danger of the phenomenon of failed states manifesting in ever-expanding contagion of generalised insecurity in the characteristically abandoned border regions of the continent, partitioned Borgu and similarly exposed Nigerian border and cross-border areas inclusive.

Anthony I. Asiwaju, MFR.
Professor Emeritus at the University of Lagos,
Imeko, Ogun State,
September 2019.

Precolonial Borgu

Introduction

Borgu typifies everything about the European scramble and partitioning of Africa. It currently straddles two West African countries, Nigeria and the Benin Republic. Within each of the two countries, Borgu is scattered in different states and provinces. In Nigeria, it is located in the western flank of the north-central region and in the Benin Republic in the north-eastern axis. The study of Borgu is undoubtedly one of the most difficult in contemporary African political and sociological studies. Located in a relatively obscure region, Borgu is scattered across borders at the fringe of two different countries with two different national/European languages cutting across two major ethnic groups, amidst a liberal sprinkling of other minority ethnic groups. Until recently, no significant effort had been made to study and understand this hitherto strategic region of West Africa. Borgu was, therefore, one of the less covered regions in the historical collection of West Africa. Although possessing a vast geographical size, its sparse population, multiple and unstable state structure and the colonial partition saw it not attracting significant scholarly attention. Until the era of the European travellers' collections and colonial documents emerged, Borgu appeared only in footnotes to the history of its Hausa, Songhai, Nupe, Oyo and Dahomean neighbours.

Before the colonial occupation, Borgu was a strategic region in international trade and politics. It stood between major pre-colonial polities – the Songhai, later Sokoto Caliphate, Oyo, Dahomey and Nupe. It particularly had a significant influence on the politics and society of Oyo. As argued in Chapter 4, the etymology of the name *Yoruba*, by which the people of Oyo and today's Yoruba language-speaking people are known, is probably linked to the Borgu region. Its early contact with Europeans and its subsequent colonial occupation significantly influenced developments in northern Nigeria. Britain's Royal West African Frontier Force (the progenitor of the Nigerian Army) was first established in response to protracted conflicts with France over the navigable stretch of River Niger and other strategic parts of Borgu. It was an important gateway for the subsequent colonial conquest of the heartland of the Sokoto Caliphate as it then was. After the effective colonial occupation, it became one of the first-generation colonial provinces in northern Nigeria. Borgu, especially the part that wound up in Nigeria, has suffered significant deterioration since the effective colonial occupation and has become one of the most excluded segments in colonial and post-colonial West Africa.

Borgu's difficult-to-access terrain and linguistic diversity have been compounded by two academic traditions (French and English) occasioned by the colonial partitioning. Major reference sources on Borgu, particularly in Nigeria, are therefore dominated by hurriedly collected and often contradictory European accounts from Barth, Clapperton, the Lander Brothers and Lugard, as well as assessment reports by various colonial officials drawn from uncritically evaluated oral history. Borgu, therefore, suffers from documentary tentativeness and outright distortions mostly bordering on assertions of dominance or supremacy of one principality, often referred to as kingdoms, against another. This is surely not peculiar to Borgu, as Crowder (1973) observes that oral traditions in most parts of Africa have become instruments of dynastic legitimisation deployed for use in claims and counter claims over land and political control. Since most colonial documents were drawn from one or the other of these oral traditions, they have continued to reinforce these claims. The colonial domination didn't only contribute to this distortion of history; it dislocated the people and invented new identities.

Generally, historical and political studies Africa have largely been on mainstream groups, marginal groups like Borgu attract limited academic attention. It is therefore not a surprise that Borgu is understudied, particularly in the Nigerian side. Even in the Benin, where extensive studies were conducted, they have been largely ethnographic surveys, limited to sampled localities. Aside from a few early generation studies (Lombard 1957, 1960, 1965; Crowder 1973; Idris 1973; Anene 1970), major studies on Borgu exist mostly as published and unpublished doctoral dissertations. Although these have contributed to increasing the understanding of Borgu in the academic, historical and anthropological community, most of these works were conducted for university certificates and largely published abroad and thus are most times not available for local consumption, particularly in Nigeria. As a result, these have not had the benefit of local academic scrutiny and validation. A lot of these have also heavily relied on colonial documentation and travellers' collections. Although some have conducted extensive field study, they often were constrained by linguistic barriers occasioned by the need for multiple interpreters due to the diversity of the region. As observed by Crowder (1973), a serious study of pre-colonial Borgu would require not only the knowledge of the two principal languages of the area but a longer period of fieldwork than most doctoral students might have. Some of these works, therefore, suffer from over generalisation and simplistic understanding, or the attempt to forcefully fit Borgu into the chronology of the history of its neighbours. As important as the oral tradition is to historical methods, historians have advised that such traditions should be critically engaged and treated with academic caution (Smith 1987; Usman 1981).

Lately, there have been attempts by local Borgu historians to document the history of the region (Lafia 2006; Mohammed and Nze 2009; Idris and Yaru 2008). While these efforts have helped to fill some gaps created by academic historians and anthropologists occasioned by their better understanding of the context and languages of the region, even some of these appear to be equally simplistic narratives, influenced by local politics and Borgu-centric sources. They are often devoid of a clear connection of how external factors shape the Borgu situation or how similar developments ensued in other places. More often than not, Borgu is simply isolated for analysis, thereby losing the larger political and economic context and how that has contributed to shaping local realities. The historicity of Borgu requires more than just giving an account of what occurred in the region and the relationship between contending groups. A systematic historiographic and political economy analysis requires a deeper understanding of the rest of the world and how developments in other places shaped the region. As observed by Mbembe (2001), the "historicity of African societies, their *raisons d'etre* and their relations to solely themselves, are rooted in multiplicity of times, trajectories, and relationalities that, although particular and sometimes local, cannot be conceptualised outside a world that is, so to speak, globalised" (pp. 9). It is generally difficult to assert distinctive historicity in a globalising world. While globalisation is often misleadingly conceived as a recent phenomenon (Fukuyama 1993, 2018), this work is premised on a strong understanding that globalisation is a historical process. The world might have been globalising probably much longer than appreciated. The emergence of the slave trade, the collapse of Mali Empire and the emergence of the Songhai Empire and its later collapse, then the colonial occupation, were all early globalising influences that shaped Borgu. These complex movements and changes make an isolative distinction of any group much more difficult to assess (Mbembe 2001).

This book is a unique political scientist's intervention in a region academically dominated by historians and anthropologists. The approach is historical, but it interprets history from the dynamics of state, power and social relationship. It provides new and critical perspectives to the state, society and politics in the region since the pre-colonial periods. It also examines how the earlier Borgu state formation combined with the colonial and the post-colonial political economy to define the region's contemporary development crisis. The book relies significantly on secondary materials published in books and academic journals, complemented by primary sources drawn from archival materials and verification interviews and discussions in Borgu communities across the two countries. The effort is to provide a single documentary resource material for both academic and non-academic readers and contribute to opening a new conversation on Borgu, with the hope that it will generate interest in further examining its different trajectories and social structures. This effort is also made to help elevate the conversation on border and borderland, rural political economy and to appreciate the developmental challenges of one of the most marginal and excluded regions of the West African sub-region.

Surely, the book doesn't explain everything about Borgu. In fact, Borgu is too complex and diverse to be covered by a single effort. It is, however, an attempt to historicise the region and provide a critical, introspective analysis aimed at eliciting more academic interest on the other dynamics of the region, especially on the Nigerian side. The book places Borgu in perspective within the larger politics of Africa. The key argument in this book is that the present Borgu is a reflection of its past: that is, its pre-colonial and colonial history.

The ideological and institutional texture of colonialism, although a relatively short interlude in the tapestry of a history that stretches several centuries, has had a profound impact on Borgu's contemporary formation. The colonial legacy had a formative impact on Borgu, as it did for the rest of Africa. It totally re-ordered the Borgu political space, societal hierarchies, social relations and even changed names of historical figures and settlements/territories. It created a new territorial grid and invented identities, which were congealed and appropriated by local actors in the post-colonial formation. Recognising the artificiality of these new structures and identities does not, however, deny them the right to exist. Every society is a product of this process, voluntary or imposed. What is important is to recognise the inventive character and see it as a product of history that can be altered by new realities. The challenge is when people present these identities as given and unchangeable.

While not losing sight of the international dimensions of some of the crises in the region, I try, in this book, to also focus on the domestic and social factors that shape contemporary developmental challenges in the region. I emphasise the importance of social and institutional structures, public policies and the role of leadership. In essence, as far-reaching, as the colonial impact is, it would be misleading to argue that it is the sole determinant of Borgu's contemporary situation. To the contrary, as observed by Lewis (1998), indigenous societies, adapted, resisted, or evaded other influences. The historicity of colonial rule should be recognised as an encounter with other dynamics, equally endowed with their historicity, which no level of imperial subjugation could obliterate. According to Bayart (2009), these other dynamics are linked to the trajectories of the pre-existing indigenous social groups, which during the colonial period acted in pursuit of their own interests and in accordance with the strategies of moral repertoires that could not be reduced solely to the new colonial order. Contemporary Borgu, therefore, reflects the lineage of both its pre-colonial institutions and successive historical changes, among which the disruptive elements of colonialism are prominent.

Borgu has been reduced from a strategically placed polity of the eighteenth and nineteenth centuries to the margin of two West African countries today. Although Borgu in the Republic of Benin may arguably be faring better due to the size of the country and its structural composition (even if it is still considered the least developed segment of Benin Republic), Borgu in Nigeria is not only the geographical fringe of the country, its different communities and local governments are also further scattered within the geographical and political margins of three different states—Kebbi, Kwara and Niger.

Within the analytical frame of this book is also a detail of the historical intricacies of developments and events in the region. This is meant to serve two objectives. The first objective is to provide general-purpose readers with human-interest stories and help enhance the understanding of the dynamics of politics and society. The second obejective is to respond to the poor documentation of Borgu. This detailing helps to put on record and present to the world, some of the most controversial, devastating and contentious moments of the history of the region.

Some of my findings and arguments could challenge existing conventions and traditions, so I expect them to be thoroughly and critically interrogated. While I have made conscious efforts to cover the French Borgu, I was obviously constrained by my iffy French and poor relationship with the Benin/French academic community and its traditions. I regret that I might have missed some political and economic nuances that shaped the political economy of the region, but I hope this effort also helps colleagues from that region to engage in more cross-border studies for a better appreciation of the developmental challenges of the partitioned Borgu.

This book is structured into eleven chapters across three broad themes/periods – pre-colonial, colonial and post-colonial Borgu. While each section of this book can be read separately and independently, the most rewarding way to read it may be to take it chronologically. The pre-colonial period is divided into four chapters and covers the earlier state formation and politics of Borgu. It discusses the ethnographic structure and the changing dynamics of the political formation in the region. The second section examines the emergence of colonial rule, looking at the colonial political structure, the resistance to colonial rule and its impact on the society and politics of Borgu. The last section is on post-colonial Borgu, and it examines the contemporary politics and dynamics of development. The book ends with a conclusion and policy recommendations on how the development challenges of the review can be sustainably reversed.

Sources and Analytical Framework

Materials leading to this book were drawn from primary and secondary sources. Its primary sources include written and oral sources. Written primary sources were drawn from documentary reports or records of early European travellers, traders, missionaries, trading companies, governments and their agents. Some of these include the travel reports of Barth, Clapperton, the Landers and Lugard. Others are political reports of colonial officials responsible for Borgu. Documented materials containing information about Borgu stored in national archives in Kaduna, Ibadan, Porto-Novo and international libraries and related depositories were also quite helpful. These sources were complemented by select validation interviews at some political centres of Borgu.

There has been an excessive elevation of the myth and history of migration of the aristocracy. The myth associated with the aristocracy has often been wrongly conflated with the history of the people and society. Some colonial documents have been uncritically accepted by the people as the history of their own communities. It is not uncommon then to hear a Baatonu in Nikki saying their origin is Bussa in Nigeria or a Boko from Kaiama stating that the people of Kaiama migrated from Nikki. The colonial attempt at periodisation and defining dates of settlements have contributed to the crisis, as such dates are largely associated with powerful migrants rather than those of the autochthones.

My secondary sources were drawn from books, journals and unpublished research reports. Since the 1960s, impressive efforts have been made to understand the political development of Borgu and its ethnographic formation. The studies have been largely dominated by historians and anthropologists. While the anthropologists and historians like Lombard (1957, 1960, 1965,1967), Stewart (1984,

1993), Morae Farais (1992, 1996, 2013), Kuba (1996, 1998) concentrated on the ethnography and political structure of the region, other efforts centred around pre-colonial politics and economy (Idris 1973; Adekunle 2004, 2008), colonial rule and resistance (Crowder 1973, 1975), post-colonial intergroup relations (Akinwumi 1997, 1998) and the impact of colonial partition and cross-border relations (Anene 1965, 1970; Asiwaju 2004; Akinwumi 1997). An extensive body of work has also been done on pre-colonial trade, particularly the role of the Wangara in the kolanut and long-distance trade in the western Sudan (Lovejoy 1971, 1978, 1980). Borgu has also featured prominently in the pre-colonial dynastic politics of its neighbours, particularly Songhai and Oyo. This work,, therefore, benefits from a multitude of sources, from official archives to secondary materials.

Many of these Borgu-specific works understandably relied on oral traditions, travellers' accounts and colonial archival documents. Uncritical use of these documents can be problematic, as can be discerned from some of the works. The challenge with these sources are not necessarily the reliability of the facts but the framework of analysis, which defines how questions were posed and how responses were generated and interpreted. Colonial data collection and management was influenced by the brute power of colonial officials (the associated risk of speaking out of fear or for patronage) and the challenge of language and interpretation. Data was often collected from people who were less informed and probably not able to communicate in any language other than theirs. The interpreters were almost often uneducated individuals, with little or no knowledge of the history, custom, traditions and context of the subjects of this class of materials. The manner of processing the information and the bureaucratic approval process appears to have also distorted history. Observing data collection and the interpretation processes by colonial officers, in the case of Yauri, an important Borgu neighbour to the north, Mahdi Adamu noted:

> Most of the interviews were group discussions conducted in the open air where the Administrative Officers used to sit in one place and then gather some old people round them and start asking questions. My experience of this system of recording oral traditions shows that wrong versions could be recorded by officers without their knowing [sic] that they were wrong. It is rare that an informant in such a

group will hear something wrongly put by another informant and raise objections (cited in Crowder 1973, 249).

Also, as a policy, the colonial officers didn't record anything that would arouse the hostility of people or a section of the people (Crowder 1973). It was on the basis of some of these gaps that Hoskyns-Abrahall's *History of Bussa* (1925) was returned for rewriting (Crowder 1973).

The colonial documentation of oral tradition of history was also deeply influenced by the European travellers' approach, which was sometimes rooted in race and a particular Eurocentric perspective of history. The works of Barth, the Lander Brothers, and Lugard on Borgu have been quite influential in this type of flawed documentation of history. Their research questions were built with a view to eliciting a particular kind of response.

I agree with Crowder that the biggest challenge for contemporary scholars of Borgu is that the colonial documented version of the history has become widely recognised and therefore easily narrated as the authentic history of the people. The history of the region has thus been reduced to a synthesis of the oral traditions made by Theodore Hoskyns-Abrahall in 1925. Not surprisingly, even the most educated people have kept copies of that document as the authentic history of the region.

My intention is to reconstruct the political economy of Borgu by assessing and re-interpreting the available primary and secondary sources to help understand the essence and processes of the historical development of the region. History is interpreted as a process of economic and social contradictions. Social structures and dynastic politics are seen as elements of the substructure but could have their own specific dynamics, which becomes evident in the course of social interaction. In this approach, social structure and forces of production are given primacy as determining the dynamics of the society and history. I consider the society of Borgu in its totality: the existence and reproduction which is based on the economic or material conditions of production and exchange. Accordingly, no aspect of the society, from culture, political institutions, ethnic configuration or religion, is divorced from the material condition of production and exchange. In this context, history is interpreted as a continuum. No phase of history is independent of the other. Although a regional study, the local context is explained through international and national dynamics and influences.

Geography and People

Pre-colonial Borgu was roughly enclaved between the twelfth and the ninth parallels of the latitude and the first and fourth meridian of the east longitude. It stretches from the north-eastern banks of the River Niger westwards to the Atakora Mountains and then south to the forest area of the Yoruba, the old Oyo Empire. The region is ethnically bound to the south by the Yoruba, to the north by Hausa of the Kebbawa and Yaurawa extraction, and to the east by the Nupe with the Songhai to the west.

Borgu is geographically located in the Guinea Savannah belt of West Africa. Its hinterland is covered by an undulating landscape, with chains of hills and a few mountains, except for the valley of the River Niger and some of its tributaries. Other physical landmarks include the Atakora Mountains in the extreme west, which provided cover for communities during foreign invasions. Similarly, the River Niger was not only a major source of livelihood, but it was also an important barrier against invaders from Songhai and Hausa in the north as well as a major source of transportation.

Riverine Borgu exhibits low and swampy soil, particularly in the flooded plains of Bussa and Illo. The tributaries of the Niger include the Mekroa, which starts from the slope of Atakora Mountains and flows northward into the River Niger; the River Alibori flows from the district of Nioro northward and terminates in the Niger around Karimama; the River Soto, with source has a northward flow and terminates at Malanville. River Oli flows eastwards from Nikki and terminates at Gbajibo. The Mosi River starts its eastward journey from the area around Kenu (Idris 1973). Other important rivers include Okpara, Swashi, Tese, Wessa and Pissio. These rivers, though not navigable, were a major source of water and fish for the interior of Borgu. Most of eastern Borgu is located within the Lower Niger Trough along which the River Niger flows south-eastwards. From Yelwa, it turns southwards, piercing through a basement rock complex, which outcrops at Bussa and forms the famous Bussa rapid. It is at this spot that the Kainji Dam is located (Idris 1973).

In the hinterland are intermittent undulating hills ranging from 1000 to 5000 metres (Adekunle 2004). Among these rocky/granite hills are Zakana, Kubkli, Sarsako, Puissa, Konko, Oziya at (Kaama) Kaiama and Kuro-Boko at Seru Kperu (Okuta), Kabaru at Gurai, among others.

Like most places in the Guinea Savannah belt of West Africa, the area has two major seasons: a wet and a dry season. Borgu has rainfall measured at 70 to 100 inches per year. The rainy season is characterised by torrential rains accompanied by violent winds and thunderstorms. The dry season is characterised by the dust-bearing Harmattan trade wind, particularly from December to February.

The southern part of Borgu is interspersed by tall shrubs and trees almost close the vegetation in the rain forest zone. These trees and grass have been a major source of construction for the ever-moving people of the area during the pre-colonial period. The vegetation gets shorter as you move northwards, almost as short as that in the Sudan Savannah vegetation.

Problem of Etymology

The origin and etymology of Borgu is still contested. While strong political ties existed between the different societies of Borgu, the use of the name might have been popularised by Borgu's northern neighbours and later Europeans. Although there is limited documentation of Borgu before the colonial times, it is not clear if the people actually called themselves Borgu. Each territory in the region referred to itself by its name. In Bussa and Kaiama, the term was believed to have been applied to Boko people around the Babanna region. It was also applied to Nikki, as it denotes the region comprising the ancient kingdom of Kenu, which were the Baatonum-speaking areas of south-western Borgu (NAK 1936). While some etymology linked Borgu to *Burugu* (Hausa for *Panicum stagninum*), a succulent aquatic grass associated with the banks of the River Niger, others linked it with Borno, *Borgu* being the south-western phonetic expression. The plant-related etymology is improbable as most of the areas called Borgu are not in the riverine (NAK 1936).

Others believe Borgu might have been derived from the Boko word *Baru* (settlement) and *Guu* (place). Borgu is also believed to be a corruption of *Baruwu*, meaning settlement of Baatombu (Baatonu people)[1] (Lafia 2004). Nevertheless, there are also external (non-Borgu) sources to this etymology; Hausa or Songhai. A Songhai folk etymology recorded by Barth presents Borgu as a derivative of *bari go* (five horses). This implies the only survivors of Askia Mohammed's troops that invaded Borgu in the sixteenth century (Kuba and Olayemi 2005). What is also clear about the etymology of Borgu is its locational geography and political structure than its ethnic formation. As with plural ethnic formations, it is difficult to associate the term with any of the multiple ethnic groups that constitute the geographical and political Borgu.

Ethnogenesis and Pluri-ethnic Formation

Although the people are collectively described as *Bargawa*, *Bariba* and *Bargance* by their respective Hausa, Yoruba and Songhai neighbours, Borgu is a plural ethnic formation (see Idris 1973; Crowder 1973; Kuba 1998; Kuba and Akinwumi 2005; Stewart 1993). It consists of several ethnic groups, with different linguistic origins and history of migration into the area. There are conflicting categorisations of these ethnic groups among scholars. Crowder (1973), drawing heavily from Lombard (1965) and Idris (1973), categorised Borgu into six main socio-linguistic groups. These are the Wasangari, Baatombu, Gando, Dendi and other immigrants. Other scholars categorised the ethnic groups based on their history of settlement in the area—those considered autochthonous and those described as immigrants and their occupational engagements (Kuba and Akinwumi 2005).

While these are good classifications, they do not necessarily explain the dynamics of society and ethnic formation in the region. Categorising ethnic groups based on occupations doesn't allow for proper historicisation of the different ethnic groups and appears to

---

[1] Farooq Kperogi, a lingiest and a native Baatonu, provides an interesting explanation: "Baru is the combining form for the Baatonu people. *Baru tem* means the land of the Baatonu. *Baru bibu* means Baatonu children. So Baru wu means the town of the Baatonu".

relegate minor ethnic groups that possibly didn't fit properly into the defined categories. Furthermore, the approach appears to give ethnic colouration to non-ethnic categories like Wasangari and Gando. Wasangari is more of a political class than an ethnic category. As presented in chapter 1 and 2, there is no sufficient historical and sociological basis to define the Wasangari as an exclusive ethnic category. While not denying the historical presence or leadership of non-autochtones in this group, to ethincally define it outside or different from the two major ethnic groups, is problematic.

The Gando were ethnically Baatombu (Baatonu people), and, to a lesser extent Boko, although they could be Fulfulde-speaking. They were considered as social outcasts due to the circumstances of their birth and childhood physical development. This was largely practised by the Baatonu people with lesser presence among the Boko and other northern Borgu minority ethnic groups.

Although Dendi and Fulbe are, in all historical and anthropological accounts not indigenous or autouchtonous to Borgu, they have been parts of Borgu history since arguably the sixteenth century or earlier and have constituted a separate historical category of Fulbe, not necessarily in a genealogical form (Bierschenk 1993, 1996). The spread of Wangara (Dendi) also dates to about the same period. These are also ethno-economic groups that have different degrees of the ethnic geography of Borgu, just like they have been in Hausa and Kanuri land.

The ethnic structure of Borgu is complex. The common origin that each of these ethnic groups share is mainly territorial and political, not genealogical. Ethnic identity was not prominent in the early periods of Borgu society. In most places, ethnic or language categories bisect with limited consciousness. Amselle (1998) observed that ethnic identities gained pre-eminence only when conditions of social and political production elapsed. "Political formations are, therefore, divided into ethnic forms only because their modes of appearance, functioning and disappearances are lost in the mist of time – this memory loss allowed ethnologists, colonial administrators and politicians to negate the historicity of African societies and obscure the common features of their customs" (1998, 57). From all indications, Borgu was largely an amalgam of ethnic groups in relation to domination and subordination to one another. The Baatombu and the

Boko are the largest ethnic groups in Borgu. The Baatombu are predominantly in the western and southern flanks while the Boko are more predominant in the eastern and northern flanks of Borgu.

For the purpose of this work, we categorised Borgu ethnic groups according to their geographical location, thus the south-western and the northern and eastern clusters. This is for the convenience of analysis. This is not denying that some of these clusters are cross-cutting.

****

The Baatombu (Baatonu people) are the largest ethnic group in the Barutem districts of Gbanaru (Gwanara), Senru Kperu (Okuta), Yaasikiru (Yashikira) and Desa (Ilesha Baruba) in western parts of Kwara State of Nigeria[2]. In the Benin Republic, it is spread across four states (Alibori, Attakora, Borgou and Donga) but with more concentration in Borgou Department particularly in Nikki, Parakou, Kandi, and Natitingou among others. The Baatonu are referred to in French colonial documents as 'Bariba', while the British colonialists called them 'Borgawa'. Baatonum, was previously known to belong to the Voltaic language group, recent studies have defined it as an isolate within the Savanna languages[3]. A tradition associates them with Dosso, in the River Niger valley, particularly a settlement, called Nikki, where people there also speak Baatonum (Robin 1947, cited in Idris 1973; Stewart 1993).

The language was once believed to be related to the Senufo group in Ivory Coast and Sudan (Welmers 1952, 82). It was considered the easternmost representation of the family. It would appear the Borgu name of 'Bariba' is actually in reference to Baatonu people. The actual speakers of the Baatonu language refer to themselves as Baatombu. Their Boko neighbours call them *Zonna*[4].

---

[2] Politically, this axis along side other none Yoruba speaking parts of Kwara is categorised as northern Kwara. However, they are geographically in Western Kwara.

[3] See https://en.wikipedia.org/wiki/Bariba_people

[4] The origin and meaning of *Zonna* is not clear, but it has however grown to acquire a derogatory connotation since the colonial period.

There are slight variations in Baatonum dialects across the different Baatonu locations and towns, but the Nikki dialect used to be the mainstream. Apart from national variation in dialect between Nigeria and Benin since the colonial period, other dialects include the Parakou dialect and the Bonikpara dialect. The Bonikpara dialect, which is close to Burkina Faso, is the furthest from the rest, but all are largely mutually intelligible[5]. Baatonum is not the only language in the region. There are many other minority groups; including the Pila-Pila (Jara or Yom), the Taneka, Woaba and Somba are linguistically and culturally closer than the Gurma, Berba, Sorubu (Bi-Yobe), Somborgu (Natimba) and Bouba (Stewart 1993).

The Baatonu pressure has historically shrunk the population of the other ethnic groups in the region. They were heavily raided for slaves during the early periods. The Woaba (Yoabu in Baatonum) are found mainly in the western areas of Kouande and near the Atakora Mountains. Traces of Woaba are still found around Nikki and Bembereke areas. The Taneke have also been scattered around these areas. There is also the Mokole, a small Yorubaphone group linked to the ruling houses of Kandi (Kuba and Akinwumi 2005).

****

The largest of the northern and eastern Borgu languages is Boko. Boko is mainly spoken in the hinterland of Borgu, stretching from riverine Bussa through Nikki, to Segbara in the north, Puissa, Babanna, Wawa to Kaiama to the south. Nikki is on the borderline of this linguistic division between the Mande-speaking Boko to the east and the Baatonum people to the west.

The Boko people had mingled over several centuries and were mutually influenced by different other ethnic groups in the region, particularly the Tienga, Baatonu, Laru, Nupe, Zabarma, among others. This can be seen from the mutation of the language and emergence of different dialects spread across different geographical clusters of the region, for example, the Boo, Bissan, Bokobaru and Tienga dialects.

Tienga-speakers are found on the banks of the River Niger from Illo to Alibori. They are recognised as one of the oldest groups in the

---

[5] With comments by Farooq Kperogi, 6th July 2019

area. Bokobaru appears to be the newest mutation of the Boko language. It was largely influenced by the original settlers around Kaiama, the Yoabu[6], Tienga people from Kanibe and possibly Kambari, Nupe and Baatonum. The Bissan, another variant of Boko, is found in the riverine Borgu in Nigeria and is spoken in Bussa and its surrounding areas of Kabigera to Kagogi, and Wawa, with slight differences. Bissan is influenced by Kambari, Nupe, Laru and Tienga, which are some of the ethnic minority groups in riverine Borgu. Boko (Boo) is often arguably described as the original of the Boko Language, spoken in Babanna, Marami, Dekana, Kabe, Konwosso, Puissa in Nigeria and Segbana, Gbasso, Negazi and in the *cantons* of Dunkassa, Bouka, Hidarou and Jerou in the Benin Republic.

The Boko people refer to themselves as *Zogwe/Zogbe* (Plu. *Zogweno/Zogbeno*) and call their language *Zogweya/Zogbeya*. It is, however, not uncommon to hear them describe their different dialects as *Bissanya* (Bissa-langauge, *Bissagwe* = Bussa person), *Bokoya* (Boko language), *Kaamaya* (Kaama Language) amongst others. They are collectively called *Boko* by their Baatonu neighbours. Early British colonial documents categorised them as *Bussawa* (Hausa for Bussa people) and their language as *Bussanci*, which is also Hausa for the language of the Bussa people. Bussanci, at a point in British colonial documentation, was wrongly included with other minority languages of Bussa. The three dialects of Boko are, therefore, not necessarily genealogical but socio-political and linguistic categories defined by geography and politics.

The Boko language is an isolated Mande language. It hasn't got a relationship with any language around it. It is, therefore, categorised as Eastern Mande and it is believed to have migrated into the area around the thirteenth century or earlier. This linguistic island is believed to have been occasioned by wars associated with the establishment of the Mali Empire and the migration of Mande-speaking people into the various parts of Western Sudan, or "were vestiges of a very ancient extension of a Mande linguistic group" (Stewart 1994, 48). However, some scholars do not see any major relationship between the western and this isolated Mande language in the east. They believe that the

---

[6] Now probably extinct in the region, but I understand that there is still a sprinkle in the Benin Republic side of Borgu. Whether the language is still spoken or not is not clear.

Boko group may be an independent Mande category that migrated to its current location but not necessarily linked to the western Mande cluster (Kuba and Akinwumi 2005).

The Boko share this region, especially the riverine areas, with the other minority language groups like Shanga, Laru, Lopawa, Gungawa and Kambari. The Shagawa and Kengewa are believed to be of the same roots. Kengawa are of eight branches – four in Argungu Emirate including Kwassoro (Kwokwoba and Kengakoi), Mushirri, Bonda (Fanne) and Bate. There are also other groups in Borgu, around Illo, including Kassati, Lumma and Makata (Stewart 1993). These categories are believed to have migrated to these areas from Argungu (Kebbi state, Nigeria) and settled in different parts of the region including Konkwesso in the Babanna area, Komi and Faku. The Gungawa (who speak the Reshe language) live on the bank of the River Niger between Agwarra and Illo. They were believed to have migrated to the area from the Yauri and Kontagora axis. The Laru are also riverine people closely related to the Lopawa: their language is classified within the Benue-Congo category. The Laru are believed to be founders of the villages of Kanibe (Dogon Gari), Lashibe, Lumma, Sansanni and Shagunu Kurum all around Bussa and Wawa (Stewart 1993).

The Kambari are a diverse Western Plateau sub-group of the Benue-Congo languages. There are two categories of Kambari in Borgu—the earlier Kambari and the late Kambari. The earlier ones are settled around Bussa and Wawa and are believed to have predated the dynastic period of Borgu and to have even been incorporated into the political structure of Wawa. They are believed to have migrated from the Auna area in Kontagora Emirate (Niger state, Nigeria) many centuries ago. The Kambarin Beriberi, found around the bank of River Oli, are of a different origin and call themselves Ashingyini (Stewart 1993).

The late Kambari groups are found around Agwara. They migrated into this region from Yauri across the Niger in the nineteenth century, a lot of them escaping the slave-raiding activities of Umaru Nagwamatse, and later on, in search of arable land (Stewart 1993). The Kambari people are called Shereno (sg. Shere) by the Boko people.

Dendi and Fulbe (Fulani) are spread across the different parts of Borgu. They are not anthropologically autochthonous but have been migrating into the region over centuries. The Dendi have been subsumed under the Wangara group. *Wangara* was a generic term used to describe the long-distance traders of Borgu and other parts of Western Sudan. Their origin is connected to the Mali and Songhay empires. They are believed to have migrated into Borgu from the Kingdom of Dendi in the sixteenth century. Dendi Kingdom was, at a point, a province of the Songhay Empire and the last refuge of the Songhay kings after the capture of Timbuktu in 1591. According to Stewart, "At this time, the Dendi become [sic] part of the *Wangara* community and their language, which had earlier been introduced by those *Wangara* with *Silla* patronymic from Kassati across the River Niger from Illo, became a more important trade language" (1993, 57). Dendi was generally used to describe Borgu Muslims from the sixteenth to the twentieth centuries. They were of a different origin but linguistically connected, their differences only identified by their patronyms as will be seen succeeding chapters.

Borgu has a large population of Fulbe (Fulani) who probably settled in Borgu since the sixteenth century or slightly later[7], from the Senegal region. Like the Dendi, their migration may be associated with the crisis in Mali and later in the Songhay Empire. The Fulbe may constitute up to one-fourth of the Borgu population and have been the second largest ethnic group in some Borgu towns, *cantons* and local government areas. In Kaiama, for instance, the Fulbe are regarded as the second largest ethnic group. Although there are no census figures to confirm this claim, the Fulbe constitute the most politically represented group after the indigenous Bokobaru people. People of Fulbe extraction have been elected or appointed local government chairmen, vice-chairmen and councillors and have represented the Local Government in the state House of Assembly since the restoration of democracy in 1999[8]. As one of the largest ethnic groups in West Africa, the Fulbe have been widely studied. We, therefore, do not need to be detained here by the details. Although largely known to be a nomadic pastoralist group, the Fulbe-Borgu are

---

[7] It is common in the literature to date it to eighteenth century (Lombert 1965, Hahonou, 2015)

[8] Discussions in Kaiama, including with politicains of Fulbe extraction.

mainly sedentary, combining pastoralism with small land cultivation. Unlike other ethnic groups, the Fulbe, despite their centuries of presence in Borgu, never claimed any land or territory. Although they were incorporated into the pre-colonial state structure of Borgu, they were largely categorised as a socio-economic rather than a political group.

The Fulbe of Borgu were a distinct Fulbe category, not in a genealogical sense, but in territorial conferment just like the Toronkawa or Turdbi in the Futa Toro, Rumawa in Ruma, Fulanin Jahun in Jahun, Fulanin Adamawa among others. According to Usman (2006), the way lineages are identified with particular territories or towns reflects one aspect of the complex process of community formation in Central Sudan.

SECTION ONE

PRE-COLONIAL BORGU

CHAPTER ONE

Early States and Societies

There is no single early period. An earlier period has to be seen as a process or a continuum in which different forms of socio-political and economic arrangements, state or non-state structures existed at different times. The early period in this context refers to the pre-dynastic formations of Borgu. Defining a chronology of this period has been difficult for historians and anthropologists. It is not clear when human activity started in the geographical area that now constitutes Borgu. There is, however, a consensus that such activities probably started in the coastal parts of the River Niger and then spread westwards and southwards. Oral and documentary sources refer to different phases of migration to the area. While movement from other places to the Niger Valley is acceptable in relation to the riverine communities and the later southward and westward movements, there appears not to be one migratory story around Borgu. As a diverse collection of people, the groups that makeup Borgu might have settled in the area at different times. The formation of the Baatonu people in the south and west of Borgu appears to be different from that of the Boko in northern and central Borgu.

Studies have recognised that the Pleistocene lived in the Borgu area (Adekunle 2004). Archaeological evidence also suggests settlements in the middle/upper Niger Valley circa 150 AD. It is probable that the earliest settlement was in the Niger Valley, in the region of Illo. Evidence of interaction with neighbouring communities and the development of iron technology and advanced material culture were suggested. This archaeological evidence has also established a connection between the early settlements of Borgu and the Nok Culture.[9] Nok-like pebbles were discovered around Shagunu and Foge Island (Adekunle 2004). Metallurgical works might have developed at places with large iron ore deposits like Bussa, Wawa and Kubli near Babanna. Similarly, artefacts and terracotta linked to Nok culture dating back to circa 100 – 700 have been found around Kainji Lake. Some of these artefacts include pottery, iron weapons, terracotta figurines and human skeletons (Adekunle 2004).

In this early period, the Borgu was surely not a political community. Therefore, there wasn't a collective Borgu communal identity. Although Idris (1973) suggests that the Tienga leader Kirikasa was the sole Chief of Borgu during this early period, there is no evidence that the area was structured enough to warrant an overarching leadership. The structure of these early polities would have gone through different transformations and changes leading to the emergence of a state in the late fourteenth to the fifteenth century. It is more likely that at the period, people lived in groups of families. The eldest in each family was entrusted with both spiritual and political leadership. The production relationship was collective, relying on family labour. There were also Earth Priests who served as intercessors between the living and the ancestors on one hand and between the deities and the living on the other.

Hunting, agriculture and fishing in the Niger Valley was probably the major preoccupation of the people. As families grew and moved around, contacts across families and ethnic groups increased and with this came the possibility of cooperation and alliances. This led to the transition from single-family structures to lineage and later, villages. These more complex structures were often strengthened around specific cultural practices. Shifting cultivation, combating diseases, the search for water, slave raids and the quest for security were major drivers of movements. Through increased contact, linguistic changes

---

[9] The Nok culture was a sophisticated civilization of the Iron Age. It involved the use of iron and stone materials. The last phase of Nok Culture was suggested to be at 925 BC +/- 70 and AD 200 +/- 50.

might have occurred and new ethnic groupings built. Most of the major early settlements in the region appear to have relocated several times. The social organisation in the earliest periods, therefore, revolved around family, lineages and villages.

Tamtaro[10] was believed to be the first settlement of the Baatonu people. They settled in that area around 1350 AD. Other early settlements include Deema, Wenususu and Nikki, which later became the political centre of the Baatombu (Lafia 2004). A chronology has been difficult for historians and anthropologists because efforts have been centred on political centralisation, ethnic categorisation and contact with the external world. The focus has, therefore, been on major events and changes in the area rather than the context and dynamics of those events, and the power structure that supported them.

On the Boko side, the earliest period of migration from the Niger Valley was probably led by the Tienga people around Illo area. It was from this region that they moved and settled in the hinterlands, in the region around Segbana – Gounji – Puissa, and from there to the south-eastern areas of Kanibe, Gbere, Lasibe, while others went to the Bussa region.

Other early settlements in northern Borgu include Kibegra, Kagogi, Karabonde and Monai. Although the Boko-speaking people were thought to be the aborigines of northern Borgu, it appears other ethnic minority groups like Kambari, Laru and Nupe have shared space with the Boko at some point in history. As indicated earlier, Boko is a Mande group and its language is spoken in most parts of northern and eastern Borgu. This isolated eastward presence of Mande speakers as in Borgu, hundreds of kilometres away from Mande-speaking groups in the west, has raised some historical and linguistic curiosity. Some have attempted to link Borgu's Mande speakers to the Mali Empire, drawing evidence from the empire's suzerainty over the entire Niger bend and even further downstream at the peak of its power in the fourteenth century. Linguistic evidence, however, confirms that the Northern Mande (the Soninke and Malinke languages) and the Southern Mande of Borgu developed independent

---

[10] This was etymologically derived from *tem tore* – beginning of the word, in Baatonum. See Hussaini Lafia, 2004, pp. 14.

of each other, thousands of years earlier (Kuba and Akinwumi 2005, pp. 323).

State and Political Formation

The process of state formation is always a long and complex socio-economic and political process. Amselle (1998) describes it as history in itself. It is difficult to assign a precise origin to a state. According to Amselle, the process is either a result of chains of reaction or an inter-societal realignment. All states are, therefore, to an extent, secondary states. They are products of a dialectical process involving emergence, dissolution and re-emergence in different forms but to serve the same purpose.

In essence, the process involved a period of formation of a state, its growth, decline and the emergence of a new successor state. It is thus difficult to provide a historical beginning or an end to a particular form of state organisation or even a stateless structure, as the two are not necessarily the exact opposite of the other. Amselle correctly argued that stateless societies never existed in a real sense in the pre-colonial period, taking the period as a spectrum. Sometimes societies considered as stateless were actually dissident societies escaping states and were in the process of building new state structures – therefore oscillating between "statelessness" and being a state.

As products of the social contradiction of society, states reign supreme over all other forms of social organisation. It reflects the development of society from a simple family or lineage structure to a more complex all-encompassing mechanism. A state is characterised by four major features. The first is that a state has unequal power relations described as public power, often expressed by the most powerful groups, but it could even be above both ruler and the ruled in some situations. The second is an identifiable geographical territory over which it holds jurisdiction. Thirdly, a state has maximum control over resources and a monopoly of force. The fourth feature is a supreme authority, a sovereign.

A state is a society of individuals submitted, sometimes by compulsion, to a certain organisational system. The roles which settle their characters are laws of the state, and by an obvious logic, they have necessary primacy, that is to say, the sovereign rules (Laski 1961,

11). Above all, the laws ultimately serve the interest of the dominant class, even when it sometimes stands above all groups.

****

The historiography of political organisation and state formation in Africa is largely viewed from two perspectives—whether the state is a product of external influence or a consequence of the social process and organic development. European or colonial historiography of pre-colonial states in Africa gives the impression that states or organised political systems were products of external influences, particularly the influence of 'superior' races outside Africa. The consensus among these colonial scholars is that pre-colonial Africa lacked the capacity for the effective political organisation beyond family and kinship. States and socio-political innovations were, therefore, attributed to racially different outsiders, called Hamites (Mamdani 2012). This colonial historiography is what is referred to as the Hamitic Hypothesis.

The Hamitic Hypothesis ascribes every important element in the cultures of sub-Saharan Africa, and more especially elaborate state structures, to Hamites, who were believed to have immigrated or invaded sub-Saharan societies from outside, often from Egypt or the Nile Valley, whether directly from those locations or having transited through before moving on to other locations (Sander 1969; Law 2009, 293 - 294). A classical assertion of this was C. G. Seligman's argument that "the civilisations of Africa are the civilisations of Hamites" (cited in Law 2009, 294). Hamites were believed to be racially white, most of them pastoralists, who conquered indigenous agriculturalists. Roland Oliver and John Fage (1962) were influential advocates of this thinking, through what they termed 'Sudanic Civilisation'. They explicitly drew their argument from the works of Hermann Baumann and his findings on structural similarities of African kingdoms (1940). They suggested that during the early post-Meroitic period, propagators of Egyptian and south-west Asian ideas of the state moved south-west and established new states, using cavalry warfare to conquer the agriculturalists south of the Sahara (Oliver and Fage 1962; Lange 2009). Specifically, they suggested that:

Stretching right across sub-Saharan Africa from the Red Sea to the south of Senegal, and right down to the central highland spine of Bantu Africa from the Nile sources to Southern Rhodesia, we find the axis of what we called the Sudanic Civilisation. The central feature of this civilisation was the incorporation of the various African peoples concerned into states whose institutions were so similar that they must have derived from a common source. At the head of such states, there were kings to whom divine powers were attributed...The 'Sudanic' state was a superstructure erected over village communities of peasant cultivators rather than a society which had grown up naturally out of them. In many cases, such states are known to have had their origins in conquest; in almost all other cases conquest must be suspected... Essentially, the 'Sudanic' state was a parasitic growth fastening itself upon the economic base of the pre-existing agricultural societies. To these societies, it contributed certain new ideas of political organisation and certain new techniques, notably in the field of mining, metallurgy, trade... (Oliver and Fage 1962, 44 – 45).

The hypothesis is largely built on white racial superiority and the denial of the historical achievements and developments of Black Africa. Although repudiated by the academic historiography that emerged in the 1950s, it was this framework that influenced early historical data collection, particularly those by European travellers and colonial collectors of oral traditions. It is, therefore, largely on this basis that several histories of origin and political processes were documented. African states and related political organisations were ascribed to Berbers, Egyptians, Arabs, Greek invasions, conquests, infiltration, assimilation or peaceful accommodation (Lange 2009). It is based on this that major African polities have been associated with external heroic legends like Oduduwa among the Yoruba, Bayajida for the Hausa and Kisra for Borgu, Kabbawa, Jukun (Kwararafa) amongst others (details of these are contained in the succeeding section) and Sayf bin Dhi Yazan for the Kanem-Borno.

This approach is not limited to only Europeans. Versions of this Hamitic hypothesis are found in West African Islamic historiography. There are elaborate collections made by medieval Arab writers. The Timbuktu manuscripts *Tarikh al Fattash* and *Tarikh al Sudan* made elaborate reference to elements related to this theory, particularly as it relates to North Africa and central Sudan (Meyerowitz 1972).

Mohammad Bello's *Infaq al-Maisur,* written in 1812, associated many Middle Eastern origins – usually Egypt, Yemen and Palestine – to a number of West African peoples (Law 2009). Also, as early as the twelfth century, the Kings of Ghana were claiming descent from a man called Salih, who was believed to be a great-grandson of Ali the nephew and son-in-law of the Prophet Muhammad. Ali was the fourth of the rightly guided caliphs of Islam.

According to Abdullahi Smith (1987), who is one of the leading critics of this Hamito-centric perspective, the argument is not only racist, it fails, also, to tell us how these individuals managed to produce the state and from where they derived their 'magical' powers. With the growing criticism by Africanist scholars, the idea of a foreign source of the state formation process in Africa and the related idea of widespread forceful conquest was modified in favour of a process of infiltration by pastoralists who were accommodated by agriculturalists. The state was, therefore, an outcome of a harmonious borrowing rather than forceful imposition (Oliver and Fage 1988, 37).

To be sure, state formation process is not an easy, linear one. It is a messy progression that can involve heroic or military leadership and action, but not necessarily. Major contradictions within a socio-political system could generate conflict with resultant implications of violence, such as wars and even conquest, in which individuals and groups play significant roles. Wars and conquests were not, however, necessarily enough to establish a state until some institutional transformation ensued which often involved a broader range of people. The historical conditions and the socio-political organisation of the people were key drivers of the state formation process in pre-colonial Africa.

Kisra Myth and Politics

The Kisra legend is an important example of the Hamitic Hypothesis and one of the most studied traditions of origin in West Africa. Versions of the legend have been associated with the riverine people in western Sudan from the Jukun in the middle of the Benue River, the Borgu on the eastern end of the Niger as well as areas under the Songhai Empire that held sway in the middle Niger (Stevens 1975). The common rendition is about the journey of a famous and great

Arabian/Persian ruler who, on resistance to Islam and Prophet Muhammad, fled the Arabian world and led a great migration of his people across the Sahara. In most of these places, Kisra was reported to either have visited, founded or his descendants are considered the founders of the state. In Nigeria in particular, Kisra is associated with over twenty different polities and societies. Of this number, only Borgu and probably Kebbi directly associate their dynastic history with Kisra himself (Stevens 1975).

There are contradictory accounts of Kisra in Borgu. Most of these accounts border on differential perceptions of Kisra as the original founder of the Borgu dynasty and whether or not he was physically present in Borgu and other places of settlement. According to Leo Frobenius[11], Kisra didn't only live and die in Borgu; he subjected the whole of Borgu after an extensive war.

> ... He subjected the whole of Borgu. He put kings over them everywhere, and, according to Albrecht Martius' researches in 1912, these were: Boa (three day's march to the west of Nikki), King Birjerima (Jerima in Houssa equals Crown Prince); in Kika (four days west of Nikki), King Bruka; in Lessa (two days from Kissiden), King Wagana; in Wue-nu (three days west of Nikki), King Kora (this Wu-enu is not identical with the one to be named later); King Djaru, in Dari; in Borish (five days from Nikki), King Saka; in Teme (four days west of Nikki), King Scheme; in Madeguru (four days from Teme), King Kora. Kisra made the first King of Nikki and at the same time his brother and afterwards his successor, Sheru Shikia ruled in Wu-enu, three hours distant from Nikki. (Frobenius 1913, 618).

Frobenius argued that Kisra lived and died in Bussa after departing Paiko in Gwariland (now in Niger State of Nigeria). According to him, Kisra only lived in the district of Paiko in Gwariland for ten and a half years. He then founded the city of Karishi, which lies three days march to the north of Kontangora in Dakarekareland. He resided there for

---

[11] Leo Frobenius, a Germen traveler, while on tour of Borgu and neigbouring regions in 1909 instituted what he called a Kisra Commission. The Commission was made up of a number of individuals believed to be knowledgeable about Kisra. His report on Kisra was a product of the deliberations – see Leo Frobenius, 1913, *the Voices of Africa*.

four and a half years, and then he went to Bussa. He resided alternatively in Karishi and Bussa. His brother represented him whenever he could not be available. After ruling for a further sixteen and a half years, he died and was buried in Bussa 28 years after the Hijra (650 AD) (Frobenius 1913, 619). Although in this narrative, Kisra was believed to have died in 650 AD, some of these identified settlements were nineteenth-century settlements and the oldest may not be earlier than the fifteenth or fourteenth century.

Fage, one of the key proponents of a Sudanic state, apparently drawing from this rendition, added that Kisra eventually conquered Borgu and Yorubaland. Similar traditions were recorded by C. L. Temple who claimed Kisra followers "settled all over Bussa and the west of the district." Accordingly, those he referred to as "principal men" settled in and around Bussa itself, while "the poorer people extended westward" (Temple 1922, 496). Apart from Frobenius' elaborate account, all other accounts, including those collected in Bussa, assert that Kisra himself never reached the city (Stevens 1975, 188). This can also be seen from the different Borgu variants of the legend.

****

Different narratives of Kisra are reflected even within Borgu. The differences are largely based on Kisra movements and the claim of seniority and authenticity of origin. The Bussa tradition, which is arguably considered the most common and mainstream, holds that Kisra, in resistance to Islam in the seventh century, migrated westward through Borgu and settled at the Niger bend. The Niger was then a narrow stream, which got expanded through Kisra's magical powers. Kisra died leaving three children – Woru, Sabi and Biyo (Bio)[12]. While Woru succeeded his father and settled in Bussa, Sabi and Biyo established Nikki and Illo respectively (Crowder 1973).

Another Bussa version, recorded by Temple, provides that Kisra, on a chase by his enemies, crossed the Niger, which was then a small stream. This served as barrier between him and his enemies. For this

---

[12] In Boko and Baatonu traditions, the first male child bears a protoname of Woru, the second is Sabi, third is Biyo or Bio, fourth is Boni (Bani in Boko).

reason, no king of Bussa was allowed to cross the Niger until the twentieth century. One of Kisra's brothers settled at Karisen (Sakaba); another, Woru) at Illo, while the third, Sharu, left the main camp in Gaunji to Nikki and Kisra himself turned eastward and founded Bussa (Temple 1922).

A related version was recorded in Illo. Although Kisra was believed not to have personally settled in Borgu, his descendants founded Illo, Nikki and Bussa, with Bussa being the senior; and the founder of Nikki was believed to be a brother-in-law to the other two. Bussa, therefore, received presents from Illo and Nikki (Temple 1922). Some "Kisra relics," which Heath (1937) called regalia, were believed to have remained in Bussa. Amongst them include a *gangan Kisra*[13] (big drum), kettledrums, spears and brass bowls. The authenticity of these artefacts may need to be archaeologically studied as most of them can be found in almost every Borgu principality and undoubtedly the cultural artefact of Borgu.

A completely different tradition was recorded in Nikki. One of the versions provides that after crossing the Niger, the Waziri (Minister) of Kisra settled at Gbewalla from where he sent emissaries to the kings of Nikki and Bweru. In return for the hospitality of the people, the leader of the Kisra party sent horses to their host. The leader of Nikki and Bweru later visited with the Kisra party and showed respect to the leader who was a very old man. This was believed to be the origin of tribute the King of Nikki pays to Bussa in form of *Gindi* (fodder) and *Konto* (sickle) (Idris 1973). Another tradition in Kaiama holds that Kisra died before reaching Bussa: that Bussa was founded by Kisra's lieutenant, whom the Kisra children regarded as a father. Before Bussa, Kisra's children and followers first settled at a different place, probably Gbewalla[14]. It was from there the Waziri went eastward to establish Bussa, while Woru went to found Nikki and his brothers, the smaller towns of Sandilo and Bueuy (Idris 1973).

A related tradition was recorded in the early period of colonial subjugation by an Acting Resident in Kaiama, Kemble. This version

---

[13] This translates to "Kisra's Drum" in Hausa. It is called Tambari (Tambura), and found in almost every Borgu principality. It is only played for kings and princes.

[14] Musa Baba Idris reported that it was a place not far from present-day Babanna and not also far from Bweru. See Musa Baba Idris 1973, pp. 137

attributes seniority to Nikki and a servile status to Bussa. According to this tradition, Kisra, along with his followers, wives and slaves, after crossing the River Niger, which was then a small stream, settled in Bussa where he lived for many years and had two sons. The two sons were out on a long hunting expedition toward Nikki when their father died. The slaves sent to deliver the message of their father's death found them in Nikki. They requested that all burial rites be performed at Bussa and Nikki.

> ... one of the brothers was then made King of Nikki and whatever he wanted done at Bussa, he told the slaves and it was done. The King of Nikki now had two sons and they went out hunting; and while they were away, their father died. Messages were sent out to look for them, but they were not found for a long time and therefore a younger brother who had been born during their absence was made King. When the two brothers heard that their father was dead and a younger brother made King, one brother said let us fight for the throne, but the other said no, as our younger brother has been made the King of Nikki, we must go to other places and be made King there. The Elder went to Buai and the younger to Kaiama where they were made kings. (Idris 1973, 158 -159).

The Kisra legend doesn't only show us the difficulty of relying on oral tradition; it clearly reveals how these traditions can be instruments of politics, in bolstering the claims and counter-claims of superiority. Each of these versions was meant to serve a political purpose. While the Bussa-related versions served to reinforce the paramountcy of Bussa in the Borgu political structure, the Kaiama, and to some extent the Nikki version, try to deny that, seeking to assert not only the independence of these polities but also to delegitimise Bussa by questioning the authenticity of its Kisra origin. Generally, these varying traditions are reflections of peer competition and tension between the major principalities.

There are extensive accounts of Kisra generally, particularly in Arabic writings. The character of Kisra in Arabic literature and historiography is of a powerful anti-Islamic symbol and a major opponent of Prophet Mohammed in the seventh century. Kisra is actually the Arabic name of the Sassanian Chosroes. The first of the Chosroes reigned between 531 AD and 579 AD and the second reigned from 590 to 628 AD. Several other kings of Persian origin used the name right up to the twelfth century. Arabic writers since the first century appear to have adopted Kisra as a generic name for all Persian kings. It is not clear how and when the Kisra legend became a major historical account of Borgu. It, however, became popular among the ruling class, whom the European travellers and colonial officers interviewed. This narrative appears not to be popular among peasants and in rural communities even up to the present.

As with all the major Arabic sources, Frobenius (1913), Palmer (1928) and Mathews (1950) associated Kisra movements with the seventh century, which coincided with the inception of Islam. Others have associated the Kisra with the Songhai invasion of Borgu in the fifteenth century; purported migration of Mande-speaking people (Boko) from Mali Empire during the reign of Mansa Musa (1308 – 1331) into Borgu (Steward 1985) or the emergence and movements of Wangara from Songhay in the fourteenth century (Adekunle 2004).

Meek (1925) suggests that the Kisra tradition represents early Mandikan or Songhai and perhaps Nubian influence. He observes that the tradition is strongest in Bussa, where Boko, a Mande language, is spoken. He attempts to derive Kisra from two Boko words – *Ki* (king) and *shira* or *sira/sia* (black). Therefore, etymologically, Kisra could mean a "black king." Meek also suggests that Kisra could be derived from the Hausa word *Sarki* (King). "Kisra may possibly have been Ali Kilnu of Songhai, who captured Timbuktu AD 1468 ... or maybe ... the Mosi emperor (called Nasira in his own country – *na* being a royal title = *ki*) who pillaged the territory of Ali Kilnu AD 1480" (Meek 1925, 72; McCall 1968). He, therefore, suggests 1480 as the apparent date of the arrival of Kisra in Borgu, which totally contradicts the seventh century narrative of Kisra movement.

Although there appears to be agreement on the possibility of migration, the legend of Kisra is largely a myth. Analysing a 1910 letter from Kitoro Gaani[15] to G. R. de Gironcourt, Moreas Farias just about dismisses the Kisra legend as a fabrication of Muslim scholars who were close to the aristocracy. He alleges that it was the Muslims in the Kings' courts who had the means – education and exposure – to

---

[15] Kitoro Mahman Gaani, colonial-era Emir of Bussa, although unlettered, wrote to G.R. Gironcourt on his visit to Bussa explaining the origin of Bussa. The letter was written in Arabic in 1910.

produce Kisra tradition linking it with the Islamic history of the production of the Kisra tradition. The manuscript was, therefore, evidence that local Muslims were active "thinkers, who shaped theories of distant origin so as to grasp local African realities, and who used in creative and topical ways, the Islamic learning available to them" (Moraes Farias 1992, 128).

Similarly, Phillips Stevens conceives the Kisra as an ideological ploy against external threats. For him, the legend has created what he called a 'Kisra effect' – the distortion of historical tradition in response to a real or imagined external threat (Stevens 1975). Writing specifically about the existence of an elaborate Kisra legend in Borgu and Birnin Kebbi, Stevens speculated that it was a response to the isolation the two polities suffered due to their military strength and independence over a long period of time. The states had militarily maintained their independence from Songhai and later, from Fulbe jihadist incursions but in the process, they had become isolated from their neighbours and allies. The popular attachment to the Kisra legend, with the recognition that similar tradition existed among their foes, not only justified the maintenance of independence but also raised a new banner of social identity and unity (Stevens 1975, 194).

A couple of scholars disagreed with Steven's suggestion (Stewart 1980; Kuba and Akinwumi, 2004; Adekunle 2004). Kuba and Akinwumi observed that the hypothesis fails to adequately account for the legend in context. For Stewart, the issue of ideology is worth considering as long as it is based on the "changing ideological emphases of various versions reflects the political relationships that developed between the rulers of the three Borgu kingdoms and between each of the rulers and their subjects – relationships which was grounded on the right to rule over the local indigenous people" (Stewart 1980, 53). She noted that the differences in the narratives of the legend contributed immensely to the illumination of the Borgu political process as it developed over the centuries. Stewart further associated the Kisra group with Boko language, even if they weren't indigenous to Borgu, "in that they speak Boko, a Manding language, which is different from Bargu [sic] ...the language spoken by indigenes of the state" (Stewart 1980, 54).

Apparently drawing from Meek's Songhai hypothesis, though limited by evidence, Stewart (1980) suggests that the pattern of movement of the Mande people corresponds with the Kisra legend. The original Mande language was located in what is now Mali and was spread by traders to all parts of western Sudan from at least the thirteenth century onwards. This dispersal of traders led to the establishment of discrete Mande-speaking regions in western Sudan, of which Borgu is believed to be the farthest east from Mali. Nevertheless, as noted earlier, there are newer arguments that the relationship is at best very remote. That Boko, the Mande language in Borgu, has become distinct in its dialectal and lexical features attests to the fact that this language was already in existence for several centuries. The origin and early history of the people speaking Mande languages, including the eastern division of the Mande language of which Boko belongs, is unknown, but Welmer suggests that the upper Nile Valley is the original Niger-Congo homeland and that the Mande language as part of the Niger-Congo conglomerate is, therefore, associated with the area. While these suggestions are unsupported by empirical evidence, they do correspond to the pattern discussed in Kisra legend (Stewart 1980, 54).

Associated with the Kisra legend is a Bussa tradition that links the Bussa ruling class with Borno. Although reported in several colonial documents, Kuba (1998) leads the post-colonial reconstruction of this tradition. While dismissive of Stewart's hypothesis of possible Songhay origin, Kuba holds on the possibility of tracing the origin of the Borgu ruling dynasties to Kanem-Borno. Kuba relies largely on colonial sources, oral tradition and associated elements of the Kisra migration, particularly the element that Kisra first settled in Borno before proceeding to Bussa. It was reported during the early colonial times that the rulers of Bussa sent tributes in form of gifts of a number of sickles, choppers, horses, herbs or medicines, firewood to the King of Borno and received in return camels, horses and suites of cloths (Duff 1920; Cary 1907).

Kitoro of Bussa (1814 -1830) was reported to have told Hugh Clapperton on a visit to Borgu in 1826 that the inhabitants of the Bussa region were "Cambrie [Kambari]" but added that his own ancestors were from Borno and that the "Sultan of Niki was descended from a younger branch of his family" and that they paid tribute to Borno until the eruption of the Fulbe Jihad disrupted movement to Borno. To prove that this tradition is still associated with the Kisra legend, Clapperton further reported that "Youriba, Niki, Kaiama, Wawa and Youri, paid tribute to Bornou." John Lander, who continued the return journey after the death of his principal in Sokoto and later visited with his brother, reported thus:

> The people of Boussa [Bussa], the principal state in Borgoo (Borgu), together with those of its sister provinces of Youri [Yauri], Wow [Wawa] and Khiama [Kaiama], are indebted to the Bornouese [people of Borno] for their origin; or at least the traditions of the natives intimate that Borgoo was colonized from Bornou at a remote era, in which opinion all classes implicitly believe; and, like the Carthaginians of old, but send annually a number of presents by way of acknowledgement to their ancient country; although of late years, owing to the disturbances of the Falatas [Fulbe], the accustomed presents have not been received in Bornou with the same punctuality as formerly. (Lander, pp. 286 – 287).

The closeness in names were also major points of convergence – Borgu and Borno or Beri-beri and Bariba. Governor Moloney of Lagos claimed the language of Borgu is closely related to that of Kanuri of Borno. He tried to prove this with a number of Borno and Borgu words for one, two, three, four, body, child, dog and rain. Anene (1965, 212) found the correspondence "remarkable but hardly conclusive." While it is not clear which of the Borgu languages Moloney tested, for Boko and Baatonum, the two main languages, it appears absolutely far-fetched.

Borgu and Borno, apart from the closeness of their names, are believed to share a joking relationship (*yobo* in Boko, *gonnaru* in Baatonum). The existence of this relationship is a matter of contention as it is not as pronounced as the joking relationship between the Nupe and Katsinawa, Tiv and Fulbe or Fulbe and Kanuri people of Borno. Even if confirmed to exist, a joking relationship is not necessarily evidence of kinship affinities. It is also suggested that Borgu may also have been a vassal of Borno based on the expansion of the Kanem-Borno from the Lake Chad region south-westward to the River Niger in the thirteenth century (Kuba and Akinwumi 2005).

Beyond the origin, wars and related adventure of Kisra found in Islamic history and folklore, there are other elements of the legend that are believed to have a local origin. It is, therefore, probable that pre-existing narratives of migration and names phonetically close to Kisra combined with later contacts with Muslims to shape the Kisra legend. The legend could, thus, be a "reshaping of existing dynastic tradition according to Muslim world view" (Kuba and Akinwumi 2005, 327).

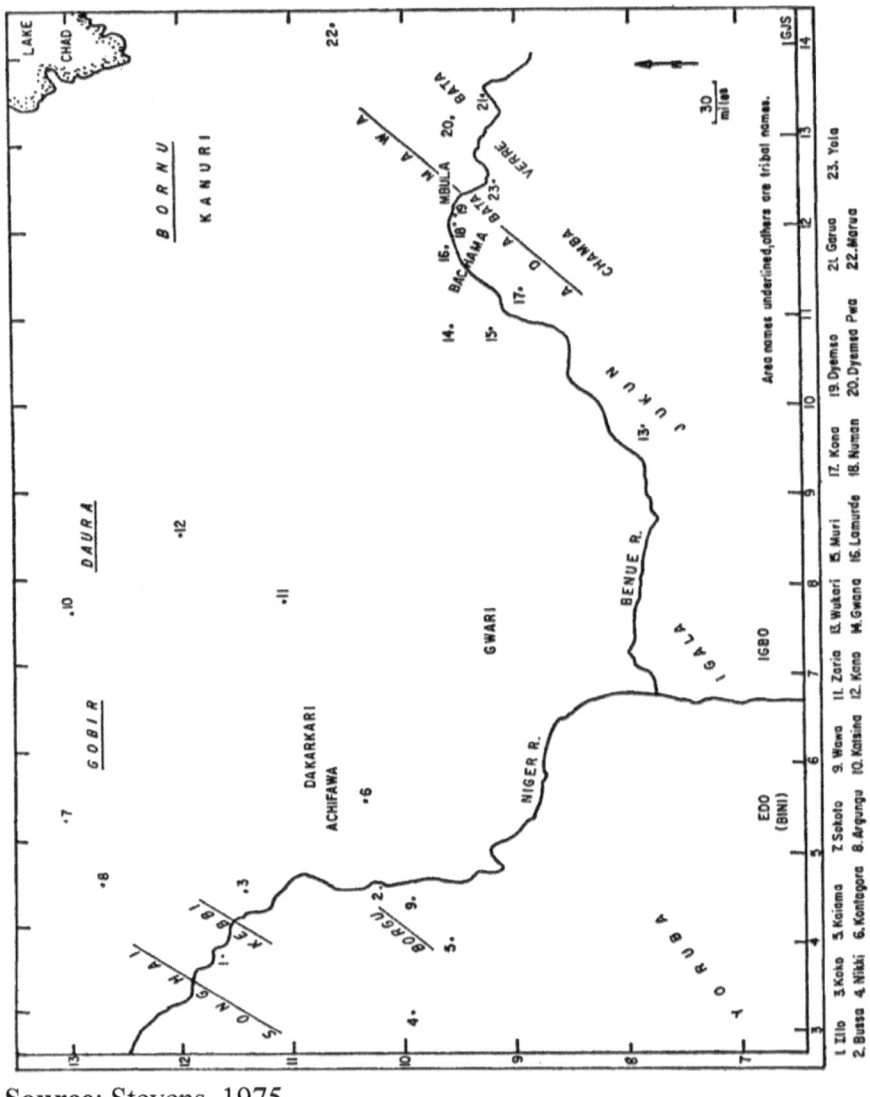

Source: Stevens, 1975

Accordingly, I agree with Stevens (1975) and Idris (1973) that the Kisra tradition is a myth and a fabrication. It should be cautiously accepted as an interpretative event that might have been distorted or influenced by later events or powerful forces in the history of the area, or something brought about through "some sort of comparable word-play" (Idris 1973). Idris observed that the structural features of Borgu made it receptive to the Kisra legend. However, he suggested that the Kisra legend cannot be treated as a historical account. "... approaching the legend by historiographic methods can only continue to mislead the historian.... Legends have their own logic. It is important to distinguish between legends which simply romanticise historical events and legends that belong entirely to the realm of myth, even if they make use of names and events of proven historicity" (Idris 1973, 130).

Myths are largely located in the realm of traditionality: they are not necessarily a lack of science or failure of reasoning. They are also rooted in racial ideology, which the Hamitic Hypothesis shares. In traditional African societies, this ideology is characterised by what Mbembe called *"facticity"* and *"arbitrariness."* Facticity is about the immediacy of *truth* – simplistic fact that requires no questioning or justification since it has always been like that and people believed it. Arbitrariness, on the other hand, is in contrast to reasoning, where "myth and fables are seen as major definers of order and time in traditional societies, they, therefore, require no justification and cannot be questioned" (Mbembe 2001, 4).

It is in this context that colonial anthropologists, historians and administrators documented Borgu oral history without critical questions and sometimes with embellishments.

Pre-Dynastic Political Organisation

To understand how a state emerged in Borgu is to examine the historical processes and political evolution, the local power structure and its dynamics, the economic structure and the nature and character of external contacts in the different phases of the history of the area. The pre-colonial states in Borgu, like those in other pre-colonial societies, were products of long political and economic processes. They were a reflection of the peculiar value system, social structure, religion and economic structure of the society that created them. The characteristics of each of the political systems evolved at different times and can be better understood with reference to historical processes and events that shaped them (Kuba and Akinwumi 2005).

Generally, the discourse of the state and state structure in pre-colonial Borgu revolves around the centralised formation led by the Wasangari. Although scholars have made reference to an earlier structure, the details of these are often missing. Some seem to assume that there was no centralised state formation before the Wasangari. Crowder (1973) suggests that some elements of a state system might have existed for Borgu to have resisted major empires like Songhai and Mali in the late fourteenth to early fifteenth centuries.

According to Adekunle (2004), there was no "centralised or unified force and no well-preserved state system in the pre-dynastic period. Hence, the Borgu region didn't have any recognisable political identity" (pp. 436). Because of a perceived lack of evidence of an elaborate centralised political structure, Adekunle further suggested that "presumably, clan or lineage heads who were not entrusted with political authority led the people. In other words, the people existed in acephalous or stateless societies" (2004, 78). In apparent self-contradiction, he recognises that the social and political organisation of the pre-dynastic period "indicated the existence of a closely-knit society. Like other parts of West Africa, village democracy constituted parts of the settlement's unique organisation. Under the lineage administration, elders met to discuss village problems" (2004, 90). While he acknowledges archaeological evidence on the material culture of the people, he suggested a gap of information on the political organisation. It is quite puzzling that people can develop an appreciable material culture without political organisation. A further study could easily reveal the relationship between social relations of production and the political organisation of the people. In the run of history, Borgu exhibited different political systems and its identity revolved around these systems at different times. The dynastic formation only helped to create a pan-Borgu identity occasioned by the myth of Kisra, but not necessarily the rampaging influence of Wasangari, as important as they are to the dynastic structure.

While it could be correct that societies of Borgu have not always been politically centralised, it is important to recognise that centralisation was a process, not an event. Therefore, the processes leading to that might have passed through different phases. It is in recognition of this that other scholars appear to suggest that such structures were small – family, village and lineage-based. Borgu, in this early period, didn't have an overarching political structure encompassing the entire geographical area. Settlements were expanding, villages were growing and social structures and occupational groups growing. Acquisition and use of slave labour might have also developed. There were inter-communal skirmishes, if not outright wars, as can be seen from the reported Songhai invasions in the fifteenth century. The political systems in Borgu were highly localised. It is probable that sovereign control was limited to villages and towns and this might have expanded as the villages grew and clustered around each other.

In northern and central Borgu, *Kibe* or *Kina* (King or Leader) had developed among the Boko people, while the Baatombu had *Suno*. Each village or settlement had a leader. Geo-political identities were restricted to villages and their surroundings called *busu* and *tem* among Boko and Baatonu people respectively. There were Bussa *busu*, Gbere *busu*, Illo *busu* and Makara *tem* comprising Tomtaro, Deema, Wenu-Susu and Nikki (Lafia 2015). Citizenship or membership identity was not necessarily ethnic as some were territorial, such as village settlements. Among the Boko-speaking people, this is called *Gbee* (person) or *Ne* (son), thus Bussa-*gbee* or Bussa-*ne,* and this territoriality was collectively referred to as *Zogbe* (Boko people, as self-referred).

The political system across the region significantly differed. Idris (1973) and Adekunle (2004) erroneously reduced the system to a village or lineage and gerontocratic administrations. While lineages were important in the early phase of settlement in the area at the point of formation, in time, lineages intermixed and heterogeneous polities emerged. In Nikki Wenu, for instance, Dendi settlements have developed just like the emergence of other ethnic groups like Laru, Kambari people in Bussa and Illo. While kinship may be relevant in defining occupational groups, all occupational groups were part of the social structure that defined the state. Adekunle (2004) got it wrong when he referred to the head of a lineage as *Baa*. *Baa* is a patronymic for an elder or father: it is not necessarily a title. It is significantly different from *Ki* or *Kibe* (*Suno or Yinni* in Baatonu), which means king. Its use as a prefix for some political tittles was just a recognistion of the partriachal and gerontocratic character; as such titles are both masculine and age-determined (elderly).

The predynastic state structures were deeply localised. The Boko political system was probabaly different from that of Baatonu. Among the Baatombu, the head of the village or community was *Suno*. It is not clear how the political system was structured or the relationship between the villages. Idris (1973) was certain that the *Suno* Barisonga of Dema had political control over a wide territory of what later became the metropolitan area of Nikki. Wenu-Suno, the custodian of the deity of *Wuuru* in Nikki-Wenu, was believed to be the spiritual head. According to Lafia (2015), Wassa had Wassa Suno, while Kpandesuno was responsible for Kpande. There was also Bagou Suno for Bagou, Nam Suno for Banikpara and Sina Sarougi for Maratem, which comprised Tomtaro, Dema, Wenu-Susu and Nikki.

On the Boko side, early settlements of Gbere (Wawa), Kanibe, Kabaru and Wozibe among others also had a localized kingship system. Bussa in particular provided a relatively decentralised system when compared to the early structure in Nikki and other early Baatonu settlements. In the Bussa region, political leadership was observed to be among the Boko, while some occupational activities combined with spiritual leaderships are provided by Badaburude. (*Daburu* means fishing hook. Badaburude could therefore literarily, means head of fisherfolk). The role appears to be more of a head of the fishing community in the area. Idris (1973) noted that the Badaburude probably represented a vestige of earlier occupants before Ba-Karabonde whose people migrated from the middle of the Niger and served as Earth Priests in the Wasangari era.

The Karabonde were probably originally Tienga people (early extraction of Boko), and possibly linked to the Mandigo from Mali. The Karabonde were the original custodians of the Zekara or Zekana shrine – a hilly shrine highly consulted for fertility. It is arguably the oldest and most patronised shrine in the region, especially among the Boko-speaking people (details in the succeeding section on religion). The shrine was led by a Ba Maso (*Maso* means oracle in Boko, *Ba Maso* could, therefore, mean Head of Oracle). What later became the territorial and sovereign coverage of Bussa was a loose structure of leadership involving two principals: Bakarabonde as the head, and his brother, Bamode, who lived in Monnai (Idris 1973). Other ethnic formations in the area had a different leadership structure that was nonetheless linked to the Bakarabonde. Each village around this area had their leader.

The head of Kagogi was Namubere. The settlement was made up of indigenous Kambari, Nupe and Laru speaking people. Lumma had Beresara, while the head of Zali was Beresaru. The heads of Shagunu, Shagunu Gwagwa and Shagunu Duga were Sombede, Manabere and Bereduga respectively (Idris 1973). The relationship between Bussa and Gbere (Wawa) was not clear during this period, but they appeared to be of the same ethnic origin. The head of Wawa was Magai Weragi and was responsible for other settlements such as Fakum and Kanibe. The later generation of Tienga settlements in and around contemporary Kaiama like Lashibe had Kilashi, Wozibe had Kiwozi as the political and spiritual head, while Kabaru had Ki-Kabaru, who was also the Chief Priest of Konko Shrine (Idris 1973, Adekunle 2004).

Kaiama, although often referred to as an eighteenth-century settlement, might have been there much longer. The eighteenth-century date was an apparent reference to dynastic history, rather than to the history of settlement. It was, at different times, called Gbegazi and later Mewi (the name Mewi is still popular amongst the surrounding villages). The name Kaama/ Kamma/ Kaiama, is probably linked to dynastic history. Kaama has been transformed to Kaiama as a result of a misspelling of the original name first by European travellers and later colonial officials. It appears Kamma is a latter-day invention derived from *mewi* (rest), to provide an etymological source for the name, just like Gbasorro or Bussa[16] (from *ma Bussa*). All were attempts to associate settlement names with 'rest'. The name of a village or settlement doesn't need to make immediate meaning or etymological sense. Names are largely what others call a settlement, not necessarily what the settlers call it. Settlements, particularly of early generations, were also not essentially named by the settlers.

The same applies to several other Borgu settlements; their names were distorted through wrong spellings and adoption of non-Borgu rendition. As a result, Yaashikiru, became Yashikira; Desa became

---

[16] There is a general tendacy in the region to associate the etymology of names of settlements to "rest". Kaiama, Bussa, Gbasoro etc. have been questionably linked to this.

Ilesha Bariba, Seru Kperu became Okuta, Tikandu became Chikanda, Taberu, became Tabera, and several others across the region. Nevertheless, for consistency, I have adopted the official and recorded names despite the obvious distortions.

****

The political structure was ideologically sustained by the material and spiritual (ritual) system. Religion played an important role in defining the state and the power and character of the political leadership. Therefore, the emerging polities were based on the duality of political control and ritual hegemony, supported by agricultural production, which was supplemented by fishing, hunting and pastoralism by the Fulbe. Ritual and the political system acted dialectically and complementarily in reinforcing and reifying each other. In most cases, the leadership of the two is different, but in some instances, the political leadership also exercised some spiritual leadership, mostly under the supervision and control of a ritual structure. The spiritual leadership, or the Earth Priests, was that of intermediaries between the living and the spirit world, including local deities and ancestors.

It appears that leadership was not deeply monarchical during this early period. Age or birth status in the lineage was more important, but it was not a major determining factor. Leaders' claim to authority was also spiritual. Family size, hunting prowess and warfare were other key determinants. The leader, in consultation with the spiritual head, determined a lot of community decisions and actions including migration, warfare and control/response to epidemics.

The social relations of production revolved around families and villages. Land was collectively owned and the production system was largely subsistent. Metallurgical technology had developed and smithing lineages had emerged, called *Siya* in Boko and *Seko* in Baatonum. The blacksmiths produced all the agricultural tools and war equipment, including spears and poisonous arrows. They also produced domestic utensils like knives. Bussa, Wawa and Kubli, Wozibe, among others, had large iron deposits and were major centres of metallurgy (Adekunle 2004).

It is not clear whether a strong medium of payment had developed, but barter trade was still very strong up to the eighteenth century. Agriculture was an all-encompassing vocation. Almost every member of the society was involved. Other occupational activities were part-time and seasonal. For instance, the blacksmiths were available in their factories, called *siya kpen* in Boko and *seko gbaburu* in Baatonum, only during the dry season. The blacksmiths also had spiritual relevance. They were believed to have ritual control over thunder and served in oath-taking and exorcism of witchcraft.

There were strong fishing communities in the riverine areas, while drummers and entertainment lineages had also developed. Butchery and butcher clans were a latter development, with a strong association with the Fulbe pastoralists. It appears the butchers were originally a lineage of hunters who transformed their vocation to trade in the eighteenth century.

Settlement Pattern

It appears each of the Borgu settlements had a complex network of people with multiple identities. They were either in the *wu* and *wete* (towns in Baatonum and Boko respectively). There are three categories of towns and settlements: *maro* and *wete* (city in Baatonum and Boko respectively). There were also the surrounding *lakutu* (villages) and *bura-lakutu*, (farm settlements in Boko). Up to the eighteenth century, Nikki was the only settlement classified as *Maro* (city). Others were *wu*, *barukpaaru* (villages) and *gberu* (farms settlement in Baatonum). In Kaiama axis, *Mewi* is misconstrued to mean a city or big town, but in reality, it is one of the original names of Kaiama, which of course happen to be largest in the region.

The Fulbe community and their Gando slaves were settled in cattle camps, called *kpasa* in Boko and *gaa* in Baatonum, which were more remote than even the *barukpaaru* or *lakutu*. Each of these settlements was attached to different occupations relevant to the lives of the people. While the villages and farm settlements were largely peasant settlements producing food, they also contributed to the military force and produced some farm implements and weapons of war. Most shrines and places of divination were located around these village settlements. They produced medication for the treatment of illnesses and combating epidemics. The Fulbe settlements were largely pastoral. Through their cattle, they were linked to both the ruling classes and other occupational groups. They provided the major source of beef protein for the communities.

The eighteenth-century witnessed an extensive growth of towns and villages. This expansion was associated with the increase in caravan movements across Borgu and the violent succession conflicts and wars that pervaded the region. New settlements emerged to access new opportunities, while others were set up by disgruntled groups and others emigrating from war and related disasters. The social composition of most Borgu principalities also changed in the eighteenth century with the expansion of long-distance trade and Islam. This period saw another wave of immigration from neighbouring and even distance polities. This wave of migration and social contacts had a significant influence on the culture and economic activities of the people. People who dwelt in the principal towns were believed to be smarter and more engaging. A slight change in the way they spoke was noticed, due to contact with other languages and cultures. This created a distinction between the town dwellers and the rustic people in the villages, not only in terms of social organisation but also in economic activity and identity. By the close of the eighteenth century, some of these immigrating groups have been incorporated to the governance structure of the state as the case of Dendi people in Nikki or the Kambari in Wawa. The towns became the most cohesive socio-political entities in Borgu.

Occupational Groups

The occupational groups were the most distinctive units formed around economic activities. Six main occupational groups can be identified during this period. They were the farmers, pastoralists, blacksmiths, butchers, fisherfolk, drummers/griots, merchants and priestly/clerical groups. There were also other vocational groups like hunters, artisans (woodcarvers, weavers, dyers) musicians/singers and related artists. The structure of these occupational groups differed based on historical and social composition.

Borgu was an agrarian society. Farming was the first and primary occupation of the people. It seems almost everybody was involved in food production at least for family subsistence. Each family had a *bura* or *gberu*, (a farm in Boko and Baatonum). Farm labour was collective family labour and sometimes it was possible to draw on community labour to support the family particularly during the planting and harvest season. Yam, sorghum, cassava, potatoes, maize, rice and millet were the principal crops. Indigo was also a very important plant in Borgu. It was used by the local textile industry for dyeing.

Famers were supported by blacksmiths who produced the necessary farm tools and war weapons. The blacksmiths were, therefore, very important to the three major preoccupations of the Borgu community— farming, hunting and warfare (Idris 1973). With good iron deposits, iron smelting developed quite early in the region.

Pastoralism was an important occupational group and a major economic activity linked to the political economy of Borgu. Pastoral activities were largely an occupation of the Fulbe people, who were widely spread across Borgu. They were the major source of meat and *gasaru* and *gasi* (cheese in Baatonum and Boko respectively). The Fulbe Borgu have probably been in the region since the sixteenth century and have been deeply attached to some of the cultural and political systems of Borgu. The butchers were attached to the pastoral groups. They were responsible for the killing and sale of meat in the region. The griots were involved in the entertainment of the aristocratic classes.

Occupational groups like blacksmiths, drummers and butchers have historically ossified into almost a semi-caste structure, with all the characteristics of exclusiveness. People were born into these occupations and it remained their occupations even if they were not practising it. They, therefore, had clan names such as *yari*, *seko* and *mako* for butchers, blacksmiths and drummers respectively. These occupations might have started as voluntary vocations but historically got crystallised through the process of state formation, becoming a principal category in the socio-political structure. This was a means of monopolising the occupation and also guaranteeing occupational services to society.

The Merchant Group – Wangara

The merchant group were largely the trading community called *Wangara*. This group played an important commercial and Islamic role in Borgu. The earlier usage of Wangara was both territorial and ethnic. In a geographical sense, they covered the commercial space of the Sudanese region of West and North Africa. As a people, they were believed to be Mande-speaking but of different origins. According to Levtzion (1968, pp. 3), this group of Muslim traders were known by different names. They were called "Dyula among the Malinke of the Upper Niger, Marka by the Bambara in the region of Segu and Jenne, Dafing in the bend of the Upper Black Volta River, and Yarse by the people speaking Mole-Dagbane language." Wangara was a derivation from Arabic sources, and that was the name they were known by in Hausa and Fulfulde. They were largely responsible for both commerce and Islamisation in Hausaland in the fourteenth century (Palma 1908; Al-Hajj 1968).

In Borgu, as in Hausaland, the Wangara were the prime drivers of trade and Islamic activities. Until the late nineteenth century, the Wangara controlled most of the commercial activities of Borgu, leading the kolanut trade, gold, and related foreign goods. Although a distinct cultural and religious group, the Wangara had economically and politically integrated with the larger structure of Borgu. The Wangara and Fulbe formed the economic nerve wire of Borgu society and had built a complex symbiotic relationship with the aristocracy. As a lettered group with a better knowledge of regional and world affairs, the aristocracy and the kings relied on them for advice, communication, interpretation and external affairs. The aristocracy depended on them for information about the movement of caravans to enable them to prepare for tolls or criminal pillage. In the later years, the Wangara became symbols of spiritual power. The aristocracy relied on them for charms and divination in support of political ambitions. The Wangara, in turn, received protection from the aristocracy for their internal and external trade (Idris 1973).

The Wangara retained their traditional patronymics of *Ture, Silla (Sira), Taruwere, Fofana, Sisse, Manne* or *Mande*. Those of Silla patronymic were believed to have immigrated from Kasati on the River Niger near Illo and were ancestrally linked to the Dendi language. As would be seen in chapter 4, the Dendi may have founded communities in Borgu during the Songhay Empire in the sixteenth century, especially in Djougu in the west of Borgu. They controlled the external trade of Borgu and dealt primarily in slaves, textiles, kolanuts, salt and potash (Lovejoy 1971). The Dendi language played an important role with the arrival of different Songhay groups after the Moroccan invasion of Songhay in the sixteenth century (Idris 1973). Some of their earlier settlements were around Godebere, Tomboua and Nikki. From there they dispersed to other places.

The Wangara were an immensely hierarchical community with the Imam at the top. The Imam was the leader of the Muslim faithful and, therefore, the leader of the Wangara community. He was responsible for all Islam-related activities. The Imam, later in the nineteenth century, became a member of the king's courts in almost all the Borgu states. He was followed by the *Baa-parakpe, Annaini, Ladani-Madiwu*. On the feminine side was *Yon Wokpe*, who was responsible for Wangara women, coordinating marriages and ensuring Islamic discipline and Wangara morality among women. She was more like the *Yon Kogi* of the Wasangari aristocracy. They also had the *Wokpe* who was responsible for girls or younger women, who coordinated social activities and facilitated young people's support during marriage. The young men had *Sabebe,* who was called *Sarkin Samari* in Kaiama.

Other major commercial groups were the Hausa and Kambarin Bariberi, especially in the late nineteenth century. These communities often assimilated with the Wangara and adopted the patronymics of Manne or Mande (Idris 1973). The Hausa (Gambari or Gambaru in Borgu) came under the banner of Islam. Their integration with the Wangara community was enhanced by their entrepreneurial skills and Islamic faith. At the end of the nineteenth century, the Hausa overthrew the original Wangara in long-distance trade dominance.The Difference between Hausa and Dendi traders was largely around residency. While Dendi became more settled in the eighteenth century and became politically integrated with Borgu, Hausa were more itinerant. The Hausa trade dominance was, therefore, more in international trade than the domestic trade in Borgu.

Kinship and Lineage Groups

Several patrilineal households formed lineages and clans. These lineages might have been drawn from across several generations. Apart from settlements and patrons, family genealogy and patronymics were major means of identifying clans. While these clans were identified by names, they did not appear to have formed any effective cohesion in the economic and political system of the Borgu. In some towns and villages, though, people belonging to the same group or clan might cluster together, maintaining considerable cohesion and providing mutual support for each other.

The social structure of the Baatombu was largely built around clans and sub-clans. Amongst them were *Dorosika, Baare, Sessi-Baru, Wonko, Tossu, Nari, Seko* and *Yoo*. Others were *Yari, Doo, Kenu, Buro, Kio* and *Kusso* (Lafia 2006). There were three types of descent groups in Borgu: the occupational groups, servile groups and the aristocracy. To a lesser extent, the Muslim clerical establishment transformed to clans, as *Imams* within the traditional setting, were appointed exclusively within this group.

As stated earlier in this chapter, in Borgu, some occupational groups were also lineage groups. People were born into them and it remained so, whether practising or not, and they were expected to perform all the rituals and taboos associated with such a descent group. The occupational descent was largely associated with drummers/griots, butchers, blacksmiths and priests. Baatonu and Boko had the same clan name for butchers – *Yari, Mako* for the griots/drummers and *Seko* for the blacksmiths. This is further evidence that the structural consolidation of these occupations had a strong relationship with the state formation process.

The members of these occupational groups were from autochthonous communities. These clans were made up of extended families of unilateral patrilineal descent, having putative common ancestry. The primary social unit amongst the Baatonu and the Boko was the extended family, and these were composed of people of different generations, male and female, old and young. Children were named according to the hierarchy of their birth. The family was the first place of socialisation for all categories of people. Different cultural mechanisms were instituted to ensure the strength of family bonds such as adoption, joking relationships, folklore and storytelling, among others. Every child was trained to be like its father or grandfather or some other family hero. Children were also adopted by others within the larger extended family or across families. Adoption was instituted as a means of ensuring family and community discipline and for strengthening social and family bonds. Children were largely brought up by uncles, aunties and grandparents, immediate or extended. Through this, they developed a better appreciation of the extended family – its values and culture, including taboos, ethics and expectations.

There were also joking relationships, called *gonnasiru* in Baatonum or *yoboo* in Boko. It helped break the age gap, creating access, accountability, encouraging generosity and allowing for free expression amongst various members of the community, ultimately strengthening the bonds between them. Respect for family issues, hard work, commitment, humility, heroism, contentment and modesty were built into the folklore and stories of the Borgu people. These were told at night, mostly by the elders of various groups. It helped in moulding the character of the young.

Names were important to the society and politics of Borgu. People were named based on place of birth, circumstances of birth, social hierarchy and generation. Additional names could be attained through personal achievement and family history. The commonest and standard ones that applied to all were birth rank and generational names. Every child was named primarily based on the hierarchy of birth. In addition, every child also received a collective praise name based on his/her generation. As showed in table 1, there were both feminine and masculine birth ranks. While these names were commonly practised in Borgu, they varied according to regions and even linguistic category.

In Kaiama, the names end at the sixth birth. Subsequent names, up to the twelfth, involved adding the suffix of *Siya* to the any of the names. Starting from the first, it could be *Woru-Siya* for a male seventh child and *Yon-Siya* for a female child. It is not clear why the names were so limited, but it does appear that the birth rate in Borgu was relatively low[17] and this could explain its low population density. Spiritual support for fertility was also a major issue in Borgu. There were shrines and priests purely responsible for fertility, *Zakana* in particular. To be sure, children whose births were associated with divinations had their names linked to that particular deity, such as

---

[17] Borgu had a relatively low population density, and household sizes are relatively small compared to other polygamous societies in Africa. This may require a rigorous scientific analysis for any conclusive findings.

Kana or *Biokana*, which meant the child was linked to *Zekana*. Others include names like *Kabo, Nonbo* and *Ojo,* which were associated with the deities of Kemanji and Gwaria, all in the Kaiama region.

Table 1: Names according to Hierarchy of Birth

HIERARCHY	FEMININE	MASCULINE
1ST	Yoo/Yon	Woru
2ND	Bona (Bana in Boko)	Sabi
3RD	Bake	Bio
4TH	Biyon	Boni (Bani in Boko)
5TH	Dado	Sani
6TH	Nari (Beru in Kaiama)	Tori
7TH	Koda or Bakiri	Meere (Koda in Boko)

Source: Compiled by Author

Generational names were *Wure* and *Kpai*. These names alternated across generations. A person whose father was of *wure* generation was automatically *kpai*, and a *kpai's* child was *wure*. There were, therefore, only two socially active generations in Borgu world-view. These collective/praise names were largely used by praise singers and elders in regular or ceremonial greetings. Ability to define people based on the generational difference was a good indication of knowledge of the person. The names were often cited along with personal birth-rank names like – Bio-Wure, Sabi-Kpai, Bana-Wure, Yoo-Kpai etc. In some contexts, *wure* was slightly rated higher than *kpai*. Amongst the aristocracy, this generational identity was important in determining who ascends the throne, as it was often expected that the elder generation was considered first (Schottman 2000).

Wasangari – the Aristocracy

As would be seen in Chapter 2, the most important of these descent groups which were also at the centre of the political systems of Borgu was the ruling dynasties. They are called *Wasangari* mainly by the Baatonu and *Ki-neno* by the Boko. Wansangari could also mean a smart, enlightened, urbanised, urbane or even a shrewd person. As discussed in chapter 4, the origin and meaning of Wasangari is traced to Songhai, but institutionally linked to the Kisra legend. It is structurally associated with the dynastic state formation process in Borgu. They were spread across Borgu, in the major principalities and kingdoms traced to Bussa, Nikki and Illo, considered progenitors. It had a complex genealogy with different clans and dynastic branches emerging since the seventeenth century. As examined earlier in this chapter, the narrative of the Kisra legend is complex. Its origins are not clear and the authenticity is surely dismissible. It may also not be correct that this group was a different ethnic stock that migrated enblock to Borgu and later assimilated.

Table 2: Common Princely Names for Nikki and Kaiama[18]

Nikki		Kaiama	
Male	Female	Male	Female
Sero	Gandigi	Biside	Biegede
Sime	Yinre	Bwede	Duwe
Bagidi	Kpaa-Yenro	Gunu	Gaiya
Kora	Yanki	Koto	Gandugi
Yaaru	Brekogi	Mora	Ganki
Bate	Manu	Sane	Kpanyero
Mora	Kida	Sogee	Manu
Kisira	Azuba	Wenne	Suswade
Lafia		Yaru	Yanki
Gene		Yazide	Yinre
		Zume	
		Bagidi	

Source: Compiled by Author

Although they were all believed to be descendants of Kisra, layers and different aristocratic branches have emerged in not only the principal states of Nikki, Illo and Bussa, but also in the provinces and dependencies of second and third generation Borgu states. In Nikki, for instance, there were six dynastic branches – *Karawe, Kwararu, Gbassi, Gbasso, Makeraru* and *Lafiaru*, while Bussa had four – *Eteboro, Gbemusu, Gambui, Fuin* or *Fuyin*. Similar dynastic divisions are found in other kingdoms. Nevertheless, the aristocratic groups were differentiated from the commoners through facial marks – two cuts on each of their cheeks[19], the possession of copper or iron stirrups (bangles) and a princely name received during the *Gaani* festival and

---
[18] This is just an example – it could be slightly different from the two.
[19] This has been long discontinued, even before colonial times.

in some cases wearing of a turban and a red cap (Idris 1973). Examples of some of these princely names in Kaiama and Nikki are provided in Table 2. These names are not exhaustive, they could be different from one major Borgu principality to the other. The Kaiama-Nikki example provides broad example covering a typical Baatonu and Boko context.

Servile Group and the Gando System

The dynastic state formation process created aristocratic and servile groups. Between these two extremes were other other layer of the society. Scholars have often view the servile class from the prism of cultural practice, in reality, the class is inseperable from the dynastic state formation of Borgu. Although generically called *Gando*, a reference to the settlement where slaves were kept close to the seat of their masters, different terms have been used to cetegorise this group; *Yobu, Mare-yobu, Gandogibu, kiriku* in Baatonu and *Zzo* (pl. *Zzono*) in Boko. In Fulfude, they were called *Gannunkeebe, Jiyaabe* or *Maccube* (Lombert 1965, 1968, Hahonou 2015). Borgu was a deeply stratified society. Hierarchically, it composed of the aristocracy (Wasangari), free people (Baatonu and Boko), the Fulbe slave owners and slaves in that order (Lombard 1965). The *Mare Yoobu (*generally called *Gando)* were rejected Baatonu and, to a lesser extent, Boko children, due to some circumstance of their birth and some abnormality in physical development. Particularly, children who cut their teeth first from the upper side were regarded as witches, bad omens or abominations for the family. Such children were, therefore, rejected and sent to the *Kpasa* (Boko),*Gaa* (Baatonu*), Gure* (Fulfulde) Fulbe cattle farmsteads.

In periods before the consolidation of the dynasties and Gando institution, such children might have been abandoned or killed. They become more or less Fulbe slaves, adopted Fulbe languages and culturally or circumstantially became Fulbe (Idris 1973; Lafia 2006). Others were slaves captured during punitive expeditions and sold to the Fulbe people. The *Yoobu* were individual slaves of the indigenous Borgu people, they were called *Zzono* (plural) in Boko. They were a major source of family labour, both at the farm and domestic level.

There were also state slaves, called *Wete Zzono* in Boko, who were kept in separate locations to serve the state. Depending on territorial location, each Borgu principality, province or dependency had different sources of their state slaves. In Kaounde for instance, most of them were of Gourma origin, while those in Kaiama and Parakou axis were of Oyo origin.

The *Kiriku* were domestic servants of the kings, mainly differentiated by the nature of their haircut[20] (Idris 1973). The *Gando* people were endogenous; they married among themselves. A female of a servile class could marry a free person and become free. The *Gando* were a very important component of the state and society of Borgu. They were a major source of productive labour, particularly for the aristocratic classes who didn't like to farm. Farming grew to be considered belittling for them. They, therefore, relied on slave labour, particularly since slaves were prohibited from war[21]. Their presence at home during the perpetual wars of Borgu helped to sustain many families.

The Fulbe and the aristocracy built strong political and socio-economic relations over time. Like most of the other economic groups, the Wasangari provided security for the Fulbe in the incessant wars of the region. In return, the Fulbe looked after the cattle of the Wasangari and offered tributes with cattle to sustain the lavish lifestyle of the aristocrats. According to Bierschenk (1993), the Fulbe in Borgu weren't an ethnic group in the classical sense, as they hadn't a defined and autonomous political or territorial control of their own. They were therefore considered as a "status group, which specialised in cattle raising." Their status in the pre-colonial social and political system was "relatively low" and their language and endogamous practice isolated them from the other groups in the area (Bierschenk 1993, 224).

Religion and Society

Right up until the late nineteenth and early twentieth century when Islam became a major religion, the Borgu people were largely

---

[20] Only one side of the head is shaved. All others have both sides shaved and the middle left.
[21] This might have been a deliberate measure to ensure slaves don't bear arms.

animists. They believed in an overarching god, called *Gunsuno* in Batonou and *Luda/Lua* in Boko but their daily or regular divinations were associated with ancestors and community deities. Clapperton, during his visit to Kaiama in 1826, recorded that the inhabitants of Kaiama were "pagans of easy faith; never praying but when they are sick or want something and cursing their object of worship as fancy serves" (Clapperton 1829, 73 – 74). He observed that the Hausa slaves were "allowed to worship in their own way." He reported seeing Muslims attending mosque on Friday and the pagans took "advantage of the day, and spend it in showing their fine cloths, and paying and receiving visitors" (Clapperton 1829, 71).

The animism in Borgu had four different features: state rites, ancestral worship, horse cult and occupational cults (Idris 1973). The state rites consisted of devotion associated with the entire or a large segment of Borgu. Such processes had a strong connection to the politics of the Borgu states and principalities and were major ideological instruments that defined the Borgu political system. The coordination in such worship was done centrally, with the strong leadership of the kings. The Kibe, that is the king of Bussa, invoked about 365 deities (NNAK 1910) for good health, prosperity, and children for the people of Borgu. Bussa received representation from all principal towns of Borgu during the period. The *Gani* was also an important state festival where ancestral cults and deities were worshipped.

Borgu people believed in reincarnation. Between death and reincarnation, there exist the *genwa*, (ancestor in Boko, pl. *genwadeno*; *gori* in Baatonum, pl. *goribu*). They were worshipped and refreshed through sacrifice by family members. Neglect of ancestors could result in spiritual reproach. Ancestors could be seen in dreams or through other spiritual processes. The *Maso* (oracles in Boko) were the intercessors with the ancestors. Family members would not want to offend the ancestors as it was believed the ancestors could fight back in the same way they had the capacity to protect the living. Ancestor worship was also associated with cult heroes, including the *Sunon Sero* at Nikki-Wenou and *Sabi Agba*, the progenitor of the Kaiama ruling aristocracy. In Bussa, the tombs of the ancestors of *Kibe* were venerated twice a year. Even at the individual family level, ancestors were venerated. The ancestors were important and had to be factored into every family decision. Families did not necessarily create an ancestral shrine, as done by the aristocracy, but they performed rituals and poured libations to their ancestors.

Such worship processes were major areas of interface between the Earth Priests and the aristocracy. Because horses were so important to the aristocracy of Borgu, the *N'Pera* was invoked for the good health of horses. The horses were treated to libations at the shrine. *Ki-lashi* was an important occupational deity for hunters amongst the Boko people.

There were also therapeutic cults, like *Weregu* and *Bori*. When possessed, they were believed to have foreseen calamity, wickedness or to provide remedies for societal challenges. The *Bori* and *Werengu* were connected to the clan organisation of society. It was, therefore, hereditary. According to Palmers (1914), "animism is the religious basis of *Bori*, a philosophy which, through the agency of spirits or demons, endues every object, and especially parts of nature such as stones, trees and rivers, with a soul" (p. 113). Different types of practice were prevalent among all the ethnic groups of Borgu, including the Kambari and Gungawa in northern Borgu. *Bori* is believed to be of Songhay origin, although the name is Hausa. It was imported into Borgu, according to Lombard, by Zima (the chief of the Songhay cult of the Holey). He was believed to be of Dendi/Zerma origin (Stewart 1993, 99).

Adherents of *Bori* believed they are possessed by their individual spirit through whom request can be made for several human needs and against different calamities. *Magiro* was also related cult worship in Borgu. *Magiro's* origin dates back to the thirteenth century. The centre of the cult was believed to be in Kwatarkwasi, near Gusau, which is now in Zamfara State in Nigeria. The influence of the cult was believed to have extended south to the Middle Niger. *Magiro* shrine was one of the prominent shrines in the hills of Kaiama. It was largely worshipped by Kambari and Boko people around Bussa, Wawa and Kaiama.

It also appears that each Borgu state, and villages too, had its own deity. These were called *tana/tara* in *Boko* and *bun* in Baatonum, and were invoked by their inhabitants while *Ki-Lashi* and *Jekana* were more like national deities. There were many shrines across Borgu, such as in Malami in the Babanna region where *Zaputa* was centred on a pool on top of a rock that never dried. *Lashi* was also worshipped at Dhazi (Zazhi). The Dhazi shrine was believed to be the original shrine. There was also *Dandu* in Puissa. There was *Daudu* in Kagogi, *Takama* at Shagunu, *Gauji* at Sollai near Gomji. Bazaru was served by *Tandi* at Sambaburi, and Swanbodi, a Laru diety (NAK 1921). Dao at Wozibe was served by Kiwozi, *Antsa* at Kemanji was an important deity served by Kisura. It was consulted in cases of fertility and was an important shrine for oath-taking. *Antsa* was represented by a small piece of iron at the foot of a tree.

Most shrines and gods of Borgu (particularly in south-eastern Borgu) had a peculiar and puzzling 'dislike' for the Yoruba. A lion that regularly visited Kali was believed to have stopped "because of the smell of Yoruba" (NAK 1921). It is/was an abomination for a Yoruba woman to give birth in Kemanji. This aversion was often attributed to the servile status of the Oyo in southern and western Borgu, probably starting after the Ilorin war (NAK 1921). The Borgu, particularly Boko, spiritual aversion to Yoruba (originally Oyo) is probably linked to the social and political relationship between the two polities. As would be seen in chapter 4, Borgu had a significant influence on political development in Oyo. As one of its closest neighbours, it is not unusual that there were mutual raids for slaves and wars and cooperation between the two.

Ojo and *Nombo* at Gberia in Kaiama area were represented by a pot containing twenty round stones and three pieces of metal (about the diameter of a finger and nine inches in length with a tapering flat head, somewhat like a chisel) that had two rings round them. *Numbo* was represented by a tree. The shrine at Kabo near Kenu was dedicated to the spirit of *Siano* and was believed to be the most important in the south-west of Borgu. Another was *Bana,* believed to be an offshoot of *Siano*, which was largely used for oath-taking. There was also *Worukana* shrine at Woron-kowari and Wenri.

These gods and related activities defined the taboos of the society and provided the ideological justifications for the social structure. The servile practice of *Gando,* for instance, was based on superstitions associated with childbirth and development where a particular "abnormality" was considered an abomination and the child had to be abandoned. The same applied to the birth of twins (*sika*) and the spirituality associated with twins. The belief in the spiritual powers of twins was common in Borgu. They were believed to protect families, identify thieves and cure illnesses. This mystification of twins was probably associated with the relatively low fertility of some parts of the region and rarity of twin births. A twin birth was a bonus and, therefore, venerated. The spiritual power of the king was also an ideology supported by religion. A king was believed to have a divine capacity to destroy recalcitrant members of his domain through curses and his blessings are significant for every endeavour.

Other dimensions of animist religion were witchcraft, charms and other spiritual engagements. They were considered major sources of power and protection and were widely sourced and considered necessary for a political contest and personal survival. Borgu was well known for witchcraft and it was a major instrument of individual and family conflicts. Families invested time and resources seeking protection from witchcraft. Other times, it was the first resort in feuds, family or political struggles. It was only when witchcraft had failed that they went physical. Even wars were fought with strong doses of witchcraft, superstitions, fetishism and spirituality. During this period, fetishism was part of social reality. "To deny them (spirits) was to deny your reality" was a common saying in Borgu.

Trade and Islam in Borgu

Although Islam didn't grow to become a dominant religion in Borgu until the twentieth century, it has been in the region since the late sixteenth century or earlier, first through the Wangara who were later joined by the Hausa in the eighteenth and nineteenth century. Islam had, for instance, been a major religion in Djougou since the eighteenth century while Nikki, Parakou, Bussa, Illo and Kaiama had been interacting with Muslims since the seventeenth century.

Some scholars (Adekunle 2004), using the Kisra legend as evidence, tried to paint an "anti-Islamic" picture of Borgu. Evidence showed that though the ruling class and the Earth Priests had historically resisted Islam, it wasn't different from the initial resistance to any new faith by any human community. It was, therefore, not necessarily about Islam but more about power, politics and resources. Borgu was historically ambivalent towards Islam. On one hand, it showed a strong tradition of resistance to Islamic pressures since the sixteenth-century Songhai invasion and its nineteenth-century resistance to the Fulbe Jihad. On the other hand, the Borgu aristocrats were deeply influenced by resident Muslims (Levtzion 1968). Up to the close of the eighteenth century, it was difficult to find a Baatonu or Boko Muslim and the generic name, *Bariba*, was believed to be associated with "unbelievers." Levtzion, was told in Dahomey that "it is impossible of a Muslim Bariba [Borgu person]; as Bariba who becomes a Muslim is referred to as Dendi, a term which covers most Muslims residents (excluding the Fulani)" (Levtzion 1968, 174).

The Dendi Wangara people, called Dendawa, didn't come to Borgu on a purely Islamic mission. They were largely traders connected to the caravan routes that passed through Borgu. While they formed a strong Muslim community, they were also careful not to cause disaffection among their hosts. They settled in centres on the caravan routes leading from Hausaland to Gonja, in such places as Djougou, Nikki and Kandi, amongst others. There was a considerable difference between the influence of Muslims in places where Islam was a minority religion and places where they were predominant. Unlike Nikki and other places in Borgu, Parakou and Djougou had a large Muslim Dendi presence. They were believed to have settled there even before the emergence of Wasangari rule (Levtzion 1968). Settlements with considerable Muslim Dendi presence, in addition to the Wasangari kings, had a *Baparakpe* – a leader of the Muslim community – who was appointed and served as the interface between the indigenous leadership and the Muslim community. Djougou comprised two sections, the Wangara and the Kilir, which was the residence of the Borgu chief and settlement area of most Borgu natives.

In the nineteenth century, Hausa long-distance traders became the major drivers of Islam in caravan routes that passed through Borgu from Hausaland to Asante. Scholars have recognised the strong relationship between long-distance trade and Islam in West Africa (Lovejoy 1971, Cohen 1969, Wilks 1968, Olayemi and Raji 1990, Adamu 1980). In almost everywhere along the caravan routes, the Wangara, Hausa and Kambarin Beriberi set up stations and transit camps that created strong Muslim posts and networks that were primarily for trade but also helped in spreading Islam.

In the nineteenth century, Hausa merchants travelled through Borgu from the area of the newly founded Sokoto Caliphate in order to access the markets in Asante. Muslims travelled through other communities, especially on the trading routes, not just for trade but also to study. Mohammed "Baba" al-Ghamba of Kumasi, the son of the Imam of Gambaga, was believed to have transversed Borgu and the Volta region both as a trader and a student. He later moved to become the head of the Muslim community in Kumasi in 1810 (Lovejoy 1971). In Kilir-Wangara (Djougou), another Muslim scholar, Alhaji Idris, taught high profile Muslims like Al-Hajj Umar b. Abu Bakr al-Kabbawi, who emigrated from Kano in 1870s. He is believed to have written over forty works in Arabic and Hausa. He was later responsible for the spread of Tijaniyya among Muslim communities (Lovejoy 1971). Djougou, Nikki and Parakou were major centres of Islamic learning along the trade routes. The dispersed Hausa Muslim settlements across the trading routes relied on Islam as a unifying ideology. On this ideological connection, Lovejoy correctly noted thus:

> Islam encourages social connections between trade centres, which buttressed economic links. Islam provided a status system which supplemented the emphasis on wealth since education and religious piety were respected more or as much as commercial success. Furthermore, Islam and its status orientation furnished a religious rationalisation for the hospitality which landlords extended to passing traders for economic motive. (Lovejoy 1971, 543).

Other Muslims groups were the *Gesere*, griots who were believed to be Dendi Muslims of *Taruwere (Traore)* patronymic who had served in the courts of Borgu kings (Levtzion 1968). They were believed to have migrated to Borgu from Songhai. They performed in *Wakpaarem*, a language believed to have been derived from the Soninke, but borrowed their patronymic name from the Mande-speaking areas (Farais 1995). The Fulbe were generally identified as Muslims in the literature, but in most parts of Borgu, during this period, only a few of them were practicing Muslims. They didn't have any influence on the people of the region because of their exclusive spatial pattern and endogamous culture and generally in the lower ladder of the social hierarchy.

This period preceded the season of Islamic jihads of the nineteenth century. At the start of the jihads, of course, attempt incursion or internal revolt in Borgu territory was resisted by the state in almost all the kingdoms, as was seen with the invasion of Illo by Gwandu and even the participation of Borgu in the Ilorin war, which was essentially a pre-emptive action against possible Fulbe attack on Borgu. Despite the religious differences, there was a strong symbiotic, if not opportunistic relationship between the Wangara Muslim community and the aristocracy who depended on the Wangara for the procurement of their horses and related aristocratic accessories. The aristocracy also approached the *Alfas/Mallams* (Muslim scholars) for spiritual help to secure the throne. A letter from Sabi Nayina, the twenty-third king of Nikki, to *Alfa* Kiro of Djougou, who was believed to have helped him to the throne, was a typical example of such relations (Idris 1973). The Wasangari in turn provide security and related political cover and support to the Wangara.

It appears the growth in economic activities and the prosperity of the Wangara in the nineteenth century created friction between the Wangara Muslim communities and the aristocracy in Nikki, leading to increased distrust between the *Sina Boko* Sero Kpera, the twenty-fourth king of Nikki, and the Wangara merchants which eventually resulted in an attempted Jihad against Nikki, which was effectively crushed. The attempted Jihad appeared to be a collaboration between the Wangara and the urban-based clerical Fulbe. The Wangara were believed to be in solidarity with Fulbe clerics, who were further suspected of threatening the security of Borgu. The leader of the Jihad was one Alfa Mohammed Gani, who mobilised the Wangara and secured their cooperation across Borgu, except Nikki. Most of those alleged to be involved in the failed Jihad escaped to Djougou (Idris 1973).

CHAPTER TWO

Political Centralisation and Dynastic Politics

The political system in pre-colonial Borgu was deeply connected to the entire social system, which was reinforced by other elements of the society as already discussed. The system was particularly shaped by the character of the state or social structure within which it operated and in turn influenced by the level of technological advancement, culture, values and social institutions.

The earlier political structure, as discussed in chapter 1, provided the foundation for the emergence of a centralised Borgu-wide political system, which revolved around kingship. There was no single centralised authority across the region, but each formation had a central authority that had a strong network with others in the region. The kings were sovereign monarchs, limited by institutional checks, traditions and religion of the society. The succession to the office was limited to the ruling class, Wasangari, that is, the social class connected by a myth of common ancestry.

It would appear the use of the term *Wasangari* was more pronounced in historical documents and within the aristocratic ranks than the everyday conversation in Borgu. Princes among the Boko are referred to as *Kine* (pl. *kineno*) or *Wee ne* and *Sina bibu* by Baatombu.

Wasangari was of limited use in the common vocabulary of the Boko people, even in Bussa, where it was believed to have originated. The concept of Wasangari might have been popularised by colonial anthropologists, particularly the French, as part of the process of the characteristic ethnic categorisation and redefinition as would be seen chapter 10. The use of the word is quite limited, if not unavailable in British colonial documents.

As seen in chapter 1, the meaning and origin of this Hausa-phonic word, Wasangari, which some scholars associate with Songhai, is not clear (Morae Farais 2013). But it is often linked to the Kisra legend. Scholars are also not in agreement as to how the institution emerged. They are believed to be part of the fifteenth century Mande immigrants into Borgu, particularly following war encounters between the Mali and Songhay Empires. Adekunle (2004) suggests that the Wasangari might have gained control of Borgu settlements through strong military action and in some cases, willful surrender to militarily powerful immigrants. The Wasangari are believed to have first established themselves in the north-eastern part of Borgu. It was from there that other parts were incorporated. To that extent, it is argued that the original Wasangari were Boko-speaking, even if they may not have been genealogical Boko (Stewart 1993; Kuba 1997; Crowder 1975; Asiwaju 1993, 2004).

The popular Wasangari–Kisra rendition believes the Wasangari first settled or conquered Bussa, and later Illo and Nikki. These were the first-generation principalities. They are believed to have settled alongside other autochthonous communities and adopted their beliefs and languages. To ensure effective integration, they shared power with the Earth Priests and the related pre-dynastic power structure (Idris 1973). In Nikki, the Wasangari were believed to have appropriated the land rights of the Earth Priests and left them with only spiritual powers. In most cases, the Wasangari king and the Earth Priest counterbalanced each other: the Earth Priest installed the Wasangari king, while the king appointed the Earth Priest.

The political structure and power arrangement in major Borgu principalities do not provide adequate evidence of forceful conquest. There were power-sharing arrangements, with a strong connection to the pre-dynasty structure. In some cases, especially in Bussa, it was a relatively decentralised structure with some layers of horizontal power relations. It was, therefore, suggested that the Wasangari peacefully penetrated Borgu communities and then established themselves as a ruling aristocracy. They gradually integrated through inter-marriages and amalgamation with the culture of the inhabitants (Lafia 2006, 12).

While the foreign origin of Wasangari and even the Kisra legend is highly contestable, as already discussed in chapter 1, a possible mutual political influence, particularly the Bussa origin of the dynasty, may be plausible, not necessarily in the ethnic sense but in terms of the history and dialectics of political development. Apart from the archaeological findings in the Bussa area as early as the Pleistocene period (Adekunle 2004), the location and access through the river and proximity to other state systems and polities, to the west of the river could have influenced contact and cross-breeding that could have influenced the state formation process.

The Kisra Legend tends to obscure these dynamics of state formation by presenting it as an externally propelled process. State formation might have also developed its contradictions, resulting in emigration to other locations, possibly leading to Illo and Nikki. It does not appear to be correct that state institutions developed within the same generation across Borgu. It could rather have been a gradual process that resulted in movements of people across the different settlements. Crowder (1973) and Stewart (1978) contestably attributed a sole Boko origin. The historical contentions and contradictory narratives appear to be a colonial creation. The Boko-speaking origin of the Wasangari is hard to admit as the colonially invented identities have reshaped inter-ethnic relations over time, such that the place of each ethnic group is important in the politics of the region as would be seen chapter 10.

Nevertheless, it is important to recognize that membership of the Wasangari is not necessarily genealogical. It is deeply political and probably involved different ethnic groups of the region. It is also important to note that at the period of the institution of dynastic politics in the region, ethnic boundaries were fluid and cross-cutting, and contemporary ethnic identities had not emerged. Even, if they, were external, their social and political organisation was not ethnic and never constituted an autonomous ethnic group in any sociological sense.

The three earlier principalities have different characteristics. They possess different versions of the Kisra Legend and each of them played different socio-economic and poltical roles: Nikki was believed to be the biggest with a high number of second and even third generation "dependencies" especially since the eighteenth century. The extent of control over these dependencies will be examined later. Bussa, as the "progenitor" was the spiritual centre and it had only three dependencies. Illo was, at a point, the emporium of Borgu, deriving its importance from the trade caravans that passed through its territory to Gonja and Hausa states in the north (Stewart 1978).

Borgu was never a consolidated dynasty or a unified kingdom, but rather a region with several kingdoms. Although power had at different times gravitated among Bussa, Nikki and Illo, in the earlier periods of the dynastic history, changes in economic and military strength in the later centuries altered the balance of power in favour of newer principalities like Wawa, Kaiama, Kandi, Perere and Parakou.

******

There are several misconceptions and fallacies in the discourse of the state and political system in pre-colonial Borgu. First is the impression that Borgu was a stateless society until the emergence of dynastic politics. While it is true that the dynastic system created a more or less totalising power structure, elements of state and political system had emerged in the Borgu area over a long period of time before the Wasangari dynasty. There was strong political leadership at different settlements. There was *Kibe* or *Kina* among the Boko and *Suno* or *Yinni* among the Baatonu people, as examined in Chapter 1. The Wasangari dynasty also helped in building pan-Borgu system and identity, without necessarily consolidating it as a political entity.

The second of these misconceptions of Borgu was defining the political system on the basis of ethnic origins, largely drawn from the Kisra Legend. Therefore, the ruling aristocracy was conceived as an immigrant group that got assimilated in their new settlements. Consequently, Borgu was believed to have one dynasty that started from Bussa. While it is true that a combination of forces and processes led to the emergence of the state and political system, which included migration and contacts with people of different backgrounds, the eventual ruling class was not necessarily a product of a single ethnic origin or even of the same genealogical roots. Borgu emerged probably in the fifteenth century, as a conglomerate of politically independent states with Bussa, Nikki and Illo as the initial major power centres. The Wasangari dynastic state formations were a result of a merger of the existing political system with those of immigrant groups, probably of Mande-speaking origin, (Lombard, Crowder 1976; Stewart 1978, 1980, 1993; Kuba 1998; Asiwaju 1979, 1989). The Wasangari only helped to promote a leadership network across Borgu, using the Kisra legend as a gluing or unifying ideology. The Wasangari episode should, therefore, be considered a distinct, but long episode in the political evolution of Borgu.

The third misconception and fallacy is the description of the political or state structure as feudal. Borgu didn't have a feudal system as obtained in Europe, or as a mode of production. The political system in Borgu was not based on land ownership, even if the social relationship was asymmetrical. Kinship ties were never replaced by ties of personal dependence, force was not a necessary means of expanding territory. There weren't landed class and land tenure and control were not the determinants of dynastic power; marriage, voluntary declarations and alliances were.

The dominant relationship was that of clientship, and it was constituted by a voluntary declaration of allegiance to a particular king in exchange for political protection (Stewart 1980). While it is true that the early state structure collapsed and aboriginal leaderships were either incorporated or subordinated, land was a territorial issue not a production one. Land ownership and control was not a major issue in Borgu. It was freely available and people were able to move and switch from one area of political control to the other. The power of kingship was more about control over people situated in a land than over the land itself. It was actually for this reason that the Wasangari did not appropriate land. This was left for the Earth Priests, and not necessarily for the purpose of control or tenure, as often portrayed by Borgu historians. Land in Borgu was a spiritual and identity issue linked to ancestors and the religion of the people. The priests were the interlocutors in the relationship with the spirit and ancestral world.

Political and Governance Structure

All political formations in Borgu operated a segmented and hierarchical political system. Although the ruling class was believed to be from the same root, each Borgu kingdom possessed somewhat distinctive characteristics. However, drawing from the experience of the first-generation dynastic power centres of Bussa, Illo and Nikki, there were strong elements of commonality in institutional structure and governance system. The systems were a fusion of the old, decentralised but structured leadership with a new monarchical system: It retained almost all the earlier political offices and added new ones to reflect the change in social dynamics. It was more like a power-sharing arrangement between those considered autochthonous and the new ruling groups believed to have immigrated.

The authority was in the *Kibe* or *Ki* (king) in Boko and *Suno* in Baatonu language. This authority was exercised through a governance structure involving a distinct category of people including the ruling class, such as princes, princesses and other members of the dynasty; autochthonous communities, such as Earth Priests, occupational groups; and the provincial leadership. This political structure is, therefore, classified into two: the central administration of the kingdoms and the administration of the settlements, dependencies and provinces.

Central Administration

The kings in Borgu had enormous spiritual and political power, although these were circumscribed by certain trappings of power and religious provisions or obligations. Their roles were sacerdotal and protectionist. They were considered divine and their blessings and curses meant a great deal to their subjects. In Bussa, the *Kibe* ruled through a number of ministers and his *Kiwotede* (the one who seeks to be king), that is, heir apparent. The system required the king to share his political power with three nobility groups: *Ki-neno* (princes and princesses); the *Ki-talakano* (subjects King) and *Busu-deno* (owners of the land).

Among the *Ki-neno* were honorific title-holders like *Kikyankyan*, *Kikparo*, *Kisanta*, *Kigwase*, the *Kiwatede* already mentioned, *Ki-*

Kawa, *Zhi-ki* and *Yon Magara*. Each of these had a specific function or value to the central administration. It appears some of the titles have been abandoned since the colonial period and institutionalisation of Islam. Among the *Ki-talakano* were *Ba-taku*, who was the Chief Minister of the king; *Ba-marubere*, Chief Scribe and the keeper of the *Kibe*'s records and instructor of youth; and *Beresondi*, keeper of the city gates of Bussa and also responsible for fetishes of the Earth Priests. Others were *Madoro*, a royal messenger to the provinces; *Ba-maso*, the Chief Priest responsible for major shrines, particularly the *Zakana* shrine and *Ba-ziki*, Minister of War and Head of the Army. Among the *Busu-deno* were *Ba-karabonde*, Head of the Earth Priests and Head of Karabonde Settlement, and *Ba-daburude*, who was responsible for royal burials and custodian of sacred cob-skin used to enrobe a new king.

The King of Bussa had combined executive, judicial and legislative powers. He was, however, circumscribed by a rigorous regiment of etiquette, such as not being able to freely move around as ordinary people did. He couldn't cross the River Niger. It was also a taboo for him to visit Nikki. So was meeting the *Neretege*, the Chief of Gaunji (Idris 1973). As a result of some of these restrictions, the political power of the *Kibe* was exercised through his ministers, particularly the *Ba-taku*.

The political structure of Nikki was a derivative of Bussa, with distinct contextual variations. The central administration of Nikki was led by the *Sina Boko* who was Supreme King, with support from his ministers. Like Bussa, the ministers were chosen from all segments of the society, including the Wasangari ruling class, the autochthones, the migrant communities and occupational groups. All the ministers acted in the interest of the *Sina Boko* and were expected to follow established protocol.

Among the ministers from the ruling class were—

- *Bosussi-Suno*: Chief of Bosussi Village and judge of the Supreme Court.
- *Sunon-Boni*: The Chief of Police, also a bodyguard to the *Sina-Boko*.
- *Sunon-Gbonsio*: The Minister of Justice.

- *Sunon-Konde:* Responsible for toll collection from people on behalf of the king. He was also responsible for the welfare of the royal stable.
- *Sinrari-Sunon:* Traditional seen as the "senior" of the king, this official appears and speaks to the king with authority, quite like the King's Whip[22].
- *Sunon-Toto*: War Minister, also responsible for the security of Nikki town.
- *Tomtaron-Suno*: Chief of Tomtaro and member of the royal court.
- *Yon-Kogi*: Head of Women. It is a feminine office. She performed various functions, including overseeing the initiation of young princes and princesses (Idris 1973).

The King's ministers from the autochthonous communities included—

- *Sina-Donwiru*: Head of the Supreme Court, also Head of the Council of Senior Ministers. He stood in for the king during transitions until a new king was appointed.
- *Wenou Suno*: Responsible for the *SinaBoko's* ancestor's shrine in Nikki Wenou, also sanctified a new king on appointment.
- *Sina-Gorigi*: Earth Priest, a descendant of *Sunon Barisonga*. He was responsible for land issues, including all the rituals and rites associated with food planting, harvest and storage.
- *Sina-Bonno*: Managed candidates for the throne during the transition and announced a new king on appointment by kingmakers.
- *Sunon-Bousio*: king's doctor, responsible for atonement.
- *Bio-Boukoseme:* Chief of Kpelle[23] and judge of the Supreme Court.
- *Ndali-Sunon:* Chief of N'dali[24] and judge of the Supreme Court.

---

[22] No historical reason was determined for this role but it appears to be a corrective mechanism, ensuring that there was somebody who could speak truth to the King.

[23] A province of Nikki.

- *Sunon-Bounon:* State Counsel. Gave legal interpretations of legal matters. (This office was also called *Takou-kpe*).
- *Makararun-Sunon* Chief of Sounaru[25], a minister without portfolio.
- *Maru-Bushi:* Responsible for royal visitors, this official had access to the king at any time.
- *Sina-Doberegi:* State Counsel who managed the king's temper and often pleaded on behalf of defendants.

For the occupational groups and specialised functionaries, a number of positions supported the *Sina Boko* in central administration. These positions, those with the suffix *kpe*, were of Dendi (Wangara) origin and, probably an eighteenth-century development, suggesting an integration of Dendi in the political system, in the political structure of Nikki, Parakou and Kandi. *Baagesere* or *Ba-Maru* is the chief Chronicler and head of the griots. He was believed to have a tremendous influence on the ruling class; *Bara Suno* is the Head of Drummers. He kept the genealogy of the rulers, which was repeated every Friday. Mistakes in reciting the genealogy could reportedly attract the death penalty (Idris 1973). *Arari Suno*, Head of the butchers in the entire state. Others are *Yakpe,* a special artist and Chief Jester of the king; *Wasan-kpe*, the Chief of Barbers; *Tofarkpe,* head of the Royal Drum, *tambari; and Bawarakpe*, responsible for spiritual matters and relevant rituals on behalf of the *Sina Boko.*

As Nikki received more immigrants due to expansion in trade and Islamisation, particularly since the eighteenth century, the immigrant communities were also incorporated into the governance structure with the following positions:

- *Baa-Liman* (*Imam*): The Head of the Muslim community and Chief Scribe at the King's Court is also a member of the *Asakpa* (Council of Kingmakers).
- *Sonkoro:* Head of Customs, responsible for visitors in transit. He was assisted by *Sina-bondore* and *Ba-wankpe*.

---

[24] A province of Nikki.
[25] A province of Nikki.

- *Foudunga:* Minister of Finance and collector of tributes from Fulbe settlers and *gaa* (cattle camps).

From the servile class was the *Gando Suno* – Chief Chamberlain, responsible for the general control of the palace and the *Gando* community where he originated. Also of *Gando* background was the Chief Messenger of the king as well as the *Kirukuban Sabi*, who served in the King's Palace. They constituted the bulk of the palace population. They are differentiated by their hair cut, which was half-shaved (Idris 1973).

The replica or a combination of Bussa and Nikki models were found in all the major Borgu principalities, particularly in Kaiama, Wawa, Parakou, Kenu, Kandi, Bouay, Kika, Sandiro, Kouande, Puissa, among others.

Illo was part of the three-state Kisra Legend. In Illo, the Chief Priest was *Kirkasa* and he was the custodian of the land. He performed the libation of *Doguwa*, a female spirit. The second-in-command was *Kikparude*. *Kirkasa* and *Kikparude* were both involved in the appointment and installation of the Illo king. The title of king was *Sonni Ali*, defining the relationship with Songhai. The Illo kings were believed to be descendants of the first king, Aguza.

In Kaiama, one of the dependencies or vassals of Nikki up to the late nineteenth century, there developed a central administrative system that was more or less like those of Nikki and Bussa. The aristocracy of Kaiama were descendants of Nikki who had migrated to the Kaiama area in the mid-eighteenth century. The settlement of Kaiama surely predated this period and it might have changed names several times. Kaiama was probably originally named Gbegbazi, and at some point was also called Mewi[26], from which its Bokobaru expression of *Kaama* was derived and later transformed to *Kaiama* through European travellers and colonial documentation. Up until today, villages around Kaiama still refer to it as Mewi.

The new ruling class occupied the Kaiama area, dissolved the earlier political system, spread out and then subordinated all villages and settlements around them. The king, called *Kina* or *Dii,* was the

---

[26] There is an erroneous impression that Mewi meant "a large town". Mewi and Kamma both mean "rest" in Boko.

head of the administrative structure of Kaiama. A Council of Ministers and other officials provided support to the king. The structure was a combination of the old and the new. Amongst the positions occupied by the dynastic class were the *Gbensi-Ginda*[27] the head of *Ki kai no*, (kingmakers) and Head of Sinsi-musu, a settlement south of Kaiama. From another nearby community was the *Gbaagizi ki*, who was the head of metropolitan administration and as well the Head of Gbaagizi Settlement. *Dhazi-ki* was also responsible for administration. The *Bede-gbana* was part of the party that migrated from Bweru and was responsible for the entire Kaiama from Gbaabe to the south-west of the River Niger. *Ki Taku* was also one of the migrants from Bweru and was the War Chief and priest of *Zakana*[28]. During the war, the *Ki Taku* never returned, regardless of whether the war was won or lost. An associated role was *Kama-zhiki*, commander of the army in Kaiama metropolis. Like *Ki Taku*, he never returned home, regardless of whether the war was won or lost. *Gbesasi ki* was also a war chief.

Others were *Gene Atta*, who was responsible for construction-related works, while the *Ki-gebekorede* was in charge of territorial waters and its resources. *Gene ynon* was the eunuch responsible for the king's wives: the office later became the Village Head of Venra. *Ki Zandude* was the head of the Council of Elders responsible for adjudication[29]. *Ki Kpasi* was reserved for a close friend of the king. Every king appointed his *Ki Kpasi*. *Kiwaride* was a war chief. The first and last holder of the title was believed to have been a Nikki prince from Wari, west of Nikki. He was believed to have migrated on self-exile to Kaiama after a dispute with the king of Nikki. He was later to be a leader of the failed plot to remove the king of Kaiama, after which he went on further exile to Boriya.

The *Ynon Kode*[30] was in charge of initiating young princes during the *Gaani* Festival. As examined in Chapter 4, *Gaani* has a Songhai

---

[28] Zakana is a common shrine for all Boko people. It was worshiped in Bussa, Kaiama, Wawa, Lashibe and other Boko settlements. Each of these settlements had a priest responsible for interlocution.

[29] The last *Kizandude* went on self-exile to Imileya, after a failed attempt to overthrow Mora Tasude in the late nineteenth century. He was believed to be one of the planners (Idris and Yaru 2008).

[30] This later changed to *Kiyezinde*.

origin. It is the most celebrated festival in Borgu; although linked to the Muslim celebration of the birthday of Prophet Muhammad (*Mawlud*), its practice actually predates the wide Islamic practices in the region. The position was similar to those of *Yon Maga'a* of Bussa and *Yon Kogi* of Nikki. The *Ynon Kode* led the female aristocrats and was the custodian of the culture, norms and etiquette of the ruling class. Under her were other women title-holders like *Kimeborodi, Ki ghazide, Ynon-toiji, Ynon Barimusu, Ynon-Bisamare, Kidare-Zakanano, Kidare-Kukunano* and *Kidare-Ghansindo.* Of all the titles, only the *Ynon Kode* and *Ki-Ghazide* played strategic official roles. The others were honorary titles.

There were also other titles reserved for special princes, including *Yerima Bakaru*[31] (Senior *Yerima),* often held by the oldest of the royal family and regarded as the most senior prince. *Kilishi Yerima* was exclusively for the firstborn of a king during his reign. Others were *Yerima Jorojoro, Yerima Gene* and *Mora Gene*. Their functions were defined by the king of Kaiama and could include military functions like escorting trade caravans that had official permission to pass through the territory of Kaiama. There were also other military-related positions reserved for the senior princes of Kaiama.

The autochthonous communities or original settlers also occupied a number of positions in the political structure of Kaiama. *Kiopara* was more or less the chief Priest, responsible for the Oziya Shrine. *Ki wozi* was also a priest and the head of Wozibe. *Kabaruki* or *Ki-Kabarude* was the head of Kabaru village, one of the original settlements in Kaiama area. He was also the custodian of *Magiro* shrine. *Ki Sura* was the Head of Kemanji. *Ki-Gberia* was in charge of Gberia deities, *Ojo* and *Nombo. Kiototode* was the Chief Messenger of the king, also responsible for the investiture of the Kaiama king and other appointed officials with special regalia (now called a turbaning). *Kijano-wetede* was responsible for the widows of dead kings. He led all the rituals associated with widowhood. *Gbekerade* was responsible for the palace gate and managed the entrance and exit of the palace.

---

[31] This is a Baatonum word for senior Yerima, it is not clear at what point it got infused into Boko aristocratic title. Yerima is also obviously Kanuri. These are probably changes associated with either colonial rule or immediate period before colonial rule.

On the professional or occupational side were *Bata-Ki,* head of griots and drummers. He was also responsible for *kpa-kpa* (town criers). *Laki* or *Laga ki* was the head of butchers. He was entitled to portions of all cows killed in Kaiama and he was expected to remit some to the king every Friday. *Siyaki* was the head of blacksmiths. The *Wanzan Ki* was the chief of Barbers. Under the supervision of *Ynon Kode*, he shaved the head of all eligible young princes and princesses during the *Gani* Festival. *Ere Ki* was the head of the markets, responsible for collecting market tolls from traders on behalf of the kingdom. The *Fudunugan* was a title reserved for Fulbe people. This official coordinated the Fulbe people and collected tolls or taxes on behalf of the king. All tolls were collected either in cash or in kind.

Territorial Organisation

The affairs of the various settlements and villages around the major principalities were managed by their respective heads and resident title-holders. Some of the heads were parts of the central administration, like the *Ba Karabonde* in Bussa, who was, in addition to his principal role in the central administration, also the head of Karabonde. There existed a variety of relationships with the centres.

While there were clear provinces, some were dependencies. Provinces were under the direct supervision of the kings while dependencies were largely independent. They paid allegiance to the principal king but the management of such entities, including the appointment of kings, was done independently. The relationship between Kaiama and Nikki was a good example. At different times, Kaiama was a vassal, buffer zone and probably a dependency of Nikki but it was never a province, as is often portrayed. This relationship found affinal justification: the aristocracy of Kaiama was believed to be part of the Nikki ruling class.

A similar situation applies to the Bussa and Wawa relationship. Towards the close of the nineteenth century, Wawa and Illo had been reduced to a tributary status in relation to Bussa. They, however, retained their independence and the political power of the Bussa state was shared with the kings of Wawa and Illo (Crowder 1973). Bussa was relatively small in terms of geographical size. By the close of the nineteenth century, its influence and territorial space was largely around the core of Bussa with some political alliances with the principalities of Wawa and Illo. For Wawa, it was because of the geographical proximity and some genealogical relationship, while for Illo, it was more or less a relationship of convenience in response to the increasing military pressure from Hausaland, occasioned by the Fulbe Jihad.

Although Wawa had existed as Gbere, long before the arrival of the Wasangari Dynasty, the dynasty was said to have been established in the eighteenth century during the reign of Dan Toro in Bussa, when a family branch of *Bamarubere* led by Mallam Toga established itself in Wawa. A different tradition claims he was a Kambarin Beriberi merchant who was invited to help manage merchants passing through Wawa. Idris (1973), however, observes that irrespective of the traditions, Mallam Toga had a probable matrilineal connection with *Bamarubere*. The King of Wawa was the descendant of Toga, but the ministers represented different segments of the society. Althougha t a point in history, the King of Wawa received investiture from the King of Bussa, Wawa enjoyed absolute autonomy and had its own administrative system, with a functional military that was believed to be one of the biggest in the region at the close of the nineteenth century[32].

Clapperton, in 1826, felt obliged to visit the King of Bussa because, according to him, "all this part of the country is nominally under him. The Sultan of Nikki is next to him and equal to him in power." The Lander Brothers reported that Wawa received about eight hundred cavalry soldiers who came to take refuge following the war of succession in Nupeland in 1830 (Hallet 1965; Crowder 1973; Idris 1973; Adekunle 2004).

Nikki had a complex territorial organisation, apparently because of the expansive size of the kingdom at the close of the eighteenth century. Idris (1973) identified five different territorial structures in ensuring effective allegiance to the king: the Nikki metropolis and its environs, the districts, old divisions, new divisions and provinces. Each of these territorial structures had a different relationship with the principality of Nikki.

---

[32] Wawa even used its military against Bussa in 1897 when it sided one of the factions during a succession crisis in Bussa. Wawa supported Kwara to the throne of Bussa against Kisan Dogo, who had already been elected to replace Dan Toro.

The metropolitan Nikki was under the direct control of the *Sina Boko* and it included all the surrounding villages of Nikki. The heads of villages were appointed by the *Sina Boko*. He exerted direct control over them and the resources therein. Most of the village heads, in this regard, were from the royal family and they appear to have been those with a good relationship with the *Sina Boko*. Unfriendly and ambitious princes did not dwell very near the capital, for fear of being co-opted or closely monitored (Idris 1973).

The districts were areas administered by descendants of the different dynastic lineages or branches. They too were appointed by the *Sina Boko* but enjoyed relative autonomy. They were expected to be loyal to the *Sina Boko,* who was believed to be their benefactor. The *Karawe* (a Boko dynastic clan) were around the north-east of Nikki, alongside the *Kwararu*, *Gbassi* and *Gbasso* in areas known as Gbassoland in the east of Nikki. The *Makararu* (Baatonu dynastic clan) were responsible for the western side, in the area around Gbengbereke, while the *Lafiaru* (Baatonu dynastic clan) were in the south-eastern and later south of Nikki (Idris 1973). The autonomy enjoyed or exerted by these princes was reported to have created tension and abuses in the region. According to Idris:

> ... although the King of Nikki appointed the chiefs of these villages, he had limited influence over them as they were constantly under the cover of mighty princes who took laws into their hands. These were not only areas of political manoeuvring and armed conflicts, but also the areas where princes were able to accumulate wealth, mostly by extortion from caravans as the king could not control them especially if he was weak. The situation accounted for the growing strength of Koto Moro, the Chief of Pelle (Perere), who in 1891 completely overshadowed the *Sina-Boko*... (Idris 1973, 243).

What Idris called the older divisions could actually be the real provinces of Nikki. The political structures of these settlements were believed to have been established by the children of the first *Sina Boko*, Suno-Sero. They were Bouay, Puissa, Sandilo, Kika and Bweru. They were autonomous entities with full kingship powers and elaborate political structures just like Nikki. They had all the necessary paraphernalia of power, including *Kakaaki* (royal trumpets). Their relationship with Nikki was at the level of appointment of leadership and initiation of their young princes during the *Gaani* Festival.

Towards the end of the nineteenth century, Puissa and Bouay became the suzerains of the *Kwararu-Gbassi* and *Kwararu-Gbasso*, while Sandiro and Kika were under the control of the *Lafiaru* (Idris 1973). A similar structure was applied for the new provinces like Babanna to the east and other Baatonu settlements in the south-east of Nikki, like Ilesha, Kenu, Okuta, Yashikira, and Gwanara in the nineteenth century.

The administrative structure of Nikki dependencies, which some Borgu historians (Idris 1973; Kuba 1994; Adekunle 2004; Lafia 2004, 2008), wrongly described as provinces, were totally different from the other territorial political structures. These dependencies, including Kaiama, Parakou, Kandi and Kouande, had no direct influence on any of Nikki's dynastic branches. Although the aristocracy of Kaiama has a Nikki origin, the genealogy predates the emergence of dynastic branches of Nikki, therefore, not directly linked to any of the six branches. They were independent polities that had voluntarily or involuntarily submitted to the coverage (political alliance) and protection of Nikki, which was the largest and most influential polity in the region in the eighteenth century. They were led by independent kings of almost equal political status to Nikki and controlled wide territory, with a strong and independent military formation. They had all the regalia and political structure of independent kings. Nikki had no control over them as they independently appointed their kings, even if the King of Nikki on some occasions, depending on the state of the relationship, carried out the investiture. Idris reported that all the kings of these dependencies received their investiture from Nikki, but new evidence has shown that not all went through that. It largely depended on the relationship with the King of Nikki at the time and how a king emerged.

Tributes were paid on a voluntary basis. Towards the end of the nineteenth century, with the diminishing capacity and status of Nikki, some of these dependencies, principally Kaiama and Kounde, refused to pay tributes to Nikki, which Nikki tried unsuccessfully to enforce[33]. As observed by Idris (1973), the relationship between these dependencies and Nikki was that of continual contestation. The degree of control or influence of Nikki was largely determined by the character, personality, political skills and even the military capacity and ruthlessness of the King of Nikki and those of the dependencies at a given time.

Fiscal System

The fiscal system provided economic support for the politics of the region. The system was largely based on the structure of the political economy of the states, which was ever-changing (details in succeeding chapters). The state revenue and expenditure pattern were, therefore, influenced by the character and size of the kingdom and also the level of economic activities therein.

The political system was expansive and probably expensive for the economy. The major sources of revenue were proceeds of the slave trade in the early periods of the seventeenth and eighteenth century, tributes and gifts from districts, provinces and dependencies, war booty, as well as caravan and market tolls. The community tax and tributes were not clearly defined but each of the subordinate Kings remitted to the principal kings through assigned officials. In Nikki, the *Baa Agban* was responsible for tribute collection from individuals, while each of the territorial heads paid directly to the *Sina Boko*, except those from the south-eastern part who paid through the King of Kenu (Idris 1973). The kings often retained parts of the revenue for both official and personal use. Tributes were also received from the pastoral Fulbe community through the *Funduga*. These payments were made with cattle. Markets tolls were collected on market days while caravan tolls were received from merchants passing through the territory of Borgu. These were also received in either cash or kind. Other sources were mandatory military contribution during wars and war booty from defeated territories. Individual princes also made extra

---

[33] When these two principalities refused to pay tribute to Nikki under Sero Toru Wonko, he resorted to war against Kaiama in particular.

resources from raids, pillage and banditry on villages and trade caravans.

The kings were responsible for the management of the revenue. The major expenditure was on construction, particularly city walls in some principals towns, particularly Bussa, Kaiama and Wawa. Substantial parts of the resources were spent on the lavish ceremonial lives of the kings and princes, especially during festivities like *Gaani,* and later the two Muslim *Eids*.

Defence and Military Organisation

Borgu had been historically presented as a pugnacious country with an apparent joy for violence. Being a relatively small state surrounded by large polities, it was forced to contend with different levels of aggression since the thirteenth century. It, therefore, fought a series of battles but had never succumbed to any imperial conquest until the nineteenth century with the European colonial subjugation (Clapperton, 1829, Lugard 1895, Anene 1965, Akinwumi 1995).

Borgu held up against Songhai invasions twice in the fifteenth century[34] (Crowder 1973, Stewart 1996, Kuba and Akinwumi 2005). It invaded the Oyo Empire under Alaafin Oronpoto in the sixteenth century and resisted Dahomey in the eighteenth century. It also repulsed Habe onslaughts and later the Fulbe Jihad from the Kabawa. Borgu also provided military assistance to its neighbours in strategic wars of self-defence and aggression. The development of iron weapons and mounted cavalry might have contributed significantly to the upsurge of states and military capacity of Borgu. Borgu's war-like nature was well established and held in dread and awe by its neighbours.

Mockler-Ferryman, travelling through the Niger in 1889, noted some popular sayings by Borgu's neighbours: *"Masudawaki goma na Burguwa sun issa kore masudawaki dari na filani."* Translated, ten Borgu horsemen are enough to defeat one hundred Fulani horsemen. Also: *"Ekpa Burgu de noshe gaya."* This, in Nupe, states that the Borgu arrow is very poisonous, setting out the Nupe view of their neighbour. In Yorubaland, old women would say *"Olurun gbami lowo*

---

[34] Borgu was attacked by Askia Mohammed in 1505 and in 1555 by Asia Nuhu.

ogu Bariba;" God delivers one from a Bariba war (Mockler-Ferryman 1892, 145).

The defence structure and military organisation of Borgu was a major contributory factor to its invincibility. Borgu also had a natural defence with the River Niger in the north and the Atakora Mountains to the west. The Guinea Savannah terrain and vegetation of Borgu made it easy to withstand battles from the Sahel or Sahara Desert regions, while its open and vast territory easily overwhelmed its enemies. Each Borgu city, especially since the seventeenth century, had city walls[35] with access gates. These served for both caravan toll collection and defence purposes.

Each state in the region, including districts, provinces and principalities, had its own independent army and could deploy the army for self-defence or aggression. In most cases, there were no standing armies but reserves mobilised within a very short time. All able-bodied males were eligible for recruitment. The army was led by the members of the ruling class. The bulk of the foot soldiers were from the other layers of the society, except for slaves. The military formation was made up of cavalry, archers, spiritualists and griots. The cavalry were largely members of the Wasangari ruling class and they were followed by their respective groups of archers and griots. The spiritualists were largely priests of different deities, "medicine men" and clairvoyants. The griots were the morale and confidence boosters who sang the praises of the warriors, related them to previous heroes and veterans and pushed them to keep fighting until victory was attained.

The military was led by the king of each territory, unless he was indisposed, which might be occasioned by ill-health or old age. He could then appoint a representative from the senior members of the ruling the class. The Wasangari were responsible for the horses. Each important member of the ruling class had at least three horses, with a retinue of followers and warriors. Heroism was important for the ascension of the throne. This was even more important in the nineteenth century when violence became an important means of ascending the throne in most of the Borgu principalities. The kings and

---

[35] Hugh Clapperton and the Lander Brothers both reported the city walls of Bussa, Kaiama and Wawa. Ruins of the walls can still be found in Kaiama.

chiefs assembled and managed the military through the support of other princes and the war minister, an official with the title *Zhiki* in Boko, Kaiama and Bussa. This official was called the *Sina Toto* in Nikki.

Military weapons consisted of swords, spears, bows and arrows. As reported by Clapperton (1829, 106), in Bussa, "a heavy club of about two feet and a half in length, bent at the end and loaded with iron" was also employed. This may be the weapon known as *gbemba* in Kaiama. The archers and some Wasangari wore special uniforms with different forms of protective charms and amulets around them. Borgu was renowned for poisonous arrows and biological warfare. Akinwumi (2004) chronicles the details of the nature of biological warfare, which included the use of poisoned arrows. Clapperton was also told how the dreaded poisoned arrows were made from the seed of *"Kongkonie"* (likely *Konko li.* In Boko, *li* is the word for a tree).

> The tree is a parasitic (meaning probably a creeper), and about the thickness of a man's thigh at the root, from which shoot up several stems, that ascend the large tree at the root of which it grows, twisting itself round the stem and branches to the top of the tree ... the part which grow from the flower contains the seeds is about a foot and a half in length, and one and half or two inches in circumference in the thickest part. The seeds are like caraway seeds, and are surrounded by a silky substance; they are boiled until they turn into paste, when they fit for use and put on the arrow (Clapperton 1829, pp. 88).

The arms were largely prepared locally by blacksmiths and hunters. The defensive amour was a "tanned leather shield, of a circular form and ... large shirt gathered in folds round the body, and made fast round the waist with a belt" (Clapperton 1826, 109). Each military went through different forms of collective and individual fortification. Some were individually procured and others centrally provided by the state. Bravery was a major issue in Borgu, a Wasangari hero could easily become a king and a commoner hero could dine with a king and become influential. Every young man was brought up and trained to be a warrior. War games between communities were prevalent, especially after harvest season[36].

War was, therefore, a serious business. Defeat was never an option. Defeat in battle often meant suicide for the war commanders. "Warriors must never be captured or enslaved" was the prevailing ethos. Ambush, night raids, hypnotism and courage were some of the military tactics of Borgu. The military was structured in small columns led by a Commander, each given a responsibility in the larger scheme. Some columns served as advance attack teams. Borgu relied on the speed of its cavalry, ambush, night surprise attacks and full frontal attacks in sections. Lugard attributed the success of the Borgu military to two reasons:

> First their reputation for a knowledge of witchcraft and the deadly poisons, which render their poisoned arrows very dreaded. Second, to their fighting tactics… I am told, when they attack by day, is to make a feint of attack simultaneously on front and rear, reserving the bulk of their strength for a strong attack on the centre of a long caravan. This mode of attack by ambush would generally succeed in dividing their enemies' forces and inducing panic. They, however, love most to effect a night surprise (Lugard 1895, 219).

Confederacy and Interstate Relations

The pre-colonial political system and territorial administrative structure and relations between the states of Borgu were a classic example of a confederation. There is a tendency among Borgu scholars to reduce this confederation to a relationship between Illo, Bussa and Nikki, as provided in the Kisra traditions. However, the dynamics of the structure in the mid-eighteenth and nineteenth-century indicates that more states of different sizes, history and power were recognised members of the confederation and played complementary and distinct roles in the politics of the Borgu states.

The Borgu confederacy was based on these following characteristics:

---

[36] Interview in Kaiama on April 23rd, 2017

Loose and Decentralised Structure

The states of Borgu didn't have a central authority and had to contend with strong centrifugal tendencies. Nonetheless, it was a league of territories united for common action and common interest. The relationship was shaped by the changing dynamics of the political economy of each of the states, irrespective of history and size. It was, therefore, wrong to refer to Borgu as a whole as an 'empire' or a 'kingdom' in the strict sense of these terms. There were several component kingdoms within the entity. Some of the kingdoms grew, others mutated and multiplied and some shrivelled up right up to the final colonial annexation in the late nineteenth century. The confederacy was, therefore, a journey of several centuries in which different segments played some primary roles but none was consistently dominant in the run of history. Governor Ballot of Dahomey, in 1895, noted thus:

> ...it was only in the minds of European geographers that Borgou (Borgu) existed as a centralised "Kingdom". In reality, Borgou was a loose political federation of local rulers, a society in which a series of local power centres had emerged and were permanently at war with each other under constantly changing alliances. (cited in Bierschenk 1993, pp. 221).

When Clapperton passed through Borgu in 1826, he was told that the King of "Bussa could, after the Hausa, raise more horses than any other prince between the Hausa country and the sea, and could take the Yoruba country anytime he wanted it." It was on this basis that Clapperton concluded that Borgu was made up of "petty states of Nikki, Kaiama, Wawa and Boussa (Bussa), of which Boussa is considered the head". Even after asserting the seniority of Bussa, Clapperton recorded that a Dahomeyan messenger told him "... Nikki was the Capital of Borgu, not Kaiama." (Clapperton 1829, 83).

However, in the treaty leading to the annexation and eventual balkanisation of Borgu, Lugard, even after signing an earlier treaty with Bussa, described the King of Nikki as the "King of Nikki, and of all Borgu" (Crowder 1973, pp. 30).

To be sure, in the course of history, especially since the late seventeenth century up to the middle of the nineteenth century, Nikki had become the most dominant polity in the region, even if Bussa remained the spiritual or ancestral root of the kings[37] (Crowder 1973; Idris 1973). Nikki experienced a massive territorial expansion, with new tributaries and dependencies during the reign of Zume Dobidiya. The Kingdom extended from "the River Niger in the east, excluding Bussa State, to the Atakora Mountains in the west; and from Guene in the north to Save in the south" (Idris 1973).

In 1830, Lander reported that there were "not less than seventy considerable towns dependent on the state of Nikki, all of which have several smaller towns and villages under their control and management" (Lander 1936, 152). Of course, within these boundaries were independent entities with voluntary political alliance with Nikki.

Military Alliance/Defence Pact

Each of the states, including the provinces and dependencies, had their own military which they deployed individually or collectively in defence of their territorial integrity. It was probably a result of this that Borgu was never defeated until the colonial occupation[38]. They responded to territorial defence collectively, especially in the eighteenth and nineteenth centuries. Wawa and Illo collectively resisted and frustrated the Fulbe jihadist invasion of Kaiama[39]. The invading forces were defeated in Wawa by Ki- Mohammed Lafia, King of Wawa, and eventually frustrated by Ki-Taku, a senior minister of Illo (Hermon-Hodge 1937; Idris 1973, 217). When the Fulbe forces reorganised, with the support of Gwandu[40] and occupied , Illo, the invaders were dislodged by Nikki. In 1880, when the Bussa and Yauri forces failed to subdue rampaging Kambari forces, Bussa requested and received support from Kaiama, led by *Kilishi Yerima*, Mora Amali

---

[37] Clapperton reported in 1826 that the King of Nikki was equal in power to the King of Illo, but subordinate to the King of Bussa.

[38] The defeat in the Ilorin War was Oyo's defeat, not Borgu's, as Borgu was only supporting the Oyo to prosecute the war against the Fulbe Jihadists in Ilorin.

[39] The Fulbe Army was believed to have been led by Mallam Magaji, the son of Mallam Dendo, the Fulbe ruler of Nupe.

[40] Mohammadu, the son of Abdullahi, Emir of Gwandu, joined the earlier dispersed Fulbe forces and crossed the Niger through Gaya and occupied Illo.

Dogo, who eventually defeated the Kambari forces at Gebi. Kaiama provided similar support to Ilesha against Shaki in 1884.

Earlier, in 1837, when the Oyo requested military support against the Fulbe Jihadists in Ilorin, almost all the major principalities of Borgu contributed forces. These wars were important drivers of the political relations that brought these different entities together in defence of their common interest and destiny. Despite the elaborate history of military alliance and defence pacts, Borgu did not have a central military command and control. As Anene observed:

> In all these wars of defence and offence, there is ample evidence that in the face of national danger, the rulers of the principal Borgu centres of Bussa, Nikki and Kaiama co-operated fully. There is however no evidence of the existence of an organised national military machine controlled from the centre. The Eleduwe (Ilorin) War no doubt emphasised Nikki leadership and no one in Borgu had questioned the assumption of the powers of Commander-in-Chief of the Borgu forces by the King of that important Borgu focus of political power. (Anene 1965, pp. 216).

Despite this level of military alliance and defence cooperation, the relationship between the Borgu states was not always cordial. There were a series of wars and skirmishes between them. Ilesha and Nikki were embroiled in intense conflicts in the late nineteenth century. Okuta and Ilesha were also involved in a war in the same century, leading to strategic alliances between Ilesha, Kenu and Taberu against Okuta (Stewart 1993). A similar conflict ensued between Gwanara and Ilesha in 1843. Bussa was also involved in a war with Wawa from 1855 to 1859. This was ostensibly to avenge the killing of a relative in Wawa[41]. As a result, Wawa was observed to be the only principal state in the region that didn't participate in the war against Kaoje and later the Gebe war, even when non-Borgu states like Shaki and Kishi were involved (NAK 1925). There were also tensions between Bussa and Kaoje in the later part of the nineteenth century. The Landers reported an expected invasion of Kaiama by Wawa during their visit in 1836.

---

[41] The king of Wawa actually had a tense relationship with Gajere of Bussa for supporting Bawalaki against him, among other issues of relationship.

Kisra Myth as Unifying State Ideology

The myth of Kisra was a major source of bonding within the Borgu elite claims of affinal relations flowed from it. The dynastic leadership across the Borgu states associated themselves with common ancestry, using it to strengthen relationships and build solidarity. The geographical entity called Borgu was largely areas with leadership that associated itself with one version or the other of the Kisra Legend. Once you removed the Kisra Myth or Legend, what remains would be mere panoply of different people within a particular geographical area. According to William H. McNeil, myths are important elements of any human society. He described myths as the human substitute for instinct supporting a unique way of acting together. "In the absence of believable myths, coherent public action becomes very difficult to improvise or sustain" (cited in Midgal 1988, pp. 26).

Citizenship in Borgu was, therefore, not just about culture. As discussed earlier, there were different cultural and linguistic groups. It was, in fact, a geographical area covered by entities with a Kisra-related dynastic leadership, either by direct relationship or voluntary alliance. In this context, some scholars defined pre-colonial Borgu as simply a federation of three kingdoms – Bussa, Illo and Nikki. The Kisra myth helped promote brotherhood among the ruling class. It was on this basis that Mora Tasude, King of Kaiama, told Lugard in 1894 that "his elder brother was the King of Nikki and he was in a sense under Nikki, but paid no tribute to him, in fact, was independent. He said Bussa (the eldest of the three and looked up to by all), Kaiama and Nikki were all independent Kings and the only Kings of Borgu" (Crowder 1973, 36).

Earlier, the King of Wawa had told Clapperton in 1826 that "he owed allegiance to Boussa, as Kaiama, Niki, and Youri did… Kaiama was a province of Borgoo, subject to the Sultan of Borgu" (Clapperton 1829, 90). Similar assertions were recorded by different kings across Borgu. This brotherhood was not necessarily genealogical, but political, built on the Kisra Legend. To strengthen solidarity, the ruling class exchanged children and inter-married across kingdoms and ethnic groups. These inter-marriages also spread across the entire states. The inter-marriages between Boko and Baatonu and Baatonu and Dendi have been very strong and influenced the dynamics of inter-ethnic relations and have enriched the languages with mutually borrowed words.

Tributes and Exchange of Gifts

The relationship between the principal states was maintained by the payment of tributes and exchange of gifts. This was not a reflection of subordination but a historical sense of friendliness, goodwill and mutual respect. Gifts were exchanged across all the principal states. Even the most powerful gave gifts to the weaker polities. Although part of the gift culture was built around the Kisra migration, these gifts were largely political. For lesser states, tributes were never fixed but expected anyway. Payment of tributes determined friendship and voluntary commitment to the principles of the confederation.

The supremacy of any of the polities was not based on its political strength or extensive domains. Payment of tribute was largely dependent on the strength of the king. According to Stewart (1993), a strong ruler had little or no problem ensuring payment of tribute for two reasons: "first, if tribute was not forthcoming, retaliatory action would have occurred, and second, the benefits of security and protection which accrued from an alliance with a strong ruler constituted an added incentive for payment" (pp. 208).

National Days and State Festivals (Gaani)

Different national days were set up for state worship and festivities. The *Gaani* Festival was one of the most prominent. As observed in chapter 4, *Gaani* is associated with the birthday of Prophet Muhammad and was widely practised across many West African polities. *Gaani* had a Songhai origin and might have been introduced in Borgu around the fifteenth century, a period when Islam was least practised by Borgu autochthons. It was celebrated as a state and aristocratic festival.

It was a period for assertion of the power of the kings and a confirmation of their suzerain control. The *Gaani* conduced to the preservation of the unity of the state. All the subordinate chiefs, princes and provincial heads were expected to pay homage, tribute and confirm their loyalty and allegiance to the kings of Borgu. Failure to attend the festival for no justifiable reason was an important confirmation of dissent, which could lead to an appropriate sanction. The solidarity of the Wasangari aristocracy and its reaffirmation of common origin was a major driver of the festival. During this festival, young princes were initiated into royalty as they would have their heads shaved (*miiboo* in Boko, *kona* in Baatonum) and be assigned a royal name.

Gaani was therefore, a political, judicial, economic and religious festival at which the structural elements are brought into a strong display and served as a unifying force that contributed to the perpetuation of the Wasangari aristocracy. Although *Gaani* was held in almost all the states of Borgu, Nikki's *Gaani* was one of the most prominent in the nineteenth century. Each state's *Gaani* attracted representation from other member states of Borgu. Failure to send representation was considered an important sign of a diplomatic crisis.

Coordinate Economic Policies and Foreign Relations.

Each state developed its economic policies, particularly as it related to the slave trade and later caravan trade across the region. The custom duty and commercial treaties were independently determined. The *Sina Boko*, that is the king of Nikki, was believed to have "established commercial treaties with Hausa, Nupe, Yoruba and Asante and became widely acknowledged by the neighbouring people" (Adekunle 2004, 11). Similarly, Clapperton observed during his visit to Kaiama in 1826 that "Kaiama had a direct trade with Dahomey, Youri [Yauri], Nyfee [Nupe] and Yourriba [Yoruba]. There is no fixed duty for the Merchants to pay, but the Chief [king] takes just as much as can be squeezed from them" (Clapperton 1929, 107). Foreign relations and external engagement were also independently coordinated but for dependencies, it required coordination with the major principalities to avoid suspicions of a conspiracy.

Dynastic Politics and Succession

Kingship was the apex political institution in Borgu. Each state, principality or province had a kingship structure, with succession, lineages and an independent succession process. While there were strong elements of commonality in the succession structures, the process of appointment was diverse, particularly among the principal states of Bussa, Kaiama, Illo, Nikki, and Perere amongst others. The death of a king marked the end of the reign. Until the colonial time, the kings were never deposed. More often, they were either killed through violence (which was more or less the rule) or through poisoning. The history of Borgu is replete with these two cases. Violent deaths were a result of the rigid political structure and etiquette that defined the king as not only the Commander-in-Chief but he was also required to physically lead battles, irrespective of age. Self-poisoning, on the other hand, was considered an honourable death by kings (Idris 1973).

Interregnums were often difficult for the polities; the system was sorely stressed and there were hardly any peaceful transitions in most of the states. Contenders and pretenders threw themselves into the ring and everything was fair – poison, charms, violence etc. Serious civil strife could ensue. But ultimately, the unity of the ruling class was maintained.

The rules of succession were operated to distribute power among the various segments of the aristocracy in a manner that fostered the cohesion of the ruling class. In almost all the states, through succession politics and contentions, the dynasty expanded from a mono-dynasty to a poly-dynasty structure involving multiple ruling houses. The dynasty in Nikki had, over the years, increased to six while Bussa had four. In other Borgu states, the dynasties might not have mutated to several numbers but micro-dynastic politics created internal fissures that were sometimes difficult to mend.

The underlying schism generated by the process of complementary filiation, though particularly destructive, served to emphasise the value of preserving the unity of the individual houses in their effort to retain their claim to the throne (Stewart 1978). The contentions were, therefore, between different dynasties, while each dynasty's structure strived to maintain its unity often with extreme difficulty. In Bussa and Nikki, the houses were believed to have stemmed from the different mothers of the princes. Half-brother relationships that existed between a group of sons were sufficient to cause them to break apart and establish their own separate claims to the throne, backed by their matrilineal kin groups (Stewart 1978). However, the right to claim the throne was patrilineal. This rule expectedly produced a large number of eligible candidates on each occasion of succession. In Bussa, the competition was often between half-brothers across dynasties. Full-brother competition was discouraged.

While the throne was restricted to the ruling house/houses as the case may be, "only houses connected by direct descent with previous kings through the senior male members of each generation have a chance of retaining a continuing claim to the throne. If the individual members of a ruling house eligible to succeed do not actually do so for whatever reason, the right of that particular ruling house to the throne is irretrievably lost" (Stewart 1978,170).

Each of the Borgu principalities had a council of kingmakers that comprised senior state ministers and officials who formed an electoral college. In Nikki, at the death of a king, the *Sina Donwiru* would assemble all the members of *Asakpa* (electoral council). They constitute an interim leadership committee, chaired by the *Sina Donwiru*, until a new *Sina Boko* was appointed. In Bussa, there were eight members of the Kingmakers' Council, representing the autochthonous community and the ruling aristocracy. These were the Bakarabonde, Badaburude, Bamoide and Madoko representing the autochthonous groups, while the aristocracy was represented by the Bataku, Beresondi, Bamaribere and Beresoni. Succession in Bussa was often horizontal, between the initial two (later four) dynastic branches. The eldest in the senior generation often succeeded. While the council of kingmakers managed the selection process, the tradition of Bussa and other Borgu states holds that the selection of kings was decided by deities.

At the end of the *ge-i-kunma*, that is the mourning period in Boko (called *Kanana* in Batonu), the new king was revealed to the princes of the dynastic branches and their *Ibano* (supporters, followers, subjects) at the outskirts of the town. From that moment, after all the salutations from the other princes, the new king commenced all necessary rituals, including wearing of antelope skin and *felele* (a traditional dress) and being made to walk to his horse unaccompanied. This was expected to be a show of bravery by the new king, as he could be killed by other contenders. If that were to happen, the process started afresh (Idris 1973).

A similar process applied in Nikki, where the new king was expected to travel to Nikki-Wenu, the ancestral home of the aristocracy. He travelled through a secret route with a small group of supporters. On his safe return to the city, the new king would live in celibacy for a week in a specially constructed hut and, thereafter, go through three-month-long confinement in the house of his closest supporter or friend.

This process of selection and conferment also applied to Kaiama. In Bussa and probably Kaiama, the senior *Yerima* (heir apparent) of the most senior generation was often chosen. The Yerima had to be at least fifty years of age and his mother must have died: this is considered a sign of maturity. He must have been baptised, been given a princely name at a *Gaani* festival and introduced to the ancestors. The kingmakers would confirm the genealogical roots of the candidates and the link to previous rulers. Once these are confirmed, other non-dynastic criteria like military prowess, generosity and charisma were put into consideration. The appointment processes were politically intense, comprising political manoeuvres, a balance of forces, witchcraft and violence. The interregnums were obviously turbulent. In some cases, it could result in revolts and sedition. The selection of the Electoral College had first to be confirmed by the local deities. With the coming of Islam, especially from the twentieth century on, Imams became important members of the Electoral College. Before the colonial period, a new King of Kaiama must first be approved by the village heads of Kemanji, Wozibe and Venra and the elders of Kaiama. These three villages, in addition to Kabaru in Kaiama, were considered autochthonous and, therefore, the owners of the land.

Nikki had the largest number of dynastic branches at six. Although, as indicated earlier, the kingship has been dominated by two, Nikki happened to be the only principality where power was not only shared between the dynastic groups: the kingship itself was rotated between the two major ethnic groups, the Baatonu and Boko (Idris 1973, Stewart 1993). This can probably be traced to the process of the emergence of the Nikki aristocracy. Although Baatonu was the major ethnic group and an autochthonous community in Nikki, the origin of the aristocracy was linked to Bussa in the east. The political system that emerged in Nikki was, therefore, a fusion of Boko and Baatonu.

In Nikki, as in Kaiama, where any eligible candidate of a dynasty was female, such a candidate was overruled for a male in next dynastic branch. However, the appointed king would be expected to appoint the woman as the *Yon Kogi* (in Nikki and other Baatonu principalities), or *Kiyezide* (in Kaiama), anytime the position became vacant. Where a prince emerged whose father or grandfather was never a king in the family, such a person could be overlooked for one whose father or grandfather had ruled. In this case in Nikki, such candidate would be given a large province to administer.

The maternal homes and relationship of the princes were always important in the contests. They provided the first layer of solidarity and a place of refuge for unsuccessful candidates. Unsuccessful candidates were required to return to their maternal homes. This was aptly summed by a Nikki expression "*Toko kon da yenuo, Nikki ma yina*" which translates to "Old man, I shall be back home: Nikki has refused/rejected me" (Idris 1973). Historically, on return to their maternal homes, these princes indulged in raids for slaves and in the pillage of caravans. This happened in the case of Yerima Baba, the son of Kpe Gunu *Giribusiko,* when he returned to Gbassi after his rejection by the kingmakers for Sero Tasu.

The process and mechanism of the political system was tense and conflict-ridden. While the oral tradition recorded most of the ideal, albeit embellished systems and processes, evidence indicates that the system was severely tested and stressed by different layers and processes of engagement. One of the major process challenges Borgu had to face was the ever-expanding dynasties in the principal kingdoms of Nikki and Bussa, and associated dynastic rivalries. In Nikki, the breach of existing rotational succession arrangement between the six dynastic houses created a huge rivalry among and within royal houses. Certain dynastic lineages were believed to have unfairly dominated the throne of *Sina Boko*. According to Idris (1973):

> The genealogy of the Kings of Nikki shows that *Kwararu-Gbasso* had presented three successive rulers to the throne whereas the *Tosu* was completely eliminated and had to contend itself with the Chieftaincy of Okuta district. Common happenings were the

enthroning of a junior [sic] branch before the senior ones. The succession order should have been *Karawe, Kwararu Gbassi, Makararu, Lafiaru, Tosu* and *Kwararu-Gbasso*.(Idris 1973, 277).

As a result, especially in the nineteenth century, violent successions became the order of the day. Sero Kpera overthrew Sabi Naina and ran a massive terror campaign on Nikki's districts and provinces. The internal crisis in the royal houses resulted in rebellion in some provinces[42] which began to assert their independence. The metropolitan Nikki also had to contend with the suspicion of a Wangara rebellion and a suspected alliance with the Fulbe to launch a new jihad. This was one of the reasons Sero Kpera decided to support the Oyo against the Fulbe in Ilorin and eventually died in that war. As shown in chapter 4, the death of Sero Kpera and other prominent Borgu leaders in the 1830 Ilorin War was believed to be a big loss to Borgu. Sero Kpera was believed to have been a great unifier of Borgu (Idris 1973). After his death, Nikki found itself in an unprecedented political crisis.

In addition to the raging challenges of dynastic struggles, new fissures and layers of conflict within the ruling class emerged. The first of such was the appointment of the successor to *Sero* Kpera. Kpe Gunu Bakpari was appointed, instead of Sero Sorou[43] who was believed to be Sero Kpera's preference. Kisan Dogo[44], the King of Bussa and the only principal king of Borgu who failed to participate in the Ilorin War, was believed to have been instrumental to the installation. He got Gejere, a veteran of the Ilorin War, to lead a delegation to Nikki for the installation. Gejere himself was to later be involved in a violent coup against Gbewanlaki in Bussa. A violent conflict was later to ensue between Gunu Bakpari forces and those of Sero Sorou, leading to the defeat and overthrow of Kpe Gunu Bapari.

---

[42] Sandiro was believed to be one of the provinces of Nikki that began to assert its independence.

[43] Sero Sorou was a veteran of the Ilorin War. He was one of the survivors and it took him 14 days to return to Nikki from Ilorin. According to Idris, his appointment would have been "unconstitutional" because he was of the *Lafiaru* dynastic branch and his father was a *Sero Kpera* predecessor.

[44] With the death of *Sero Kpera* and other prominent kings in the Ilorin War, Kisan Dogo was believed to be trying to claim the leadership of Borgu.

Sero Sorou controversially installed himself at Koro-Woko[45]. Kpe Gunu Bakpari fled to Sono-Bonnikari, from there to Sunon-Wonke, then Gbemgbereke and later Ganouru (Gwanaru), where he tried to regroup against Sero Sorou. He was believed to have mobilised up to five thousand soldiers to attack Nikki, but his plans were foiled by Sorou's forces. He died in Ningurume, his final refuge after three years (Idris 1973).

The crisis at the centre resulted in massive rebellion and intransigence by Nikki districts, provinces and dependencies. Many began to reject the authorities in Nikki. The situation remained so for a long time as the centre continued to be embroiled in a succession crisis between Sero Kpera, Darukpara[46] and Sabi Purukaru. Even after the defeat of Darukpara, the allied forces couldn't agree on leadership. This resulted in another round of crisis between Sabi Purukaru and Sero Sorou. Eventually, he made it into Nikki and became the *Sina Boko* with *Kpe Lafia* as his title. Even after this, Nikki was engulfed in different wars – civil and international. It was during the reign of Sero Toru Wonko that the Nikki state collapsed, leading to an almost total breakup with the provinces and the collapse in the solidarity of the Borgu states (Idris 1973). The political alliances of Djougou, Kouande, Kandi, Kaiama and Parakou all collapsed and they became independent states. Even the metropolitan province of Nikki was "taken over by Perere, which has grown immensely powerful toward the end of the nineteenth century" (Idris 1973, 293).

In Bussa, competition for kingship fragmented the dynasty from one to three between 1792 and 1900 with most of the splits occurring in the latter century. Stewart classified them into four, with the fourth one not having a proper label (1978). The fourth was believed to have been founded by Kisan Dogo (1892 – 1902). This didn't get entrenched possibly because it overlapped with the colonial period and colonial interference with the dynastic system. From the original *Eteboro* Ruling House, there emerged *Gbemusu, Gambui* and *Fuin (Fuyin)*. Kitoro was the first to break away from the *Eteboro* Ruling House in 1792 and established the *Gbemusu* Dynasty. Kisan Dogo, another member of the original dynasty founded the Gambui Ruling

---

[45] The rebellion continued as his authority was rejected by most districts of Nikki.
[46] As the *Sina-Boko*, he decided to stay at Darukpara instead of the metropolis of Nikki for fear of subversion.

House. A violent dynastic tussle between the Gbewanlaki of *Gbemusu* and Gejere (1844 – 1863) led to the establishment of the *Fuin* by the victorious dynastic house (Stewart 1978, 1997; Mohammed and Nze 2009). Each of these succession processes has historically been violent.

With the growing crisis in each of the principalities and the increasing exclusion of several members of the ruling class, cases of raid, pillage and banditry on caravans increased, especially in the nineteenth century. Succession crises and competition among the dynastic branches created the need to maintain a huge army and a retinue of seekers and courtiers, which was very expensive. *Gaani* Festivals and related activities were also opportunities for princely exhibitionism. Most of the princes weren't involved in any economic activities and, therefore, relied on pillage, banditry, intimidation and influence-peddling to accumulate necessary resources. This wasn't a classic primitive accumulation of capital, as the resources were neither saved nor invested for capital growth.

Borgu also went through intense social, political and economic pressure. The advance of Islam and the Fulbe jihadist forces placed tremendous pressure on the north and south-east of Borgu. Illo, in particular, had to contend with several pressures and eventual capture by Gwandu, while the interior had to manage the relationship with the Fulbe-Borgu and the Wangara merchants who were the drivers of Islam in Borgu. At the economic level, banditry was beginning to affect businesses as new caravan roads were identified and Hausa merchants had taken control of trade from the Wangara. Intermittent upheavals and external pressures increasingly dominated Borgu in the middle years of the nineteenth century and "continental Borgu, became, as it were, enveloped in obscurity" (Anene 1965, 216).

Women and the Dynastic System

Although a deeply patriarchal society with strong patrilinealism, women aristocrats played a very important role in the leadership of Borgu's dynastic politics. The political structure recognised the role of princesses. They were assigned strategic roles in the central and territorial administrative system. These roles were both formal and informal. At the formal level were official functional positions provided for in the dynastic administration and informal roles were the political support roles mothers of princes played in inter-dynastic contestation and politics of accession to the thrones.

At the formal level was the position of *Yoo Maga'a*, in Bussa, *Yoo Kogi*, in Nikki and its provinces and *Yoo Kode* (and later *Kiyezinde*) in Kaiama. Every Borgu principality had a formal role for women in the administration of the kingdom. They were of aristocratic background and occupied one of the most powerful positions. These women were heads of the women communities in their domains. They had a hierarchy of other women who were responsible for different functions under them. They played strategic roles in the *Gani* Festival as they led the initiation/baptising of all eligible princes and assigned royal names to them. They were also members of the Council of Kingmakers.

In Bussa, Clapperton and Lander reported that *Yoo Maga'a* had a considerable influence over the King as she played a major part in the negotiations with the visiting party. He further recorded that she kept a separate institution from the king and had a great deal of influence over the King of Wawa who she defined as her brother (Crowder 1973). In Kaiama, the *Kiyezinde* was among the signatories to the 1894 Treaty with the British Government (Idris and Yaru 2008).

The mothers of princes also enjoyed tremendous influence in dynastic politics. The maternal home played an important role in the political development of princes. While in power, the younger children of the king were kept away from the capital. They, therefore, grew with their maternal uncles before going to their paternal uncles where they received basic education on social skills for their future roles. For almost ten years they learned horsemanship, warfare and the princely code of conduct. They, thereafter, returned to their maternal home: the same place they returned to after losing the contest for the throne. As noted by Stewart (1993), the dynastic houses in Bussa and Nikki stemmed from the different mothers of the sons of kings and "the half-brother relationships that existed between a group of sons being sufficient to cause them to break apart and establish their own separate claims to the throne, backed by their matrilateral kin group" (1978, pp. 169) even if the right to claim the throne is patrilineal. It was based on this that she suggested that five of the six houses that emerged in Nikki were inspired by women who were probably mothers of the princes. They include *Mako* I (*Gbasi*), *Mako* II (*Gbaso*) *Sannu* (*Yari Lafiaru*), *Sannu Tossu* and *Sessi* (*Makararu*)[47].

Some of the princesses were believed to have participated in some of Borgu's wars and performed exceptionally. Idris (1973) provided the names of some of these brave women warriors: Bake Iya the daughter of Sero Kpera, the 24th *Sina Boko*, and Yon Wehene, daughter of Kpe Gunu participated in several wars. Sime Sika and Tondi Sika, the two daughters of Yon Wehene and her husband Sina Worigi, were said to have caught a lion with their bare hands at Dunkasa, to stop the beast from preventing the inhabitants of that village from drawing water from the stream (Idris 1973, 104).

Similarly, Kiyezide Duregi was reported to have led the home guards of Kaiama against the invading Nupe warriors and succeeded in repelling them (Idris and Yaru 2008). Women have played an important socio-economic role in dynastic politics. They owned slaves and were believed to be major links in accessing charms and medicines and even witchcraft for the fortification of the princes in the struggle for the throne.

---

[47] Although this was questioned by Kuba, we have no reason to disagree.

CHAPTER THREE

Pre-colonial State and Economy

The growth of state apparatus in Borgu was closely connected with the shift towards more active exploitation of internal resources and greater inter-regional exchange. The state, in Borgu, appears to have developed and transformed at the period of convergence, or integration, of the desert and ocean-centric commercial systems. This was the period when the trans-Saharan trade routes met the trans-Atlantic trade route. Structurally and historically, the state and economy were mutually reinforcing. The global commercial development from the eighteenth century might be associated with the wave of state-building along the West African coast (Moseley 1992). This growth was later interrupted in the last half of the eighteenth century by the savannah draught and the Islamic jihads. It resumed in the nineteenth century with increased expansion of trade, production and the exploitation of slaves for both the Sahara and the Atlantic markets. The expansion of trade in Borgu might also have increased the hunger for European goods and for even more horses for the cavalry of the aristocracy. This most likely explains Clapperton's claim to have seen more European items in Kaiama than he had seen in Yorubaland. He had also seen some of the best horses "from Bornou and Houssa merchants" (Claperton 1829).

The economy and the state in Borgu were, thus, mutually reinforcing. The structure of the economy depended on land, mercantilism and the exploitation of slave and family labour. The key economic activities were, therefore, agriculture, trade and cottage industry.

Agriculture and Peasantry

Pre-colonial Borgu was largely an agrarian economy. The society was deeply attached to the land and the practice of different land-related economic activities such as agriculture, pastoralism, fishing and hunting. The agricultural system revolved around shifting cultivation and bush fallowing. The low population density of Borgu was very suitable for this form of farming. Land was used for a period of time and abandoned for another location. This abandoned piece of land could then be revisited after natural re-fertilisation had occurred, or it could forever be left fallow. Land was never a problem because, as indicated earlier, Borgu never had a landed class. Land was communal, and to some extent, managed by the state through the kings. What was classified as communal land was actually the farms of such family or clan. It was their land to the extent that they were cultivated. There were very limited conflicts over farmland and where such arose, it was resolved by the political or community leadership.

Farm labour was largely sourced from family members and domestic slaves. The social and economic organisation was around the family. Often, extended families of people lived in compounds and each segment of the family could have separate farms and could rely on the larger pool of kinfolk. Polygamy was a major means of increasing the size of the family. Men were the major cultivators with women supporting and participating largely during harvest time. General community labour was used to enhance productivity as members of the community were mobilised to support individual family farms on a rotational basis.

Only limited economic surplus was extracted from agriculture and most production was for subsistence. Nevertheless, excesses were sold in the various markets along the caravan routes. Settlements in Borgu, particularly in the nineteenth century, were influenced by security and farmlands. Villages moved, in some cases, as farms changed. Because of shifting cultivation, farms began to get further away from town and village settlements. People, therefore, camped in the farms during planting season and only went back home at the end of the season. As the clustering around the farms increased, villages shifted to new locations. Many of the villages around the major principalities of Borgu were products of farm settlements or rebellious princes.

The Guinea savannah vegetation of Borgu and the generally favourable climatic conditions allowed for the cultivation of different species of crops. Farming was seasonal. Planting was done at the start of the rains and harvesting was done towards the end of that season. The principal crops in Borgu were yams, sorghum, corn/maize, cassava, rice and indigo. Rice was mainly produced in the riverine parts of Borgu, along Bussa and Illo. Farming was a trans-community venture as almost every member of Borgu community, except the itinerant Wangara and the Hausa long-distance traders were involved in farming. The expansion in long-distance trade in the eighteenth century transformed agriculture in Borgu as the demand for food increased and an avenue for sale of excess incentivised increased production.

The Fulbe pastoralists also cultivated small farms through their *Gando* slaves. They were largely involved in producing corn and sorghum for family consumption. Sometimes, they exchanged cattle, sheep, milk or cheese for other food products. Clapperton was fed with "milk, eggs, banana, fried cheese, curds and *foo-foo* (probably pounded yam or cornmeal)" during his visit to Kaiama in 1826. The pastoralists were not only taking care of some of the cattle of the ruling aristocracy, but they also developed a symbiotic relationship with the community where animals were allowed to feed on the remnants of the farm harvest. The movement of cattle in the woodland of Borgu also helped in building access roads and linking villages through animal paths.

Farming was complemented with seasonal hunting and fishing in the riverine areas. There were two types of hunting: individual and community hunting. The individual hunting was largely by experienced hunters with their children or apprentices. Community hunting was led by the local head of hunters. *Damaru,* that is community hunting, appears to be peculiar with the Batonu. It was led by the *Dama-suno*. This was conducted during the dry season when farming activities were over. It could run for a couple of days. Borgu people were believed to be great hunters. Clapperton (1829, 78) saw one of them at Barakina (Barkani?) on his way to Wawa from Kaiama.

He relates: "As I arrived at this village, a hunter came in from the chase, he had a leopard's skin over his shoulder, a light spear in his hand, and his bow and arrow slung over his shoulder. He was followed by three cream-coloured dogs, breed as if between the greyhound and cur: they were adorned with round collars of different coloured leather... he was followed by a slave carrying a dead antelope that he had killed this morning."

Fishing was also one of the preoccupations of Borgu. Commercial fishing took place on the River Niger, in the areas around Bussa and Illo. Smaller but substantial fishing was also carried out in the smaller rivers and tributaries of the Niger that criss-cross Borgu.

Local Industries

Small-scale industrial activities contributed significantly to the Borgu economy, especially in the eighteenth and the nineteenth centuries. Borgu was a major shea butter producing country in the West Africa region. Iron smelting also supported agriculture and the war efforts of the Borgu states. Weaving and dyeing was also a major artisan-led industry, supporting the local economy.

Blacksmithing is the oldest industry in the region. This industry was important to the major preoccupations of the Borgu people – farming, hunting and war. The industry is associated with the discovery of iron deposits and might have contributed significantly in the state formation process. This is because blacksmithing revolutionised agriculture and war in Borgu as iron tools and arms were produced. With iron tools, people could produce more, settle in more locations and could defend themselves. Carrying out expansionist aggression was easily the next logical step. The state formation process might, therefore, have been deeply facilitated by blacksmithing. Iron was believed to have been obtained in the north of Borgu, primarily in Bousakou, which is east of Kandi and Segbara. It was also found in Kamre, near Djougou. Iron was collected from these locations and used to produce the necessary tools, weapons and utensils. Farm implements were also used as means of exchange. Farmers were known to exchange food produce for farm implements. Blacksmithing skills were transmitted from father to son. It also had a religious connotation, associated with Iron and Fire Priests.

One of Borgu's biggest exports was shea butter. It was produced through the local milling system called *burare*. Shea butter was exported to Salaga, Hausaland and Yorubaland. It was largely a women-led industry. Shea trees grow wild and are found all over Borgu, particularly between latitude 9° and 10°N. The spread of the trees reached up to twenty-five to thirty per hectare in the areas around Kaiama, Nikki, Dunkasa, and Perere (Idris 1973, 46). The shea tree produces the shea nuts, which contain the shea kernel. Women systematically picked the shea nuts from the bushes and farms surrounding their communities. This was processed and refined into oil. Other oil milling activities include groundnut oil milling and its related by-product, *kulikuli* (groundnut cake/cookies), were also carried out by women. Women were involved in brewing beer, distilling gin and in the production of earthen pots and locust bean cakes (*kparo* in Boko)).

Another important pre-colonial industry in Borgu was the weaving industry. The origin of weaving in Borgu is not clear. It was believed to have been imported into Borgu through Yoruba slaves and captives and/or through trade with the Songhay. The industry was believed to have grown and spread across all segments of Borgu. Wawa and Djougou were key centres of weaving (Idris 1973). This industry was largely controlled by Wangara merchants, as well as the Pilla-Pilla and Dompago women. The slaves, of different origin, formed the bulk of weaving labour. Different variants of these cloths were produced and sold within and outside Borgu and generally called *Barubekuri* in Baatonum (*Zogwe-bisa* in Boko), but key types of cloths include *taru, kiribi, baboko, alkilla, laruba* and *kurakura,* amongst others. A related industry to weaving was dyeing. Some of the woven cloths were dyed into different colours. This is called *osi* in Boko. The dyes were produced from Indigo plants, also cultivated in Borgu. In places like Kaiama and Wawa, dyeing was done in a pits called *osi-were*.

Means of Exchange

Means of exchange varied, depending on the period. However, over time, they revolved around barter trade, cowry shells, gold and kolanuts. Barter was employed in both local and trans-national trade. People exchanged goods for others. Cowry shells in West African commerce have exclusively been the Indian Ocean shell of *cypraea moneta* and *cypraea annulus* from the Maldives, later from the East African coast and islands, especially Zanzibar. These were different from olive shells, somewhat similar to cowries, but lacking in some of the features. Olive shells were found in large numbers in some West African countries. Cowries were known to have been imported into the Niger Bend a century before the Portuguese brought them to the coast of Benin. The *cypraea moneta* specie of cowries was believed to have been in use as a means of exchange in different parts of the world for at least one thousand years (Johnson 1973). At the beginning of the nineteenth century, the English were shipping some 100 tonnes of cowries a year to Africa. This dropped with the abolition of the slave trade in 1806 and later recovered with the development of the palm oil trade.

The earliest currency area for cowries in West Africa was the Upper and Middle Niger in the medieval period. The cowries were believed to come through Sijilmasa, which appears removed from any other currency area. It would, therefore, seem they were introduced deliberately by the state, as in nineteenth-century Borno, or by a well-organised group of merchants (Johnson 1970). Cowries reached Mali and Gao in the sixteenth century and later Hausaland in the eighteenth century. In the nineteenth century, they were used on the west-east caravan route through Banduku, Salaga, Djougou, Nikki, Kaiama and Bussa. Most of these cowries came through Morocco; some might have come to Hausaland through Tripoli.

It has been suggested that the Hausa cowries might have come through Nupe and ultimately from the coast of Guinea. There is evidence of northward movement of a considerable amount of cowries into the Sokoto Caliphate in the form of tributes in the nineteenth century. It was believed that cowries came to Hausaland either as booty or given as an exchange for captured slaves (Johnson 1970). Cowries were moved in large quantities by donkeys and head loads. A donkey load in Kano in the nineteenth century was, for instance, 50,000 cowries (Johnson 1970).

Table 3: Cowries Values to Mithqal with Days of Journey

Journey	Days	Changes in Value of Mithqal	Change %	% Per day
Salaga-Yendi	6	4,300 – 4,200	4.8	0.4
Yendi-Zhogou	8	4,200 – 4,000	5.0	0.6
Zhougou-Nikki	10	4,000 – 3,800	7.9	0.5
Nikki-Niger	13	3,800 – 3,500 or 3,400	10.5	0.8

Source: Adapted from Marion Johnson, 1970

It was at about this time that Lugard travelled to Borgu. He used donkey loads of 84 Ib. each - two to a donkey from Jebba to Nikki. They were initially packed in 53 donkey loads but he had to sort out the cowries after losing most of the donkeys. The small ones were then bagged in sacks containing 16 heads (32,000 cowries), making quite a heavy head load of 76 Ib. each. The price of a donkey in Nikki in 1894 when Lugard visited was 60,000 cowries. This was conditional on the price being paid in cloth. Lugard's donkeys were probably carrying 40,000 cowries each before they were sorted into bags of 30,000 large cowries. That was half of the value of a donkey carrying the cowries. Transport by donkeys was efficient and economical only when they were believed to be healthy, with a good chance of survival for resale at the end of the mission (Johnson 1970). Lugard lost almost all of his donkeys. The cost of transportation grossly undermined the value of a currency. The value of cowries was, therefore, determined by days of the journey. Cowries could lose up to 10% of its value after a 13-day journey from Salaga to the Niger. By the end of the nineteenth century, the depreciating value of cowries had become a source of concern for long-distance traders. According to Johnson (1970, 32), it was so bad that carriers needed something like 1,000 cowries a day for subsistence "and would consume his whole load in under three weeks, even without payment.. Although carriers were usually paid on return, this was quite telling.

In places like Nikki, cowries were used in exchange for gold *mithqal*. There is no adequate information on the exchange rate in Borgu, but for a period of two centuries and probably longer, the exchange rate for gold *mithqal* to cowries was 1 *mithqal* to 3,000 cowries in Timbuktu (Johnson 1970). In Borgu, like in Hausaland, cowries were counted in numbers: fives, tens, hundreds, two hundred and so on. They were packed in units of 20,000 called *zika* in Boko (from *jaka*, meaning bag, in Hausa) and *boru* in Baatonum. Nikki and Djougou were believed to have developed their own gold coin, *mithqal* in the nineteenth century and was exchanging with other *mithqals* and cowries. Early in the nineteenth century, the Wangara were involved in the gold trade. Dupuis was reported to have handled two gold coins minted at Kalinga (Djougou). The coins were believed to be current in Jenny, Sago, Yauri, Wawa, Bussa, Kaiama, Kamba Mangho and all the neighbouring countries. The Nikki *Mithqal* was said to be current in Katsina and probably contributed to its emergence as a major trading city in the eighteenth century (Idris 1973).

Slavery and Slave Trade

Slavery and the slave trade were important to Borgu's economy right up to the early twentieth century. Slave labour was a vital factor in the production chain. As in every other society during the period, there were two types of slavery: the domestic slaves and those captured for export through the Atlantic slave trade network. The extent of Borgu's involvement in the trans-Saharan slave trade is not clear, but the trade may have contributed significantly to the political economy. Domestic slavery was always part of Borgu society and this may be associated with state formation. The different layers of the *Gando* system were very important for domestic production. The Wasangari, the common people, the Wangara and Fulbe owned slaves and these slaves supported domestic work, animal husbandry (including pastoralism and taking care of horses) as well as crop cultivation. Slaves were owned by both males and females. In Bussa, Clapperton, in 1826, saw "numerous slaves – male slaves were employed in weaving, collecting wood or grass, or on any other kind of work; while female slaves were engaged in spinning cotton with the distaff and spindle, some in preparing the yarn for the loom, others in pounding and grinding corn, some in cooking and preparing cakes, sweetmeats, natron, yam and *accassons,* and others selling these articles at the markets; the older female slaves are principally the spinners" (Clapperton 1829, 94).

The domestic and Atlantic slave trades were not mutually exclusive as the domestic slave structure was an important source for the transatlantic slave trade. The true extent of Borgu's involvement in slave trade was not clear but there is no doubt that Borgu was a source of slaves for both the local West African market and for the trans-Sahara market. Although the major source of slaves for export was from war, some of these slaves might also have been sourced from the servile class of Borgu, that is, the *Gando* people. Some might have been judicially sent into slavery. Borgu was also both a beneficiary and victim of slave trade. Slavery was important to the political economy of most pre-colonial states in West Africa from Central Sudan to the coast. The fifteenth-century Mande movements to Borgu and the raids from Songhay and the Hausa/Fulbe in the eighteenth century all had slave raiding as a core motivation. The southwards movement of people and the setting up of new settlements in the hinterland were also associated with the resistance to slavery. Through its numerous wars, Borgu might have exposed some of its people to capture who were eventually sold out as slaves. War was a major source of slaves all over the world. Captives were often sold. Borgu had surely captured even more slaves from their neighbours or even via internecine conflicts. In the early seventeenth century, Ahmed Baba, the Timbuktu jurist, had Borgu and Bussa[48] amongst the list of non-Muslim countries that were considered legitimate for enslavement. Others were Yoruba, Mossi, Kotokoli, Gurma, and more (Law and Lovejoy 1999). In the eighteenth century, Borgu was considered a minor, but a significant supplier of slaves to Europe through the West African coast. Its involvement in the European slave trade has not been properly documented and its significance to the trade not properly measured.

Lately, Law and Lovejoy (1999), relying on early European travellers' reports, slave documentation in the Americas and the testimonies of Borgu victims of war, painted a compelling mosaic of Borgu's role in the Atlantic slave trade. Among these travellers was Hugh Clapperton, who passed through Borgu, particularly Kaiama, Wawa and Bussa, in 1826. Clapperton's account provides an

---

[48] Some early Arabian and European sources defined Bussa as separate from Borgu. Some presented Borgu as a town – almost referring to Nikki. Borgu, in some cases was just referring to the Baatonu people.

interesting anecdote on slave trade in Borgu. In Kaiama, he reported seeing Hausa Muslim slaves praying in "their own ways." Clapperton saw extensive European articles in Kaiama, Wawa and Bussa. He was told the articles were brought from Dahomey. He believed this because he had "seen great abundance of rum, pewter and earthen ware" (Clapperton 1829, 84). In Kaiama in particular, he saw more European items than he had seen in Yorubaland (Oyo). He believed that slaves were important exports of Borgu and that it was through the sale of these slaves that Borgu received European items in return. This may not be totally correct, as Borgu played an important middle role in the long-distance trade, which might also have been a major source of these items.

At Wawa, Clapperton met a party of Dahomean traders who pretended to be emissaries of the King of Dahomey on a trade mission to buy camels in Yauri. They claimed "that the King of Dahomey had sent them to get camels, but the war between the Yaori [Yauri] and Fullatas [Fulbe] prevented any camel to come to Yaori." He later found out, after crossing the Niger to Nupe, that they were actually slave merchants and had bought 100 slaves in Yauri and intended to buy 100 more in Wawa. Dahomeans were generally presented as both slave raiders and as victims of slave raids. They had been involved in the slave trade probably since the seventeenth century and, principally, as a state trade, since the eighteenth century. Dahomey was originally a hinterland state, bordered to the coast by the kingdoms of Allada and Wydah. It, nevertheless, became a significant supplier of slaves through the southern kingdoms. Its eighteenth century conquest of these southern kingdoms provided it direct access to the coast and to European trade (Law 1989). The West African coast between the Volta River and Lagos, called the Slave Coast, was a major source of slaves for the Atlantic trade and probably supplied between seventeen to twenty percent of the total slave export. Dahomey was a significant contributor (Law 1989). In Dahomey, the king had the monopoly over the sale of war captives. Soldiers were, therefore, expected to surrender their captives to the king for a fee at the end of every war. Clapperton's visit to Borgu was during the reign of King Gezo of Dahomey (1818 – 1859), who had changed the monopolistic policies of the past and allowed for middle-men to access the coast and the European traders. He relaxed the earlier restrictions on foreign merchants and permitted Muslim traders to travel to the sea. This period was believed to have been a boom period in the search for slaves by these middle-men in the interior of West Africa. So, the visit of the Dahomey merchants to Wawa was not an isolated event. It can be understood as a part of the growing slave trade with Dahomey. Clapperton's report on slavery in Borgu may also have been influenced by the decline of Oyo and the consolidation of the Sokoto Caliphate (Law and Lovejoy 1999).

In trying to determine the extent of Borgu's involvement in the Atlantic slave trade, Law and Lovejoy (1999) traced the ethnicities or origins of Africa-born slaves in the Americas since the seventeenth century. They were largely identified as 'Bariba' or 'Barba'. This was the name Borgu people were called by their southern neighbours - the Fon people of Dahomey and the Yoruba. The earliest trace of Borgu slaves was in a 1627 book published by Alonso de Sandoval, a Spanish missionary in New Grenada, where he listed "Barba" among the caste of slaves that arrived through Sao Tome. Bariba were again traced in records of ethnicities of Africa-born slaves in the French colony of Saint Domingue (now Haiti) between 1760 and 1800. Bariba were described to have constituted less than 1% of the total and less than 2% of those shipped from the ports of Bight of Benin. These were roughly comparable in numbers to the Tapa (Nupe) but much less numerous to the Nago (Yoruba). The latter represented around 9% of the total and 26% of those from the Bight of Benin. In 1790, they were outstripped by the Hausa (Law and Lovejoy 1999). In another set of data covering 1721 to 1797, a similar proportion was attributed to Bariba, but in this case outnumbered by Tapa (Nupe), Hausa and the Nago (Yoruba) whose numbers significantly increased. Four Bariba were identified in the Louisiana Estate inventory database of 1719 to 1820 – two males and two females of ages between 30 to 35 years (Law and Lovejoy 1999).

Some Borgu slaves were also traced to the West African coast. Although Borgu didn't feature earlier in the database, there were suggestions that Muslim slave traders in Quidah, called Male or Mallais in the 1870s, were actually Wangara or Dendi from Borgu (Law and Lovejoy 1999). Others claim they were Hausa from

Zamfara[49]. Borgu elements were believed to be part of the Muslims of Abomey, believed to have been captives obtained in the Borgu-Dahomey war during the reign of King Tegbesu of Dahomey (1740 – 1774). According to Law and Lovejoy (1999):

> European traders operating along the Atlantic coast of West Africa later in the eighteenth century ... did occasionally hear explicitly of the Bariba. This may reflect an increase in the numbers of slaves from Borgu entering the Atlantic trade at this period – as is perhaps also suggested by their renewed visibility in the Americas after the mid-eighteenth century. But it was also, and probably more critically, due to shifts in the routes whereby slaves were delivered to the coast, which were ultimately due to Dahomian conquest of Quidah in 1720 (Law and Lovejoy 1999, 77).

The experiences of former slaves were also quite revealing. Testimonies exist of ex-slaves who had either passed through Borgu to the coast or those actually from Borgu. The experiences of Matteo, believed to be a native of Daura (now in Katsina State, Nigeria), and Benedito from Gaya, explain the dynamics of slave trade in the nineteenth century. While Matteo was captured during the Jihad, Benedito was picked by robbers. They both passed through Borgu while being transported to the coast. Similarly, Mohammed Manuel from Kano was captured during a war in Borgu and transported to Lagos. Karo Manuel, from Borno, was imprisoned in Wama (Wawa) and Cayawa (Kaiama?) in 'Borba' (Bariba or Borgu) country before passing through Yoruba country to Lagos (Law and Lovejoy 1999).

Specifically, on Borgu slaves, it was also recorded that among free slaves resettled in Freetown, Sierra Leone, were particularly Borgu-originated slaves. Baita (John Williams) and Wuene (William Cole) from Kaiama were Baatonu and Boko informants respectively to a German linguist, Sigismund Koele, around 1850. They were both captured during wars: Baita in Nikki and Wuene during the Oyo-Borgu War against Ilorin. They were both sold and later freed and resettled in Freetown (Law and Lovejoy 1999). The account of Mahommah Gardo Baquaqua provides a fascinating insight into slave trade in the Borgu region. In his 1854 biography, *An interesting*

---

[49] The term "Male" means "Muslim" in Fon and also Yoruba.

Narrative: Biography of Mahommah G. Baquaqua, a Native of Zoogoo, in the interior of Africa. From the title, Baquaqua was from Zoughou. At about the age of 30, he was captured and transported as a slave to Pernambuco in north-eastern Brazil and sold on to Rio de Janeiro. He was liberated after two years of slavery and later moved to New York. While Baquaqua implied that Borgu had weak linkage to European trade, he made several references to judicial enslavement. That is, prisoners were sold out as slaves instead of serving capital punishment. He also indicated that prisoners could be ransomed by relatives, rather than being sold abroad (Law and Lovejoy 1999).

Local historians in Bussa (Mohammed and Nze 2009) have attempted to claim for Bussa[50] the leader of the Barbados slave rebellion of 1816. It was believed to be the first slave rebellion in the region, after about 189 years of colonisation by English. The rebellion was the first of three slave revolts that took place in the British West Indies between the abolition of slave trade in 1807 and the emancipation in 1838 (Beckles 1985). Without any evidence beyond the names, reference was made to him as a Bussa hero. Bussa (or Bussoe) was an Africa-born slave. He was a chief driver at the Bayley's plantation in St. Philip. Biographical dates on Bussa are not available, but Beckles raises some inductive points:

> Firstly, it is (of) much significance that an African born man should be the prime leader of predominantly creole rebellion. In 1816 at least 92% of the slave population was creole, and all the other leaders of the rebel contingents were creole. Secondly, that an African should have achieved the status of chief driver, suggests that he probably was not a young man in 1816, since the slave trade was abolished in 1807, and it in general took at least 10 years for Africans to acquire the language and managerial skills, plus their masters' confidence, in order to become the chief slave personnel on estates (Beckles 1985, 90).

It will require more biographical details of Bussa to determine whether he was actually from Borgu and Bussa in particular. Considering the scale of misspellings of African names and towns during this period, a simple similarity in spelling is not enough. After

---

[50] His photo was displayed in a book among prominent names linked to Bussa.

all, until the colonial period in the twentieth century, Bussa was variously spelt as "Busa", "Boussa", and "Borsa".

The structure of the slave market in Borgu is not clear. It would appear the state played a leading role in the enslavement and export of slaves. The kings and princes of the various dynasties, in collaboration with the Wangara, were the main drivers of trade in Borgu. War captives were surely held by the different warriors and pooled together as state slaves, were probably traded through intermediaries in Borgu or outside Borgu, such as the Dahomey and possibly Hausa and Yoruba slave traders. The Wangara were believed to have, at a stage, combined both long-distance trade with slave trade and were a prominent part of the West Africa slave trade network. Borgu might not have provided a significant amount of slaves to the international slave market but the slave trade did shape the economy and society of Borgu from the seventeenth on to the nineteenth century.

Long-Distance Commodity Trade

Borgu was strategic to the long-distance commodity trade between coastal West Africa and the savannah areas of Hausaland and the Kanem-Borno. Geographically, Borgu was the midpoint of the caravan routes that transversed the area, depending on the destination or start point of the caravan. The settlements around the routes developed the necessary infrastructure to support trade. This involvement in long-distance trade became more noticeable in the eighteenth century. Three important developments might have contributed to this: first was the expansion in trade along the coast and the integration of this into the trans-Sahara trade network, second was the growth in demand for kolanuts, particularly its increased consumption in Hausaland, and third was the expansion in settlements across different segments of Borgu in that century.

As indicated earlier, the Wangara were the major drivers of trade in Borgu. They were later joined by the Hausa and Kambarin-Beriberi who eventually took over the trade by the nineteenth century. The Hausa long-distance trade was preceded by three Muslim commercial networks in the Borgu and the Middle-Volta basin – the Mande Dyula, the Yarsa and Dendi. Each of these networks had its own trade language. The Dyula trade network was founded around the early fifteenth century and they were linked to Jenne gold trade and settled in Borgu, Borno and Hausaland. The Yarsa was set up in the sixteenth century and had its trading network covering the Mossi states, connecting to Asante, where they exchanged livestock and slaves for kola. The Dendi were largely concentrated in Borgu and had probably migrated into Borgu from Songhay in the sixteenth century as well. The Dendi dealt mainly in slaves, textiles, kola, salt and potash (Lovejoy 1971, 540). It should be noted that these three groups were sometimes collectively called Wangara.

The Wangara, as an economic category, were divided into two—the sedentary and the itinerant Wangara. They built a strong symbiotic relation to support their trade network and spread Islam. The Wangara sold their goods locally while the richer and more itinerant and enterprising extended their trade to Hausaland. The earliest reference to Wangara in Hausaland, according to Idris (1973), was during the reign of Abdullahi Burja, when a trade route was opened from Borno to Gonja. During the fifteenth century, they were largely limited to the Borgu "ports of ever shifting metropolis of Bussa, Illo and Karimama" where traders from Borgu, Nupeland and Hausaland exchange their merchandise. Skinner described a traveller's account of Illo market as follows:

> The Dendi (Wangara) have a little of everything, the Zeberma (Songhay) have only livestock and potash. The Bengou people (from Sudan) have only the salt, the inhabitants of Illo foodstuff which they produce and the Hausa the cotton cloth which they weave. As it is, the Zaberma go to sell their livestock in exchange for salt which they carry to Ilo. At Ilo, they meet the Hausa who bring cotton cloth there to exchange and thereby procure merchandise, part of which they sell afterwards to the Dendi. Then the Zaberma and the Dendi go to Kano (Kandi?) where they meet people from Togoland with whom they exchange their merchandise for kolanuts, which are then sent off to Sokoto (Skinner, cited in Adekunle 1994, 11).

The Dendi also traded in salt with the Dallol Fogha and with major centres of Yolon, Bana, Bengu in exchange for shea butter. It appears the activities of Wangara traders first expanded westward to Gao, Timbuktu, with Djougou and Sansanne-Mango as major centres until the collapse of the Songhay Empire. In response to the economic consequences of the collapse, the Wangara shifted eastwards to Katsina and Kano, which had already been opened up by Wangara Islamic missionaries since the fifteenth or sixteenth centuries (Idris 1973). It was through these places that the Wangara connected the trans-Saharan and trans-Atlantic trade with some strategic networks in Borgu. Until the dominance of Hausa and Kambarin-Beriberi traders in the eighteenth century, two sets of Wangara became important to this trade. These were the diaspora or itinerant Wangara and Borgu Wangara.

Several trade routes connecting the coastal and kolanut producing areas to Hausaland passed through Borgu. These routes become an extension of the trans-Saharan and trans-Atlantic trades, linking to some of the major centres in western Sudan. Borgu was, therefore, an "economic middle zone between the gold mines of Bonduku and the kolanut fields of Gonja on one hand, and the salt centres of northern Sudan on the other" (Adekunle 2004,9). These routes were not necessarily stable nor even standard compelling routes. The decision on which route to take was determined by the nature of goods, security and weather, especially during the rainy season. For instance, the relatively peaceful and well-patronised Nikki to Gonja route was badly affected by the nineteenth century political crisis in Nikki so, traders diverted to the Djougou route through Kounde, Kandi Illo or Gaya.

Some of the several other routes include Djougou – Nikki – Bussa – Kano, which was quite prominent for gold carriage. Kandi – Illo – Sokoto and Nikki - Bussa – Zaria – Kano were patronised during the rainy seasons. Another option during the rainy reason was Nikki – Yauri – Sokoto. The Kandi – Nikki – Parakou route was more prominent for agricultural products and shea butter. The Parakou – Kaiama – Bussa route was used more during the dry season and linked up with Yorubaland (Idris 1973; Lovejoy 1971; Adekunle 1994).

At the close of the eighteenth century, the route linking Djougou to Hausaland through Kounde, Kandi, Illo or Gaya became the most frequently used, especially during the dry season when the rivers had receded and was largely for the movement of kolanuts (Idris 1973). According to Idris (1973), the caravans from Hausaland first congregated at Jega. From Jega, the route passed through Karaho, Guiro, Dakin-Gari, Sabon Gari (the Niger Passage), Illo, Logou, Kandi, Bagou, Sinende, to Ouassa where the route split. One went directly to Salaga through Djougou, the other through Kouande before Djougou.

Through these routes, Wangara and Hausa merchants travelled overland with long caravans from Hausaland through Borgu to the markets of Asante where they exchanged textile, potash, leather goods, dried onion leaves (*gabu*) and other products for kolanuts, hats, and fans of different colours. It was a gruelling journey taking six months to one year to complete a round trip from Kano to Asante (Lovejoy 1971). A complete circle of trade included Borno. Each caravan could have between one thousand to two thousand people. In 1826, Clapperton saw a caravan of more than one thousand people in Kaiama, involving men, women and children, with an equal number of donkeys and mules. The goods were sold along the route and to central or big markets like Djougou, Nikki and Salaga.

The kolanut trade significantly transformed the economy of Borgu. For one thing, it increased the number of caravans passing through and enhanced access to other commodities, including European items from the coast. Other items include salt, natron, as well as exotic goods from Europe such as earthenware jugs, brass, pewter dishes, wool and cloth also came into Borgu. Borgu became a major link between growing kolanut-producing areas in Gonja and the ever increasing demand in Hausaland. Through this trade, Borgu benefited and gained access to horses that helped strengthen its cavalry and paradoxically, also probably contributed to the political turmoil and criminality that later ensued.

Although the Wangara had dominated the long-distance trade in Borgu since the fifteenth century, they were eventually overtaken by the Hausa. The expanding kolanut trade and the growing markets in the Sokoto Caliphate had edged out the Wangara and a lot of them became sedentary in the late nineteenth and the early twentieth century, concentrating more on local trade and on Islamic teaching and propagation.

****

The long-distance trade was a well-organised one with an expansive structure and elaborate power relations. Although largely driven by profit and Islam, it was also an ethno-economic system organised around endogamous commercial descent groups, each of the different players with a different ancestry. They preserved their individual identity through facial and body markings, patronymics, marriage arrangements and tightly held stories of origin (Lovejoy 1971).

The patronymic of the Wangara was a major issue of identity and their political and social structure, as seen in chapter 1 and 2, was clearly different from the Baatonu and the Boko. The Hausa groups were dominated by the Agalawa, Tokarci and the Kambarin Beriberi[51]. Others were Sherifawa, Beriberi[52], Katsinawa and Adarawa. The trade was centred around Jega, Sokoto, Gummi, Katsina, Zaria and Kano. Although they were all Hausa-speaking, each of these groups claimed a different origin and such differences were considered important. This ethno-economic segmentation was counter-balanced by the trans-ethnic occupational and religious identity provided by Islam, which facilitated cooperation and reinforced their specialised occupational roles (Moseley 1992, 532). Islam didn't only provide the required unifying ideology, it also extensively redefined social relations, rationalised certain goods and extended markets for certain products. For example, charms were largely produced by Hausa Muslims, cloth was important for modesty and concealment of the body and kolanut was an important substitute for alcohol and become a standard gift item for hospitality in Hausaland (Moseley 1992).

The trade depended on upon several Hausa commercial settlements along the trading routes. These connected with pre-existing trading routes instituted by the Wangara trading structure. In each of the settlement, there were *maigida,* that is a host or a landlord and then the *dillalai* (sing. *dillali*) who were agents or brokers who would provide passing merchants with accommodation, support their feeding and facilitate the local market through interpretation, warehousing and other intermediary services (Lovejoy 1971). The caravans moved in hundreds of people and animals.

The movement of caravans was properly structured, with a clear leadership and support mechanism. The group is led by the *Madugu*

---

[51] Originally of Kanuri descent, (Kanuri is Beribari in Hausa) but settled in Gummi around 1800.

[52] These were different from the Kambarin Beriberi who have Hausaised. The Beriberi formed the Borno wing of the kolanut trade.

(*Madugu uban tafiya* – Madugu the leader of the journey). He was responsible for security and regulating movement and providing directives that had to be followed. He also responded to challenges on the route, such as dealing with hostile communities, settling local chiefs and paying tolls. The *Madugu* was supported by *Jagaba*, who was the vanguard and navigator of the routes, determining the shortest and safest. He was also supported by the cavalrymen and other armed groups of individuals. There was also the *Ubandawaki*, responsible for the merchandise, the major body of the caravan and women. He was also in charge of *cimaka,* food and negotiating in different *Zangos*, (stopping points). Like a parade, the *Madugu* was in front, followed by load carrying beasts, then the women led by the *Maduga* (leader of women). The *Madugu*, the *Jagaba* and the armed men patrolled the rear of the caravan, largely made up of the weaklings—the sick, pregnant women, and children (Lovejoy 1971; Idris 1973). The size of the caravan depended on the reputation of the *Magudu*. An experienced *Madugu* could lead more than 2000 people in his caravan. Each merchant could have more than thirty donkeys and the length of a caravan would then depend on the number of merchants on the caravan. A caravan could start small and end up growing larger as other merchants joined in along the route.

****

The impression in the literature is that Borgu was a passive or minor participant in the long-distance trade. The major towns along the trading routes were presented as just hosts and recipients of products without giving anything in exchange. It was apparently a result of this that Lord Lugard, in 1894, described Borgu as being of poor commercial value and the Lander Brothers described it as un-enterprising, arguing that Borgu people "never quit their towns except in case of war, or when engaged in predatory excursions…" (Hellert 1965, 112). Scholars often reduced trade to the source of goods and the end market, without looking at the dynamics between these two ends. Yet, this is precisely what propelled the long-distance trade. The benefit to those entities along the trade route could be as beneficial as those of the ends, if not more, as they added value at every stop. Surely, the states of Borgu benefitted from the trade not as happenstance, but as active participants who tried to take advantage of the economic activities and the opportunities provided.

The Borgu people participated in the long-distance trade both as middle-men and as real entrepreneurs. As stated in the preceding section, the Wangara Borgu were part of the trans-Sahara and trans-Atlantic trade network in Borgu. They had been involved in these trades since the fifteenth century, becoming prominent actors by the eighteenth century. Although their level of participation diminished significantly in the nineteenth century with the rise to dominance of Hausa traders, they remained the major traders in Borgu, building up the Dendi language as the trade language across the region. The Wangara didn't only lead trade on salt, natron, cloth, kolanut and European articles; they were also involved in the cattle trade. The Wangara with the *Ture* patronymic were believed to have specialised in the cattle trade. This trade was believed to have started since the Fulbe settlement in Borgu in the sixteenth century. Trade in cattle played a significant role in the political economy of Borgu. It was intricate to the Wasangari aristocracy, providing a major means of exchange for procuring foreign goods and the needed cavalry and arms (Idris 1973). Through the cattle trade, *cinikin jebu* was instituted, that is trade without the middle-men like the *mai gida* or *dillali* (Idris 1973).

The growth of long-distance trade had a significant influence on the politics and economy of the major Borgu principalities, Nikki in particular. Trade deals were entered into with different states in the north and south. Bussa, Kaiama, Nikki and Parakou all had trade relations with the Hausa, Nupe, Dahomey and Yoruba countries. Nikki had some trade relations with Portugal in the sixteenth century (Dupuis 1824). The trade boom in the eighteenth and nineteenth centuries might have contributed to the political turmoil in major Borgu states, particularly Nikki and Bussa, and led to the chains of wars in the southern Borgu states of Okuta, Gwanara, Kenu and Ilesha. In 1830, Richard Lander described the King of Nikki as possessing one thousand horses, with his soldiers forming a good part of the population of Nikki. In the eighteenth and nineteenth centuries, the Borgu Wangara covered about five different trade routes: the kola trade from Salanga to Hausaland, the route from Sassanne Mango, that of Fogha and those of coastal cities of Dahomey and Yorubaland (Idris 1975).

Market cities like Illo, Nikki, Djougou, Bussa, Parakou, Wawa, Segbana, Kaoje, and Kaiama were important centres of trade in the eighteenth and nineteenth century and were regularly visited by Hausa and Wangara traders. They provided important stopover markets for caravan merchants, not only to sell their wares but to also buy produce from Borgu. Clapperton recognised one of these markets in Wawa where he observed the plentiful necessities of life and luxury items "some of which they could do without." Being on the direct road from "Bornou, Houssa and Nyfee (Nupe) to Gonja, Dahomey, and Jannah ... they are able to procure plenty European articles, such as pewter, jugs and dishes, copper, pans, earthenware, Manchester cottons etc" (Clapperton 1829, 93).

A similar situation was reported about Kaiama, which was believed to have direct trade relations with Dahomey, Youri [Yauri] Nyffe [Nupe] and Yourriba [Yoruba]. They also exported products from Borgu including shea butter, cheese, and pots of different sizes, locust beans and butter, indigo and woven cloth (Idris 1973, Adekule 1994). The Hausa merchants also bought foodstuff, hides and Borgu textiles in exchange for their goods. Between 1854 and 1859, Samuel Crowder met some Borgu traders who arrived from Ilorin at Zugoshi on the Niger. They arrived with "donkeys laden with merchandise: They travelled to and from Ilorin by land, crossing the Niger twice, once below Busa to Kabba in two days, to avoid circuitous river-passage, which in their canoes would take several days ascending" (cited in Idris 1973, 191).

The long-distance trade significantly impacted on the economy and society of Borgu as it became the principal source of income for the states and kings of Borgu. The caravans were arbitrarily taxed by the governments of Nikki, Bussa, Wawa, Parakou and others. Special gifts were also received by the kings. Non-payment resulted in delays in the movement of caravans and possible pillage by vandals and criminal princes. The state also provided extra security to the caravans on payment of required tolls and gifts to the kings and principal political players.

Idris described how these escorts were conducted:

... caravan coming from Hausaland through Gaya, after crossing the river Niger would be escorted by the Wasangari (Princes) of the area to take them to Kandi whose chief [kings] would give the Wasangari the *gidi* (or staff of chief) to lead them all the way to Kouande. The Wasangari of that province might lead the caravan to beyond Djougou, even to Salaga if this was necessary (Idris 1973, 208).

Some of the trade Routes to the Volta Basin

Sometimes, there was a non-provision of escorts despite payment of necessary tolls and gifts. Such situation exposed caravans to robbery and banditry. The Borgu people also played important intermediary roles such as providing interpretation services and hosting merchants. Some of the porters were also Borgu slaves.

The polities grew, as there were more resources for state activities such as building of the army, erecting and rehabilitating city walls as well as grandiose state ceremonies like the *Gaani* Festival. The prosperity of the kings and princes also increased. Leo Africanus was believed to be referring to the King of Nikki when he reported to have met a powerful King "who commands 7,000 archers and 500 horsemen. He has considerable revenue from tolls on trade. The inhabitants of the Kingdom are very rich, as they go with their merchandise to remote countries" (Africanus 1956, 447).

Aristocracy, Banditry and Economy

The demographic growth in the aristocratic class, expansion of trade and resources access saw to increased political turmoil and succession crises and this resulted in criminal exhibitionism rooted in the sense of entitlement of members of the ruling class. One such exhibitionism of aristocracy has been variously described in the literature as "highway robbery," "raiding," "pillaging," "brigandage," "plundering," "freebooting," "marauding" and "banditry" (Clapperton 1826; Lugard 1895; Crowder 1973; Hirschfield 1979; Akinwumi 2001). At heart, this was a deliberately planned and forceful acquisition by seizure of other peoples' properties. It included everything from raids on villages to organised robbery of trade caravans. This activity was largely led by princes of the principal towns around the caravan routes that criss-crossed Borgu. This was not necessarily perceived as a crime but aristocratic privilege. It was called *ze-blee* in Boko and *swadio* in Baatonum[53].

Borgu in the nineteenth century became renowned and almost synonymous with banditry. Every traveller to the region had something to report about this.It appears that during this period Borgu,

---

[53] *Zee blee* and *swadio* in Boko and Baatonum respectively literally mean "one who eats road". More like feeding on roads.

because of these armed groups, was perceived with extreme dread. Clapperton was not only advised to leave Kaiama by the leader of the caravan he met there, he had this to say about the official escort that came to receive him on his way to Kaiama:

> They were [a] despicable, lawless set of fellows; for as soon as they had delivered their master's compliments to me, they began to plunder the village of goats and fowls. One fellow rode in at full gallop through the fence of matting which surround the huts, brandishing his spear, those on foot following him, and making a prize of everything they could lay their hands on (Clapperton 1829, 65).

Lugard had a similar experience all through his travel in Borgu in 1894. The entire travel from Yorubaland to Nikki through Kaiama and return to Saki through Ilesha was heralded by incidents of attempted banditry and robbery. His porters were in total dread of Borgu as they had had violent exchanges with the marauders. He spent a lot of time "patrolling" his transit camp in Ilesha "with a strain of anxiety and responsibility which the situation naturally produced ..." (Lugard 1895, 220).

While the state did not have any major control of the activities of these princes, in some cases, the kings were directly involved. For example, there was the case of Kaonde, in 1890, when the chief, Dangana Gurou Kuari (1883 – 1897) led some Wasangari princes including his children, to pillage a huge caravan. This led to the killing of several Hausa traders including the leader of the caravan, Mijinyawa Mai Hakori (Idris 1973).

Idris (1973) also reported an encounter between the Kilishi Yerima (Mora Bakaru) of Kaiama, who later became the Ki-Mora Tasude (seventh King of Kaiama) and Woru Yaru (Ojo Kiro) of Yashikira, who also later become the King of Yashikira and later Nikki. Kilishi who led the escort of merchants to Gberawusi (near Nikki), was attacked by the Ojo gang resulting in a huge battle that culminated in the death of several merchants. Ojo was believed to have lost 53 horses while the traders lost over 1,000 donkeys. The entire merchandise was looted by the Nikki princes.

Mora Amali Dogo, who was also later to become the eighth Emir of Kaiama, was believed to have also led a similar pillage between

Yashikira and Nikki in collaboration with "Bakin Jaki," a Gbasoro-based Nikki prince. Over 2,000 pack animals were believed to have been raided in that encounter. The duo is believed to have waited for years[54] to execute their plan. Bakin Jaki was later killed in Morai in a battle with French's army of occupation. Other prominent princes believed to have been involved in banditry were Baa Kombiya, a prince of Okuta, who was believed to have raided and captured over 240 slaves (NAK 1924; Stewart 1993). Some of these princes eventually became the kings of their respective domains.

Raids of this nature was a major preoccupation of the princes and, when not state sponsored, it was presented as a legitimate act. Some of these robber princes actually claimed to be enforcing the collection of tolls which some traders had tried to circumvent by avoiding major routes. Of course, the traders had their own incentives. At the bottom of it all was the fact that this activity provided a major source of income for these princes. As the Wasangari grew in number with notions of superiority that could not be backed by economic means, since many felt farming and similar occupations were beneath them, pillage furnished substance. Occupational engagement was not considered aristocratic and princes were literally above the law, unless if it was for a sovereign offence such as an attempted coup.

Further, building a pillage gang required bravery, princely courage, leadership and an ability to take on risk, which were major requirements for being a king as far as the Borgu and the Wasangari were concerned. It was, therefore, not surprising that some of these leaders ended up becoming kings. It was through these activities that they amassed resources, built followership and an army that could propel them into power. Some of the gangs had up to four hundred men and scores of horses. Recruitment was largely based on bravery, loyalty and previous experience.

The surge in banditry and brigandage was a reflection of the changing dynamics in the economic and political structure of Borgu. The emergence of new settlements in the eighteenth and nineteenth century, the expansion in the demography of the Wasangari and multiplication of dynastic wings in almost all of the principal kingdoms side by side with the expansion of economic activities are

---

[54] Some claimed 12 years.

intricately linked with the growth of long-distance trade. Before the eighteenth century, Nikki, Djougou, Kaonde, Bussa, among a few others, were the principal political centres along the trading routes. New power centres emerged in the eighteenth century in Kaiama and Parakou and later in places like Okuta, Ilesha (Desa), Kenu, Tabera and Gwanara

The expansion of trade across, particularly of Borgu to the south of Borgu might have contributed to this, as new polities were set up with new layers of princes who weren't economically engaged, but aspired to be kings or wanted to exhibit their aristocratic status through shows of power. Brigandage and banditry thus became an essential tool in aristocratic exhibitionism. For one thing, it made the common people dread the princes and it was thus easy for them to exert control and assert their aristocratic identity over the commoners. In consequence, the more brutal princes were often rewarded with kingship and other senior princely status. The raids were not only reminiscent of slave raids of an earlier century; it appeared to be a continuum of it in a different economic system.

The governments of each of these states tried to respond to the situation that had contributed to escalating the political turmoil in Borgu. As more princes gained access to resources to finance their armies, they undermined the state and ran huge, violent campaigns of sabotage and rebellion. This was the case in Nikki, Wawa, Kaonde and Bussa in the nineteenth century. Some of the responses included further militarization of the state, developing military escorts and setting up of anti-robbery guards in strategic locations. These had a limited impact. The situation rather escalated. In reaction to the situation, traders began to avoid Borgu by the late nineteenth century. This led to the massive decline of the principal states of Nikki, Wawa and Bussa as caravans stopped plying their routes in favour of more secure ones. By the late nineteenth century, most of the Wangara and Hausa traders had abandoned these towns. Economic activity plummeted significantly and the capacity of the states declined correspondingly. This was the situation until colonial occupation.

CHAPTER FOUR

Pre-colonial Borgu and its Neighbours

Borgu's relationship with its neighbours bordered on two related issues. First was the reciprocal political, economic and social influences between Borgu and its neighbours. The second was the complex inter-state relations that were sometimes peaceful and mutually beneficial and othertimes turbulent. While there is limited documentation to support these relations, evidence of diplomacy and international relations were very clear (Smith 1973). There were exchanges of emissaries across states, letters, written especially since the nineteenth century, trade, cultural exchanges and integration for example. Tributes were received and gifts exchanged with the neighbouring states as well as with distant states such as Borno. The long-distance commodity trade was the major driver of Borgu's foreign relations. The eighteenth and nineteenth century mercantilism led by the Wangara and the Hausa illustrates the relationship between trade and diplomacy. The trade network, as indicated in the previous chapter, passed through several states: from Ashanti through Gonja, to Dagomba connecting through Borgu and then Hausaland unto Kanem Borno. In each of these states, there existed different formal and informal state representatives.

Borgu was surrounded by powerful neighbours. In the north-west was Mali, and later the Songhai Empire, where the very enterprising Wangara had migrated from. To the north were the Hausa states and from the nineteenth century on, the Sokoto Caliphate. To the east was Nupe, with which Borgu shared political and social relations even before the institution of the Sokoto Caliphate's rule in that region. To the south were the empires of Oyo and Dahomey. Borgu built different layers of diplomatic, political, social and economic relations with these entities. These relationships were sometimes in amity and but most times were locked in conflict.

Songhai in Borgu History and Politics

The Songhai were significant neighbours of Borgu to the north and north-western axis. It would appear that Borgu had a very long historical relationship that oscillated between alliance and hostility with Songhai. The history of the two appears interwoven. Building a chronology of the relationship will be difficult, as some of the phases of engagement have not been properly recorded. It is safe to say that the Borgu relationship with Songhai was built over years of cross migration, trade, cultural exchange, religion, including Islam, as well as joking relationships and wars. There might have been two major waves of migration from the Songhai region to Borgu. The first was the contestable migration of the Mande-speaking Boko people from the region, probably in the twelfth or an even earlier century. The second was the migration of Wangara traders into Borgu, probably in the fifteenth century. The first migration was still at the level of hypothesis, drawn from the isolated presence of Mande language in the east. There exist other arguments about the unlikely or remote linguistic connection between the eastern Mande languages and those of the west (Kuba and Akinwunmi 2005).

A strong indication of the Songhai relationship with Borgu, whom the Songhai called *Bargance,* can be found in one of Songhai's mythologies of integration (Kuba and Akinwumi 2005). In Dallo Boso and Zarmaganda in the far north of Borgu, there are oral traditions referring to the Borgu as the original people to have settled there before migrating out of the place. There is also a joking relationship (called *gonnasiru* in Baatonum) between the Zarma and the Baatonu people.

Kuba and Akinwumi (2005) suggest that the two states shared common or related pre-Islamic religious practices; particularly the existence of *Harakoi*, the "Mistress of the Water" worshipped by the Songhay as well as by riverine Borgu people. There also appears to be a relationship between the Songhai god of thunder, *Dongo,* which was believed to be of Borgu origin just as Yoruba's Sango. Sango shares some common attributes with *Dongo,* including being believed to be of northern origin. Although largely associated with Nupe, this origin could as well be Borgu (Law 1977 and 1984; Stewart 1993; Agiri 1975; Kuba and Akinwumi 2005).

Elements within the Borgu aristocracy have been associated with Mande origins, probably the Soninke and Malinke Diaspora (Stewart 1993; Kuba 1996). A number of words and phrases in the Borgu cultural vocabulary are believed to have been derived from Songhai. The name, "Wasangari" was probably derived from the Songhai word for a warrior, *Waangari*. Some of the political titles, terms and paraphernalia related to horses and the aristocracy was associated with the Songhai (Kuba and Akinwumi 2005). Although Wasangari is often linked to Kisra in the popular Borgu mythology, Moraes Farais (2013) provided a fresh and interesting relationship between an early (probably thirteenth to fifteenth century) Songhai–Borgu long-distance trade relationship and the Wasangari. The Wasangari traded slaves in exchange for horses. During this period Borgu was a major source of kolanuts for the Songhai. Although not known for producing kolanuts, *Ta'rikh al-Fattash* refers to Borgu (barku) as a source for kolanuts and gold for the Songhai (Moraes Farias 2013).

Gaani, the most celebrated Borgu festival, also had a Songhai origin. Songhai-Muslim traders spread the festival across different regions of West Africa, including Borgu. However, in a typical integrative manner, the practices were blended with existing cultural festivities and cultural practices of the region. Although Gaani is linked to the Muslim celebration of the birthday of Prophet Mohammed (*Mawlud*); its practice actually predates the wide Islamic practices in the region. Gaani might have been introduced around the fifteenth century, a period when Islam was least practised by Borgu autochthons.

Another interesting cultural assimilation of Songhai in Borgu was the role of *gesere* (pl. *gesereba*; Baatonu, *djassere*) in the Borgu political system. The *gesere* were palace griots and chroniclers of the Wasangari dynasty. They praised the king and kept the royal genealogy of the palaces in which they were located. They were believed to have been Songhai refugees of Soninke origin, praise-singers in the Askia's court (Kuba and Akinwumi 2005). Some of them were believed to have moved to Borgu as praise-singers attached to the Songhai Empire military leaders or as individuals seeking new opportunities (Moraes Farias 2013). They performed in *Wakpaarem*, a dialect of Soninke language, but bore patronymics borrowed from Mande-speaking areas. They called themselves *Taruwere* (*Traore* in Mali) and *Fafana* (*Fofana* in Mali), amongst other patronymics (Moraes Farias 1995, 1996, 2013). The *Wakpaarem* language is unintelligible, except to the auxiliary *gesere* who helped interpret it into Baatonu or Boko. These griots were largely found in the royal courts of Kouande, Kandi, Buay (Gamia), Yashikira and Nikki. They were believed to have been introduced into the royal court by the eighth Sina Boko of Nikki, Kpe Sumera Tokobu (Kuba and Akinwumi 2005).

Borgu had also built a strong economic relationship with the Songhai through the activities of the Wangara, who are believed to be an old Soninke Diaspora (Massing 2000; Stewart 1993). As discussed in chapter 2, the Wangara Muslim traders were of Mande stock, who integrated with Borgu and other migrant trading communities and developed Dendi, an obviously Songhai language, as a major trading language in Borgu. According to Kuba (1996), Dendi language is hypothetically linked to the fall of the Songhai Empire and the movement of refugees down south into Borgu. It could also be a relic of "older times" in which Songhai dialects were the *lingua franca* of a north-south trade network.

The Wangara were the major links between Borgu and other major centres of power in the southern and central Sudan, from Songhai through Hausaland and Borno. As indicated earlier, they were also responsible for the spread of Islam in Borgu. The Wangara in Borgu spoke Dendi and are believed to have been the "foundation of Wangara settlement in Hausa cities and the spread of Songhai-oriented commercial diaspora. They brought the Hausa states into contact with the Western Sudan" (Lovejoy 1978, 176; Massing 2000). The role of the Wangara, Dendi, in particular, is the most sustained evidence of the historical relationship between Songhai and Borgu. Moraes Farias (2013, 22), while looking at this historical relationship between the two regions, concludes that "it is not the impact of Songhai's 'imperial' conquerors that has lasted in Borgu, but that of the Songhai-speaking traders who created the Dendi-speaking communities in the region."

Until the collapse of the empire, Borgu experienced several military invasions from the Songhai. According to Kuba (1996), in order to understand the relationship between the "imperial" Songhai and Borgu, we need to appreciate the strategic role of the Dendi region, that is, the southernmost part of Songhai, which adjoins Borgu. With the fall of Songhai to Moroccan powers in the late sixteenth century, the Askia Dynasty retreated southward and operated from the "Gourma-Dendi, with Lolo, the outermost border town, north of Borgu, becoming the last capital of the empire. Lolo lay in the north of present day Borgu, not far from Illo on the right bank of the River Niger" (Kuba and Akinwumi 2005).

Earlier, in 1470 – 71, Sunni Ali was believed to have drawn a large military assistance from Borgu, probably against the Mossi during the first year of his rule. Although the army was believed not to have been for an aggressive military campaign, such support was surely a product of an existing relationship between the two (Stewart 1993; Kuba and Akinwumi 2005). Stewart also suggests that although Songhai never had any suzerain control of Illo, Illo might have paid "symbolic" tribute to Songhai at the height of the empire, considering its proximity to a powerful neighbour.

Songhai's aggressive engagement with Borgu probably started with the ascension of Askia Muhammed (1493 – 1528). Although there are no detailed accounts of Songhai aggression, there were probably two abortive campaigns to take Borgu in the sixteenth century. The Timbuktu Chronicles does mention attacks on Bussa. These campaigns of aggression were largely associated with Askia Muhammed and Askia Dawud. Askia Muhammed was believed to have suffered a huge defeat in the 1505/6 battle and barely managed to escape. Five decades later, in 1555/6, Askia Dawud ran another devastating campaign against Bussa. This campaign was believed to have lasted up to 1559 (Pardo 1971). Although they failed to conquer Bussa, the city was reportedly destroyed with a huge number of people believed to have drowned in the River Niger.

A similar belligerent relationship continued under Askia al-Hajj (1583 – 1586). The devastating defeat of Askia Muhammed was not only deeply engrained in Songhay mythology, but it also defined their etymology of Borgu as derived from *bari go* (five horses), meaning five horses that returned out of several that went into the battle. Borgu probably didn't enjoy any friendly relationship with Songhai until Songhai's defeat and consequent decimation by Morocco. There was probably cooperation between the two by the time Songhai moved its capital to the border town, Lolo. The eventual collapse of the empire might have led to the submergence of some Songhai territories by Borgu. Kuba and Akinwumi (2005, 340) suggest some relics of Songhai in Borgu to include "the title of *Fari Mondyo*, Songhai for a high-level prince, which appears in the title of the Wasangari King of Kerou as well as in the title of an important dignitary in Banikoara."

Borgu - Hausa Relations

Borgu didn't directly share borders with a major Hausa state until the nineteenth century Sokoto Caliphate was instituted and some of its non-Hausa or non-Fulani neighbours were co-opted into that hegemony – the Yauri, Kontagora and Nupe are good examples of such new Caliphate territories.

Since the eighteenth century, several pull factors encouraged migration to the Borgu area, especially on the bank of the River Niger. The collapse of the Songhay Empire was one of the first as the political centre moved southwards. Others were the increase in trade and emergence of major trade centres on the Niger, including Illo, Bussa and Kaoje, which became renowned for the cattle trade. The Sokoto Jihad of the nineteenth century was also a major disruption in Hausaland which affected the political and economic structure of the region. Several groups migrated southwards into Borgu areas, including the Fulbe, Hausa, Kambari, among others. These migrations changed the ethnic composition and settlement pattern along the River Niger, making an impact on social relationships in the area.

To be sure, even before the creation of the Sokoto Caliphate, Hausaland played an important role in the political economy of Borgu. This relationship dates back to the fourteenth century through the activities of the Wangara, who were settled in both polities. The relationship was one of cultural influence, religion (including pre-Islamic animist religion) and trade. Borgu only securely bordered the Hausa of Kebbawa (Kebbi) extraction to the north and Yauri, but trade led by the Wangara had been possible through a network of relationships between the Hausa farther afield and Borgu states.

While there had always been some cultural exchange with the polities north of Borgu, the Sokoto Jihad and post-jihad developments created an uneasy relationship with other ethnic groups, including the Fulbe, Kambari, Hausa and even the Gungawa. For instance, at the height of the Jihad, Bussa and Yauri came under tremendous pressure from Gwandu. The subsequent annexation of Yauri and some Borgu territories into the Caliphate made Borgu vulnerable to attack. However, Borgu responded with extreme surveillance and monitoring of its own large Fulbe community. In this period, it was believed that the Fulbe constituted almost one-fifth of the Borgu population (Crowder 1973). Borgu resisted the jihadist invasion into its territory from all angles of the north and north-west through Nikki and to the north-east through Bussa, Wawa and Kaiama. The pressure continued until the colonial conquest.

In 1820, Magajin Malam, the son of Malam Dendo, the first Emir of Nupe, was believed to have invaded Wawa and Kaiama and was defeated in both places. The battle in Zakuru near Wawa was believed to have been a fierce one. Following the crisis of the later years of the Sokoto Caliphate and the pressure on the aristocracy, adventurers and sometimes brigands emerged and operated on the fringes of the Caliphate. It was on this basis that Umar Nagwamatse, the son of Ahmadu Atiku, the fifth Emir of Gwandu, conquered parts of Gwari territory and launched a campaign against Yelwa Kotunkoro and Ngaski and established his political capital in Kontagora. He was believed to have attempted to invade Bussa but was repelled by Kigera II. The activities of Nagwamatse increased the Kambari's westward migration into Borgu territory, especially in the late nineteenth century (Anene 1965).

Borgu's military activities in the region were not only defensive: there were also offensive actions. It was through these offensive actions that Borgu extended its sphere of influence farther, to areas around Illo, including Kaoje and Koenji, in the nineteenth century. These two locations came under Bussa's suzerain as vassals, under its control alongside its largely Fulbe and Hausa population. Borgu had strong historical and cultural relations with Yauri. Bussa, being the closest, led Borgu's interface with Yauri and helped in building a strong and harmonious relationship until the late nineteenth century. Both Borgu and Yauri came under severe pressure from the Fulbe jihadists in the nineteenth century, until Yauri succumbed to Gwandu and accepted to pay *jizya* as a non-Muslim state. Bussa maintained the relationship though, despite the change in the political status of Yauri. In 1880, Dan Toro, the king of Bussa, and that of Yauri, Gallo, agreed to wage a decisive military action against the recalcitrant Kambari in Gebe (1881 – 1883). It was one of Borgu's last wars before the colonial conquest. The war was successfully prosecuted through the traditional alignment of Borgu military forces, involving Kaiama, led by Mora Amali Dogo (Mora 1994).

After the Ilorin War, Gajere, the new king of Bussa, kept a very cordial relationship with the Fulbe leadership across the River Niger. This policy was followed by his successor, Dan Toro. There were reported exchanges of messages and gifts including "a magnificent horse, valued at ten slaves, which Nagwamatse always rode until his death, was given to Dan Toro" (NAK 1925). With the political developments in Nupe, Dan Toro kept a close watch on the situation and its implication for Borgu. Around 1880/4, Etsu Baba was defeated at Leaba in Zugurma on the bank of the Niger and drowned as he tried to escape. Thousands of Nupe crossed the Niger and surrendered to Bussa. They were encamped close to Faku. Some of the refugees were sold into slavery while others were allowed to settle and found Leabe in Bussa territory. Etsu Baba's brother, Dalibu, as well as his son, Shaibu, and their followers were given the island of Komi. The developments in Nupe during this period led to the formation of various Nupe settlements around Bussa (NAK 1925).

The successful military expedition was a major turning point in the Bussa-Yauri relationship, as friends suddenly turned into foes. Yauri and Bussa couldn't agree on the control of the conquered territories.

As soon as the war ended, Dan Toro, who led the final phase, appointed Berdi Bello as the Chief of Gebbe, while Yauri appointed the village heads of Kalkami and Kawara to serve under Bello. Conflicting understanding and assertion of sovereignty resulted in a new conflict between Bussa and Yauri. Yauri claimed sovereignty based the origin of the people settled in the disputed area, while Bussa insisted that its sovereignty was based on ownership of the land (Crowder 1973, 38). This impasse defined the relationship between the two, with resultant tension, until the colonial conquest.

As indicated earlier, Hausaland played a significant role in the long-distance trade especially in the nineteenth century when the influence of the Wangara receded. Through trade they also contributed to the spread of Islam and had a significant influence on the aristocracy. The Wasangari significantly relied on the Hausa in accessing horses and related accessories especially after the collapse of the Songhai Empire. Clapperton and the Lander Brothers traced the sources of Borgu horses to Hausaland. It would appear the Hausa had a much longer relationship with the Wasangari than often recognised. One of the dynastic branches of Nikki aristocracy had Hausa origin. It is reported that Suno Dobidia (second Sina Boko) and arguably the founder of the Nikki principality had a Hausa wife believed to be from either Katsina or Zaria. The Lafiaru dynastic branch is a product of this marriage and revolved around her through her children.

Borgu Factor in Yoruba Political History

Borgu was one of the two most influential and difficult northern neighbours of Yorubaland[55], particularly Oyo, the other being the Nupe. Borgu might have had strong political/religious influence in this region, beyond what is recognised. Borgu was probably the etymological origin of the name 'Yoruba', originally used as a name for Borgu's Oyo neighbours until, eventually, in the nineteenth century, it became the pan-ethnic name of the peoples and area linked

---

[55] Yoruba is in this regard referred to as the Oyo Empire. Until the nineteenth century, "Yoruba" was largely associated with the Oyo. Its name "Yoruba" could probably have been associated with Borgu, as the Baatonu would appear to be the first to call people of that region *Yoru*, while the Boko called them *Yuru*. Yoruba in Baatonum is a plural of *Yor*u (*Yoruba* or *Yorubu*).

to the Oduduwa legend and speakers of the language. Until the nineteenth century, the contemporary Yoruba region was variously called Lekumi, Elukumi, Nago, and Aku, among others. The different Yoruba peoples answered different names – Oyo, Ekiti, Egba, Ijebu, among others.

The earliest use of the name 'Yoruba' was perhaps in a seventeenth century book written by a Timbuktu scholar, Abu-al Abbas Ahmad Baba al-Timbukti (Hodgkin 1975) and later in the nineteenth century by Mohammed Bello of the Sokoto Caliphate. The earliest instance of its use in its modern, general sense is in J. Raban's *The Vocabulary of the Eyo, or Aku, a Dilect of West Africa,* in 1832. It appears that Borgu (Baatonu in particular) is the only Oyo northern neighbour that has historically called Oyo "Yoruba." The Boko called them *Yuru* (singular, pl. *Yuruno)*, while the Baatonu called them *Yoru* (singular, pl. *Yoru bu,* the third person plural being *Yoru ba)*. The name was probably sourced from Songhai contact with Borgu, later reinforced through interviews with Baatonu slaves in Sierra Leone and popularised by European travellers like Clapperton and missionary documentation, such as the works of Samuel Johnson in the nineteenth century.

While appreciating the historiographic differences in the account of the state of Oyo (see different accounts by Johnson 1921; Biobaku 1955, 1973 Smith 1965; Law 1977; Atanda 1971; Agiri 1975), Borgu has been associated with the three historical traditions of the state and dynastic history of Oyo—the Oyo-Ile period, the Igboho period and the post-Ilorin War period. It is based on this that the "northern factor" has become an important element of the historiography of Yorubaland/Oyo. The similarity of the tradition of origin associated with Kisra might have been a product of a strong political relationship that might have developed over a long period of time. According to Agiri (1975), the Oranyan Dynasty of Old Oyo was from Borgu. The conquest of Old Oyo, whose capital was just about a day's travel from the Borgu border, might have taken place in the fifteenth century, about the same period Borgu repelled Songhai forces led by Sonni Ali in Bussa.

> It seems possible that Bussa established satellite dynasties in the Yoruba towns including Oyo, replacing the former Nupe influence

there. Bussa's domination may have extended as far south of Ife, which was then well established as the centre of a highly complex civilisation (Agiri 1975, 10).

It was probably the weakness of Bussa, occasioned by the second invasion of Songhai in the sixteenth century, that provided the space for the return of the Nupe to Oyo and the defeat and eventual destruction of Old Oyo. This early invasion and conquest of Oyo by Borgu was probably the origin of the Oranyan myth. According to Johnson (1921), Oranyan succeeded his father Oduduwa in Ife but attempted a military expedition to Mecca, which was aborted partly because of disagreements between his bothers and partly because of the difficulty in crossing the River Niger, blocked by the Nupe. Oranyan, therefore, consulted with the King of Borgu (Bussa) who gave him a magic snake, which led him to the site of Oyoro, where Oranyan built his new capital (Johnson 1921). According to Agiri (1975), the "story of Oranyan as recorded in Oyo traditions is very much a Borgu myth of conquest into which account Nupe influence has been woven."

The second phase of probable Borgu political influence was the event following the Nupe invasion and destruction of Oyoro and the eventual collapse of the state of Oyo. Alaafin Onigbogi fled northward to Gberegburu (Gbere for short) in Borgu and was received by a Borgu king of the region. His wife, *Iyalagbon* (mother of the *Aremo,* or the eldest son), was believed to be of Borgu origin (Smith 1965). Different traditions have identified the receiving king, called Eleduwe[56], to be that of Nikki, Bussa or Kaiama (Smith 1965). The number of years the Alaafin spent in exile in Borgu is not clear but it was believed that Alaafin Onigbogi died there and was succeeded by his eldest son, Ofinran, whose mother was also of Borgu origin. The changing dynamics of the relationship with Borgu was believed to have compelled the departure of Ofinran southward, first to Kusu and later, Igboho. Alaafin Abipa, the 14th Alaafin, was believed to have ended the years of exile by relocating to Oyo-Ile with the support of Borgu forces.

---

[56] Eleduwe appears to be a general name used among the Yoruba to describe the kings of Borgu, as the same name was used for Sero Kpera, the King of Nikki who led the allied forces of Borgu-Oyo against the Fulbe jihadists in Ilorin.

The processes of this movement have been examined in different ways by historians. While some historians give Johnson's narrative a literal interpretation and saw the movement as just a return from exile, others viewed it as an implied dynastic change and the beginning of a new dynasty. The Igboho experience was, therefore.viewed as a period in which new Borgu dynasties were instituted in Yorubaland (Kuba and Akinwumi 2005). Agiri viewed this process of dynastic change as the support given by Borgu forces to Alaafin Abipa in successfully re-establishing his dynasty who then decided to reward the Borgu warriors by permitting them to "replace the rulers of some former Yoruba settlements such as Kishi, Igboho and Igbetti. Others became rulers of new settlements like Ogbomoso, located in strategic areas to guard the state against further Nupe incursions" (Agiri 1975, 10). For Law (1977), Igboho had a Borgu foundation and the return to Oyo-Ile was neither a return of Yoruba refugees or exiles, nor was it simply a Borgu-supported action, "rather, we should think of (this as) a conquest by the Bariba (Borgu) invaders" (Law 1985, 46). Law's Borgu invasion hypothesis was corroborated by the tradition of several Yoruba settlements that trace their dynastic origins to Borgu. Shaki in the north-west of Oyo which was believed to be linked to the reign of Ofinran has a royal dynasty that claims a Borgu origin. Kishi, with a foundation linked to Igboho, is of Borgu dynastic origin linked to a Borgu warrior, Kilishi Yerima. The Lander Brothers actually described the King of Kishi as a "Boorgoo [Borgu] man" (Lander 1967, 208). Ogbomosho, or Igana, also has a dynasty linked to Borgu. Similar accounts are associated with Igboho and a group of people living in Ketu, particularly known to be exceptional warriors (Kuba and Akinwumi 2005). A similar process of conquest by invading Borgu forces, probably in the sixteenth or seventeenth century, was also recorded in Save (Sabe) area (Asiwaju 1973; Agiri 1975). This was not only recognised by the various Sabe traditions, the rulers' names and hierarchy or order of birth and naming practices are typical of Borgu.

It would appear that the Borgu invasions of Oyo had greater ramifications not only in Oyo but on Yorubaland generally. According to Agiri (1975, 11), "the attacks on existing Yoruba settlements came in waves and were widespread, resulting in the re-establishment of new dynasties that still claim direct kinship with Borgu." Like the early Borgu conquerors during the Oranyan period, these Borgu conquerors were few in number, leading to their cultural and linguistic absorption over a period of time (Agiri 1975; Law 1985). The Borgu invaders were believed to have introduced the use of cavalry and even some structure to the monarchy in Yorubaland and to have contributed to the strength of the empire until its eventual collapse in the nineteenth century.

According to Agiri (1975), the non-Yoruba origin of the ruling dynasty of Old Oyo was also supported by the traces "of the relics of the extinct (and probably Yoruba) dynasty in the lineage of the Basorun." Like the process of the institution of the state in Borgu, where the Earth Priests were absorbed into the political structure as secondary players, the Basorun were next in rank to the Alaafin.

> He wears a beaded coronet while the Alaafin wears a beaded crown. He has his own small throne and his wives were called ayinba (those who sing the praise of the Iba?); the Alaafin possesses a larger throne and his wives are called aya'aba (wives of the King). The Basorun is head of the Oyo Mesi, the seven most important traditional chiefs in Oyo, who constitute the royal council. Beside this exalted political status, the Basorun holds a very important religious position of the state (Agiri 1975, 8 – 9).

On the religious side, the worship of Sango as a patron god was, according to Agiri, probably made easier because the worship of the god of thunder was common amongst the Borgu people.

The invasion and dynastic domination of Borgu over Oyo might have been followed by huge population movements as seen in south-western Borgu, an indication of a prior presence of Yoruba-speaking groups in places like Parakou, Kika, Sandiro, Tchaouru and Mari-Maro (Kuba and Akinwumi 2005). Existing local traditions still refer to the conquest of Yoruba in those locations and their push further down south. Until the end of the nineteenth century, Borgu was still involved in different military activities around its southern border. The distinctive anti-Yoruba tradition of some of the shrines around Kaiama area in Kemanji[57], Gberia and other locations may be associated with

---

[57] Until probably very recently, Yoruba could not give birth in Kemanji. They also didn't have access to the healing powers of the traditional orthopedic surgeons in

this period. There were obviously a few northward movements too; particularly the Mokole (*mo ko ile* "I rejected my homeland") believed to be of Oyo origin and the Yoruba-speaking Nyantruku people. While the Mokole are found around Kandi in northern Borgu, the Nyantruku, who claim to have migrated from Ilesha, are settled in the south of Djougou near the Togo-Benin border (Kuba and Akinwumi 2005).

Although these events were believed to have occurred in the sixteenth century (Smith 1965; Law 1977, 1984), Agiri questions the methodology used in arriving at the date and believes it could have happened earlier. "For our purposes, the most important point is that these events took many centuries rather than a few generations" (Agiri 1975, 11). Determining the time frame and the probable ancestries will require deeper archaeological and genetic analysis in both Borgu and Oyo.

Johnson reported a change in power dynamics in the region, in which Oyo had sovereign control over some southern Borgu and Nupe regions. In 1826, Clapperton also reported the claim of the Alaafin of Oyo that he controlled and collected tributes from as far away as "Yaru" which Clapperton believed may be referring to Kaiama, where the king was named Yaru. This was not only dismissed by Clapperton himself; the dynamics of power relations in the region didn't favour such an argument. Clapperton reported that "the sultan of Boussa (read Borgu) could take Yourriba whenever he chose" (Clapperton 1829). As observed by Kuba and Akinwumi (2005), the Alaafin's claim was not only exaggerated, it appears not to be in congruence with the balance of power in the early nineteenth century as Oyo would, in 1835 just a few months after the meeting with Clapperton, seek the support of Borgu in its war against the Fulbe jihadists in Ilorin. The Ilorin War and its aftermath constituted the third phase of Borgu influence in the politics of Oyo.

The Ilorin War

The Ilorin War, also known as the *Eleduwe* War, was one of the major wars of Borgu in the nineteenth century. It was a war in support of the

---

Kemanji. In fact, it was an abomination for some families/communities around Kaiama to marry Yoruba.

Oyo against the invading Fulbe jihadists. Although it was not necessarily the first of such alliances (Akinwumi 1992), it was arguably the first that involved an extensive mobilisation of the military across the entire Borgu. The military alliance was an attempt to finally check the expansionist drive of the Fulbe jihadists at Ilorin and possibly reclaim or regain control of the town that had, for all intents and purposes, seceded from Oyo and was then seized by forces aligned to the Sokoto Caliphate.

The alliance was at the invitation of the Alaafin of Oyo, Oluewu. The reason for the invitation may not be farfetched. Oyo was already in decline. Previous attempts to retake Ilorin had failed. Nupe had already been incorporated into the Caliphate and was in alliance with the Fulbe jihadists of Ilorin. At the time of the war, only Borgu, among Oyo's northern neighbours, was independent of the Caliphate. Borgu's war prowess was also well known. It is also possible the Alaafin was aware of and relied on his dynastic link to Borgu. This alliance was reminiscent of the Oyo alliance with Nupe under King Majiya II (1819 -1826) against the rebellious town of Ilorin. They collectively fought Ilorin in the *Mugba-Mugba* wars of 1824 – 1826 (Jimada 2005).

Borgu's participation in the Ilorin War was both for strategic and egocentric reasons as it was not under any formidable or immediate threat by the Fulbe jihadists. The Niger River was an important buffer although there were skirmishes to the north of the river and the attempt by the Wangara and Fulbe-Borgu to instigate a rebellion was adequately suppressed. Nupe's attempt on Bussa, Wawa and Kaiama were also decisively handled. While it was strategic to keep the Fulbe jihadists at an arm's length, the decision to participate, according to Nikki tradition, was driven by motives that were largely egocentric. These motives revolved particularly around Sero Kpera, the king of Nikki who was, at the time, the most powerful of all the Borgu kings. Five of these egocentric reasons were identified as follows. The first was to, as usual, attract war booty. The Wasangari had grown to derive joy in violence and booty sharing. The war provided an important opportunity for both. Second, the war was an opportunity to attract external attention. Sero Kpera was already a local autocrat, with his name resonating across Borgu. His external adventure and potential success in the war would attract greater internal and external respectability for Nikki as well as personal fame. This would allow him achieve the third objective of consolidating political control of Borgu. As the war commander, his political influence across Borgu could reverberate easily and earn him a lot of political leverage. The fourth and fifth reasons were more strategic: to address the possible future internal Fulbe jihadists threats and to help the Yoruba fight a common enemy as the defeat of Oyo would make Borgu more vulnerable. Borgu would, were Oyo to fall, be surrounded by the Caliphate to the north, east and south (Idris 1973; Anene 1970).

It was also believed that Sero Kpera, like other Borgu warriors, had territorial ambitions. Oyo was at its weakest moment politically and on the brink of collapse. The defeat of the Fulbe in Ilorin would have emboldened the Borgu to possibly take Oyo (Akinwumi 1992). This may not necessarily have been correct, as Sero Kpera was unable to even fully consolidate his political hold of Borgu. In the period before the Ilorin War, a couple of provinces were asserting their independence and some dependencies and vassals like Kaiama, Parakou, and Kouande, had practically pulled out. Such control might have been made possible in south-western Borgu, but Sero Kpera was already dealing with serious political issues in Nikki.

The allied forces were led by Sero Kpera, also known as *Worukura* and posthumously *Ilorin-Kpuno* (Baatonum for one that lies in Ilorin). Before his accession to the throne, he was known as *Saka Tonna, Saka Yayarekowo* (Baatonum for wanderer). He was from the Sessi Makararu Dynasty of Nikki and from the *Wure* generation (Lafia 2006). With him were other prominent Borgu kings and princes from Ilesha, Parakou, Okuta, Gwanara, Gwette, Kaiama, Wawa and Bussa, amongst others. Although Borgu was believed to have mobilised extensively for the war (Akinwumi 1992), it would appear it was a relatively small elite force drawn from all the major towns of Borgu (Mockler-Ferryman 1892). The bulk of the fighters were apparently sourced from the Oyo.

In response to the increasing threats from Oyo and Borgu, the Fulbe drew support from Gwandu and the Nupe axis of the Caliphate, particularly from Lafiagi and Shonga. As reported by Imam Umaru Salaga[58], the initial response came from Gwandu with the arrival of

---

[58] Imam Umaru Salaga (1858 – 1934) was a prominent Hausa scholar and poet. He trained a number of students across West Africa. He was an informant to two German researchers, Gottlob Adif Krause and Adam Mischlich. Through their

some senior Fulbe leaders including Mohammadu Buhari, the son of Usman dan Fodio who had founded Tambuwal and Mohammadu Buhari from Jega. He was the son of Abdusalam, the leader of the revolt in Sokoto who died in 1818. There was also Mohammad Abdullahi from Gwandu, son of Abdullahi dan Fodio who was believed to have conducted several campaigns in Nupe. The combined Sokoto and Gwandu forces were led by Mohammadu Buhari and Mohammad Sambo (Reichmuth 1993) and probably, later, by Ibrahim Khalil, the third of Emir of Gwandu.

With the defeat of the Fulbe being eminent, they struck a desperate but strategic alliance with some Oyo chiefs, particularly Atiba, a prince of Oyo, who had his eye on the throne and who apparently was disenchanted with Alaafin Oluewu. This Atiba was to later establish the new Oyo (Akinwumi 1992). With the new alliance of the jihadists, several Oyo towns like Ogbomosho, Ikoyi, Ede, Ago Oja withdrew from the allied troops and thereby reduced the number of its army in the Ilorin battle which eventually got overwhelmed by the Fulbe forces. Prior to this, the Fulbe forces had withdrawn to Ilorin in a desperate defence of their last stronghold.

The Allied forces lost the war at Ilorin after recording success in battles in Gbodo and Otefo in particular. It was a fierce battle that ended with the death of Sero Kpera, the Sina Boko of Nikki, who had led the combined allied force. Other prominent Borgu leaders that fell in the battle includedSuno Ali, King of Gwanara, King of Illo, Ki Yaru (posthumously *Yaru- Ilorinde*) of Kaiama, King of Gbette, and Koto (posthumously *Gbodokpuno)*, King of Okuta (he was killed in battle at Gbodo). Others were Mora Lafia, King of Ilesha, Magai Kabe and the Kings of Wawa (Idris 1973, 281).

The war had a significant impact on the state and society of Borgu. It also shaped the character of the Oyo kingdom and redefined the power dynamics of the region. The defeat affected the relationship between Borgu and Yoruba generally as they held the Yoruba responsible for the defeat. They accused the Yoruba of cowardice and treachery, two unpardonable offences in Borgu culture. Oyo, on the other hand, accused the Borgu of rapacity and greed. The Borgu forces

---

encouragement, he documented accounts of the history, culture and economy of different Hausa communities (Reichmuth 1993).

were believed to have had an overwhelming control of not only the allied forces but also of the Alaafin, who practically surrendered his leadership to Sero Kpera, the Sina Boko. The Borgu were in total disdain of the Yoruba forces. They raided villages of livestock which they voraciously consumed. This earned them an epitaph of *Ikoko* ("wolves" in Yoruba). According to Akinwumi (1993, 165), "the Borgawa (Borgu people) considered themselves as superior to the allied friends and the Oyo soldiers were made to believe this. It was, therefore, an abomination for any Yoruba man to spill the blood of the Borgawa, even at the point of self-defence..".

It was also a case of impunity. Borgu people got away with every atrocity. According to Abrahall,

> The fear inspired by Sarkin (king) Nikki and his army on friends and foes alike made many of the Yoruba chiefs, whose allegiance to the Alafin was far from strong, wonder whether they were not exchanging a Filani (Fulbe) menace for a Borgu one. These dissensions delayed an attack on Ilorin and steadily weakening the fighting value of the allies (NAK 1925, 12).

It was probably these fears and suspicions that made Atiba succumb to Fulbe entreaties and eventually make a secret pact with them. The war was a major turning point in the relationship between Borgu and Oyo. The old relationship of cordiality gave way to hostility and a "bitter contempt of Yoruba, on one hand, a deep-rooted fear of the Borgawa" (NAK 1928, 8). The hangover of the Ilorin defeat also encouraged cross-border skirmishes between Borgu towns in the south-west and northern Oyo towns like Shaki and Kishi. Ilesha was embroiled with Saki, while Kaiama raided Kishi and took many slaves. These hostilities continued until the colonial conquest in the late nineteenth century.

Although Fulbe forces celebrated their victory against Borgu and left the Borgu in the agony of an unprecedented loss, they never pushed further to conquer Borgu. They rather returned to the offensive against the capital of Oyo, Katunga, which led to the desertion of the city. Eventually, Atiba, the prince who had cut a deal with the Fulbe at Ilorin, founded a new Oyo with a capital in Ago Oja. This was in apparent recognition of Borgu military strength even in defeat. Nevertheless, Borgu still had to contend with the jihadist forces from its northern and eastern flanks, bordering the Bussa areas, especially to the north of the River Niger.

SECTION TWO

BORGU UNDER COLONIAL RULE

CHAPTER FIVE

European Scramble and Partitioning of Borgu

West Africa had a long historical relationship with Europe, lasting over 500 years before the formal institution of colonial rule, starting from the arrival of Joao de Santarem and Pedro de Escobar, two Portuguese sea captains, at the Cape Coast in 1471, all through the periods of slave trade and commodity trade. The resort to colonial conquest and subjugation was a late nineteenth century development. Although Borgu had received European travellers since the eighteenth century; this was largely a relationship of trade, friendship and mutual respect. Borgu's initial contact with Europeans stemmed from the European interest in tracing the course of the River Niger.

In 1796, Mungo Park journeyed the river from Segu in south-west Timbuktu and reached Bussa where he died at the rapids. Between 1822 and 1830, other European travellers passed through Borgu. The travels of Clapperton and the Lander Brothers have been extensively referred to in the preceding chapters. However, until 1894, when Lord Lugard went deep into Borgu, travelling from the east to the west and south of Borgu, no European had successfully travelled through the hinterland of Borgu. Wolf, Duncan, Hess and Kling were believed to have either lost their lives or were forced back. Wolf and Duncan went some distance into the interior but never returned. Kling was forced to return while Hess was killed by a poisoned arrow before he even crossed the boundary (Lugard 1895; Anene 1970).

Colonialism emerged at the point that African states and societies were undergoing major political and economic transformations. The "old Africa appeared to be in the dying throes, and a new and modern Africa was emerging" (Boahen 1987, 1). The abolition of slave trade in the middle of the nineteenth century had a profound impact on the pre-colonial economies of some West African states, especially the coastal states. As indicated in the previous chapters, there is no evidence that Borgu played a significant role in the trans-Atlantic or trans-Saharan slave trades and the extent to which it might have depended on it was likely minimal. However, Borgu benefitted from the slave trade and appears to have played an important role in the commodity trade.

Although the shift to commodity trade didn't result in an immediate end to wars or even slavery in the region, it reduced the commercial importance of slaves and helped reduce commercial slave raids on rural settlements. This helped to stabilise rural Borgu, even while the major principalities were embroiled in internecine violence and succession crisis in the late nineteenth century. The shift to commodity trade allowed for a more equitable distribution of wealth, especially in the rural areas. Most of the products traded for export were actually growing wild. They were only picked and processed by the people. Shea butter, for instance, was a major Borgu export. This was unlike the slave trade which was largely controlled by the aristocracy. As a result, a merchant class began to emerge in Borgu. While some slave merchants like the Wangara transformed into commodity traders, the nature of their trade changed significantly, as they needed to trade more with common people than with the aristocracy. The commodity trade was responsible for the integration of parts of Africa into the world capitalist system; a development that encouraged colonialism and consequently intensified it.

Commercial unification had also emerged with the increasing dominance of Wangara and Hausa traders through the different trading routes that criss-crossed Borgu, linking it to other important states like Nupe, Hausa, Oyo, Ghana and Gonja. Borgu was beginning to become an important player in the long-distance trade. The River Niger was also becoming a major link to the Lower and Middle Niger states. Politically, as raids on rural areas reduced, the polities began to centralise more. Although political unification was never achieved, the states of Borgu became relatively more centralised and autonomous.

The circumstances leading to the colonial subjugation of Africa has been a subject of contention amongst historians and political economists and has been extensively discussed and documented. We will, therefore, not be detained by these details but rather emphasise that colonialism was primarily a product of the change in the political economy of Europe, especially in the last two to three decades of the nineteenth century and how those changes were enhanced or hindered by the dynamics of politics and society in West Africa (Boahen (1987).

Economic competition among the European powers saw to the development of neo-mercantilism, infused by elements of protectionism and the building of market spheres for raw materials. The spirit of nationalism grew following the unification of both Germany and Italy, particularly after Germany defeated France in 1871. With these, European nations began to think not only of their powers and development but also of prestige, greatness and security (Boahen 1987) as would be seen in the scramble for and partitioning of Borgu. The number of overseas colonies a nation possessed became a significant determinant of its European and global relevance. Thus, each European country rushed to Africa and other parts of the world in search ofcolonies.

The entities that made up colonial West Africa were conquered or proclaimed by different colonial powers, particularly the British and French, at different times, with or without the involvement of the constituent people. Before the colonial conquest, the Borgu area had largely escaped direct incorporation into the expanding world capitalist system. This is primarily because of its relative inaccessibility to the probes of capital. Situated in the centre of West Africa, its contact with the capitalist world was mediated by the commercial cities of the Maghreb to the north and the coastal states to the south.

The Scramble for Borgu

The scramble and partitioning of Borgu should be approached from the broader context of the scramble for Africa, which was an intensification of competition between the principal industrial states of Europe for their share of the world market. It was a hysterical reaction to the crisis in industrial capitalism; feeding on the fear that the economic and political future of the European countries depended on the exclusive control of markets and raw materials (Boahen 1987). According to Crowder, the scramble for Africa took place when it did "because the mutual suspicions of the interested European powers of each other's intentions had reached such a pitch that none of them was willing to stave off the undesirable for fear that their own interest might be pre-empted by another" (Crowder 1978, 39). This period was a dramatic change from the ambivalence towards colonialism a few years earlier as remarked by Lord Salisbury on his return to the British Foreign Office in 1885 "...when I left the foreign office in 1880 nobody thought about Africa. When I returned to it in 1885 the nations of Europe were almost quarrelling with each other as to the various portions of Africa they could obtain" (cited in Crowder 1978, 35).

Borgu was a major theatre of this intense politics between the major powers, Britain and France primarily and, to a lesser extent, Germany. The scramble took place in three phases. The first phase was that of entering into different treaties between Borgu rulers and European imperial powers. This was followed by the signing of bilateral treaties between European powers, based on the earlier treaties with rulers, defining the spheres of influence delimited by respective boundaries. The third was the conquest and subjugation of their spheres. In between these three phases were intense politicking, strategic engagements and even threats of war between the contending powers.

The Anglo-French scramble for Borgu was for the ownership and control of the navigable parts of the River Niger and expected economic opportunities in the interior. The political engagement concerning Borgu, including military and off-field engagements in Europe, started around 1885 and lasted up to 1898. Initially led by the Royal Niger Company on the British side, treaties were signed with Bussa. Not minding the multi-state structure of Borgu, Goldie, on behalf of the Royal Niger Company, first in November 1885 entered into a treaty with Bussa. Another was entered into five years later, after realising the vagueness of the first (Lister's Treaty of 5 August 1890). Earlier boundary negotiations between the powers recognised Borgu as a political unit under the suzerain control of the King of Bussa.

The negotiations between the two European powers passed through three phases. During the first phase, France was the underdog and, therefore, defensive. It hadn't achieved political control of Dahomey, while Britain was fully armed with Lister's Bussa Treaty of 1890 and also with the Anglo-French Say-Barruwa Line Declaration (Anene 1970). The second phase was after France conquered Dahomey and got its access to the hinterland. Colonial confidence was built that it could control the Niger and France began to advance the argument that Borgu was not a single political unit, and, therefore, questioned the validity of the Bussa Treaty. The last phase of the controversy was described as that of "extreme bitterness, in which rising tempers almost completely obscured the original question of whether Borgu was a nation or an incoherent agglomeration of separate states" (Anene 1970).

Initial engagement with the West African issues culminated in the West African Conference in Berlin, Germany. The conference started on 13 November 1884 and ended on the 26 February 1885 with thirteen European powers in attendance. Also represented were the Ottoman Empire, the United States of America and King Leopold's International African Association. It is important to note that the conference didn't initiate the scramble for Africa; it only gave international recognition to the already ongoing scramble for Africa. It was an attempt to manage the situation and bring a level of discipline to the confusion and conflicts associated with the scramble in the interest of the European powers.

The first week of the conference was focused on establishing rules of navigation for the Congo and Niger rivers. Freedom of navigation was to be maintained on the Niger and Congo rivers. The second phase of the conference focused on defining valid title to territory on the West African Coast. Although the purpose of the conference was largely coastal Africa, the decision became the basis for the occupation of any part of Africa. It provided that any power wanting to claim any part of Africa should inform the signatory powers "in order to enable them, if need be to make good any claims of their own" (Crowder, 1978, 42). However, for such claim to be valid, it had to be supported by effective occupation.

To guarantee enforcement and collective commitment "the signatory powers ... recognised the obligation to ensure the establishment of authority in regions occupied by them on the coasts of the African continent sufficient to protect existing rights" (Hirshfield 1979, 17). The British attempt to get the principle extended to other parts of Africa was unsuccessful. This decision was to increase the hunger for more African territories amongst the European powers, as they all rushed for the validation of their treaties, to define limits and proclaim territories. Without any African participation, the rules for the partitioning of West Africa were defined and these became the basis for the modern nation states on the continent. It was, unfortunately, the basis for the partitioning of Borgu between the two major European powers in West Africa.

Britain claimed that all territories negotiated by Goldie of the Royal Niger Company with African rulers were valid. It, therefore, unilaterally proclaimed protection over the entire areas covering the Bight of Benin and Biafra (now Niger Delta) to the Niger confluence in Lokoja and Ibbi on the Benue and called it the Niger District Protectorate with headquarters in Calabar. The company, therefore, embarked on an ambitious westwards and northwards territorial drive through its agents. It was in the course of this expansion that the first treaty with Bussa, apparently on behalf of the entire Borgu, was signed in 1890. Through this, the company, and of course Britain, hoped to strengthen their hold on the Niger Bend and beyond.

With the French concession of Zanzibar to Britain in East Africa, Britain in return agreed to a demarcation line in West Africa running from Barruwa on the Lake Chad to Say on the Niger. Although acceptable to France initially, the reaction in France to some self-celebratory statements of Lord Salisbury, saw the French turn down the offer. When it became clear that Britain actually had a limited penetration to the middle of the Niger, the abstemious aspect of the agreement became clearer (Hirshfield 1979). A major area of contention that concerned Borgu and which the French queried was whether the August 5, 1890, agreement implied an extension of the

Say-Barruwa line west of the Niger as the Royal Niger Company claimed. The non-validity of the Bussa Treaty raised fears among the British knowing full well that Borgu could be up for grabs.

> ...should France edge around the Say-Barruwa line from the southwest and scoop out of Borgu, she would secure access to the navigable portion of the Niger below Bussa Rapids and, once the conquest of Dahomey was complete, link that ocean colony with the possession in the interior (Hirshfield 1979, 29 -30).

Instead of resolving the issues, the August 5 agreement became a major subject of contention and acrimony with increasing public interest in both Britain and France.

In 1892, the Niger Commission met to discuss the issue. The Niger Commission was one of the three boundary delimitation commissions involving Britain and France in West Africa. The commission had been constituted to enforce the terms of the 5 August agreement, to define the Say-Barruwa line on the map and decide French and British spheres of influence to the west and south of the Middle Niger. In May 1892, France proposed a tentative boundary line that apparently favoured British interests in the Niger Bend. It offered Borgu and Gurma to Britain, while it retained Mossi and parts of Gurma. Britain, however, turned it down because it wanted the whole of Gurma. French ambition in the region changed with their conquest of Dahomey. The penetration to the interior of Dahomey provided an important leeway to access the navigable segment of the River Niger (Anene 1970; Hirshfield 1979). This set the second stage of boundary negotiations between France and Britain.

The Royal Niger Company insisted on the indivisibility of Borgu, and that the 1890 agreement with Kigera II, King of Bussa, covered the entire Borgu. Between 1890 and 1894, no agent of the Royal Niger Company had penetrated the hinterland of Borgu, which was assumed to be under the protection of Great Britain. The government of Britain relied on assurances provided by the Company even if they had no direct contact with Borgu (Anene 1970). In 1894, the French, for the second time, made an offer to Britain. This was often referred to as the Hanotaux Line, drawn from the coast east of Dahomey and taken northwards to Gomba on the Niger; the line followed the west bank of the Niger to Say. With this, Nikki would be cut off from Borgu. For this reason, the British rejected the Hanotaux Line and insisted its treaty with Bussa covered the entire Borgu, including Nikki. Britain was willing to make territorial concessions in 1894 but wasn't ready to part with any segment of the navigable part of the River Niger. The French, reinvigorated by the annexation of Dahomey and the opening of the corridor between Dahomey and the Niger, didn't only reject the British offer; they insisted that access must be provided below the Bussa Rapids. This resulted in the collapse of the second negotiations.

With the increasing intensity of the push by France, and not sure of their intentions, the Royal Niger Company tried to strengthen its case against future resumption of negotiations. It, therefore, sent its most experienced agent, William Wallace, to Sokoto and Gwandu to conclude more elaborate treaties with the rulers (Hirshfield 1979). Wallace's eventual presence in Borgu opened a dramatic phase in the contention between France and Britain over Borgu. As indicated earlier, the company had earlier signed two treaties with Bussa. However, Wallace's engagement in Bussa led to the understanding that Bussa didn't have sovereign or jurisdictive control over the other principalities of Borgu as previously assumed by the company and the British government. The Borgu states of Nikki, Wawa, Kaiama, Illo and Bussa were independent entities, irrespective of historical and political association. The treaty with Bussa, therefore, didn't cover those principalities and their territories. It was, therefore, imperative for the British to make immediate plans for more treaties in Nikki and the other Borgu states.

Steeplechase for Nikki

The race for Nikki was a product of the abortive negotiations over Borgu as both France and Britain came face to face with the reality of the political structure of Borgu. As a confederation, a treaty with one of the states could not cover the others. The result of this was what Anene called a comical phase of European activities in this part of West Africa, describing it as "a veritable steeplechase" (Anene 1970). Those involved in the race didn't take it as a joke; it was an important venture for their respective states. Penetrating Borgu during this period was not a joke. The commitment was to sign a treaty with Nikki, an important Borgu state. While Captain Frederick Lugard was engaged by the Royal Niger Company for Britain, Captain Decoeur acted for France. All departed from different locations, at different times, for the same destination – Nikki.

Lugard set out for Nikki with over 200 porters and forty soldiers, while Decoeur left Dahomey with one hundred Senegalese soldiers. Lugard had an initial advantage over Decoeur as he could travel by steamer from Jebba on the Niger while Decoeur navigated the difficult terrain of Borgu all through. Lugard visited all the major principalities of Borgu: Bussa, Kaiama, Nikki, Ilesha, and the northern Oyo towns of Saki and Kishi (Lugard 1895). He didn't only sign a treaty in each of these states; he tried to understand the political structure of Borgu. In Bussa, Lugard confirmed that Bussa had no control over the other territories of Borgu. This was further confirmed by the King of Kaiama, Mora Tasude who noted that the King of Nikki was his senior brother. He spoke of Nikki with admiration but concluded that the kings of Bussa, Kaiama and Nikki were independent kings and the only kings of Borgu (Anene 1970). In Ilesha, he was told by the King that "If the King of Nikki asked him (King of Ilesha) to eat sand, he would do so" (Anene 1970, 213). Lugard arrived at Nikki from Kaiama but found it difficult to access the King. For three days, he was not invited to see the King who was presumably blind and very sick. It was the *Imam*, Abdullah, advisor to the King who eventually signed the treaty.

As reported by Lugard:

> I had made a friend in need, and he proved himself a friend indeed. This was the "leman," [Imam] or Mohammedan (Muslim) missionary, who resided in this pagan town, and had much influence in the councils. Through his unwearied efforts, all turned out well, and the king, whose extreme age had rendered him blind and very infirm, deputed some three or four of these leading men – including my firm friend, the lemam (Imam) – to negotiate the treaty. This was done in the most intelligent way; each clause was discussed in all its bearings, and questions of a shrewd and practical nature were asked (Lugard 1895, 218).

Decoeur and his party arrived at Nikki five days after Lugard's departure. He gave a lavish present to the king and extracted a treaty.

The king was later discovered not to have known the difference between the two visiting Europeans and thought they belonged to the same nationality. He, however, mentioned that he didn't fear Decoeur as he did Lugard (Hirshfield 1979). Realising that Lugard had bagged a treaty earlier, France began to question the validity of that treaty and also to affirm the paramountcy of the Nikki in Borgu. One of the major French newspapers, *Politique Coloniale,* reported thus:

> The King of Nikki, it (is) true, styles himself king of Borgu, but he is far from having any power. Nikki probably, from the ruins still existing, was formerly a great centre. At present it is only an agglomeration of small and miserable villages, of which the king, covered with dirty rags, was lodged in a poor straw hut, has not even sufficient authority to make his will respected by his immediate attendants. His power is as chimerical as his budget (cited in Anene 1965, 218).

Escalation of Conflict

The treaties extracted by both powers didn't ameliorate the contention over Borgu and they both asserted their claims on the territory. Against Lugard's findings, up until April 1896, Britain continued to speak of the unity of Borgu while France continued its contention that Borgu was at best an aggregation of independent, miserably poor state (Anene 1970). They challenged Lugard's treaty on the ground that it was forcefully obtained because the king was afraid of him. In 1895, France launched an aggressive treaty-signing expedition led by Ballot, the Governor of Dahomey. He entered Nikki and made the king renounce his treaty with Britain's representative. From Nikki, he criss-crossed northern Borgu and began to explore the Niger frontage of Borgu. Another French representative, Toutee, arrived at Kaiama and signed a treaty with the king and established garrisons in both Kaiama and Kishi. From there, he proceeded to the King of Bussa, who affirmed his independence despite the three different treaties he had signed with Royal Niger Company. Leaving Bussa, Toutee next arrived at Gbajibo, where he commenced the construction of a fort in honour of Prince d'Arenberg, a principal French patriot who had funded French colonial designs (Anene 1970; Hirshfield 1979). Toutee insisted that Bussa was important to the French mission in the western Sudan and, therefore, justified his action:

> ...to make use of this access, France must have footing on the river below the Rapids where for long years at all events, trans-shipment or unloading of some sort will be necessary... we have a vital interest in bringing our zone of occupation below the Rapids; England has none in preventing us from doing so... (Hirshfield 1979, 105).

The British government was uncomfortable with the obstinacy of the French government, while the Royal Niger Company became even more nervous with this development. Goldie turned to his German friend, Vohsen, for support, with the hope of repeating the Anglo-German masterstroke of 1893 in Adamawa. It was believed that Borgu might even provide a better prospect as "Borgu was an important hinterland for the German Togoland, and so the Germans were as interested in Borgu as anybody else" (Anene 1970, 216). The acquisition of the territories to the north and north-east of Togoland and, possibly, an advance to the Niger, became an important problem of German colonial policy (Anene 1970). Two Germans: Herr von Pawlikowski and Dr. Gruner pushed further into the interior, arriving at Say and then Gwandu. From Say to Bussa, Gruner was reported to have discovered some eleven to "twelve virgin territories" that had no suzerain control. The British continued to ignore the French but made a proposal to the German government. It turns out the German government was as anxious as the French for the navigable segment of the Niger. In addition, Germany demanded compensation for letting go of Nikki, even without evidence of contact or treaty. The Germans believed they both (and Britain) had no good presence and knowledge of Borgu and so "both powers were in fact engaged in partitioning a "no-man's-land" (Anene 1970, 218). The Anglo-German negotiation produced nothing as the Germans also realised that they were being used against France.

Toutee's activities in and around Kaiama, Bussa and Gbajibo was a big revelation for the French. They had come to the realisation that the British had limited presence in the region and they had no influence outside of Bussa and Gbajibo. Though the French didn't make further moves to take the Middle Niger, they believed that it could be taken. France, therefore, posed a strong challenge to the British. Major French treaties collected by Monteil, Decoeur and Ballot, covering areas around the Niger Bend, north and north-west of Dahomey were sent to the British embassy in Paris. Britain also presented their counter treaties, resulting in French withdrawal from Gbajibo but the British celebration was cut short with news of a new French expedition from Timbuktu led by Lieutenant Hourst to "complete the hydrographic and political work recently accomplished by Toutee in the region of the middle lower Niger" (cited in Hirshfield 1979, 75.). Hourst descended the Niger at Leaba and, like Toutee, also contested British claim over Bussa.

While the open disagreement between France and Britain continued, the French developed a "new theory" of negotiation bordering on effective occupation rather than suzerain treaties. This was a notion they rejected during the Berlin Conference when the British pushed for it. They proceeded to make their claim on Borgu territories on effective occupation. The British proposed a boundary similar to what had been offered to Germany the previous year. In this case, Nikki would now go to France. But the French were not impressed with this compromise as they raised further territorial issues on the Say-Argungu-Gomba triangle, Yola and Borno. The French expected more for sacrificing those regions (Anene 1970). The French rejected the Royal Niger Company's treaty with Bussa, without any grounds. The treaty with Kaiama was also rejected for not having the real name of Mora Tasude, the King of Kaiama. For Nikki, they argued that Lugard didn't sign any treaty with the king. Referring to Imam Abdullahi who signed the treaty on behalf of the king, the French argued that they would "not accept the action of a materialistically-minded Moslem non-Bariba as representing that of the King of Nikki" (Anene 1970, 219). The British could not respond effectively to these issues but insisted that they couldn't abandon the principle of suzerainty. This "...principle was recognised in all international negotiations and we (hold) that, in treating with a suzerain, the right conferred ... extended to the whole of the territory under his dominion" (cited in Anene 1970, 220).

While the French questioned the concept of suzerainty, the British made further offers to avert the breakdown of negotiations. The fall of the French government in 1896 delayed negotiations but the re-emergence of Hanotaux as French Foreign Minister didn't fundamentally alter the attitude of French on the structure of Borgu. By mid-March of 1896, it was still obvious that the French were not shifting ground. It wanted a part of the navigable portion of the Niger, to connect the hinterland of Dahomey with French possessions on the Upper Niger through the acquisition of a portion of Borgu which included Nikki. In April, Britain made further concessions, including Gurma, western Borgu and the Dendi region of Say. This offer was unacceptable to France as it did not include any navigable portion of the Niger. The intractable negotiations, therefore, reached another deadlock.

Anglo-French Military Occupation and Hostilities

In December 1896, sudden hostility broke out between the Royal Niger Company and the Emirates of Nupe and Ilorin. With the Royal Niger Constabulary (the company's military) now engaged in Nupe and Ilorin; the Middle Niger became open and undefended. The French tried to cash in on this by despatching three missions to the Niger Bend. One was led by Lieutenant Baud, the second by Captain Voulet and the third by Lieutenant Bretonnet. By March 1897, the French had installed a resident in Bussa, after stumbling on the Bretonnet-led forces of four hundred Senegalese *tiraillers*. This angered the British who had all along claimed Bussa although without any physical presence there (Hirshfield 1979).

The British reaction to French military aggression in Borgu was relatively slow, if not negligible. This had to do with differences in approach to external military engagement of the two powers. While the French enjoyed a level of flexibility and could take independent action, the British military, including those instituted by the Royal Niger Company, were controlled by the Colonial Office in London. Even if the British had wanted to match the French, they simply didn't have adequate local forces to withstand them,. The various colonial governments on the Nigerian coast had local military units. These units were relatively small, poorly trained and ill-equipped to stand the French forces (Ukpabi 1971). The Colonial Office was responsible for the military in the Lagos Colony and its adjacent protectorate, while the Foreign Office controlled the Niger Coast protectorate through the Royal Niger Company. The company's interest in the Niger Bend appeared relatively different from that of the British government. The company appeared more interested in trade and was more concerned about safeguarding the navigable stretch of the Niger as far north as possible. It, therefore, recommended that the government concentrate on waterways and let the French have the rest (Ukpabi 1971).

The French occupation of Bussa and Joseph Chamberlain's appointment as British Colonial Secretary in 1895 marked the beginning of the British change of approach to the problems in West Africa. Chamberlain began to consider a "forceful" approach to engagement with France. To carry out this new policy, often referred to as the Chessboard Policy, he argued that "a strong force must be raised, hopefully through the Niger Company but also directly by the government of Gold Coast and Lagos" (Hirshfield 1979, 98). This was to be a counter-force represented by a small West African army that was to be raised irrespective of the cost. Chamberlain recognised the folly of Britain acting through the Royal Niger Company and its reliance on Goldie, the head of the company. He was, therefore, ready to build an alternative structure and insisted the British government must financially support the building of a frontier force of about two thousand men to be quickly deployed as counters to the French established posts in Saki, Kaiama and any other place between Nikki and Bussa not already under French occupation. He insisted that each post must be "distinctly stronger than the French force in the neighbouring post" (Hirshfield 1979, 103).

Goldie's reasoning was in terms of profit and loss. He did not see any value in such an action. He believed it was "useless, dangerous and destructive" and had no financial value (Hirshfield 1979, 103). He also believed that such a response would mean an acceptance of the new French policy of effective occupation. In defence of the navigable part of Borgu, Goldie even contemplated conceding Sokoto to France so long as the company kept the Niger Bend. The company believed that the Niger Bend was the most valuable British real estate in Africa and had to be preserved. This appears to be different from the British government's priorities as it attached more value to Egypt and the Nile Valley than what Salisbury often described as the "malarious African desert" (Anene1965, 218), the term he used to describe the Niger

Bend. While Goldie fought on, he was eventually reprimanded for embarrassing the government in dealing with France by claiming effective occupation, even when there was none, with Bussa as a case in point.

Following the initial military engagement by France's Toutee, Lieutenant Bretonnet, who was assigned to eastern Borgu, occupied Bussa with two hundred soldiers and made himself Resident. He justified his action with the prior treaty signed by Toutee. The British protested this action and referred to it as aggression into their territory (Anene 1970). In fact, the new King of Bussa, Kisan Dogo II (often called Ikki in French and British documents) solicited the support of French troops against Wawa, which had supported a rival candidate for the throne. To counter the increasing control of the region that the French were enjoying, Goldie sent a report indicating that the people of Kaiama had rebelled against their King, Mora Tasude, and beheaded him in protest against his support for Kisan Dogo. This happened to be false as the king appeared before Willcocks and the French commander in 1898 and pronounced his allegiance to the French (Anene 1970).

In January 1887, the French captured Nikki to the chagrin of the Colonial Secretary who deplored the failure of the British government to protect the King of Nikki despite his request for such action. The French, however, denied any such request had been made as the King actually supported their arrival.

While in occupation of Borgu, the imperial forces meddled in the political affairs of the region. The French supported the new King of Bussa, Kisan Dogo, against Wawa and Babanna who were believed to have supported a rival candidate, Kwara, son of Kigwassai, who, at a different time, had been a rival of an earlier king, Dan Toro, for the throne. They crushed a large force believed to have been mobilised by Kwara from Babana and Wawa. The increasing meddling of the French led to several uprisings across the major principalities and villages of Borgu. By May 1897, most parts of Borgu were in a state of disturbance. Kaiama and Wawa were the first to be brought under control. This was a big embarrassment for the French, who often pretended to be acting in the interest of Borgu. Some French strongholds such as Shori, Borea, Bouy, and Kandi were evacuated, while Kounde fell to Borgu forces led by Mora Ali (Hirschfield 1979).

The French, hiding their humiliation, insisted that the violent suppression of the revolt had been "necessary in the interests of civilisation – the Baribas (Borgu) are incorrigible robbers, playing the same role in the north as the Dahomeyans in the south" (cited in Hirshfield 1979, 109). The capture of Nikki was, therefore, the crescendo of the French attempt to clamp down on the Borgu resistance. It also exemplifies the pinnacle of French conflict with Britain over the territory of Borgu.

During this period of intense French military activities, the Lagos Frontier Force commanded by Lieutenant Colonel Allen had also become involved in Borgu. It occupied Godebere in December 1897 and hoisted the British flag there. The French, already in Nikki, vehemently protested this occupation, pointing out that Godebere was Nikki territory. The period also coincided with the death of the King of Nikki. Woru Yaru, the Chief of Godebere, happened to be a senior prince of Nikki and a possible successor to the throne. Woru Yaru was believed to be the son of Sero Lafia, who died in 1864. He had been succeeded in turn by Sero Kura, Sero Tasu, and Sero Toru (Hirshfield 1979). The British had hoped to use him to access formal control of Nikki. He was properly protected, prompted and supported to take the throne. Lt. Colonel Allen told Woru Yaru:

> The King of Nikki now being dead, the French will doubtless send for you in order to make a treaty with you. You must decide...whether you wish for French or English protection. I must tell you that under English protection, you will still be King of the Baribas in reality and not merely in name as will probably be the case if you choose the French. If you should choose English protection, you must send all your trade to Lagos and must keep the roads good to Saki. All your trade can be sent to Saki, and from Saki it will be sent to Lagos. In return for your trade the English offer their trade. I know that Kyama [Kaiama] is in the hands of the French but that will not prevent your trade being sent to Saki. The English have come here for trade only and desire only peace, not war (Hirshfield 1979, 152 – 153).

The French, on the other hand, were sponsoring Sabi Yerima, the Head of Dunkasa, whom the British argued had no connection to the Nikki aristocracy. The British insisted that Woru Yaru was the rightful successor and should be made king. The French, expectedly, refused to accept this claim on the grounds that he was being sponsored by a rival European power. They, therefore, installed Sabi Yerima as the king.

For effective response to the French, Britain decided to establish the Royal West African Frontier Force (RWAFF) as earlier suggested by Joseph Chamberlain. Lugard was appointed the commandant of the Force in 1897. This resulted in a situation where British and French forces were face-to-face with each other in several Borgu villages, a situation that fell just short of war. Although the WAFF had a slow start and Lugard was initially reluctant to place his few and relatively untrained soldiers against the French in Borgu, several events in April 1898 compelled Lugard to consider Chamberlain's Chessboard Policy.

British forces, led by Willcocks, were ordered to advance westward from Fort Goldie and occupy any territory unoccupied by the French. They were particularly instructed to occupy Kanikoko, Gwasoro, Boriya and Taberu to render any French posts to the south of Borgu untenable (Ukpabi 1987). The advance party, under Captain Welch, reached Kanikoko in early May and found it already occupied by the French. He, therefore, set up camp some distance to the town and reported the situation to Willcocks. Lieutenant Glossop also made some diversions to arrive his assigned destination of Kemanji as his way was blocked by French forces.

The Anglo-French rivalry and military activities reached its height at Gbenekpata where the two forces took positions in the town. Willcocks gave an ultimatum of forty-eight hours for the French to withdraw from the town; otherwise, he would march to Kaiama which the French had already occupied. By this time, the situation had degenerated to almost a military confrontation. This caused Lugard to demand the Reserve Force. He sent one company of the First Battalion of the WAFF to relieve the Royal Niger Company garrison at Leaba and Fort Goldie and sent the troops, who were relieved, to reinforce Willcocks. The British forces eventually arrived Kaiama on May 30, 1898. On the approach to the city, they noticed French flags hoisted over several buildings, the city gate and the king's palace in particular. As the British troops approached the city gate, French guards stood to arms (Ukpabi 1987). The two forces eventually avoided any escalation and hoisted their flags in different locations of the town.

Final Negotiation and the Partitioning of Borgu

The balance of forces and the resistance in Borgu had compelled the need to reopen negotiations. The British, once again, were set for a compromise. It was prepared to renounce parts of Borgu and give the French access to the Niger between Leaba and Gbajibo, from the Nikki area, the line of communication passing between Kaiama and Bussa. The French weren't necessarily averse to this proposal. What was important was for each of the powers to define what they wanted to keep and what they wanted to let go. At this stage, the British identified Borgu outside Bussa, Kaiama, Kishi and Ilesha, and were ready to barter places situated in the line of the direct Lagos hinterland and Nikki. A major obstacle to this agreement was the French demand for a corridor, thirty-five miles, from Nikki to the Niger. This, the British were not ready to offer. In June, the two powers settled their differences and agreed on a compromise boundary. The protocol was signed in Paris on the 14th of June, 1898. The Borgu boundary was described in Article II of the Anglo-French Convention of 1898 to include in the British sphere the territories of Bere [Godebere], Okuta, Ashigere [Yashikira] and Bete [Gbete], while Nikki and the surrounding districts remained within the French sphere. The boundary was deflected to touch the Niger at a point ten miles to the north of the town of Illo, leaving within the British sphere all territory belonging to the province of Bussa and the district of Gomba (Anene 1970).

This compromise position was deplored by the colonial interest groups of both countries on the ground that they had lost territories. Nobody considered the partitioning of Borgu and its implication for the people. The Borgu story is a telling example of imperial insensitivity. The Borgu people weren't only subjected to horrific militarist subjugation and years of uncertainty, they ended up being balkanised across two divides in a very despicable way. In the French section of Borgu, the Baatonum-speaking people in particular suffered the most from this partitioning. While majority of the Baatonu people found themselves on the French side, the provinces of Nikki ruled by different ruling houses of Nikki including Taberu, Okuta, Boriya, Yashikiru, and Ilesha were all lost to British Borgu. Other Baatonu towns, not necessarily under the control of Nikki, like Gwanara and Kenu, all found themselves in the British side. This was to shape the political developments of Borgu from the colonial up to the post-colonial periods. The Boko became an extreme minority in French Borgu and treated more like an appendage of the Baatonu.

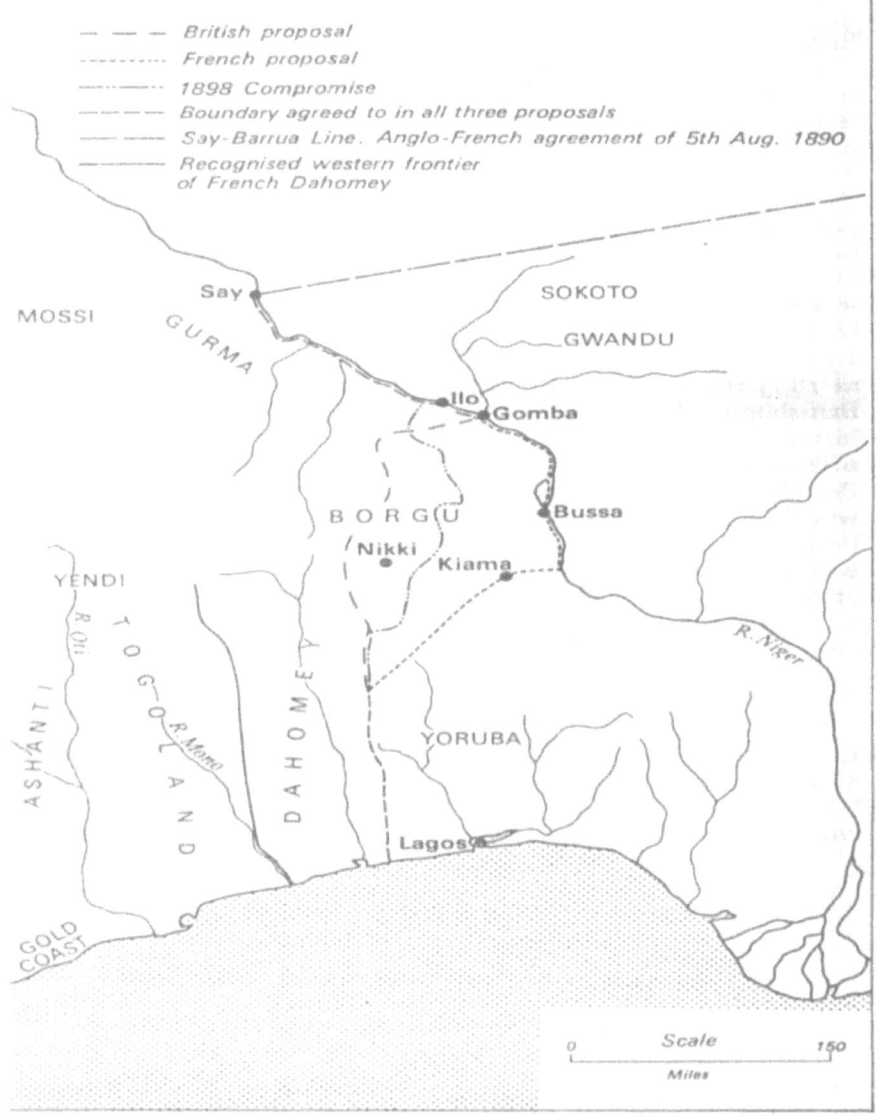

The Partitioned Borgu (Adapted from Anene 1970)

****

Borgu was going through its first major historical defeat and effective occupation by foreign forces. Although it resisted occupation by the French, it was brutally suppressed and forcedly occupied. As observed by a British officer, MacCallum, the devastation has been cruel. Anyone who refused to accept French presents was killed and the town or village burnt. On the point of final negotiation, the French had done the dirty job; almost all parts of British Borgu were effectively pacified and occupied. As the French moved to their side of the territories, the British inherited a deeply brushed, intimidated and disempowered people. From 1878, British Borgu remained under military occupation or administration. The authority of the Royal Niger Company was transferred to the imperial government in 1900 and Colonel Lugard, who had been acting as a political officer in Borgu with Colonel Willcocks in command of troops, was appointed High Commissioner of Northern Nigeria.

This wasn't necessarily an administration but a military occupation. It was an attempt to keep the region under effective British control. There were no fundamental changes to the political structure of the place except that the chiefs of the occupied territories were expected to report regularly to the military command in each location. The commanders, in turn, reported to Fort Goldie.

For effective control, British garrisons were initially situated in Bussa, Kaiama, Okuta and Yashikira. Up to 1901, these small detachments of the WAFF remained in Okuta, Yashikira, Illo and Fort Goldie, while those in Kaiama and Ilesha were removed in 1901. Borgu remained under military rule until 1902 when Mr. Kemble was appointed the first civilian officer to take charge of the province (NAK 1928).

European Scramble and Partitioning of Borgu

Areas lost by Nikki toBritish Borgu 1898 (adapted from Anene 1970)

CHAPTER SIX

Colonial Administration in Borgu

With the effective partitioning of Borgu into French and British dominions, each domain was administered based on the idiosyncrasies of the controlling power. A difference in approach shaped the character of each of the respective administrations, even if the essence remained the same. While, for instance, the British were inspired by their metropolitan monarchy, the French were more driven by the notions of the Republic and the Jacobian state. The French, therefore, ruled directly through the principle of Assimilation while the British Native Authority system was based on Indirect Rule.

Despite the differences in administrative styles, as would be seen, they shared some common features. This was largely because the organisation of the state was a response to a principal and prevailing dilemma of the "native question," bordering around how a tiny minority of Europeans could manage a large native community of indigenous people (Mamdani 1996). Nevertheless, it appears none of the colonial powers had a preconceived idea of how to manage the colonial territories. They were largely flexible, responding to context (Herbst 2014).

Direct and Indirect Rule were, therefore, responses of the two powers to an important local question based on the ideological structure of the metropolitan states in Europe. The idea of direct rule was built around a single legal and administrative system defined by the European powers based on their metropolitan civilisation. The colonies were, therefore, expected to conform to European laws and be ready to be "civilised" into European culture and practice. In contrast, Indirect Rule was the use of the local political structure to dominate and control the colonies. The dynamics of how these played out in the Francophone and Anglophone Borgu will be examined in subsequent sections.

Colonial Administration in British Borgu

After the conquest and effective occupation, the British imposed their rule on Borgu. The Colonial Office developed a system of Indirect Rule which was more of a fusion of the indigenous Islamic authority, 19th-century emirate administration, and intervention by the "Bonapartist" colonial state (Watts 1983). Lugard provides a summary of the Indirect Rule policy thus:

> The policy of the Government was that these Chiefs should govern their people, not as independent rulers. The orders of the Government are not conveyed to the people through them, but emanate from them in accordance, where necessary, with instructions received through the authority. While they themselves are controlled by Government in policy and matters of importance, their people are controlled in accordance with that policy by themselves (Lugard, cited in Watts 1983, 167).

The Indirect Rule system was, therefore, more or less a retention of the old system within a new political setting, obviously with changes that suited the new overlords. With this, although the pre-existing political system was shattered, Indirect Rule resurrected a simulated monarchical structure that built class alliances between traditional emirate officeholders and the European bureaucracy. Indirect Rule was thus not only responding to the "native question;" it was also a pragmatic necessity. It was a response to the demand for political stability and fiscal self-reliance. The necessity for forging a class alliance between the colonialists and the traditional ruling class did not mean that the aristocratic class was kept intact. The British meddled constantly in the emirate and dynastic politics, deposing and re-instating high-ranking local officials with immense regularity.

The establishment of a political system and effective political control was followed by strategic changes in the political economy of the area. This was introduced by the colonialists. In the process, currency replaced cowry, taxation was simplified, systematised and incorporated into an all-embracing system of revenue and assessment. Where it was not originally applicable in Borgu, changes were forcefully introduced. Slavery was abolished while labour was both voluntarily and forcefully recruited, largely for construction and porterage. The colonial courts were established with jurisdictions embracing the activities of the mercantile companies and agents. Colonialism transformed the pre-colonial class relations in Borgu, even if some of the pre-colonial institutions and structures like kingship, indigenous ruling classes and social structures survived and flourished, albeit with changes. They were adapted to suit the new requirement within a different structure of production relations and state.

In this guise, the British ruled indirectly through the Native Authority system controlled by native rulers. Therefore, local kings were placed as heads of Native Authority councils and were to be assisted by subordinate officials drawn from the ruling aristocracy. The purpose of this was to carry out routine administration through subordinate intermediaries who were dependent on the colonial authorities for their positions. It was also to enable the colonial rulers to manipulate, for their own interests, the intense competition for office and status by the native elites (Williams 1976).

As indicated earlier, the Native Authority was not simply an institution of local governance; it was also an institutional manifestation of a social force in the society. As a political institution, it was expected to maintain law and order, balance interests among social forces and supervise the allocation of resources in the society. The primary interest of the Native Authority was to safeguard the values considered vital for the survival of the social forces it represented (Yahaya 1980).

****

The military occupation and rule in Borgu effectively ended with the appointment of a civilian administrator and the re-definition of Borgu as a colonial province. This marked the beginning of the institution of a colonial state and its related substructures. Borgu was an unstable polity all through the sixty-two years (1898 – 1960) of effective colonial occupation. Territorial boundaries and administrative systems changed rapidly and almost impulsively, most times responding to the exigency of time, the temperament of colonial officials, the manipulative influence of political agents and changes in the overall political system in northern Nigeria. These changes were undertaken with extreme insensitivity to the politics, culture and history of the people.

However, the influence of pre-colonial political and sociological formation remained constant. Borgu couldn't fit properly into the British/Fulbe model of a centralised authoritarian monarchical system. The more the colonial authorities tried to panel-beat the system, the more instability it created.

In 1902, Borgu was made a province of the newly established Protectorate of Northern Nigeria. Henry Kemble was appointed the first civilian Resident. Kemble reported to Lugard who was the High Commissioner. The province was divided into two units – the northern division under Bussa and a southern one under Kaiama. Kaiama also doubled as the Provincial Capital. Kaiama and Bussa were respectively led by Mora Tasude and Kisan Dogo both First Grade Chiefs in the new order. While Bussa was placed in control of entities that it had a historical suzerain over or relatively strong political relations, Kaiama received a number of previous dependencies and provinces of Nikki that were never under Kaiama historically.

With this arrangement, all the provinces of Nikki and related Baatonu settlements in British Borgu – including Ilesha, Yashikira, Gwanara, and Okuta – become districts subordinate to the Emir of Kaiama, an arrangement by no means agreeable to these communities. Resistance to the new structure by the kings of these territories was met with deposition. The first to be deposed was Suno Kpera of Kenu. Kenu and Tabera were consequently placed under Okuta and the surrounding villages ceded to Gwanara. The King of Okuta, Sakogi, was also deposed in 1902 and replaced by Lafiagobi (Baakombia).

Although Lugard had a tremendous influence in defining Kaiama as provincial headquarters, he, on a visit to Kaiama in July 1904, without reaching Bussa, considered Kaiama unsuitable for the headquarters. He observed that with a province nearly 200 miles long and only 65 miles broad, the headquarters should be more nearly in the centre. According to him, Kaiama was only 30 miles from the south frontier, and being out of touch with the north and with the Niger navigation (being 50 miles from Fort Goldie) was of no political importance. Kaiama was made the station of an Assistant Resident and the capital was removed to Bussa, considered more central and strategic. With the movement, the Resident could control the customs stations in the north where the important kola caravans crossed the province, and, being on the Niger, would be in touch with the enclave at Fort Goldie and the station of exit (for French flotillas) at Illo.

Provinces of Northern Nigeria, 1906.

According to Lugard, the King of Bussa was the most important king in the province (NAK 1905). The movement to the provincial headquarters was effected on the 23rd of March 1905. While in Kaiama, Lugard selected a location for the residence of the Deputy Resident. Until then, the Residency was almost in the town, in an old fort built by the French in 1897. The relocation of the base was not only a reaction to the illnesses regularly suffered by Europeans – one of the staff, Lieutenant Ward Simpson, had died during that period – it was also part of the residential segregation policy of the colonial government. The new Residency was located way off the town. A similar system was also provided for in Bussa.

From 1905 to 1907, two major developments ensued in Borgu. First, Borgu was amalgamated with Kontagora Province in 1905. Second, the northern segment of Borgu, including Illo, Kaoje, Gendenni and other adjacent villages, were ceded to the Gwandu Division of Sokoto Province. This was done ostensibly as compensation for their loss of land to the French through international boundary adjustments. In reality, there appeared to be no serious reason except, according to the Resident of Kaiama, for the fact that the emirs of Yauri and Gwandu had gained the listening ear of a certain Captain Williams. The 1907 Annual Report of Northern Nigeria actually wrongly indicates "the area of Sokoto province has been increased by the restoration of the districts which were included in the Province of Kontagora and Borgu. This rectification has given great satisfaction to the Emirs of Gwandu and Sokoto" (NAK 1951). The Emir, and the people of Bussa, expressed their dissatisfaction with the decision to no avail. The ceded part of Borgu was not only a very important commercial section; it had a sizeable population and contributed significantly to the tax profile of Bussa.

The amalgamation of Borgu with Kontagora in 1907 was part of the larger administrative changes in northern Nigeria. Although this didn't interfere with the independence of the two emirates of Borgu, the European staff in the region were reduced to one and finally, in 1912, to none at all (NAK 1928). Although still administered almost as a two-in-one province, the absence of Europeans in the region didn't make Borgu independent or self-sufficient as the Emir continued to serve the interests of the colonial administrator and even became more authoritarian, particularly in southern Borgu led by Mora

Tasude. They ensured regular collection of taxes and resistance was often met with repression. It was during this period that the Resident of Borgu proposed the deposition of Kitoro Gani of Bussa and making Mora Tasude the sole of head of the entire division.

With the withdrawal of Europeans from Borgu, a single political office based in Yelwa administered Yauri, Bussa and Kaiama emirates. This was not minding the historical hostility within Borgu, particularly Bussa and Yelwa, and the difficulty of administering a vast area of about twelve thousand square metres by a single political officer based in Yelwa. During this period, the mainland of Bussa opposite Rofia, for 10 miles inland and with 20 miles of river frontage, were given to Yelwa. Other Bussa land ceded to Yauri includes Kunji, the northern portion of Agwara. Kwotashi Island, occupied by Nupe and Bussa, was given to Kontagora. Political manipulation and intrigues at Yelwa, with the collaboration with the Political Officer, resulted in the framing and deposition of the Emir of Bussa. A non-Bussa element and an "ex-slave," Turaki, was appointed in his place. As would be seen later, this incident, combined with other grievances, resulted in a major revolt in Borgu which was violently crushed by the colonial authorities.

A deliberate policy was designed to subordinate Borgu to Yauri and bring the two Borgu emirates to heel under handpicked men who owed their positions to the British. Agwara District was given to the District Head of Ngaski. Bussa and Kaiama were reduced from emirate to district status, paying tax to Yauri. Gwanara, Okuta, Yashikira and Wawa were reduced from district to village status. The whole of the Niger, with all the "islands" and fishing rights, were allocated to Yauri. This decision, including Ulakami Island, was reaffirmed in 1955. While Bussa lost Kunji and all islands, Yauri farmers were allowed to continue farming on land to which they had no claim (NAK 1956).

In 1917, Bussa and Kaiama regained their emirate status, but as second grade and in the same year a Political Officer was once again stationed at Kaiama. The question of Yauri's claim to these districts was raised by him. Owing largely to the refusal of the people of Agwara to remain under Ngaski, whom they had been forced to follow since 1915, this district was returned to Bussa. Kunji, however, "for other historical and administrative reasons" (NAK 1925, 28) remained under Yauri even if the historical component of the reasons for this was invalid and dubious. In 1927, Rofia was restored to Bussa but Illo and Kaoje remained in Gwandu Division of Sokoto Province with meagre revenue and little apparent hope of self-development. In another administrative change in 1923, Borgu was made a Division under Ilorin Province, with the two emirs retaining their independent status.

Native Authority Structure and Administration

Borgu, like most parts of northern Nigeria, went through different native administrative systems and structures since 1902. The constant in native administration was the role of the aristocracy, who were the central players within the native category, but taking instructions from the European officials. The political leaders, such as emirs or chiefs, were designated as the Native Authority (NA) and ruled as either the sole authority or through other administrative hierarchy of Chiefs. These native authorities were vested with specific functions including the collection of taxes (which were shared between the NA and the government of the Protectorate of Northern Nigeria) and the management of the *beit-el-mal* (Native Treasury), which kept the NA revenue. They were responsible for the courts, police, and prisons. They also provided some service functions including works, sanitation and education. The Native Authorities were also vested with legislative powers. They could legislate on traditional matters or local issues such as forest reserves, and the production and sale of liquor. Taxation, the Native Treasury and the preparation of annual budgets were managed by the emirs, their councillors and district heads. The political heads, from the Emir to the District and Village Heads, were all salaried officials (Yahaya 1980; Crowder 1973).

The NAs were supervised by British Political Officers. The extent to which a Political Officer supervised a NA depended on his competence and, to some extent, the character of the pre-colonial political system. The more hierarchical and centralised Fulbe caliphate systems enjoyed relative autonomy compared to non-centralised polities. Ideally, the Political Officers were supposed to act as advisors they meddled incessantly with the politics of local communities and sometimes took direct management of the NAs. All appointments and dismissals from positions in the NA were, in principle, under the control of the NA, though the central government had to sanction the appointment of the Chief or Emir as heads of a NA.

From the early days of the British administration, Borgu was structured into units of local government based on emirs and districts heads. Towards the end of the Second World War, the system had evolved into a powerful political force. It revolved around the European Residents and the respective emirs with stronger power vested in the emirs especially after the revolt in 1915. The Native Authority was both territorially and functionally structured. Nevertheless, in the 1930s, three types of Native Authority administration emerged. These were the Muslim governing Muslim, the Muslim governing Pagans and the Pagans governing Pagans. Pagans, in this regard, referred to non-Muslims. Borgu was a combination of Type One and Two even if majority of the people, at the early period of colonial rule, were in fact pagans or at best nominal Muslims. The pagan administrative policy was a response for some of the challenges of the early native administrative system essentially drawn from the Sokoto Caliphate and imposed on non-Muslim areas.

The colonial memorandum on pagan administration stated the reason for the new policy as follows:

> About 1907 – 1908, the form of native administration in Kano and Sokoto was imposed on the rest of the Northern Provinces, and the full system of District Heads and Villages Heads was forced on places quite unsuited to it. The result has been that a veneer of Muslim administrative system has been laid over a great part of the Northern Province and the true phenomena of local government have been obscured (NAK 1934, 7).

Type One was categorised as the best and easiest to manage as "there is not much to criticize in the form of administration and the details of its organization" (NAK 1934, 6). The colonial administrative officers were only expected to ensure justice, check oppression and suppress crime.

Territorially, Borgu Division was, at different times, structured into two emirates, that is the Southern Borgu and Northern Borgu, respectively led by the emirs of Kaiama and Bussa. Each of the emirates had a three-layered structure: Central Emirate

Administration, District Administration and Village Administration. The administrative structure was in turn structured into different functional units to meet the demands for certain services – courts, sanitation, works, police, prison, revenue and treasury.

Central Administration

Each of the two Emirates had a Central Administration led by their respective emirs. They had two members of the council. In Kaiama, it was the Waziri and Ubandoma and in Bussa, the Waziri and Abokin Mallam formed the council. Sometimes, the Emir of Bussa sought the advice of the Liman (Imam) and Karabonde, who was the Head of Bussa Town. The Ubandoma was the link between the District Officer and the Emir of Kaiama, while in Bussa, Abokin Mallam, or in his absence, the Waziri, performed the role. This was the link between the native institution and the colonial officials. Kaiama Town was divided into three quarters which were supervised by the Liman, Kilishi Yerima and Ubandoma. Ubandoma supervised his quarters and that of the Emir. In ensuring popular participation in the affairs of native governance, an elected Town Council was instituted in 1952. The members of the Council included the Waziri as the Chair, three Ward Heads, elected representatives from each of the three wards, and an elected Hausa representative and Yoruba representative each. The Council elected one Ward Head and one representative as members of the Native Authority Council.

Each of the Emirates also had a Touring Officer, who was often accompanied by a senior emirate official. This was usually the Abokin Mallam and Abokin Sarki in Bussa and Kaiama respectively. The Touring Officers were responsible for the supervision of the administrative machinery of the subordinate districts, an inspection of tax documents, court records and managing the record-keeping of District scribes, public education on sanitation and diseases and collection of information for the District Gazetteer. In districts bordering Dahomey, the Touring Officers also collected useful information about the neighbouring country. They kept a touring diary, which was recorded under classified headings. They recorded all decisions taken and orders given (all orders were given through the

Emir's representatives). Officers on tour also received complaints which were documented in complaint books (NAK 1953).

District and Village Administration

The emirates were subdivided into districts. Kaiama had five districts, including Kaiama, Yashikira, Okuta, Gwanara and Ilesha while Bussa had four. These were Bussa, Wawa, Aliyara (Babanna) and Agwara. Each district, except the metropolitan districts, was administered by a District Head. The districts had their own District Council, including Ward Heads and elected representatives. The remoteness of most parts of Borgu was a huge administrative challenge. For instance, Gwanara District, considered the most remote of Kaiama districts, had eight village areas in 1953 which were widely dispersed and communication between them non-existent. Gwanara itself was only accessible during the dry season (NAK 1953, 46). The District Council was large and believed to be representative of each of the eight villages of Gobo, Ningurume, Pura, Borobiye, Gammau, Yakiru, Bwe and Kyawu. The large council was aimed at providing a better understanding of the council system to a large number of villagers. The Town Council in Gwanara had the District Head, two traditional councillors, two Ward Heads and ten *wakilin talakawa* that were representatives of the ordinary people.

Below the district structure was the village structure. It was generally considered to be weak as compared to the district-level structure, particularly in Bussa, less so in Kaiama. This is not surprising as such a political structure, at that time, was alien to the people. There was particularly no village organisation beyond the Village Head level and the structure of power relations was not as hierarchical as defined by the Native Authority system.

The village areas were classified into three types:

1. An artificial grouping of villages ruled over by some members of the ruling aristocracy as village heads, such as Shagunu and Rofia areas.
2. An artificial clustering of villages of which the head of one has been made the Village Head of all. That was the

arrangement in most parts of Aliyara and Wawa Districts since 1935.
3. A group of villages whose village unit head is their natural chief.

In 1936, for instance, in Aliyara District, the village administration was reported to be weak with the village heads having little authority in their villages. Several villages, particularly Pissa and Kabe, were reported to be in the process of disintegration because a large number of people preferred to live in their farms where they would not be bothered by the authorities.

The village heads, like other political heads, were paid salaries. The salaries, in 1953, were increased to five percent of the tax collected in Kaiama Emirate and seven percent in Bussa. This funding arrangement had often pitched the village heads against the district head, as the district heads sometimes appropriated what was due to the village heads.

Administration of Justice

The Native Authority had partial control over the administration of justice including local police functions and the management of prisons. There were three types of tribunals in the Emirates: The Judicial Council presided over by the Emir, an Alkali court presided by an Alkali, and District Courts presided over by the District Heads. The Judicial Council or Native Courts were graded B, while the Alkali Courts and those of the districts were of Grade C. Cases not settled at the Emirate Court could be referred to the protectorate level. The Emir's Court was presided over by the Emir and was an appellate court for the district courts. There were hardly any appeals to the protectorate level. It would appear that most cases were settled out of court by Village Heads, especially with the poor road connectivity and long distances from the headquarters. Most of the adjudication was done in the pre-colonial ways, and often not properly recorded or recognised in the NA system. This reduced the number of cases in the formal judicial system. An assessment in Yashikira, for instance, shows that a substantial part of judicial work was done by households and village Heads. Therefore, district officials only received petty cases, particularly those involving non-indigenes. This was believed to be good as it saved litigation and spared the pockets of litigants from travel expenses at least. Village Heads and District Heads used the judicial process for extortion, particularly those involving pastoral Fulbe on the issue of encroachment of farmlands.

The Emirate Court in Bussa consisted of the Emir, Waziri, Kiwotede (replaced by the Abokin Mallam in 1937) and the Karabonde. As at 1953, reports indicated that District Courts were hardly operational in Bussa districts except for Wawa where the mining industry produced a number of divorce cases amongst migrant labourers. The Court Books were submitted monthly to the District Officers (DO). The treasury receipts for fines and court fees were provided for in the Court Book. All cases were numbered serially, by each court, throughout the year. Cases that had not been concluded were marked in red ink. The Native Court also kept a register of names and towns of prisoners, the date of sentence and the release date. It also kept the records of those awaiting trial. A register of corporal punishment was kept by the District Officer and the Native Court (NAK 315).

Police and Prisons

Each of the emirates had a police force (*dogarai*). The police force at Kaiama was under the command of the *Sarkin Dogarai*. A 1936 report indicates that they were all trained at Ilorin. Each District Head was assigned one or more *dogarai,* who were interchanged every three months. They wore dual-coloured gowns of red and blue as a uniform, with a red turban. Each Emirate also had a prison. Prisoners were employed for works of general utility. Prisoners' food was procured by the *Sarkin Yan Doka* who rendered account to the *Ma'aji* (treasurer).

Native Treasury

Each Emirate had a treasury headed by the *Ma'aji* and his assistant. The procedure of the treasury was guided by colonial financial memoranda. All taxes were remitted to the treasury and proper records kept, although this was often not so as the Emirs, Districts Heads and treasury officials were often found wanting on issues of financial management. Salaries were paid from the treasury. The district's salaries were collected at the end of each month by a messenger of the District Head and distributed at the District Headquarters by the District Heads. Wages of road workers were paid as directed by the *Ma'aji* or his assistant. Payment vouchers were authorised by the Emirs. Reviews indicated different forms of irregularities in relations to the approval process (NAK 315 8A).

At the end of each month, the *Ma'aji* was expected to make returns of the following: nickel coinage, the balance remaining in the votes, and, until the completion of taxation, a statement of the total collected and outstanding for every district. There were three holders of the key to the treasury strong room in Kaiama. These were the Emir, the Ubandoma and the *Ma'aji*. In Bussa, the key holders were the Emir, the Waziri and the *Ma'aji*.

Colonial Taxation

Taxation was an important feature of the colonial state in Nigeria. It was first introduced in British Borgu in 1901. Unlike the caliphate region of northern Nigeria, Borgu was not a systematic tax-paying polity prior to the colonial period. The tax was, therefore, to them, a symbol of domination and attracted different forms of revolts and resistance which, in turn, was accompanied by state repression.

Apart from serving as the main source of income for the state, taxation served as a means of instituting capitalist market relations, which was realised through the introduction of currencies and the elimination of pre-colonial forms of distribution and exchange. Through this process, also, peasant commodity production and wage labour were encouraged as people had to work to raise the required cash to pay their taxes (Ake 1981; Ekekwe 1986). Furthermore, taxation was another way of measuring loyalty to colonial authorities. The payment of a fixed amount, in cash or kind, by a weak people to a stronger one has long been historically recognised as the sign of acknowledgement of suzerainty. It was enforced by the government of Northern Nigeria, not so much on account of the amount brought in, but as a means of control.

Taxation in colonial Borgu entailed compulsory payment of specified but often reviewable amounts of money. The main forms of taxation in the first decade comprised *haraji* (poll tax), *jangali* (cattle tax), mines labour tax and *nomanjidde*. Caravan tolls were initially collected but abolished in 1907. There were several other taxes like an industrial tax levied on blacksmiths, liquor licenses, fishing tax, etc. Some of these taxes were abolished in 1912, leaving out the farmers' and non-farmers' tax. At the start of the colonial administration, the amount of tax collected yearly was not necessarily a percentage of assessable wealth of the districts, but whatever could be collected without danger of the necessity of coercion. Between 1904 and 1914, the tax incidence gradually increased. In 1915, capitation tax was based on proper assessment and estimated the percentage of the wealth of the districts, which significantly increased the amount of tax payable. Separate taxation for women was abolished in 1933. In 1935, the principles of proportional assessment were introduced and explained to District Heads and *Mallams* (in this case, tax officials) in Yashikira, Okuta and Gwanara. It had earlier been introduced in Kaiama, reportedly with "great success, and had the support of the Emir" (NAK 1936, 29).

Beyond the material and exploitative nature of the principle of colonial taxation, the process of its collection was brutal and oppressive. Tax extortion was a common thing among the Native Authority administrators in the rural areas. In 1923, in Agwara District, it was reported that a "number of people were tied up at different times for non-payment of tax and were made to pay *kudin igiya* (money for the rope used in tying them) for them to be untied" (NAK 1936). In some cases, livestock were seized for tax. Villages were often violently raided to compel inhabitants to pay their taxes.

Tax details were announced to the District Heads by the Emirs of Kaiama and Bussa. The District Heads, in turn, relayed it to the Village Heads and it cascaded down to the smallest settlements. District Heads collected taxes from the subordinate villages and they supported the Village Heads in ensuring all taxes were collected. A proper record of taxes was kept in the Tax Book consisting of the following:

1. The Census Book: This provided, by village and household, the names of all adult males and females, the number of children by gender, the amount of livestock owned by each household and the trade and industry they were engaged in.
2. The District Register: This was an abstract of the census and provided statistics of adult males and females, children by sex, the sick and infirm, livestock and professions and the amount of general and industrial tax with which each village is assessed. A copy of this register was kept with the District Officer.
3. Duplicate Assessment Note: This showed the total assessment of each village or village area and acted as a receipt for payments.
4. Village Household Sheets: These were kept by each Village Head and showed the payment made by each household.
5. District Cash Book: In this Book, all payments made by the Village Heads to the District Head and all payments made by the District Heads to the Native Treasury was entered.
6. Tax Receipt Books: Individual receipts were issued to all taxpayers who had completed their payments.

Tax collection and management was arguably one of the most difficult Native Authority engagements. The challenges of under-collection were always difficult to deal with. In 1940, for instance, the Emir of Kaiama stated that *haraji* collection had been completed in three districts, but a total of £24.14 was unpaid from Kaiama and Ilesha districts. The *jangali* collection showed a decrease of £38 on the previous year's figure which was partly due to the epidemic of black quarter in Okuta District which caused the death of a hundred and sixty cattle. Until 1937, the Borgu Native Administration received only fifty percent of the direct taxes and, except for small sums spent on salaries; there was no expenditure by government in Borgu Division. The situation only improved with the increase inrevenue by seventy percent.

Table 4: Bussa Native Administration Tax – 1940 - 1941

District	Assessment	Collected NA Share	Government Share	Total
Bussa	£475,14.0	333,11.0	142,19.0	476,10.0
Wawa	489,13.0	344, 6.0	147,11.4	491,18.0
Agwara	1,118,9.0	784,0.8	336, 0.4	1120,1.0
Aliyara	492,6.0	344,13.7	147,14.5	492,8.0
Total	2,576,2.0	1,806, 11.11	774, 05.1	2580,17.0

Source, NAK 1940: DOB/BOU/1

Against the policy of limiting taxation to adults, in many places, District Officers often assessed and taxed children. In 1935, Okuta District was particularly reported to have seen the practice of including children in the ranks of tax-paying males. The practice was a result of pressure from the native authorities as districts were given targets of taxes to be collected based on assessments that were often unsystematically done in largely mobile rural communities. In order to meet targets and sometimes to offset losses arising from emigration, children were taxed and their parents were expected to pay for them, or the children themselves worked to pay. Taxable adults often paid bribes to evade tax. At different times, many district officers and tax collectors were charged for embezzlement. For instance, in 1923, barely a few months after his appointment, the District Head of Agwara, Babaki, and two of his messengers were accused of embezzlement. The District Head was consequently forced to resign, the district Mallam was dismissed while the two messengers employed by the District Head were prosecuted and convicted (NAK 1924).

Nomajidde was a part of the general tax paid by Yauri farmers in the Bussa Emirate side of the River Niger. This was initially paid by the farmers individually. It was reviewed in 1939 to allow for an annual lump sum payment by Yauri Emirate on a three-year basis after which the amount would be re-assessed for the next three-year period. *Nomajidde* was a major source of contention between Bussa and Yauri emirates and was a source of boundary disputes between the two. This attracted the attention of the colonial authorities, resulting in a series of boundary adjustments. The mines labour tax was collected on a monthly basis from mine workers. The mine overseers collected the tax directly and paid them to the tax officials. Mining in Borgu was largely carried out in Wawa District.

With a large pastoral community, *jangali* was an important tax in Borgu. It was collected from July to October. Each district kept a *jangali* register showing names and towns of each cattle owner. The number of cattle, the amount of assessment and the number of the receipt issued to him were also recorded. *Jangali* was also collected from itinerant herders not in possession of *jangali* receipt. This was a major source of exploitation of Fulbe pastoralists by district heads and the local aristocracy. *Jangali* reinforced the pre-colonial exploitative relationship that existed between the Fulbe pastoralists and the Borgu aristocracy. Although the colonial authorities helped to protect the Fulbe against raids, they could not save them from more systematic exploitation and extortion. Concealment of cattle by the Fulbe pastoralists was therefore common. The Fulbe paid, in a number of cases, in instalments and were often ignorant of the intricacies of the European currency and had to rely on the Tax Mallam's assertion of the unpaid balance. As part of Fulbe resistance, they migrated with their cattle across the southern borders when it was time for *jangali* payment, while others crossed the international boundary (NAK 3158).

Table 5: Jangali Tax, Kaiama Emirate: 1940 - 41

District	1939 – 40 (£)	1940 – 41
Kaiama	304.18.0	306.18.0
Yashikira	331.4.0	327.6.0
Okuta	391.0.0	367.0.0
Ilesha	166.2.0	114.6.0
Gwanara	269.8.0	259.2.0
Total	1,412.12.0	1374.12.0

Source: NAK 1940. DOB/BOU/1

Exploitation of Labour

The colonial state exploited labour in two related ways: by forced and wage labour. Forced labour was one of the cardinal elements of colonial administration in most of the provinces. It involved mobilisation of labour through forceful methods and without adequate remuneration. This was the dominant form of labour in the early decades of colonialism in Borgu Province. Construction of railways, roads, prisons, courts, colonial residential houses and market stalls were largely carried out through compulsory labour. The exaction of forced labour was part of the responsibilities of European officials, emirs, district heads and village heads. The essence was to cheaply develop colonial infrastructure for effective state penetration of the hinterland and provide perquisites for the state officials. The major roads linking the major principalities of Borgu were constructed through conscripted labour.

Forceful recruitment of labour did not only generate opposition from conscripted groups, but it also created ethnic conflict. For instance, in Kaiama Emirate, the Baatonu people accused the emirate officials of discriminatory practices in conscripting labour. They alleged that most of the labour was recruited from among the Baatonu people, rather than the Boko of Kaiama.

Apart from forced labour, the colonial administration also instituted wage labour. The superstructure of colonialism did not require a large, permanent wage labour force. But, because of the system of governance and limited development of productive forces, wage labour gradually replaced the traditional family, pawn and slave labour in agriculture, even if it occurred on a seasonal basis (Williams 1976). The government was the largest employer of labour, mainly in the Native Authority and mines. In Borgu Province, the preponderance of forced labour significantly constrained the development of wage labour. The Native Authority was relatively small and the people had limited education.

Native Authority System and Borgu Aristocracy

The Native Authority system revolved around the aristocracy. The aristocracy and the kings or native rulers were at the centre of the political system. Authority was built on what Mamdani (2004) called "personal despotism." The primary consideration in this process was the loyalty of the political leaders to the colonial authorities. To achieve this, the native political structure was tailored or "supported" to meet the new political reality. In doing this, disloyal rulers were removed with ease and replaced with loyal ones while the colonial authorities promoted or tolerated the excesses of local despots who were loyal. The pre-colonial political structure of Borgu significantly suffered from excessive colonial interference and abuse, resulting in a massive distortion of the system and change in intergroup relations.

The major hallmarks of the Native Authority system include:

- Centralisation of hitherto decentralised political units: The Native Authority system tried to centralise Borgu beyond its pre-colonial limit. Governor Ballot of Dahomey realised in 1895, during the scramble for Borgu that it was only in the minds of European geographers that Borgu existed as a centralised kingdom. In reality, Borgu was a loose political federation of local rulers. It was a society in which a series of power centres had emerged and were perpetually at war with each other under, continually changing alliances (Bierschenk 1993).
- The introduction of the Emirate system in a largely pagan society: Some of the kings, particularly in Kaiama and Bussa, were Muslims, the districts were predominantly pagans at the start of colonial rule The title of "Emir" for kings was alien, as it was even in the Sokoto Caliphate. It was initially a reflection of Native Authority hierarchy, as district heads came to be called chiefs.
- Defining the territorial space of the emirs beyond the confines of their suzerain control in the pre-colonial times, especially Kaiama which was placed over some Nikki dependences in Anglo-Borgu. All of which were of different ethnic category.
- Interferences in the political system and almost whimsical removal and replacement of emirs and district heads.

Apart from the international dismemberment of pre-colonial Borgu and the displacement and distortion of the different entities, the Borgu aristocracy suffered incessant deposition and change in structure and even provincial membership. Borgu was faced with a historical challenge to the definition of its pre-colonial political system and structure. Although a monarchical society, it didn't have the functional structuralism of the Sokoto Caliphate or of Kanem-Bornu. While the kings enjoyed strong powers, their powers weren't absolute and the territorial space they controlled was limited by history and cultural constraints. As indicated in chapter 2, no Borgu principality had total control over the entire polity. Although Borgu was one of the first to be brought under colonial control in northern Nigeria, the political system and economic resources based on colonial reckoning didn't meet the material expectations of the colonial powers. The frequent changes in the political structure were, therefore, a response to this colonial dilemma.

The attitude and perception of Borgu kings were largely based on the idiosyncrasies of the colonial officials. While, for instance, Mora Tasude of Kaiama was often praised by succeeding colonial Residents, including Lugard, since their first encounter in 1894, Diggle, on arrival in Kaiama in 1912, was less impressed and couldn't understand the basis for the favourable reports on the Emir. He believed the Emir had been left alone for too long without supervision. The apparent authoritarian hold that endeared the Emir to earlier colonial officials seemed to be a problem for Diggle. He noted thus:

> His [Mora Tasude] idea seems to be to centralise all authority and all power in himself. A great number of persons have left the town of Kaiama because of his treatment of them. On several occasions during the last month, the Chiefs [district heads] and headmen of the various towns have complained to me that they were frightened to bring tribute into Kaiama because of the Emir and by his impolitic action; he has driven a whole village across the Anglo-French boundary (Crowder 1973, 94).

While some of this criticism may have been correct, the actions of the Emir of Kaiama and his authoritarian disposition were prompted and supported by the colonial authorities. Earlier resistance in Kaiama, especially amongst the Baatonu people, was met with state repression and the deposition of chief. It was, therefore, not a surprise that Blackeney, the Resident of Kontagora, came in defence of Mora Tasude, observing that he had always been "well-spoken of." While he admitted that the Emir had been left for too long to himself, he warned Diggle to be careful about listening to stories "as there are always plenty of mischief-makers around who are always against those in authority." He further reminded him that the policy of the administration was to rule through the emirs (NAK 1912). Blackeney may have been right about mischief-makers, but some of these complaints against Tasude were real. Complaints about his authoritarian disposition were common, particularly by the Baatonu people who detested the paramountcy of Kaiama. Succeeding emirs of Kaiama were very unpopular in that region. Joyce Cary, who succeeded Diggle, described Tasude as a man of "strong and grasping character, no scruples and much determination" (NAK 1928). However, if you think Diggle was pandering to the disgruntled Baatonu people, his comment on Yaru, the District Head of Yashikira, was even more scathing. He reported that the District Head was "unfitted" for his job and the whole district refused to obey him and he had no power to enforce his authority. He was so weak, according to Diggle, that he personally carried his mat and staff of office anywhere he went.

Yaru's powerlessness was a function of the error or mischief surrounding his appointment. It appears he was wrongly presented by Mora Tasude as a son of Suno Lafia, the King of Nikki, and a legitimate claimant to the throne. Yaru was, in fact, the son of Lafia, a cobbler of Bissakwera. He was eventually removed by Diggle in 1912 after years of trial and replaced by Marshi, yet another non-legal claimant, a Zabarma who was believed to be a "slave of Kaiama" and later a friend, *Abokin Sarki*, of Mora Tasude of Kaiama. He was similarly detested by the people of Yashikira. Marshi was to later become the Emir of Kaiama in one of the most controversial and far-reaching reforms in colonial Borgu.

Borgu's amalgamation with Kontagora and subsequent subjection to Yauri was the most difficult for the region and very humiliating for the aristocracy. The period of European disappearance from Borgu was heralded by drastic reforms and violent resistance. This period coincided with the death of Mora Tasude of Kaiama. Clarke, the District Officer in Bussa, who was known as *Dan Tankwa* (the peppery man) because of his rash and cruel actions, made a number of recommendations on the further reorganisation of Borgu. From all indications, Clark was impatient with alleged inefficiencies of the emirs and appeared contemptuous of the Borgu people, their culture and the political institution. His perception of Borgu was, at best, racist. He had always preferred non-Borgu in positions of authority. His reforms, therefore, stemmed partly from his arrogance and idiosyncrasies and partly from his poor knowledge of Borgu. His key recommendations were as follows:

- Deposition of the Emir of Kaiama, Sabi Ba-Yaru also known as Gimba and Kitoro Gani of Bussa and the retirement of Sarkin Yamma of Yauri on grounds of ill health.
- The amalgamation of Kaiama, Bussa and Yauri in one emirate under the Sarkin Yamma of Yelwa.
- Appointment of Sarkin Yamma as emperor of the three provinces (emirates).

Clarke held the Emir of Kaiama responsible for the troubles in the emirate. His argument was that Kaiama and Bussa required much supervision from a strong ruler. Reporting on the inability to collect tax in Kaiama, the Emir was described as unfit for his role, useless to the colonial authority and a danger to the progress of his emirate. "He reduced his emirate, which was in a comparatively high state of efficiency to which the late Emir (Mora Tasude) brought it, to a state almost of anarchy" (NAK 1915).

The Emir of Bussa, Kitoro Gani, was described as a drunk "unfitted for the post of Emir." He was accused of eight different offences, including being unreliable and a *munafiki* (hypocrite) and that his loyalty couldn't be relied upon in an emergency. He was accused of obstructing the work of European officials since his appointment. In 1903 – 4, he encouraged the emigration of people of Agwara village in Ngaski district to Borgu. He allegedly enticed them by promising exemption from forced labour.

After the initial interrogation of the recommendations, approval was eventually given for the deposition of Kitoro Gani of Bussa and Sabi Ba-Yaru (Zume Kpandu)[59] of Kaiama in April 1915. Sarkin Yauri was retired. Kaiama was placed under the District Head of Yashikira, Mashi Koro, while Bussa was subjected to Yauri under Aliu Sarkin Yamma. Hamilton-Brown, the Resident in Kontagora, who over-relied on Clarke in Bussa, proposed to replace the name Bussa with Yauri Emirate and keep the metropolitan Bussa as a District. All these changes were expected to resolve a number of

---

[59] He was exiled in Wawa and died in 1938.

problems. Primarily, it was meant to deal with the insufficiency of European staff to post as Political Officers in Bussa. It would also see to the replacement of inefficient emirs with their apparently more capable successors, deal with the lack of progress in Bussa Emirate and finally, give room for Yauri famers to expand across the Niger since they would no longer be considered as strangers (Crowder 1973).

With these changes in Kaiama and Bussa, the policy of picked men who owed their position to the British was extended to the districts particularly after the Bussa revolt. Sabi Hakuri, the District Head of Ilesha, was deposed and replaced by Kuda from Kaiama, Kwara (Bakombia / Lafiagobi), District Head of Okuta, was replaced by Bukari (Abubakar), also from Kaiama and of Wangara (Dendi) origin[60]. He was also believed to be a nephew of Mora Tasude who had no claim to the throne. In Yashikira, Shero replaced Marshi after he was appointed Emir of Kaiama in 1914. Shero was a direct descendant of Suno Lafia, father of the first King of Yashikira, Woru Yaru (Ojo). Gwanara had earlier experienced a similar deposition, when Koto Kotogi was deposed in 1913 for refusing to pay tax and later died at Bussa. Gwanara, under Suno Ali, therefore, escaped this wave of change but was incorporated into Ilesha District. The appointment of Marshi as Emir of Kaiama was reported to have led to a southward exodus. A similar trend was also reported in Ilesha. Most inhabitants of Ilesha town returned to Sandiru in French Borgu, while others made their way to Saki (NAK 1928).

After the Borgu revolt in 1915, as would be seen later, Marshi was imprisoned for various offences including acts of oppression and embezzlement. A number of court officials were removed, together with the district heads of Ilesha and Okuta, who were also fined or imprisoned for extortion (NAK 1928). The clean sweep of officials in Kaiama Emirate was completed by the tragic death of Shero, the Chief of Yashikira. He had been summoned from Yashikira to give evidence against Marshi. Somebody mischievously informed him that he too would be imprisoned. He then committed suicide by hanging himself on the roof of his lodging (NAK 1919, 1928). Shero was succeeded by

---

[60] Bukar (Abubakar), we was called *Kokoru* (a pest), in Okuta because of his despotic rule.

his uncle, Albarka, who had formerly refused the post as he had hoped to be appointed the King of Nikki. A similar incident happened with Suno Ali of Gwanara, in 1928. He was also summoned to Kaiama to answer for alleged extortion of cattle from the Fulbe people. It was generally believed that he committed suicide rather than face probable deposition. He was succeeded by Woru Tunko who took the title of Ali Kina.

In 1917, Borgu became a division of Kontagora Province and a Political Officer was stationed in Kaiama. The Emirs of Kaiama and Bussa then officially reverted their Emir's status with a grade of second class. Yerima Kura was installed as Emir in Kaiama. On his death in 1921, he was replaced by Kiyaru. Woru Gande (Konkoma), a brother of Kwara, was appointed as the District Head of Okuta. Abigoga (Abu Goga?) became the District Head of Ilesha. Despite the changes in Leadership in Ilesha, only a few of those who had left returned to the town.

Colonial Administration in French Borgu

The French operated a Direct Rule system in their West African territories. The differences between the British and French models of colonial administration have been widely discussed in the literature (Crowder 1973). The French colonial policy was that of Assimilation, centred on the French desire to make the colonies part and parcel of continental France, what it called "the French Union." It entailed a complete incorporation of African communities into metropolitan France, with supposedly complete social, civil, and political equality (Ezenekwe 1953).

Like the British, the French in West Africa also relied on native rulers, but in different roles and with a different relationship with colonial officials. The French had direct control of their colonies from Paris, with governmental control vested in the Ministry of Colonies and its bureaus. The French Parliament could legislate for the colonies by decrees, which the French colonial officers had to carry out.

> This highly centralized handling of colonial problems not only subordinates African interests to those of the French minorities in the colonies but also destroys the natural incentive of the chiefs and local

officials in dealing with affairs of their domains (Ezenekwe 1953, 169).

The French administrative structure was more like a pyramid covering a federation of its West African territories. At the top was the Governor-General who headed the Federation. This was followed by Lieutenant-Governors as the heads of the individual colonies, including Dahomey, our subject of focus. Each state was then subdivided into districts and the largest districts were subdivided into subdivisions. In the pyramid, effective power was concentrated at the third level, the District Administrators. They were described as the real chiefs of the French Empire (Huillery 2009). They supervised the native rulers and were responsible for overseeing tax collection, representing the Lieutenant-Governor at official events, conducting a census, overseeing district cartography, steering elementary schools, watching Quranic schools, planning and supervising of the construction of basic infrastructure including roads, bridges and wells, as well as justice administration.

Against the advisory role of British Political Officers, the French placed the native rulers as subordinate to their Political Officers. They were more or less auxiliaries of the colonial administrators. An African king, in relation to a French Political Officer, was a mere agent of the central colonial authorities with clearly defined responsibilities including collection of taxes, recruitment of labour and military reservists. The native kings didn't head any local government unit. Neither did they control their old pre-colonial political units. The structure of the *cantons,* in most cases, cut across pre-colonial political boundaries. The kings weren't placed over their old political units, but over *cantons*, which sometimes coincided with the pre-colonial political units. In some cases, the pre-colonial political units were broken down to suppress the power of the chiefs and subject them to effective colonial control. Native rulers weren't necessarily those who had been selected through the traditional process and procedure. Most often, they were those who had exhibited loyalty to the colonial authorities or had obtained some education, civil or military service. Since they were agents of the colonial administration, the concern was more on "potential efficiency than legitimacy" (Crowder 1978, 201). The kings were essentially reduced to mere mouthpieces for orders emanating from outside. They were, therefore, resented by their people for being willing tools and agents for unpopular colonial policies like forceful tax collection and recruitment of forced labour.

Although the French eventually abandoned their Assimilation policy for *politique d' association* (politics of association), some of the dominant characteristics of the Assimilation policy remained. According to Crowder (1978), the Assimilation policy was abandoned because the French were not prepared for the necessary changes to make the policy work. While they recognised the impracticality of the Assimilation policy, they weren't ready to let go of some of its principal characteristics. Amongst these were:

1. The goal of creating French citizens out of Africans was retained with a few modifications. Instead of it being open to all, the process was made relatively more difficult.
2. All through the colonial period, the French colonies were centrally administered within the French West Africa – from Paris to Senegal and down through the colonies.
3. The civilising mission of the French was also retained. Education was modelled along the metropolitan system, even if it was sparsely provided in the colonies. Teaching in local languages was not allowed in colonial schools.
4. The African economy remained an extension of the metropolitan economy.
5. The role of European Political Officers also remained unchanged as they were the most dominant in the colonies and didn't have any regard for the local systems or culture of the people.

Although not as frequently as with the British; the French political structure of Borgu also went through a number of changes. At the start of the French effective political occupation of Borgu, the pre-colonial Borgu territory became an administrative division. Each Division was divided into three *cercles*. The *cercle* of Borgu comprised Nikki and Parakou, with Parakou as the capital. Moyen Niger had Kandi as the headquarters and Kounde-Djougou had Djougou as its capital. With the effective establishment of the Colony of Dahomey, French Borgu was brought under the control of the Lieutenant-Governor of Dahomey in 1904. Each *cercle* was divided into subdivisions administered by Europeans. The subdivisions in Borgu largely coincided with the political units of the pre-colonial period except for Malanville in the north (Idris 1973). The subdivisions were in turn divided into cantons, also largely corresponding with pre-colonial villages.

The administrative *cercles* of French Borgu was later reduced to two. These were Borgu and the Moyen Niger, with headquarters in Parakou and Kandi respectively. The subdivisions were, in turn, divided into cantons. These last were administered by a *chef de canton* who was a Borgu chief chosen from among the pre-colonial aristocracy. In 1907, the subdivision of Nikki had twenty-five cantons.

The parts of Borgu that fell under French colonial control were largely Nikki provinces and dependencies in the north and east of pre-colonial Borgu. With this, the Nikki aristocracy were expected to play important roles in the French colonial political organisation. Although the *Sina Boko* (King of Nikki) was recognised in name, he was reduced to a *chef de canton* and placed at the same level with his former subordinate, the kings of Parakou and Kandi. As of late 1919, Sabi Purukaru, the King of Nikki, was still referred to as *Roi de Nikki*. His former designation was *chef superieur de province*, which recognised his customary and historical authority over the *chef de cantons* of other subdivisions, even if his administrative jurisdiction was reduced to his own canton of Nikki (Crowder 1975). The administrative jurisdiction of the King of Nikki unusually corresponded with a subdivision of Nikki administered by a French *chef de subdivision*, probably to keep an eye on his activities. Parakou, like Kaiama in Anglo-Borgu, was raised in status as the headquarters of the *cercle* of Borgu, of which Nikki was a subdivision. Similarly, the small provincial kingdom of Kandi had an elevated prestige as the headquarters of the *cercle* of Monye Niger. As if this wasn't enough of humiliation for Nikki, in 1911, against the Nikki tradition that forbids the Nikki from visiting Parakou, the Sina Boko, Sero Toru Wonko, was summoned to Parakou during one of the tours of the Governor-General of French West Africa, William Ponty. The death of Sero Toru shortly after that was attributed to that visit (Idris 1973; Crowder 1975). This Nikki tradition was believed to be a response to the failure of Sero Kpera Barasobe's punitive expedition against the intransigence of the king of Parakou, who refused to attend one of the Gaani festivals in the mid-nineteenth century.

The French colonial control of Borgu was built on two interrelated political philosophies which combined to rapidly erode the political powers, status, privileges and control of the Wasangari. The first was the *politique de races* (race politics) and *commandement indigène* (indigenous command).

According to a colonial circular issued in 1909 by Governor-General Ponty, *politique de races* was based on a recognition of all status groups as different "tribes." The idea was to preserve the autonomy of these tribes. In effect, the complex social hierarchy of Borgu was disaggregated into different tribes. This was particularly in relation to the lower status groups of Fulbe and Gando people. Each of these groups would have a *commandement indigène,* who would act as an intermediary between the groups and the colonial authorities (Biersschenk 1993). Chiefs were, therefore, appointed for the Fulbe, who didn't, in a real sense, have any territorial space in Borgu, while the Gando were given autonomy from the servitude of the Fulbe and the Wasangari. In 1900, a political report in Kandi argued that the appointment of Fulbe chiefs and Borgu chiefs would enhance the mutual independence of the two races. According to Governor-General Ponty, the policy is consistent with French's commitment to justice and liberalism (Biersschenck 1993) even if it also served their divide-and-rule interests. The policy also served to avert the possible migration of the ever mobile Fulbe to the British side of Borgu, as the Fulbe cattle was considered, even by the French colonial authorities, as significant to the economy of French Borgu (Biesrschenk 1993). During the early years of colonial occupation, the Fulbe pastoralists contended with multiple taxations and related symbols of control. First was from the Wasangari who continued with the pre-colonial exploitation of the Fulbe. As "protectors," they extorted tribute from them. The French colonial authorities and sometimes, the *tirailleurs senegalais* and *gardes de cercles,* also charged and collected dues on their own initiative. At the border areas between French and British Borgu, it was common to force Fulbe to pay tax at both frontiers. At this period, fiscal policy was more of political symbolism than economics. The payment of taxes was more of an expression of political loyalty and submission. The French authorities managed to stop the Wasangari's extortion by 1900 and, as the frontier got clearer, some of these multiple payments were controlled. The Fulbe were believed to have exploited the possibility of migration to British Borgu to negotiate for space and influence all through the colonial period.

Commandement indigène was, to some extent, the cascading of the French centralised colonial administration. As described earlier, power flowed from Paris down through the Governor-General of West Africa in Dakar, to the governors of the respective colonies (Dahomey in this case), to the *Commandant du cercle* (District Officer) to the French *chef de subdivision*. The *Commandement indigène* is found below the *Chef de subdivision*, and it was further subdivided into three categories. At the top were the *chefs superieur* at *cercle* level, then the *chefs de canton* at the mid-level. At the lowest rung were the *chef de village* (Bierschenk 1993). Fulbe rulers were, therefore, appointed alongside those of Borgu in the two *cercles*. Devoid of specific territories, the Fulbe *cantons* usually covered the same areas as the Borgu (Baatonu) *cantons*. In situations where the Fulbe population was small, the Fulbe *canton* could cover upto two or more Borgu *cantons*. To be sure, the Fulbe have always had a leader (*Mare Suno*), often appointed by respective Borgu territorial kings but they were subordinate officers purely serving as interlocutors with the Fulbe community. The Gando slaves were liberated and in the earlier periods decided to group themselves in camps and abandon their Fulbe and Wasangari masters. This development was a source of contention between the Gando (*Mareyo*) and the Fulbe. While the Fulbe loved their new-found freedom, they didn't think the Gando deserved a similar treatment. The system was later redesigned to create a good working relationship among the Gando, Fulbe and the Wasangari (Lombard 1967, 1970). Although the Wangara didn't get the Fulbe and Gando treatment, they received economic encouragement for their trade and had access to the earliest colonial education. With these changes, the Wasangari ruling class in French Borgu appeared isolated, with almost a complete loss of their subjects, except those indigenous to Borgu.

The powers of the Borgu kings were totally decimated. Unlike the British Borgu kings, the French native rulers were stripped of financial, judicial and administrative powers. The changes in the social hierarchy and autonomy for the Fulbe and Gando, as discussed above, reduced their status. Apart from being liable to imprisonment, the king could be summarily tried like their subordinates through the notorious *indigénat* (summary justice system). On the economic front was the change in the trade route due to the partitioning of Borgu. The old trade route from Gonja to Hausaland, which was the principal source of Borgu's wealth, was diverted by the new frontier, depriving the Borgu kings of an important source of revenue (Idris 1973; Crowder 1975). Writing on the *chef de Canton*, Geoffrey Gorer observed thus:

> In theory, these local chiefs [kings] rule under the guidance of the administrator; in practice they are the scapegoats who are made responsible for the collection of money and men. While they enjoy the administrator's favour they have certain privileges, usually good houses and land and in a few cases subsidies; but unless they are completely subservient, risk dismissal, prison and exile. (Cited in Crowder 1978, 203).

****

The 1917 rebellion in French Borgu, amongst others in French West Africa, was a major turning point in the colonial administration of Borgu. Although the rebellion was violently and decisively suppressed, the French colonial authorities were compelled to introduce some administrative changes. The French *politique des races* was held responsible for the rebellion. It was, therefore, imperative to reverse the loss of authority of the kings, as the colonial authorities relied on them as *intermediares indegenes*. They tried to improve their power base and legitimacy (Bierschenk 1993). This was not only a reform to strengthen the Borgu institutions it was also an attempt to placate the growing influence and intransigence of the growing number of *évolués*, that is, educated Africans employed in the colonial administration and European trading companies. Strengthening the kings and the traditional institutions was regarded as a means of checkmating the educated groups. This change was more like a shift from the French doctrine of Direct Rule towards the British's Indirect Rule. While the differences between the two have been widely examined (see Boahen 1987; Crowder 1978; Mamdani 2004), in reality, particularly in French and British Borgu, they were more similar than often presented. With the changes introduced after the rebellion, the appointment of native rulers was restricted to the original aristocracy. While the European District Officers continued to play significant roles in these appointments, the roles of "kingmakers" were recognised and a façade of local ownership and legitimacy created.

The second issue to deal with was the physical appearance of the kings and their attitudes to the symbolism of power. The over two decades of forceful colonial occupation and decimation of the powers and prestige of the Wasangari appeared to have affected their confidence and invariably their outward appearance and exhibition of power. The French therefore developed a low opinion of the kings' attitudes to the symbolism of power *"le prestige indispensable au commandement"* (indispensable prestige to command). They complained that the kings lived in the same huts as the rest of the population. They, therefore, insisted that the kings wear coats, which distinguished them from other members of the community (Bierschenk 1993). In some cases, the District Officers used state resources to build prestigious houses and gave the kings formal clothing as a way of boosting their prestige through external appearance (Bierschenk 1993). But even these gifts of clothing did not fundamentally change the situation as some of the kings didn't wear them. After a series of contestations on appropriate dress for the kings, a new set of garments were introduced – a uniform red fez cap of the *tirailler sénégalaise*.

In addition to the political changes, the kings were also made to play some economic roles. They didn't only collect taxes for the colonial government; the kings also played an important role in the so-called economic modernisation and production of export commodities, largely cotton, shea nut, tobacco and kapok. The level of agricultural production in their domains became a significant determinant of their standing in the eyes of the French colonial officials.

CHAPTER SEVEN

Anti-colonial Revolts in Borgu

Until colonial conquest in the late nineteenth century, Borgu was an indomitable society. It resisted its most dominant neighbours and politically expanded its frontiers and even provided military support to some of its neighbours. The process of colonial domination of Borgu was consequently very violent. It took, in some cases, the use of extreme repressive powers of the occupying forces, especially the French, to effectively pacify the region. The French carried out extensive punitive expeditions during the period of effective pacification to keep down the rebellion against colonial occupation (Anene 1965). The French military were stationed in different Borgu locations. This was not necessarily to prove effective occupation against their British competitors but to suppress any form of rebellion by Borgu warriors. At the point of the signing of the Anglo-French treaty, Borgu was effectively pacified and dominated.

While the colonial authorities succeeded in imposing their rule in the immediate period post-conquest, the situation began to change after about a decade. This was especially true in the period around the First World War. The change in the political landscape, the humiliation of the pre-colonial aristocracy, extreme repression, recruitment of forced labour, as well as obnoxious taxes and the violent processes of its collection collectively induced rebellion in Borgu, particularly in the period between 1914 and 1917. There were two kinds of revolts in colonial Borgu - violent and non-violent revolts. The communities non-violently resisted tax and forced labour by deserting their communities and moving into the vast interior, relocating to distant farms and alternating between British and French Borgu during tax collection. The chiefs, in some cases, resigned their appointments due to resistance to certain colonial structures or policies.

The most remarkable of these resistances was the violent revolt in both British and French Borgu in 1915 and 1916 respectively. Although both revolts were independent of each other and the triggers were different, their underlying causes can be traced to the colonial policies of the two powers. The nature of colonial rule significantly defined the nature of the revolts. While the French experienced a revolt directly against the colonial authorities, the revolt in the British Borgu was directed at the Native Authority system.

Michael Crowder has set out an extensive chronicling of the two revolts in different seminal works (1973, 1975 and 1978). We will, therefore, not be held back by the details and nuances of the revolts but will only concentrate on their process, nature and implications for the politics and society of Borgu.

Revolt in British Borgu

The revolt in British Borgu started as a non-violent resistance to tax and related colonial policies. After a long period of European absence in Borgu, in 1913, the British administration returned with a renewed commitment to asserting a full-scale Native Authority system as developed in the emirates of the defunct Sokoto Caliphate. New structures were created and a new tax policy, involving increased incidence and an equal share of tax proceeds by the emirates and the Protectorate of Northern Nigeria. The almost two years of European absence in Borgu was generally conceived as a cessation of European control. The return of the colonialists, almost with vengeance, was, therefore, a major destabilising factor to the people. Between 1913 and 1914, all segments of British Borgu practically refused to pay tax.

In Bussa, Kitoro Gani was partly held responsible for the agitation against tax. Indeed, his brother, Sabuke, who later led the revolt in Bussa, was implicated in the 1913 tax disturbance. He was arrested and jailed by the Emir. He, however, managed to escape, obviously with the support of the Emir and possibly the *Alkali,* as reported by the Colonial Officer, Clarke. Similar resistance was recorded in Kaiama District. As Clarke himself reported in 1914 while requesting a military escort to patrol Borgu, "... No progress has been made in the collection of tributes – the *Sarakuna* (District Heads) informed me that the people have intimated their intention of not paying until after harvest. I visited some of the more difficult towns and assisted the native administration but in West Borgu, little can be done until I get the escort..." (NAK 1914).

The approval for military patrol was received following the report that chiefs of Kaiama District had been driven out of their domains and no tax was collected during the period. Accusing the chiefs of inefficiency and lack of capacity, Clarke deposed the chiefs of Ilesha, Gwanara, and Okuta without bringing any of them to trial. This was followed by the deposition of Emirs of Kaiama and Bussa and the reorganisation and amalgamation of Bussa and Yauri.

These changes weren't just a humiliation of the Borgu aristocracy; the people felt short-changed on many levels. For instance, the deposition of Kitoro Gani and the appointment Turaki as the Emir of Bussa was deeply resented in the same way the people of Kaiama resented the appointment of Marshi as Acting Emir of Kaiama. They were both ex-slaves and not from Borgu and, therefore, had no links with the ruling families. This was considered a total disregard and disrespect to the people and culture of both places. The Bussa were worried about Turaki's ambition, his concentration of power and perquisite of office he was enjoying. It appeared to them that Turaki wanted to usurp the Bussa dynasties. The exclusion of the princes of Bussa from the new administrative structure was even more disturbing to the aristocracy. Of the four major officials of the administration, only Kijibrin, the *Kiwotede,* had a position. Others were occupied by people believed to be foreigners and ex-slaves. The metropolitan Bussa was led by Turaki, West Bussa (Babanna axis) led by Aliyara Bisalla and Agwara had Sabi Zakari. The district of Sourtir had Ajia Umoru who, though not a slave, was not of the Bussa royalty either.

This rulership by "ex-slaves and non-indigenes" was deeply resented by the Bussa princes and it was a resentment shared by other parts of Borgu.

Organisation of the Revolt

The revolt in 1915 probably started on June 16th 1915 and came as a surprise to the colonial authorities. It surely was not a surprise to the communities undergoing massive repression and forced to bear the brunt of obnoxious policies and the high-handedness of the colonial Political Officers. It came a few months after a "successful" patrol in Borgu and extensive administrative reforms. The Acting Lieutenant-Governor of the Northern Provinces, Goldsmith, expressed his surprise in a minute to his secretary:

> This outbreak was a surprise to me. Early in the year, the Resident received approval for a military patrol which escorted the Political Officer and toured the district for a month. The Resident then reported the district as quiet and no mention as far as I can remember was made of Sabukki [Sabuke] or his intriguing [sic]. No sooner have the troops left the province than the Resident reports the return of Sabukki [sic] and serious fighting (NAK 1915).

The revolt was led by Sabuke, himself a fugitive of the law. He had escaped from prison while serving a prison term after being convicted of complicity in a tax-related disturbance in 1913. He had been quiet all through the period until the dethronement of his brother, Kitoro Gani, and the installation of Turaki. It wasn't clear whether he had contact with Kitoro, who was still around Bussa. He was, however, believed to have met a number of Bussa princes to plan a reaction to all the unwanted changes. He mobilised four of his brothers—Layan Gaba, Sabi Kushi, Dodo Lilai Ggakese and Garba Gado. They left Bussa for Zali where they recruited more forces. The colonial taxes, repressive administration, and resentment against foreign and forced labour were enough to produce willing soldiers. Forces were believed to have been recruited from Babana, Shekwana, Kuta, Kankaye, Vera, Patengi, Nagazi Thumbu, Thubu Baba and some parts of French Borgu. These forces were joined by others from Kainji, Zambara, Musina and Shebenna, Shagunu and Garafini. About one thousand rebel forces might have been recruited, even if colonial records put the number of rebel forces at around 500 – 700 people (Crowder 1973). The rebel army, on foot and with some cavalry, as well as archers with poisoned arrows and other traditional Borgu weapons headed for Bussa. They are believed to have camped in Munai, near Bussa, the evening before the attack.

After an initial engagement of the rebels by Turaki, the rebel force raided Bussa, killed the *Alkali* and three district tax collectors. They took control of Bussa and the surrounding towns. Although Wawa was believed to have remained in support of the Native Authority, its people sympathised with the rebels because of their resentment against Ajia Umoru, the District Head. The revolt quickly spread to Kaiama where Woru Suku-Suku, who had earlier mounted an unsuccessful rebellion against Mora Tasude, raised an army against Marshi, the acting Emir of Kaiama. Marshi was then away in Yelwa. The forces in Bussa went on the chase of Turaki. Kiwotede Kijibrin crossed the Niger to Yelwa at Malale with the support of the Chief of Malale. Ajia Umoru was caught and killed in Kania in Mokwa District of Niger Province. Turaki, who was in company of Ajia Umoru, escaped to Zungeru through Mokwa, and later Kontagora.

Before the attack on Bussa, Turaki, who had failed to effect the arrest of Sabuke in Zali, sent emissaries to find peaceful ways of resolving the issues. Sabuke was believed to have given three conditions for peace: that Turaki resign his headship of Bussa District; that Turaki and other non-indigenous District Heads leave Bussa and, lastly, that his exiled brother, Kitoro Gani, be reinstated or otherwise another member of the royal family should be appointed as Emir (Crowder 1973). These were of course rejected by Turaki and his team. They put together a force to confront Sabuke, which failed woefully.

State Response to the Revolt

Although initially stunned by the revolt, the colonial authorities made a desperate effort to rationalise their reforms in Borgu. They called it a "necessary evil," as "progress and development was impossible in the old regime." Justifying the appointment of non-indigenes as District Heads, Resident Hamilton-Brown argued that "… there is not one of the ruling family members who is not tainted with the disqualification of drunkenness, with the possible exception of the ex-Emir's son at school in Birnin Kebbi... that this change has led to disturbances cannot be refuted but I am convinced that it will make for ultimate progress provided the authority of Yauri is backed up by us" (NAK 1916).

The immediate reaction was to gather troops for a second Borgu patrol. The WAFF detachment at Zuru immediately received a request for quick deployment at Bussa. Justifying his need for troops, Hamilton-Brown wrote: "I consider the ordering out of troops to prevent the murder of those whom we have appointed is justified under this circumstance" (NAK 1915). On receiving the approval, Political Officer Clarke led the Zuru detachment and men of the Northern Nigeria Police, in company of the district Political Agent, Abba, and Aliu, Emir of Yauri, marched to Bussa. (Crowder 1973). This force met a considerable resistance in Borgu as Sabuke's rebels scattered into different parts of Borgu, resulting in pockets of fight in areas to which the rebels had fled. A number of the rebel force was killed in Shagunu, Ganikassai, Bussa and Garafini. At Garafini, which was one of the strongest bases of the rebels, the colonial forces met considerable resistance. Nine rebel forces were believed to have been killed. Ten had been killed in Bussa.

The patrol was unable to catch any of the rebel leaders. It was reported that Sabuke and other senior members, including Sabi Kushi and Mamma, had fled across the border to French Borgu. At Kaiama, the colonial forces didn't meet any serious resistance as Woru Suku-Suku and his forces had fled across the border to Kishi in southwestern Nigeria. The colonial authorities had to work on the extradition of both leaders from French Borgu and from southern Nigeria. While Woru Suku-Suku was arrested and handed over after a long bureaucratic/diplomatic process involving the two regions of Nigeria, Sabuke and his ringleaders remained elusive.

Sabuke's possible presence in French Borgu was a major concern to the French colonial authorities in Dahomey. They were afraid that he could stir up protests in the region, with a huge implication on French Borgu. They, therefore, did everything possible to prevent the rebels from crossing the frontier. In fact, the Governor of Dahomey received permission from the Governor-General in Dakar to send troops to Nagazi to prevent the rebels from crossing the frontier. At different times, Sabuke or members of his rebel forces were found in Nagazi. At Chikanda, on the French-British Borgu frontier, one rebel was killed by British forces. Two were wounded and two were captured. Nonetheless, thirty men were reported to have crossed into Alafiaru in French Borgu. The French authorities captured one of the rebels in Bogo-Yaru and imprisoned him in Kandi. He was later extradited to Nigeria after a protracted negotiation through the central colonial government in Lagos and that of Dahomey in Porto Novo.

In the aftermath, Turaki was recalled to his position in Bussa. In Kaiama, Marshi was reinstated on his return from Yelwa. District Heads in Kaiama were removed wholesale and substituted. Bussa was, "handed over, lock stock and barrel to Yauri." Agwara District was amalgamated with Ngaski and all connection between Kunji and Bussa disengaged (NAK 1925).

Sabuke remained elusive, as he was protected by the vast woodland and his popularity among the people, particularly in Aliyara District and Shagunu. Borgu remained unsettled as another revolt broke out on the French side. There were increasing reports of refusals to pay taxes, movement of refugees across the frontier, armed robbery and the raid of caravans. This led to the request for another patrol in northern Borgu, less than six months after the last one. In December 1915, Sabuke was reportedly seen in Shagunu; allegedly preparing to attack Bussa again. Approval was given by Lugard for troops to be marshalled against the rebels. The troops marched to Shagunu, where they encountered feeble resistance from the rebel forces.

The Aftermath of the Revolt

With increasing instability, the colonial administration began a rethink of the situation and tried to make amends. They were beginning to come to terms with the reality of the crisis they had created. Crowder identified five major causes of the revolt: the administrative reorganisation led by Political Officer Clarke with the support of Resident Hamilton-Brown; the deposition of Kitoro Gani and the appointment of an ex-slave, Turaki, as his successor; the subjection and the significant loss of Bussa land to Yauri; an unsympathetic administration and obnoxious taxation. While the grievances of the rebels were not thoroughly addressed, a new understanding of the situation emerged with the appointment of a fresh Political Officer in place of Clarke. Through deliberate policy decisions and sometimes happenstance, some of the major grievances were resolved.

Turaki, the British-imposed District Head of Bussa, was removed and charged with double murder. He was sentenced to twelve years for each offence. This was later reduced to twelve years of imprisonment. The imprisonment of Turaki was a major respite for the people of Bussa. It was seen as a significant response to the grievances of the rebels. His removal as District Head of Bussa also provided the colonial authorities with a good opportunity to reform the Bussa Emirate. Turaki was replaced with Ki Jibrin, who though unpopular among the people of Bussa because of his support for Turaki, was a better candidate for the colonial authorities given the circumstances in Bussa. He was made a Second Class king after months of controversy on what class of chief to place him. After about six years of reign (1916 – 22), following persistent complaints by colonial officials about his "inefficiency" and poor leadership, he was removed, but not before Assistant District Officer T. Hoskyns-Abrahall's "regretful" conclusion that under Ki Jibrin, Bussa Emirate would never be anything but backward, unsatisfactory, dissatisfied and ridden with corruption, bribery and corruption.

With the deposition of Ki Jibrin, Kitoro Gani was restored to his kingdom after almost a decade in exile in Ilorin. This followed the dissolution of Kontagora Province and the ceding of Borgu to Ilorin Province. Kitoro had earlier been accused of being complicit in the Sabuke-led revolt, even if the authorities did not find any concrete evidence against him. He had been banished to Ilorin where he moved to with a large collection of *Iba* (coutiers/followers). His restoration created an early euphoria and optimism among the populace and the colonial officials. The District Officer acknowledged he was "exceedingly" popular and the "universal" rejoicing in Bussa. Kitoro Gani appears to have learned from his previous experience. He stopped drinking and was "efficient" in the colonial conception. He made some quick gains to the admiration of the colonial officials. His restoration was described by Governor Clifford as "a tardy act of justice" (Crowder 1973, 189). Herman-Hodge, the Resident in Ilorin, made a note of caution on the growing euphoria. While he agreed with the popularity of Kitoro Gani, he noted that he did not think Kitoro was strong and able "till he proves this to be the case." He, therefore, advised that the District Officer, Walter Nash, keep in touch with the Emir as his "duties in Kaiama will permit."

Within a short time, the colonial admiration for Kitoro began to wane. His official support and goodwill fizzled in less than a decade. He was eventually accused of a chain of offences – of being back to drunkenness and "peculation [embezzlement] from the Native Authority Treasury," fraud, poor administration of justice, obstruction of administrative processes and that "generally, he is surrounded by hangers-on whose intrigues he is always ready to assist, takes no interest in the administration of his Emirate and his efforts are directed to doing as little as possible and evading all his responsibilities" (Crowder 1973, 219). Consequently, he was once again deposed on the 25th of June 1935 and sent on exile to Mokwa in Niger Province. He was replaced by his brother, Babaki, who ruled till 1968.

Like Turaki, Marshi, the Acting District Head of Kaiama, and Abba, the notorious political agent, was brought to trial and deposed. Marshi was charged and tried for embezzlement and two other offences and given a consecutive sentence of two years and three years respectively in November 1916. After other considerations, including the possibility of deportation, Marshi had his sentence reduced to six months of imprisonment on all the three charges.

In Bussa, Abba and Aliu Sarkin Yauri were considered the architects of the crisis, including the first deposition of Kitoro Gaani and the consequent revolt. Abba was surely not different from most colonial political agents of that period. The colonial authorities in West Africa (British and French) recruited political agents or interpreters to support the administration. These agents used their positions as intermediaries to extort and built powerful influence in the colonial system. They threatened and blackmailed native authority officials, including emirs and chiefs, and extorted them (Crowder 1973). It was in this context that Abba's role was defined in Bussa. It appears that District Officer Clarke had relied heavily on Abba for all his reforms in Bussa. It was also clear that Abba connived with Yauri to undermine Bussa. He, therefore, played a significant role in the confiscation and ceding of parts of Bussa District to Yauri and Rofia and the whole controversy on seceding Bussa to Yauri. Abba did not stop at that. He moved Bussa's insignia of the aristocracy and traditional power to Yauri, including the *Kakaki* and royal drums among others. He also took an active part in the suppression of the rebellion.

Abba was eventually implicated in an investigation in Argungu Emirate. In 1913, the deposed Emir of Ngaski in Yauri Emirate, Umaru dan Aliu, wrote to the Lieutenant-Governor complaining that Abba always promised to give the Resident a good report about him, "not knowing that he was deceiving me, I always give him anything he asks for..." (Crowder 1973, 157). In 1916, Abba was also indirectly implicated in the trial of the District Head of Kunji before the Judicial Council of Yelwa for embezzlement. He was consequently dismissed from the administrative services and held for a trial covering several atrocities (Crowder 1973).

Another major gain of the revolt was the restoration of Bussa's lost lands. In 1919, Agwara, which had been administered as a sub-district of Ngaski, was returned to Bussa. After the dismantling of Kontagora Province, Yauri was made part of Sokoto Province. Following a protracted negotiation by colonial officials, Rofia was also transferred to Bussa from Yauri. With the return of Agwara, apart from gaining one hundred and forty-four square miles of its lost land, Borgu gained two thousand seven hundred and twenty-five people whose tax contributed to the increase in Native Authority revenue. These were significant gains in the colonial political economy of Borgu.

Amnesty for Sabuke and other Rebel Leaders

Ten years after the rebellion, Sabuke and other ringleaders remained elusive, under the protection of the vast land of Borgu and their teeming covert supporters. It was almost impossible to capture Sabuke and other rebel leaders in a two thousand square mile space where every single person was his "aider and abettor" (Crowder 1973). District Officer Diggle was the first to suggest an amnesty for Sabuke as part of the larger reconciliation effort. While relieving Joyce Cary in Kaiama, he wrote to the Governor-General requesting that Sabuke be granted amnesty. Recognising that Sabuke and his followers were "undoubtedly guilty of a grave offence," he drew the attention of the Governor-General to the fact that for the five previous years, no

Political Officer had been stationed at Bussa, with the exception of the period of a few months. Also, a slave had been appointed in succession to an "exceedingly long line of lawful heirs," setting the stage for the conflict. He further noted that enough punishment had already been meted out in the two patrols that had followed the rebellion. He concluded that the return of Sabuke would strengthen and popularize the resented Native Administration.

This request was rebuffed by the Acting Lieutenant-Governor, Goldsmith, who was not only surprised by the request, he didn't subscribe to the argument that Sabuke might never be captured or killed. He noted that not being able to track Sabuke down should not be seen as a weakness of the government. He felt amnesty would be a bad example for future rebels. "What an example to set to other victims of outlaws who have been the cause of unrest and crimes of violence?" he wondered (Crowder 1973; 170).

Joyce Cary, also, in one of his numerous letters to his wife before his departure from Borgu in 1919, noted that "I am trying here to get a noted rebel to surrender to me... I can't catch him ... he has been sitting in the bush for three years. One can't find a rebel in thousands of miles of bush with half a dozen police and all [the] people are his friends"(Crowder 1973, 172). He recognised that diplomatic efforts may not be acceptable to the colonial hierarchy in Lagos and Kaduna. He was, however, through private means, letting Sabuke know that "if he surrenders," he, Cary, would give Sabuke a "short sentence" (Crowder 1973, 172).

With the restoration of Kitoro Gani, amnesty for Sabuke became imminent. Eventually, almost a decade after the rebellion, on the 12th of May, 1924, Sabuke, wanted by Clarke and Hamilton-Brown for public execution as a lesson to future rebels, was pardoned and returned to Bussa. The conclusion of the authorities was that the rebellion was provoked by ill-conceived colonial policies. Sabuke, who was next in the line of succession to Kitoro Gani, made clear allegiance to his brother. The pardoning of Sabuke and other rebel leaders was, according to District Officer Hoskyns-Abrahall, the "natural sequence to the reinstatement of the Emir and a concluding chapter to the 1915 rebellion" (NAK 1925).

Revolt in French Borgu

The revolt in French Borgu occurred in 1916, about a year after the revolt in British Borgu. There isn't any evidence of coordination or a relationship between the two incidents, even if the underlying factors were largely the same. The difference could be only a matter of scale and the nature of the response. Western Borgu, controlled by the French, was largely more rebellious and had shown more resistance to colonial occupation than those in the central or eastern parts of Borgu. From looking at the principal characters involved and the issues in contention, the 1916 revolt can be seen as a continuum from the earlier resistance to colonial occupation.

The French Borgu revolt broke out during the First World War. During the period, France was already contending with a series of revolts in most of its West African colonies. Such revolts led to a temporary loss of administrative control over large segments of Mali, Upper Volta and Dahomey. These spates of revolts were directed principally against French recruitment and conscription of Africans into the military for the prosecution of the Second World War in Europe and the latent desire for independence from European control. Other reasons were the resentment of taxes, head-counting, forced labour and the appointment of chiefs without traditional rights to rule, as well as the breaking up of traditional political units to form colonial administrative structures expedient to the French. There was also an acute understanding that the French were faced with a bigger problem of war in their country as shown by the withdrawal of French citizens across West Africa to fight in Europe (Crowder 1978), and the sensing of opportunity.

As indicated earlier, French colonial policies had a more devastating impact on the Wasangari aristocracy of Borgu than did the British. The economy was shattered by the reorientation of trade and trade routes across Borgu and the social hierarchy that sustained the superiority of the aristocracy was dismantled as the Fulbe and the Gando did not only become independent of the aristocracy, the Fulbe, in particular, had their own political units almost similar to the indigenous Borgu people. The historical territorial and political formations were dismantled and new structures created, sometimes in deep conflict with the old. Nikki, a principal Borgu town and primary pre-colonial centre of power, became a minor player in the French colonial configuration, compared to its former provinces of Parakou and Kandi. As with the British administration, though, Borgu kings were appointed and deposed whimsically and sometimes subjected to the notorious French summary justice system. For instance, in 1902, the Sina Boko of Nikki used his turban to commit suicide in reaction to his imprisonment. The same year, the King of Sinade, Gunu Yerima, and some prominent princes including Mora Sabi, Gunu Tunku, Sankoro, Batiah Gobi, Deni and Kora were all jailed (Idris 1973).

Nature and Character of the Revolt

French parts of Borgu had kept a consistent, covert and small-scale, village-specific resistance to French occupation and colonial policies since the 1897 defeat of Borgu. However, until 1916, there wasn't any major revolt. Even when the revolt in British Borgu escalated, the French believed such a revolt couldn't happen in their own controlled territories, even if they showed some initial apprehension. In fact, in June 1915, when the revolt started in Bussa, Noufflord, the Lieutenant-Governor of Dahomey, wrote to the Governor-General in Dakar that the situation in *cercle* Borgu "remains good and besides our policy continues to maintain it in such a state, if not to improve it..." (Crowder 1978, 183).

Like the British, the revolt came to the French by surprise. Obviously, in this period, only incompetence, poor dialectics and understanding of context, racial arrogance and European contempt for Africans would make the French believe people could be that much trampled upon, abused and denigrated without any form of resistance. The revolt began in Gbekou, a Nikki village, thirty-five kilometres from the French post at Gbemgbereke. The post lay in between the two administrative centres of Parakou and Kandi to service the important north-south road.

The revolt was led by Bio Gbaasi Guerra (popularly called Bio Guerra, or Kaasè, his war name). He was the son of Sabi Yerima Baba and grandson of Kpe Gunu Gbassikpunon of the *Kwararu-Gbassi* dynastic branch of Nikki (Idris 1973). He had participated in the 1897 resistance to colonial occupation. Bio Guerra was the Chief of Gbekou

(Becou[61]) until 1905 when he was deposed by the French for disloyalty and hostility against colonial officials and was threatened with imprisonment but escaped and went into hibernation. The French weren't bothered by his disappearance. After all, Gbekou, his village, was not significant to their political calculations. A village head, Iribana, was appointed but never actually had direct access to the European political officers. Instead, one Ba-Gene was the pointsman. Ba-Gene claimed to have been appointed by the *Sina Boko* (King of Nikki) as the *sous chef de village* though he never had a recognised official position. He was, however, collecting taxes and interfacing regularly with the *chef de subdivision* in Gbemgbereke.

Bio Guerra reappeared in Gbekou after a decade and launched a violent campaign first against Ba-Gene whom he recognised as an impostor, and, thereafter, against the French colonial institution and infrastructure as a whole. Ba-Gene escaped to Gbemgbereke, the headquarters of the subdivision. What started as a local Gbekou issue escalated across all segments of French Borgu. The immediate reaction of the *chef du sub-division*, Duthoit, was to arrange for the immediate arrest or capture of Bio Guerra for trial at the *Tribunal de Cercle*. This was objected to by his superior, Ferlus, the *commandant de cercle*. Ferlus felt Duthoit was too inexperienced for such a delicate assignment. He, therefore, volunteered to use his "profound knowledge" of Borgu to deal with the issue (Crowder 1978). The problem lasted for several weeks without any action, until Bio Guerra invited Felix Vignox, the official interpreter in Gbemgbereke, who was then overseeing the subdivision as the European officer left to discuss the problem in Gbekou. This was agreeable to Ferlus. The two met and agreed on measures to return normalcy to the village. One of the measures was to appoint one of Bio Guerra's sons, considered loyal to the French, as the Village Head.

Without any concrete decision on this, Ferlus set out to travel to Gbekou. There, he called in on the 21st of September 1916, to report that he had been ambushed by rebel forces led by Bio Guerra. The details of what actually happened were not clear until after the investigation of the rebellion in 1919 by the Inspector-General of

---

[61] The village was called Becou in French colonial documents. Crowder, 1975, who did extensive work on the revolt, had therefore used the French colonial name of the village.

Colonies, Phèrivong. Only then did the details of what actually transpired come to light. It was realised that Ferlus actually misinformed Lieutenant-Governor Noufflard, an action for which he was punished. Crowder (1978) chronicled the incident as follows:

> Ferlus left Nikki with Baguene [Ba Gene] himself, Ali Bachabi [Ba Sabi], a *moniteur*, as interpreter, seven *gardes de cercle*, a convoy of porters and three cash-boxes with funds belonging to the administration. He by-passed Bembereke, going direct to Becou where he arrived on 17 September. There, he was installed in a hut belong(ing) to Bio Guerra, who in fact welcomed him. The *gardes de cercle* were lodged with Baguene in a compound some hundred metres from Ferlus' own hut. Ferlus did not forewarn Bio Guerra of his intention to arrest him but ordered him to come and see him. Meanwhile, Ba Gene had begun to threaten the villagers. So, at night on 18 September, Bio Guerra came to ask Ferlus to leave his house. The latter, however, was told by his cook that some people wanted to kill him. Ferlus in his report stated that he had then sent for his guards and while he was looking for his revolver in his baggage, he was wounded in the neck by an arrow. Believing his life to be threatened, he took flight, half-dressed, leaving his personnel to look after themselves, and abandoning baggages [sic] and the money in the cash-boxes. Like many villages in Borgu, Becou was 'fenced' by a hedge of thorns and he cut his legs scrabbling through them. It was established later that given the place where he had put his baggage in the hut, it would have been impossible for him to have been hit by an arrow while looking for his revolver (Crowder 1978, 184 -185).

The *gardes de cercle* that engaged Bio Guerra's men numbered about fifteen, not a hundred and fifty as reported by Ferlus. Two people were killed on the French side. One of Bio Guerra's brothers was killed and a number of his men injured. With the intervention of Ali Ba-Sabi, Ferlus' interpreter, calm was restored in Gbekou until Bio Guerra received information of an impending punitive expedition against Gbekou. Ferlus had earlier requested and received thirty *guards de cercle*and two thousand cartridges in Gbembereke on the 28th of September, 1916. The rebels reacted by cutting off all communication channels to Gbekou, destroyed the communication line with Bembereke and other outlets, attacked road construction workers, killed four persons, and boycotted European goods.

Deterioration and Suppression of the Revolt

Unlike what happened in British Borgu, the revolt did not attract a swift reaction for three reasons. First, being a centralised system, the process of deployment of the police and military had to go through a long bureaucratic channel. Second, the true state of the situation was not clear to the central authorities in Porto Novo and Dakar, as communication lines had been destroyed and most colonial officers were off-field. When Lieutenant-Governor Noufflard telegraphed Commandant Renard requesting the deployment of a platoon of the 9th Company, expected at Djougu· the latter only received the telegraph about five days later than the expected date. It took an additional two days for the platoon to arrive Gbembereke. The authorities, therefore, underestimated the magnitude of the revolt. Lastly, even if the magnitude of the revolt had been properly determined, there were other pressing demands on the small number of troops available to the French because of the Second World War. The French were also faced with other insurrections in other parts of its colonies, Dahomey in particular. The Somba of the Atakora to the north-east of Borgu and the Pila-Pila of the Senere and Ahori were involved in major revolts and the colonial authorities decided to prioritise those. The immediate commitment was, therefore, to first deal with the situation in Atakora before dealing with Borgu. "As soon as Atakora was dealt with, Semere and the Gbembereke should be tackled. Thereafter, the Ohori should be suppressed" (Crowder 1978, 186).

Guidelines and rules of engagement were an issue for troop deployment by Angoulvant, the Acting Governor-General in Dakar and a former Governor of Ivory Coast, notorious for repressive pacification. The expedition was expected to be a police action in character. The stated aim was to strike hard in order to avoid long or repeated strikes (Crowder 1978). The population was to be disarmed, for he believed there were too many guns in Dahomey. Uncharacteristic of Angoulvant, the use of arms was restricted to only when troops were attacked by the rebels. There should be no burning of villages and granaries and systematic destruction of crops. All fortifications, though, should be destroyed. Food confirmed to belong to the rebels could be used to feed the troops, but should not be looted.

Finally, deserted villages should by no means be destroyed (Crowder 1975).

The guidelines also provided the necessary conditions for submission or surrender, including total disarmament and destruction of arms, destruction of all fortifications, the capture, prosecution and imprisonment of all rebel leaders, collective fines for the rebelling communities, and payment of all outstanding taxes. Also, all young men involved in the rebellion would be forcefully enlisted as *tirailleurs*. Lastly, hostages should only be taken where they would serve a useful purpose.

Meanwhile, the situation in Gbembereke had rapidly deteriorated by the end of October 1916. Gbembereke had been attacked. A small hut near the *poste* had been burnt down by the rebels. Telegraph lines were destroyed and Gbembereke cut off from Kandi to the north and Parakou to the south. The three French men and forty-five gardes de cercle that defended Gbembereke were under siege, without water, food or the means of obtaining them. The rebellion now covered the two Borgu *cercles* (*Cercle* Borgou and *Cercle* Moyen Niger). Kandi, headquarters of *Cercle* Moyen Niger, was under serious threat.

In response to the deteriorating situation, a detachment of thirty-two *gardes de cercles* arrived at Gbembereke from Parakou on the 29th of October and managed to push back the rebels the following day. On the same day (30th of October), another detachment of five Europeans and one hundred and twelve African *tiraillers* from the 9th and 12th companies of the Senegalese *Tirailleurs* were received. In the first week of November, additional support was received from a detachment from Cotonou led by Sub-Lieutenant Kiempinski. At Berou-bouay, the escort was ambushed by the rebels and lost three African *tirailleurs* and seven were left with different injuries. This relatively high loss was attributed to the large number of rebels and poor discipline among the colonial forces (Crowder 1975). Apart from clearing the rebels from major towns, the colonial forces were also interested in clearing the rebel mounted road-blocks on major roads, particularly the one linking to the colony of Niger. This necessitated a change in their earlier plans of concentrating on Atakora. Borgu would now be prioritised.

The rebel forces were protected by their vegetation. Thick bushes and trees affected visibility and allowed the rebels to hide and ambush at will. Many of the villages were fortified by hedges of thorn trees. The rebels often engaged the French out of their villages, in difficult terrain, or by laying ambush on the rear or flank sides of their columns navigating the thick bushes. Obviously, compared to the colonial forces, the rebels were poorly armed. "They rarely used artificial defences like stone walls or stockades. Their bowmen placed themselves either in groups without any natural or artificial protection or behind large trees. Their arms were limited to a few trade guns, for which they lacked powder, and to bows and arrows which were usually poisoned" (Crowder 1975, 110).

According to Crowder, there were three major groups of rebels to contend with. The first were those who disrupted the communication between Kandi and the Niger, largely around the canton of Begou. The second were disrupting communication in Atakora around the Gbembereke –Bérou Bouay-Sinendo area. The third group were located in the Gbekou-Nikki area. Although the last didn't present any strategic threat like the first two, they were considered important because that was the area where Chabi (Sabi) Purukaru, King of Nikki, had substantial influence (Crowder 1975).

In response, French forces were deployed in two columns. The first consisted of two hundred and twenty-five *tiraillers* and eleven *gardes de cercles*. They were responsible for securing Kandi and re-opening the Niger road. The second column was to deal with the Gbembereke-Berou bauay-Sinende area. The first column arrived at Kandi on the 25th of November, 1916, and received reinforcements of an additional ninety *tiralleurs* from Niger. By the end of the operations, four *tiralleurs* had been killed. The number of rebels killed was not determined but it was believed to be large, considering the disproportionate use of force. According to *Administrateur* Géay, "the disproportion between the enormous number of cartridges fired by the French forces and the resulting damage; 9,000 cartridges at Agbo for seven or eight victims" on the French side (Crowder 1975). The second column lost one European sergeant and two *tiralleurs*, with three others injured.

After completing their missions, the two columns joined forces at Gbembereke with a section of artillery and set off for the rebels at the epicentre of Bio Guerra's rebellion, based in the Gbekou area. The French forces engaged Bio Guerra's forces at Baoura on the 17th of

December, 1916. The fierce fight was believed to have lasted an hour and twenty minutes. At the end of the battle, forty-two rebels, including Bio Guerra, his friend Sanni Guiso, Sounour Ouorou, who was the former Chief of Ouari, and Kwara Goumbo of Sikki village, were killed (Idris 1973). Only three members of the French force were reported wounded. Bio Guerra drew substantial support from Sabi Purukaru, the King of Nikki, who tried to mobilise Borgu-wide support with limited success. He also received support from the Gbasso area, which spread up to the frontier with British Borgu. This area was largely dominated by Boko people, Bio Guerra's ethnic group. Some of his brothers, Bagidi Kutu from Gberigbe village and Bio Bubari of Dari village, were part of the leadership of the revolt.

The revolt that started on the 21st of September effectively ended on the 24th of December, 1916, when Sabi Purukaru the King of Nikki, was arrested. However, up until the middle of 1917, there were still pockets of resistance to contend with. In fact, the French forces ambushed and killed a number of alleged rebel forces on the banks of the River Tansinet, some forty kilometres from Gbembereke, in an outrageous carnage. They captured thirteen rebels, ten rifles, sixty bows and some two thousand arrows. Several Borgu people deserted their villages and crossed over the frontier while some took refuge on the borders of Djougou and Parakou *cercles*. Up to August 1917, requests were being received for mop-up exercises in the bushes north of Nikki.

Aftermath of the Revolt

Unlike the British Borgu revolt, where the principal character survived, in French Borgu, Bio Guerra and all the major rebel leaders died. The rebellion lasted longer in duration of violence though it closed more quickly than the one in Nigeria. With the effective suppression of the insurrection, the French colonial authorities concentrated on ensuring submission and disarmament. The King of Nikki was arrested, although he managed to escape and was re-arrested. Sabi Purukaru was summarily convicted and exiled in Guinea for five years. The villages that participated in the rebellion were forced to pay for damages. They were charged in "proportion" to their level of involvement. At the close of disarmament in June 1918, three thousand, two hundred and twenty-seven (3,227) bows, sixty thousand, three hundred and six (60,306) arrows and thirty-three (33) guns were recovered and destroyed in *Cercle* Moyen Niger. In *Cercle* Borgu, twenty-seven thousand four hundred and fifty-six (27,456) bows and two hundred and five thousand, three hundred and thirty-three (205,333) arrows, seven hundred and twenty-five (725) rifles were also destroyed.

The revolt further confirmed to the French the influence of the King of Nikki and compelled them to begin to reconsider their relationship with the local political institutions. Part of the evidence against Sabi Purukaru, Sorokou Komani, a son of Bio Guerra, was reported to have alleged that the King of Nikki sent a message to his father stating his awareness of the incident in Gbekou and declaring war against the white people. The French believed the rebellion spread because it had the support of the King of Nikki.

Phérivong's report on the rebellion, issued in February 1919, was quite revealing. He observed that had the French administration paid better attention and appreciated the pre-colonial powers of the King of Nikki, the revolt would not have spread that much. He, therefore, recommended that the position of the King of Nikki be reconsidered, to provide more space, recognition and respectability. To win back the people of Borgu, he recommended that taxes should be assessed with greater care on affordability, that all labour should be properly and regularly remunerated. Effective and friendly actions should be taken, that words should be replaced by action, education and water should be provided for communities and children should be saved from malaria. Imported goods should be made available to the communities by providing free transport. Lastly, that French Borgu should be opened up for development (Crowder 1975).

CHAPTER EIGHT

Amalgamation of Bussa and Kaiama Emirates

The amalgamation of the emirates of Kaiama and Bussa in 1954 was the last major restructuring of the two Borgu polities before independence from colonial rule. As examined in chapter 6 and 7, all through the colonial period, Borgu was generally unstable. It went through a number of structural changes and passed through different forms of reorganisation. This spanned from being a province of its own headquartered at Kaiama to being a division under Kontagora and later on Ilorin. The NA structure also changed incessantly with the headquarters alternating between Bussa and Kaiama. The 1954 amalgamation was momentous as it redefined the politics of Borgu and probably shaped the political and social relationships across the entire Nigerian Borgu through the remaining years of colonial rule and unto the post-colonial period.

With the amalgamation, the Emirate of Kaiama was abrogated and Kaiama became a district under the new Borgu Emirate and Native Authority. It was the first time an overarching Emir was appointed for the entire Nigerian Borgu, apart from the brief period when Mora Tasude served in a similar role, though he was never designated "Emir of Borgu." He was only the most senior in the colonial political hierarchy. With this, Kaiama was made a peer of its own former districts such as Gwanara, Okuta, Ilesha and Yashikira, which had been regrouped to form a subordinate Native Authority with headquarters in Okuta. It was the most difficult moment of the colonial history of Kaiama. It was almost similar to the experience of Bussa in 1915 when it was placed under Yelwa with the Emirate of Bussa degraded and a former slave, Turaki, appointed as District Head.

To be sure, the reform had been long in coming. The idea had always been on the radar. It was earlier suggested by Resident Daniel in 1939 but was never implemented. During the period of uncertainty of Borgu in 1915, Political Officer Clarke had contemplated merging the two emirates under the Emir of Kaiama, before the Yelwa option was adopted. Again, in 1917, when Bussa was to be demerged from Yauri, Resident Hamilton-Brown proposed that Kaiama, Okuta, Ilesha and Yashikira be made districts of Bussa Emirate, but this was not followed through. It was also suggested in the 1920s that, on the death of Emir Haliru Ki-Yaru, Kaiama Emirate be abolished and merged with Bussa (Crowder 1978). However, the Emir was too young and he lived to see several colonial officials come and go. In between those periods, his paramountcy remained and he, on several interregnums, led Borgu as the only Emir.

Grading and degrading emirs/emirates was not new in the northern Nigerian provinces. Any time such an exercise was conducted, it was always a bitter pill for the affected communities. That was the case for Kaiama in 1954, as it was for Bussa when it was placed under Yelwa and had always been the case for the Baatonu people who resented their placement under the suzerainty of Kaiama. The way the process of amalgamation was managed by the colonial officers, particularly the District Officer, his official interpreter, and the Resident in Ilorin, further compounded the entrenched animosity between the different segments of Borgu, particularly the triangular conflict of Baatonu people in the south-west, Kaiama at the centre and Bussa in the north.

The politics of this period has been deeply localised, resulting in simplistic and often emotive narratives based on the interest of each of the conflicting parties. To understand this situation, it is important to look at it from a broader context of Northern Nigeria during this period. Particularly, the events since Tafawa Balewa's famous legislative motion on the reform of Native Authorities in 1950.

Abdication of Emir of Kaiama

Crucial to the amalgamation was the abdication and retirement of the Emir of Kaiama, Haliru Ki-Yaru II. The Emir retired, ostensibly due to old age. However, evidence and development in other parts of northern Nigeria suggests it was a cajoled abdication. His resignation was apparently instigated by the colonial authorities, particularly the District Officer, M. J. Campbell. The Emir abdicated during the Native Authority Council meeting on the 30th of June, 1954. It was an emergency meeting, without a particular agenda. His resignation was accepted and he was congratulated for his over 34 years of service. The council resolved that he be presented with a letter of commendation. The District Head of Okuta was appointed interim Chair immediately the Emir of Kaiama left the council meeting. With the departure of the Emir, the meeting deliberated on two important issues – the future of Emir Haliru and Kaiama Emirate (NAK 1954).

The meeting couldn't initially agree on the place of retirement for the Emir. The popular sentiment was for him to be sent on exile, which was actually the tradition in the northern region. Some of the members feared that he could still meddle in the affairs of the emirate. It took the intervention of the District Officer for him to be allowed to retire to his personal home in Kaiama. While agreeing that exile was the common tradition, he noted that the Emir hadn't committed any offences and he was too old to be an exile for no reason at all. Therefore, on condition that he would not interfere in the affairs of Kaiama, it was agreed that he should be allowed retirement in Kaiama (NAK 1954). The meeting also resolved to place him on a "generous" pension of two hundred and thirty pounds per annum and an additional twenty pounds as a mark of appreciation. His residence was also to be renovated at the expense of the Native Authority (NAK 1954).

On the future of Kaiama Emirate, the council resolved to abrogate the Emirate and merge it with Bussa under the leadership of the Emir of Bussa. In essence, Kaiama would become a district of Bussa. A new composition of the Native Authority Council was defined. The meeting resolved to quickly hold an extraordinary joint council meeting with Bussa the following day. The entire meeting appeared to have been dominated by the four District Heads from western Borgu and District Officer Campbell. The lone voice of *Ubandoma* Umaru

Babe couldn't contain the choreographed voices of affirmation in the Council. While he voted against the abrogation of Kaiama Emirate, twenty other members of the Council voted for it[62]. The Council appointed three people, Bio Kaugi, Sidi Umaru and *Malamin Sarki* (Secretary of Council), to convey its decisions to the general public (NAK 1954).

The joint meeting of Kaiama and Bussa Emirate held the following day, the 31st of July 1954, at Wawa, where the Kaiama decision was endorsed. The Joint Council recommended the creation of a subordinate Native Authority Council and a Treasury for the Baatonu districts of Yashikira, Gwanara, Okuta and Ilesha, to be based in Okuta. They also resolved on the details of representation and membership of both the Native Authority Council in Bussa and those of the Sub-Native Authority Council (NAK 1954).

****

There are conflicting arguments on the abdication of Emir Haliru. While his sympathisers, largely from Kaiama, believe he resigned voluntarily, those against him, predominantly from Bussa and the four Baatonu Districts of Kaiama Emirate, argued that he was compelled to resign by the Council or "forced to relinquish his position as the Chairman of the Native Authority Council" (Lafia 2006). Evidence from other places and the colonial archives indicate both. The Emir had apparently discussed his resignation with the District Officer even before the Council meeting. That was what informed the call for the emergency meeting. He, therefore, was not compelled to resign during the Council meeting. The first paragraph in the minutes of the Council meeting states thus:

Shugaba, Sarkin Kaiama ya tashi ya bude majalisa da gaisuwar murna don yin ban kwana da barin sarautar Kaiama, ya gode wa Saraunia, Gominan [sic] Ikko da Leftanan Gomina (sic), Resident na

---

[62] Among them were the District Heads of Ilesha, Gwanara and Yashikira; the Village Heads of Gwette and Boriya, Dade Wajibe, Boro Gwanabe, Woru Bare Gwassoro and Bio Kaugi. Others were the Sarkin Fulani of Gwanara, Yashikira, and Ilesha; Suno Boro, Kotoyari, Sidi Umaru, Waru Bae Suya (siya?); Zume Gere, Abdu Banara, Sabi Gobo, Alkali.

Ilorin, D. O. na Borgu ... ya ce yau ya bari [sic]) bisa kan ransa... kuma shi yayi sarauta misali [read *kimani*] *shekara 34... bai yi wani laifi ba, da yake shi ya gani, ya tsufa shi yasa ya roki futun [hutu] cewa shi ya gaji* (NAK 1954).

Translation: The Emir of Kaiama and Chairman of the council opened the meeting with warm greetings to express his farewell to the council. He thanked the Queen of England, the Governor in Lagos (Governor-General), the Lieutenant-Governor, the Resident in Ilorin and the D.O. of Borgu. He stated that he resigned on personal volition. He reigned for 34 years. He didn't commit any offence. He only realised he was getting old and, therefore, requested that he be allowed to rest.

The decision to resign was surely instigated before the Council meeting. In conveying the resignation of the Emir to the Resident on the 5th of August, 1954, the District Officer of Borgu referred to their earlier correspondence, two weeks before the Council meeting. He wrote:

Referring to correspondence ending with your telegram No. GEN.106089 of the 17th of July, I have the honour to inform you that Haliru Ki-Yaru resigned his office as Emir of Kaiama in the presence of the full Kaiama Native Authority Council on the 30th of July. The Emir expressed his deep regret that increasing age had obliged him to sever the very friendly relationships which he had had with the Administration since his appointment in 1921 and requested me to convey to his Honour the Lieutenant-Governor and His Excellency the Governor the expression of his gratitude for the marks of trust and friendship which they and their predecessors had shown him during his long tenure of office (NAK 1957).

In further indication of a coerced resignation, in the same correspondence, the D.O. stated that, "in accordance with the instructions contained in your telegram referred above, I accepted the Emir's resignation on His Honour's behalf and expressed the regret which His Honour and the Northern Regional Government feel at the Emir's decision" (NAK 1954).

Historically, in Kaiama and the larger Borgu, kings never abdicate. There is no history of resignation. The king either died (naturally or by suicide) or was violently removed from power. In most cases, such violent removals ended up with the death of the king. Ki-Yaru's abdication was, therefore, unnatural. There is also no indication that Ki-Yaru had discussed his impeding resignation with anybody, not even his brother the *Ubandoma,* who was the most senior in council after the Emir. At barely 70 years of age, he was not too old for an Emir[63]. For those who knew the Emir, it was not in his character to abdicate. Generally, leaders with strong personalities and an authoritarian mien don't abdicate. They could only be compelled by more powerful forces, individual or collective.

Secondly, a similar trend of forced abdication was reported in other parts of northern Nigeria during this period. The Emir of Argungu, Mohammed Suma'ila, in 1953; the *Lamido* of Adamawa, Ahmadu, in 1952; and the *Shehu* of Dikwa, Mustapha Ibn Mohammad, are examples. The *Atta* of Ebira, Ibrahima, and the Emir of Bauchi, Yakubu III, both suffered similar fates in 1954 (Yakubu 2006). Instigated abdication or abdication under duress was the trend during the period. To be sure, the abdication of Ki-Yaru was probably inspired by these earlier abdications in other parts of Northern Nigeria. In the course of the debate on the retirement of Ki-yaru in the Native Authority Council, the District Officer quickly provided the examples of four Emirs who had abdicated within the period. He specifically mentioned Argungu, Yola (Adamawa), Dikwa and the Atta of Ebira (NAK 1954).

Thirdly, the Native Authority Council meeting appears choreographed. Some of the Council members had prior information about the impending resignation of the Emir of Kaiama and had been prepared to call for the abrogation of Kaiama Emirate. Principal among the instigators was the District Officer, M. J. Campbell, who was said to be a friend of Aliyu Kperogi, the District Head of Okuta as well as the interpreter, Usman Dera, who, like most colonial interpreters and local political agents, enjoyed the confidence of the District Officer. Based on this prior information, it was reported that most members of the Council, particularly those of Baatonu extraction in the four districts of Kaiama emirate, held a preparatory meeting in

---

[63] Haliru Ki-Yaru was to live for another 31 years. He died in 1985.

Kosubosu (a junction village leading to Kaiama)[64]. The meeting in Kosubosu was to build a consensus on interim leadership of the Council and on the decision to dissolve the Native Authority. Although the Emir of Kaiama was the leader of the emirate, the majority of the inhabitants of the emirate were Baatonu. Of the five districts, four were predominantly Baatonu and former Nikki provinces who have since the inception of colonial resisted their sunordination to Kaiama leadership. Their dominance of the Native Authority Council and the sympathy of the District Officer played an important role in the decision to abrogate the emirate, not necessarily abdication of the emir. From the munites of the meeting, the discussion and decisions were skewed and the interventions of the District Officer appeared premeditated as would be seen later.

****

The reason for the forced abdication was not clear from the colonial documents. The earlier conversation between the District Officerand the Resident wasn't properly documented in the archives. However, looking at developments in other parts of northern Nigeria where similar abdications had occurred, it can be associated with two issues: autocratic rule and the quest for reform. Autocratic rule, which the colonial authorities prompted, nurtured and supported in exerting control, ensuring effective collection of tax and recruitment of forced labour, had become unfashionable among the colonial officers and the emerging counter-elites, especially in the 1950s. These educated counter-elites had, through the instrumentality of modern political institutions, pushed for reform and liberalisation of the Native Authority system. Starting from Tafawa Balewa's motion in the Regional House of Assembly, all through the successive conferences, the tendency was to democratise the system and institute effective participation of the people. Despite the earlier changes in the system in relation to the emirs and their councils, the emirs continued to rule

---

[64] Kosubosu was a usual rendeveour for most Baatonu officials on there way to Kaiama for NA related engagement. Although located in Yashikira District, it was also seen to be central location for the four Baatonu districts. Because of its centrality it eventually become the Local Government Headquaters of Barutem, in Kwara state Nigeria.

personally, with limited participation of their councils. Pushing through this reform had been difficult with the older emirs, often referred to as the "old guard" (Yakubu 2006).

The socalled "purges of the early 1950s" were thus a part of the push for reform. The colonial authorities were saddled with the contradictory task of liberalising the autocratic institution they created (Yakubu 2006). The idea was to move from the Lugardian structure to a more liberal and democratic local governance system. The likes of Emir Yakubu III of Bauchi, *Attah* of Igala, Umaru Ame Oboni, *Atta* of Ebira, Ibrahima, Mai Abba Masta (Mustapha III), the *Shehu* of Dikwa, as well as Mohammed Sheshe, Emir of Argungu who, like his predecessor, Mohamadu Sama'ila, was forced to abdicate, are examples of traditional rulers caught up in this paradox. The official explanation for removing these emirs and chiefs was the reform of the Native Authority system embarked upon, starting at the end of the Second World War. The old guard were considered obstructive to this purpose. Emir Haliru Ki-Yaru was a quintessential Lugardian emir and a classic old guard. His abdication, in that period, was, therefore, not as unusual as it might first seem.

The push for new colonial reform required that he was pushed aside. He couldn't easily be removed because he had served the colonial authorities well at the point of their need. Also, he still commanded a level of respect within the colonial hierarchy and was considerably too old to be sent on exile. In the reckoning of the colonial officers, he was not a significant threat to their interests even though the emir had an authoritarian hold on the emirate and didn't enjoy a good relationship with District Officer Campbell and his official interpreter, Usman Dera. The District Officer, in consultation with the Resident, pressed for reforms that had been originally abandoned. In instigating the changes, in a manner typical of a divide-and-rule strategy, the District Officer found good partners in the chiefs of Baatonu, who historically resented their subordination to Kaiama.

For the Baatonu District Heads and their people, 1954 was the year of liberation from Kaiama domination and those who instigated it were understandably heroes[65]. They had dramatically secured their independence even before the national independence from colonial

---

[65] Key informant Interview in Abuja, December, 2017

rule. For the Bussa people, Kaiama had been placed in its "rightful place." Kaiama's equivalence and even intermittent seniority over the emirate of Bussa through the colonial period had been a major source of resentment. Kaiama and Bussa were of the same ethnic category and evidently of the same ancestry. Before colonial rule, there was no significant history of conflict between the two. Although Kaiama entrusted itself to Nikki in the eighteenth and nineteenth centuries, this was probably because of the decline of Bussa. 1954 heralded Kaiama's worst colonial experience. They had been humbled, devastated and exposed to the scorn and humiliation of the Baatonu and Bussa adversaries. It, however, appears that the people of Kaiama were not necessarily concerned about the abdication of the person, Ki-Yaru, as his iron-fistedrule did not exempt them - a lot of Kaiama people, including some first generation educated people, left Kaiama because of him. Considering the internal politics of the Kaiama ruling class, it appears they were only worried about the drop in the status of the emirate and invariably, the status of their community[66].

Although this was not the first reform in Nigerian Borgu, it was the most devastating for Kaiama. As with the case of Bussa being placed under Yauri, different conspiracy theories and myths were bound to be minted. The so-called colonial reforms were interpreted as a personal attack by the District Officer against Emir Haliru. Similar to Political Officer Abba during the Bussa crisis, Usman Dera was believed to have played an important role in instigating Campbell who can be likened to Clarke during the Bussa crisis. For Kaiama, the reform smirked of vindictiveness and political malice. At the end of the day, the reform process was mismanaged by divergent interests. The entire process was clumsy and explicably consumed by the local politics and had become a defining moment in the politics of the region as would been seen in chapter 10.

The Emergence of Borgu Emirate

After the approval process from the Resident in Ilorin to the Office of Local Government and Community Development in Kaduna, Borgu Native authority was effectively instituted on the 8th of August, 1954.

---

[66] Key informant interview in Kaiama, December, 2017

The three major recommendations of the Kaiama Native Authority Council meetings and those of the Extraordinary Joint Meeting of Bussa and Kaiama were:

I. That no successor be appointed for the Emir of Kaiama.
II. The Emirates of Kaiama and Bussa be amalgamated and known as Borgu Emirate.
III. The Emir of Bussa be appointed the Emir of Borgu(NAK 1954).

All three recommendations were approved. It would appear the approval was just a formality as the District Officer and the Resident already had an understanding of the issues. In one of their correspondences, District Officer Campbell stated that he was in agreement with the three recommendations for reasons given in earlier correspondence. In his words "I support these recommendations for the reasons given in correspondence ending with your confidential letter No. 29735/s./SO/18 of the 3rd of November, 1953, and in my secret letter No.528/16 of the 18th of July" (NAK 1954). This indicates that processes leading to the decision started almost a year ealier. Typically, the Native Authority Councils were only used to ratify decisions already taken by British colonial officers, to give local legitimacy. It was, therefore, no surprise that the protestations against the decision, particularly by the Kaiama elite, received little attention in both Ilorin and Kaduna. District Officer Campbell did not, however, fail to address the protesters in his message during the launch of the Borgu Native Authority and its Western Subordinate Authority in Okuta on the 8th of August, 1954. He observed, in his speech written in Hausa:

> *Tun ran da aka kawo wannan shawara cewa a hada kasar Kaiama da Kasar Bussa, akwai wadansu mutane wadanda suka rubuta wasikoki zuwa Sardauna (primiya) da Gwamna cewa su kam basu yarda da wannan shawara ba. In so in sanarda kucewa lalle an duddubi wasikokin nan, an kuma binciki abin da aka fada, amma aka ga wadanna dallilai da aka ambata ba za su isa a saki tunani akan wannan alamari ba.*

Translation: Since the recommendation for the amalgamation of the two emirates, there have been a series of petitions to the Sardauna, Premier of Northern Nigeria and the Governor expressing disapproval. The issues have been investigated and it has been confirmed that their petitions weren't strong enough to warrant a reconsideration of the decision taken.

For the first time since the insititution of colonial rule, Borgu now had a single emirate and Native Authority. The new Borgu Native Authority Council consisted of the Emir of Borgu as ex-officio President; two titled members of the then Bussa Native Authority as ex-officio members (namely the Ubandoma and Galadima of Bussa); one titled member of the defunct Kaiama Emirate; an advisor on Shari'ah as well as fifteen elected members and four cattle-owning Fulbe as members. In connecting tax to representation, each elected member of the NA was to represent approximately one thousand taxpayers. The representation matrix was, therefore, stated as follows:

Table 6: Tax and Representation

EMIRATE	DISTRICT	NO OF ADULT MALES PAYING GENERAL TAX 1954	NO OF ELECTED PRESENTATIVE PROPOSED
KAIAMA	Yashikira	1,341	1
	Okuta	1,752	2
	Ilesha	590	1
	Gwanara	1,035	1
	Kaiama	1, 289	1
BUSSA	Wawa	1,273	1
	Bussa	1,164	1
	Agwara	4,941	5
	Aliyara	1,735	2
TOTAL		15,171	15

(**Source**: NAK 1954)

The new composition was very different from the previous one. The emphasis was on representation by elections. Unelected Heads of Department, District Heads and Village Heads were excluded from the new Native Authority.

A subordinate Native Authority for Western Borgu was instituted to mitigate the challenge of the great distance between that area and Bussa. It wasn't in consideration of the Nikki connection, as stated by Crowder (1973). The District Officer explained the reasons for the Sub-Native Authority as follows:

Tun da yake wadansu kasashe kamar su Okuta, Yashikira, Gwanara da Illesha suna da nesa da Bussa kwarai da gaske, za a yi wata karamar majalisna ikon wadansu kanana abubuwa, amma tana karkashin majilisar kasar Borgu duka.
Bayan haka, za a kafa wani karamin Beit-el mal a Okuta in da za a karba kudi da inda za a biya kudi. Amma Beit-el nan yana karkashin babban Beit –el na Kasar Borgu.

Translation: Considering the immense distance between some districts and Bussa, particularly Okuta, Yashikira, Gwanara and Ilesha, a subordinate council has been instituted to handle minor issues, but under Borgu Native Authority. It will also have a small treasury to deal with payments also under the larger Borgu Native Authority.

Distance had always been a major consideration. This had made all the previous attempts to merge the emirates difficult. As indicated in chapter 4, distance was what informed the relocation of the Borgu Provicial capital from Kaiama to Bussa. The descision to have two emirate in one colonial Division was still a result of distance.

The members of the Sub-Native Authority encompassed Gwanara, Ilesha, Okuta and Yashikira in that alphabetical order and were called the Federal Council (NAK 1954). The Council had ten elected members and four cattle-owning Fulbe to be nominated by their members. The President of the Sub-Native Authority was to be elected by simple majority vote of the council. The representation of the districts was on the basis of one elected member for every five hundred adult male tax payers.

From Emir to District Head: Kaiama in a New Era

The apprehension and distress of Kaiama was not just the abrogation of the Native Authority and their subordination to Bussa they were also concerned about the appointment of a leader, whether as an Emir or a District Head. Although the Native Authority Council decision had recommended that no successor should be appointed to Ki-Yaru, it didn't mean that Kaiama would be without a leader. The difference was that the new leader would be a District Head (*Hakimi*), just like the other four Districts of the erstwhile Kaiama Native Authority. It is important to note that "emir" and "emirate" were official designations or titles and territory in the Muslim provinces of northern Nigerian. People don't necessarily address their kings or community leaders in such titles, not even in the former Sokoto Caliphate where the colonialists first instituted the designation, drawing from the Arabian title of *Amir'ul Muminin (*leader of the faithful*)*. Hausa still called their kings *Sarki*, irrespective of their hierarchy. District Heads were called *Hakimai* (sing. *Hakimi*).

In Borgu, the difference between an emir and a district head was only in the political structure and hierarchy defined by the colonial authorities. The so-called Districts Heads were members of dynasties that had historical control over sometimes autonomous political formations that predated the colonial period. Therefore, what was referred to as Districts of Kaiama, were in fact principalities or territories with some notions of self-determination and autonomy. This was actually the basis for the Baatonu chiefs' resistance to their subjugation to Kaiama and the basis for Kaiama's resistance to the new Borgu emirate. Therefore, in Kaiama the leader remained *dii /kina*, whether as district head or emir.

Based on this context, Kaiama was surely going to have a successor to Ki-Yaru, just not as a second-class graded emir in the colonial hierarchy with political control over four District Heads. The delay in the appointment of a successor was, therefore, a major concern for the people. It would appear the colonial authorities delayed the appointment until the conclusion of the reforms of the Native Authority – the effective dissolution of Kaiama Native Authority and the institution of the new Borgu Native Authority structure. Kaiama, therefore, didn't have a leader until the 4th of February, 1955[67] when Umaru Bagidi, the then *Ubandoman* Kaiama

---

[67] The appointment was actually approved by the Governor on the 22nd of January 1955, but the official announcement was made on the 4th of February 1955.

and younger brother of Ki-Yaru, was appointed District Head[68]. That was almost seven months after the abdication of the last Emir. The unprecedented leadership vacuum understandably created huge apprehension not only in the deserving princes but also in the entire community. Rumours were rife that no emir would be appointed or that a foreign person would be installed. The case of Marshi Koro, a non indigenous emir appointed to the throne, was still fresh in the people's mind.

The delay in appointing a successor attracted a series of protestations to the colonial authorities in Bussa, Ilorin and Kaduna. These protest letters and petitions were written by individuals, interest groups and, sometimes, hurriedly formed organisations. One of such interest groups, *Jam'iyyar Chin [cin] Gaban Kasar Kaiama* (Kaiama Development Party) noted in their petition[69] to the District Officer on the 19th of August, 1954:

Munji shirin da ake ciki game da Borgu, tunde shi ke Gwamna bai yi approve abinda aka shirya ba tukun, muna so a nada mana sabon sarki (Emir Temporary) a Kaiama (NAK 1954).

Translation: Since the government is yet to approve the reforms, we request that you appoint a new/interim Emir.

Another group, *Talakawan Kaiama*, had earlier written to the District Officer demanding an explanation on the decision of the Kaiama Native Authority Council on why a second-class grade Emir would not be appointed for Kaiama (NAK 1954).

Despite the protest messages from different angles, there were also those who surreptitiously supported the decision of the Native Authority Council. In an apparent move to endear himself to the colonial authorities, Mallam Suleiman, *Dangaladima* of Kaiama and the Native Authority Treasurer, wrote to the District Office on the 23rd of August, 1954.

Ni Mallam Sule na goyi bayan shawarar da ... Gwamnati suka kawo duka, da dukan abin da suka umarta akan al'amarin Borgu, da ni da

---

[68] He took the title *Ki-Yaru*, even when the former Ki-Yaru was still alive. On the throne he was popularly known as *Suno Suru*.

[69] The petition was signed by the Assistant Secretary, Sale Omar.

mutane na mun goyi bayan shawarar da gwamnati suka kawo. Nine shugaba ban ko yi tsamani mutanen kauye za su iya ki Magana na ba, ko da shike ni talaka ne, amma na goyi bayan gwamnati da Kaiama ta bi Bussa..."(NAK 1954).

Translation: I, Mallam Sule, and my followers endorse the decision of the government on the changes in Borgu. I agree that Kaiama be subordinated to Bussa. I don't think people from the villages will fail to follow my instructions.

To be sure, Sulaiman *Dangaladi* was eminently qualified. He did indicate interest in the throne even before the appointment of Ki-Yaru in 1921 but lost out on the basis of age[70]. He was the first member of the royal family of Kaiama to receive Western Education. Through his attachment to the Royal Niger Company Sales Manager in Gbajibo from 1909 – 1916, he learnt English, Arithmetic and basic Book Keeping. On return to Kaiama, he was deservedly appointment the *Ma'aji* (treasurer) of Kaiama Native Authority (Yakubu and Jumare 1997).

Ahmadu Yaru Mora Tasude actually wrote to the District Officer on the 25th of November, 1954, requesting that he be made the Emir, asserting that he had the support of the people "... *jama'ar ... Kaiama birni da kauye sun goyi bayana da samun sarautar Kaiama. Saboda haka ina son ku taimakeni da samun gadon uba* [na].**Translation**: I have the support of Kaiama and its villages. As a result, I request that you help me ascend the throne of my forefathers.

Even after the appointment of the new District Head, there were a few cases of protest, particularly by one Alfa Sule, who wrote from Ibadan. He had persistently questioned the appointment on the basis of alleged "literacy and incompetence" of the new emir, until his petition was dismissed by the colonial authorities (NAK 1955)

****

Another interesting development during this period was the relationship between the new District Head and the former Emir who

---

[70] He was considered too young and his experience in Book Keeping was apparently needed for the Native Authority Treasury.

was on retirement. Surely, Kaiama had never had a situation where two kings were situated in the same city. When Sabi Ba-Yaru (Gimba) was dethroned in 1915, he was sent on exile to Wawa. As stated before, ordinarily, kings don't abdicate. Even if they were compelled to do so, they often left their domains to avoid the situation of a real or perceived power tussle between the successor and his predecessor. There was virtually no king in Ki-Yaru's era, and even after, that enjoyed such a privilege. As it turned out, he had lasted all through two succeeding emirs without any major challenge. However, during the early period of his retirement, especially within the first year, the District Head had to contend with a lot of issues. Some of these bordered on his personal fears, perceptions and understandable discomfort at being on a throne under the watchful eyes of his predecessor who had ruled over an even bigger domain for over three decades. There were stories about the friction between the two brothers. While most were at the level of the community, some were bigger and have been documented.

Although it wasn't an issue that people in Kaiama liked to freely discuss, it was clear that beyond their animosity with the Baatonu districts, some princes of Kaiama would have supported the exile of Ki-Yaru. It was reported that several of the princes of Kaiama didn't show interest in the throne because of the fear of being under the watchful eyes of the former Emir. Those who did consider the possibility of still having him go on exile. The first official issue between the new District Head and Ki-yaru was a complaint about some missing royal regalia. He complained to the Borgu Native Authority Council that three important pieces of Kaiama regalia were missing – including: "*Ragar zinariya* [golden dress], *shirdi da likafa* [horse saddle and stirrup], and *gadon Karfe* [metal/steel bed]". The Council, therefore, wrote to the former Emir on the 24th of April, 1956, requesting that those items be returned immediately (NAK 1956). It isn't clear whether the items were returned as the issue was never documented after that.

On the 17th of October 1956, the District Head again complained about the political activities of the former Emir, alleging his support for the Action Group and the Ilorin *Talaka Parapo* (ITP) alliance, a major opposition to the Northern Peoples' Congress (NPC) at the national level. He alleged that the former emir was hosting Action

Group meetings in his house and had been summoning villagers for meetings. Although he was not sure of the details of the meetings, he believed their motives were sinister (NAK 1956).

In November 1956, the ex-Emir was invited to appear before the Borgu Native Authority Council, apparently in response to persistent complaints by his brother and successor. Details of what transpired at the NA were not recorded in the archives and there is no clear information on how the situation was managed. Nevertheless, the relationship between the former and subsisting Emir, was clandestinely awry, but overtly pleasing, typical of some aristocratic politics.

CHAPTER NINE

Politics and Development under Colonial Rule

The colonial ideology was largely built around its civilising mission, that is, the benevolent act of "saving Africa from primitivity" unto "civilisation." It was a justification found in all the early colonial documents, and it was one of the mechanisms for mobilising support from the citizens of colonising countries in Europe. The economic and political dimension in the so-called civilisation mission was concealed. Even when the economics and politics of colonial control was recognised, it was often presented as a mutual gain for the colonisers and the colonised. Lord Lugard, one of the leading twentieth century ideologues of colonialism, writing in 1922 in *Dual Mandate in British Tropical Africa*, justified it as necessary for the colonies, the metropolis and the world as a whole. The colonies were expected to benefit from the civilisation mission promoted by the colonial policies and the activities of the Christian Missionaries. Secondly, Africa was to be opened up to other parts of the world and its "unvalued" resources tapped for the growth of the European industries which concomitantly enhanced the advance of the colonies. Colonialism was, therefore, a 'dual mandate' (Lugard 1922). Albert Sarraut, French Colonial Minister from 1920 – 24 argued that *misen en valeur* was a duty to the world as it was a veritable opportunity for the colonies.

"The France that colonizes does not work for herself alone, her advantage is inseparable from that of the world" (Young 1994, 166).

As stated in chapter 5, the social and economic context of colonial rule is surely linked to the development of the capitalist relations of production, especially in Western Europe. It was a necessary response for sustaining the system, especially sourcing for necessary raw materials to sustain industrial growth, draw necessary capital and the market for production. This was not necessarily recognised by the colonial powers. Their mission was often presented as noble and intended to pull the colonies out of their "backwardness" and support their integration into the world's mainstream.

Until the 1940s, colony development was not necessarily on the agenda of the colonial authorities. Some of the "development initiatives" that preceded this period such as assertion of the civilising mission, the claim to be exercising a trusteeship, the building of roads, health facilities, schools and other similar programmes were often subsumed under the rhetoric of European-inspired development. However, these were necessary actions to support their ultimate objectives (Cooper 2010). In fact, all the investments of this period were almost exclusively resourced by the colonies. The metropolitan funds were not to be invested in colonies; rather, the colonies were expected to contribute to the economies of the metropoles. To be sure, the 1929 British Colonial Development and Welfare Act was instituted more as a symbolic assertion of the development purpose of the colonial state than any other reason. Its poor funding of the initiatives eroded whatever substance it might have had.

The crisis of the inter-war and post-World War II period compelled the colonial authorities, particularly the British and French, to begin to rethink development. This was for self-preservation against the growing agitation in the colonies and the social and economic crisis in Europe. The British therefore introduced the Colonial Development and Welfare Act of 1940 and amended it in 1945 to provide for more resource investment in the colonies. One of the goals of the 1940 Act was that it specifically provided for raising the standard of living of the indigenous population, particularly wages of workers. Funds were to be invested not just on projects that provided immediate profit, but also on social services like housing, education and research. The changing dynamics occasioned by the Second

World War made it even more compelling for developmental consideration in colonial policies.

Development, to the colonial state, was, therefore, part of the wider policy of imperial legitimisation and security of control. This was done by providing the modernising local elite and the Native Authority with a stake in the imperial structure. France even declared in its 1946 Constitution that all citizens of their colonies had "qualities" of French citizens such as equivalent political and civil rights, including that of moving to France to seek for jobs. African politicians had representation in the French Parliament in Paris. Britain also developed its own framework, providing a gradual process of self-governance within the Commonwealth. It also created a second order citizenship for some of its dominions. The period experienced significant infusion of colonial metropolitan resources, largely supported by the International Bank for Reconstruction and Development (IBRD) as part of the post-war reconstruction in Europe. The resort to a new "development" policy paradigm was,therefore, a major crisis response mechanism as the post-war economic reconstruction in Europe was deeply attached to developments in Africa. It was based on this that colonial development was to be closely coordinated within the British post-war reconstruction and development plan (Zelaza 1985).

However, this changing dynamic didn't have a significant impact on the political economy of Borgu. The structure of colonial development investment corresponded with the local political economy. Most of the development concerns were around areas that benefited the system directly, particular urban segments, and the raw materials producing areas of the colonies. The rural areas were left with the basic services that could only help sustain the colonial extraction of value.

The colonial authorities, particularly the British, appeared to be "disappointed" by their apparent failure to meet their immediate economic objectives in Borgu. The partitioning of the region between the British and their French rivals, along with their succeeding policies, profoundly affected trade, production and the income of the people, resulting in massive emigration. Borgu slowly became a shadow of itself within the first two decades of colonial rule. The subsequent resistance and state repression further pushed the region to the margins of the two colonies.

In the inter-war period, colonial officials were exasperated by the so-called "backwardness," "parochialism," "primitivity" and "closedness" of the region. They ignored the fact that it was their occupation and policies that destroyed a relatively prosperous and proud society. Several colonial reports in the 1920's and 1930's complained about "backwardness" of the region. In fact, some British colonial officers used manifestly racist and derogatory terms like "backwardness", "parochialism," "barbarism" and a "laid back attitude" to express their displeasure and disenchantment. In this case, the people were held responsible for the situation the colonial powers created.

****

As seen in chapter 4, the initial colonial interest in Borgu was anchored on the importance of the navigable parts of the River Niger for trade across the region. Lugard also considered the possibility of a plantation on the "exceptionally fine" land of Borgu. In his report on Borgu in 1904, Lugard observed that:

> Shea trees are abundant, but with the exception of a small quantity sold to the Niger Company, the fruit is allowed to rot on the ground. There are unlimited areas of exceptionally fine land suitable for cotton, with a waterway (the Niger) close at hand, but the population is small, and mile after mile of well-timbered and fertile land is without a village. As its population increases owing to the cessation of war, and by immigration, Borgu should offer great possibilities of development. (Lugard 1905, 75).

He also suggested that Borgu's forest contained silvan resources of value as well as good timber and that he knew "of no locality in Nigeria which offers better prospects for experimental rubber or cotton" cultivation. He argued that labour could be brought from Yorubaland close by and stated that he had already started such a colony at the junction of River Tese and Moshe (Lugard 1905, 77).

As the colonial authorities extended northward and consolidated in the south, their interest in Borgu began to wane, especially after the first decade of colonial occupation. This could be seen from the management of the politics of the area. Borgu became arguably the most unstable part of northern Nigeria. It transited from being a military province in 1898 to a substantive province up to 1902, and ended up as a division of an emirate in 1954. This last transition was after a series of scandalous changes and reforms that only helped in dissipating and impoverishing the people. The situation was so bad that even some colonial officials noticed it. Governor General Hugh Clifford, in 1924, described Borgu (Bussa) as an—

> ... example of one of the most inept pieces of mismanagement of native affairs that I remember to have encountered in Nigeria. The sacrifices of native institutions, desires, tribal sentiments, tradition and customs to the mere administrative convenience of the Government and its officers can hardly ever have been carried out with more cynical indifference and ineptitude" (NAK 1924).

In fact, in 1929, the Resident at Ilorin, Hermon-Hodge, felt that "some reparation should be made to Bussa (and indeed the entire Borgu) for the suffering and sacrifices which have reduced a proud and comparatively populous race to a soured and sporadic handful" (cited in Crowder 1978, 172).

The partitioning of Borgu was the beginning of the crisis, as trade was hampered by the different and divergent policies of the two colonial powers. The re-orientation of caravan routes led to the reduction in caravan movements and had a devastating impact on markets, local production and the income of the people. As seen earlier, this was part of the reason for the revolt in French Borgu in 1916. Within the first two decades of colonial occupation, Borgu practically became a tired, poor and insignificant region to the British. The French, linking their Niger territory with coastal Dahomey via a road network that passed through Borgu, helped in resuscitating their side of the severed Borgu.

At independence, British Borgu was probably poorer than it was at the start of colonial occupation in 1896. Although the area was now connected to the world economy through monetisation, commodification and wage labour, the productive base hadn't changed in any significant way. The society was largely agrarian, based on peasant production and subsistence. The markets were largely to source cash to enable people to pay their taxes. Except for French Borgu, where the colonial power had introduced cotton production for export, the only major export in British Borgu was shea butter, which at a point was sold across the French border. Gold mining in Oli River was started in the mid-1930's and abandoned after a few years.

Forced Migration and Depopulation of Borgu

Labour migration was a major colonial phenomenon that hugely impacted Borgu. Generally, statistics about migration in West Africa is limited. It is more so in relation to Borgu, a society on the margin of the two colonies. To be sure, Borgu was historically a sparsely populated region and the devastation might have started even earlier than previously imagined. Clapperton, in his expedition to Borgu in 1826, estimated the population of Kaiama to be thirty thousand people; Wawa, eighteen to twenty thousand with Bussa having between ten to twelve thousand inhabitants. He particularly described Kaiama as a walled town of considerable size and a hub of an east-west trade which had grown in importance as a result of wars in Nupe and Oyo (apparently referring to the Jihad). He reports having come across a Hausa caravan numbering over one thousand merchants (Clapperton 1829; Lockhart 2008). By 1904, the population of the entire Borgu, with over eleven thousand square miles of territory, was estimated to be only twenty-five thousand, three hundred persons. This was just about the population of Wawa and Bussa seventy-eight years earlier.

Lugard, on his visit to Kaiama in 1904, particularly dismissed it as a "mere village of about three hundred persons" (Lugard 1905, 76). While Clapperton might have exaggerated the population in the early nineteenth century, as he only had an immediate impression after a few days of visit, the gaps between his figures and those of the colonial authorities in the early twentieth century are too wide to be ignored. It tells a lot about the development and population crisis in the late nineteenth century. Wars, brigandage, a water crisis and disease were later compounded by colonial occupation.

The initial colonial assumption was that as societies like Borgu became more secure and free from wars; people would settle and produce more for themselves and the economy. This appears to have failed in Borgu. While some of the internecine wars in the region did end during the colonial period; wars of resistance and recruitment for the two European wars, as well as the near constant forced labour, undermined the expected gains of cessation of wars and brigandage. In the early years of colonial Borgu, emirs and chiefs were assessed based on their capacity to recruit forced labour for road and rail construction, the construction of European residences and porterage. In French Borgu, the revolt of 1916 was largely associated with the extensive French military conscription and recruitment for the First World War.

Even after the earlier period of forced movement of peoples, the pressure to raise tax monies, the difficulties of paid labour and a desire to escape from state and elite repression compelled people to move. According to Osoba (1969), the groups involved in these movements had their origins in areas that were remote from the markets, where the economy was predominantly subsistence and opportunities for cash was limited (Osoba 1969). Internal migration was built on three major trends and manifestations. First was the movement of people from Borgu to areas with greater economic activity and opportunity. This included the disappearance of most Wangara and Hausa traders from Borgu with the cessation of caravan trade. Many of them relocated northwards to the Kano and Katsina area while others moved southwards to Ibadan, Ilorin and even Abeokuta. Second was the movement of young people, either seasonally or permanently, to different mines and plantations in the south and north. Borgu miners were, for instance, identified amongst tin miners in Jos in 1941. Cocoa plantations were also major attractions to Baatonu people in the west of Nigerian Borgu. Third was the drift from Borgu to urban centres of commerce and administration, especially to the provincial headquarters in Ilorin and the capitals of northern Nigeria, first in Zungeru, Lokoja and later Kaduna. Some Borgu people were believed to have settled in Yelwa and Kontagora. From the 1930's onwards, some of the educated few, frustrated farmers, craftsmen, persecuted princes and other victims of the authoritarian Native Authority found their ways out of Borgu. Externally, most migrated across the often-ignored artificial frontiers to the west into French Borgu. Trading opportunities and lesser demands for taxes attracted British Borgu people to the French Borgu towns of Parakou, Kandi and Djougou in particular. Several people, especially those from Kaiama, moved to French Borgu in the late 1920's and 1930's.

Different colonial reports accounted for this mass emigration of people out of Borgu but it was never considered a problem until 1933 when District Officer Heath wrote his first development report on Borgu. His 1935 report was even more alarming. Heath reported that the population of Borgu was decreasing and unless something drastic was done to remedy the situation, Borgu was going to become a "derelict area" (NAK 1935). Earlier, in 1934, he had noted that "Borgu was decaying and to prevent it from becoming a liability, bold experiment and policy will be required."

The problem was one of population. Already in 1931, it was the sparsest area in Nigeria. The 1934 population figures show a drop of three thousand, three hundred (3,300) persons in three years (NAK 1935, 4). He attributed the crisis to scanty population, the tsetse fly, high taxation, economic depression, lack of social amenities and falling revenue. While some of these reasons may be correct, the problem was more structural than presented.

The colonial state's insistence on "self-sufficiency" in the context of Eurocentric colonial interest had resulted in incidences of onerous taxation in Borgu. As a sparsely populated area, people were compelled to pay more to meet its budgetary commitment to the colonial government. This was often justified by a low cost of living, without taking into cognisance the limited market. With fifty percent of the revenue going to the centre and only fifty percent retained by the Native Authority, Borgu was continuously taxed even higher than some more prosperous provinces. The incidence of tax per adult male in Borgu as of 1935 was 10. 2 shillings while neighbouring provinces like Gwandu, Yauri and Kontagora had 7.71 Shillings, 9/9.1 Shillings and 7.11 Shillings respectively. It was even lower for Oyo Division, where it was between 6 and 8 Shillings. Oyo, in the Western Region, had been a city of attraction for Borgu people since the inception of colonial rule and attendant colonial taxation as the region was free of tax in the first decade of colonial rule. It wasn't clear what the incidence of tax was in French Borgu, but with the exchange rate of four to five francs to the shilling, it was clear that French Borgu were paying less than the English. Above all, the British Borgu native could migrate across the border and pay nothing for close to five or six years or even more as the French did not do annual revisions of assessment. Their assessment was linked to the census, which took place only after several years. Immigrants could, therefore, live tax-free until they were captured in the register (NAK 1935). This was a major attraction for British Borgu natives who were paying neck-breaking taxes. Over the years, as the population stagnated or plunged, the number of tax-paying adults also dropped with significant implications for the economy of the area.

Despite the high incidences of tax, Borgu had the least salaries and related wages compared to the neighbouring emirates. The *Dogari* (Native Authority police) was the least paid across northern Nigeria. They received £12 per annum as against £15 per annum in other divisions. All other salaries, especially in Kaiama Emirate, were much smaller than elsewhere.

Table 7: Population Distribution of Borgu 1933 - 1934

District	Population 1933	population 1934	+ or -
Aliyara	4,011	4,001	-10
Agwara	9,846	10,228	+382
Bussa	4,358	3,923	-435
Wawa	4,389	4,185	-204
Kaiama	3,714	3,781	+67
Yashikira	4,264	4,272	+8
Okuta	5,373	4,995	-378
Ilesha	1,949	1,864	-85
Gwanara	3,095	2,896	-199
Total	40,999	40,145	-854

(**Source**: NAK 1935)

The details in table 7 are quite striking. Only Agwara district made a significant gain in population and this was the result of the influx of Kambari farmers from Yauri into the region. The most remarkable was actually the drop in numbers in Ilesha, Gwanara and Okuta, three Baatonu communities sharing a frontier with Oyo Division to the south and French Borgu. Within a year, Borgu had lost over eight hundred people. In 1932, Heath wrote that the "younger generation is said to be leaving the emirate for large towns on the railways, where it [sic] finds life more enjoyable and casual work are easier to obtain."

He noted that the failure to grant more tax revenue to the Native Authority was stagnating development. As "no development equals no casual employment, which again results in emigration and consequent further reduction in taxation revenue. A vicious circle for Kaiama, however much larger places may benefit by cheap Kaiama labour" (NAK 1935, 10). Neighbouring divisions, provinces and countries, therefore, became the biggest beneficiaries of Borgu labour, places such as Shaki and Ibadan in Oyo Division, as well as Ilorin, Sokoto, Kano, Jos, Zaria, Kaduna, Bauchi and Dahomey.

The decrease in the population impacted the revenue for social development. 1934/35 recorded the biggest drop as even itinerant Fulbe *Jangali* tax, as well as market and related dues, were abolished. The abolition considerably reduced the revenue base of the two emirates, a situation that was considered more beneficial to "foreign" traders and pastoralists than to Borgu (NAK 1935).

Table 8: Tax Revenue 1928 - 1934

Year	Bussa Emirate	Kaiama emirate	Total
1928 – 29	2,400	2,676	5,076
1929 – 30	2,414	2,589	5,003
1930 – 31	2,165	2,415	5,580
1931 – 32	1,735	2,303	4,038
1932 – 33	2,503*	2,261	4,764
1933 – 34	2,059	2,163	4,764
1934– 35 (Estimate)	1,763	1,840	3,603

Source: NAK 1935. *This included large arrears tax for 1931/32

Economic Stagnation and Social Services

The world economic depression of the inter-war period only reached the Nigerian Borgu in the early 1930s as the market and price of shea butter, (Borgu's major export) dropped. The market only picked up in 1934. French Borgu appears to have had a better response to the situation as they introduced the compulsory growing of cotton and processing of shea butter, together with the construction of a network of roads, which brought relative material prosperity to the region. The French had, during this period, developed a better communication system including roads and a rail line. In fact, due to the French's relatively better understanding and greater economic interest in the region, some of the markets in British Borgu collapsed. Boriya in Okuta District which had the biggest market in Kaiama Emirate collapsed as traders found easier routes and better markets on the French side. Market went where it could grow best and these traders avoided the difficult roads and higher taxes on the Nigerian side.

The authorities in British Borgu could not have claimed ignorance of this development. In a memorandum on the 22nd of December, 1926, the Secretary of the Northern Provinces predicted this situation. He observed that "...the natives of British Borgu and of French Nikki are ethnically more or less homogenous ... good communication in either (way) would tend to attract the population and trade of the other" (Heath 1935, 9).

The British and French colonial authorities never seriously invested their resources in the colonies until probably the late 1950s. Prior to this, infrastructure was financed through locally generated revenue. The nature and size of infrastructure, therefore, depended on the resources generated by the local administration. In English Borgu, until 1935, the Native Authority retained only fifty percent of its revenue; the other fifty went to the regional government. The French financial system was structured in three levels – the federal (French West Africa), colonies and the local budgets. The federal budget was financed by custom duties generated by trade between the federations and the rest of the world. This budget largely covered administrative and governance expenses, central services, and large-scale public works covering several colonies, like railways, and sometimes subsidy to poor colonies like Mauritania. Each colony and its local institutions generated its resources through taxation and related sources. Local budgets covered all costs except military and large-scale public works (Huillery 2009). Generally, the cost of colonisation was borne by the people rather than the metropolitan governments.

In French Borgu, the colonial administration nonetheless invested in education, health and other infrastructure including roads and railways, which was provided by the Federation of French West African colonies. The colonial officials reported on the state of these facilities in their respective domains. The British instituted something similar through their annual assessment reports, development reports, annual reports and later departmental reports. But British Borgu was a catalogue of problems of infrastructure until the mid-1940s when all-season roads began to open up in some of the districts.

Colonial Education

The two colonial powers provided education based on their interests and idiosyncrasies. The essence of education generally, in every society, is to sustain and reproduce the social, economic and political relationships that exist in that society. Colonial education was not different in this respect. Education was only required to sustain the colonial powers goal of economic and political domination. It was never interested in stimulating local development. Instead, it was designed to maintain the status quo. Nevertheless, the approach to education between the French and British was completely different. While the British policy corresponded with the Native Administration policy of localising education, the French appear to have prioritised standardised education and the French language as the sole language of instruction. Bunche (1934) reported a saying that "when the Germans first arrive in a new colony they build a garrison when the English arrive they build a customs house, and when the French arrive they a build a school" (74). This explains the priority given to education by the French, even if the purpose was to serve colonial interests.

In the early days of colonial occupation in French Borgu, education was left to missionaries, who sometimes received government subsidies. It was for this reason that the first sets of schools were established by Catholic missionaries in Perere in 1898, and Kouande in 1901. Another was led by an African translator and a French sergeant in Kandi, who established it in 1900. These schools were later closed down when the government took total control of education. The first effort at state control of education was through the *decree arrêtés* of 1903 issued by the Governor-General of West Africa. The second was in November 1918 and later again in May 1924. These frameworks defined the foundation of French colonial education in West Africa. The organisation of education in Dahomey was based on the general configuration in the federation of French West Africa as a whole. The foundation of primary education was in the village or elementary schools, which was built on two instructional courses – *cours préparatoire* and *cours élémentaire*. This structure was intended to spread the use of the French language among the natives. While the first level was offered wherever thirty pupils below the age of eleven were found; the second layer was available to only the best produced by the first. Elementary schools were managed by a native teacher (*instituteur*) and assisted by a native monitor (Bunche 1934). The next layer was *école régionale*, established in each important *cercle*. In Dahomey, the *école régionale* comprised of three different curricula – preparatory, elementary and intermediate. The most distinctive feature of French educational system was accessibility even if the colonies had to bear the burden of the cost. This accessibility was, nevertheless, at the elementary level as students were carefully weeded out as they progressed through the system.

The widespread of village schools was believed to be a response to the pervasiveness of Islamic education in most of French West Africa. The idea was to counter the spread of Arabic as a language of instruction and arrest the possible resurgence of a Mahdi-type rebellion. Budgetary allocation was made for this purpose and shared across the colonies (Oloruntimehin 1972). Through this process, Muslim clerics and teachers were trained. The objective was to influence the content of their curriculum and the orientation of their schools. Islam had not widely spread in French Borgu during the early period of colonial rule. The French authorities, therefore, targeted the Dendi Muslim and incorporated them into the system.

It is claimed that the objective of French education was to "produce strong, honest and intelligent individuals." Looking at the curriculum of these, the ideological character of education in the colony is easily exposed. The system, therefore, revolved around physical, moral and intellectual faculties of the child (Bunche 1934). The moral studies (*morale*) appear to be the indoctrinating segment of the education. It was the most important part of a curriculum designed to produce a pliable society that is accommodating of colonial domination. It ran through the preparatory, elementary and intermediate courses as well as at the domestic schools (*écoles ménagéres*) for girls. It wasn't taught through class lessons but aimed at inculcating "good morals" on children including cleanliness, exactitude and regularity, politeness, truthfulness, honesty, respect and obedience. The second most important subject was French language and grammar. Other subjects included reading, writing and arithmetic in the metric system, drawing and singing, physical education and agriculture. At the elementary level, the handling of tools, modelling of pottery, carpentry and other vocational activities were taught. Generally, school attendance was only obligatory for the children of royalty and notables. This was aimed at privileging the class in support of colonial domination.

The first colonial primary school was opened in Parakou and Kandi in 1910. For a long time, these schools were attended only by children from Dendi *cercles*. As the Muslim Dendi became more independent of the Baatonu; their support for the European colonialists increased. All the colonial administrative reports recognised the support and understanding they received from the *Imams*. They were, therefore, the first to benefit from French education (Lombard 1970). In 1918, they held their first examination for the *Certificat d'Estudes Primaries* (CEP), which none of the students passed. It was not until the demobilisation of African troops after the First World War that a sizeable number in Borgu was able to speak French. They were employed largely as translators and gendarmes (Bierschenk 1993). Although missionaries weren't allowed in other French West African colonies, Dahomey had a significant number of missionary schools because the level of demand soon exceeded the number of schools available (Huillery 2009). The French Parliament had, in 1903, voted for the secularisation of social services in the colonies and stopped the subsidies accorded to Christian missionaries. Dahomey appears to have been an exception, as missionaries were allowed to operate with a measure of control.

The experience in British Borgu was quite different. Like most parts of northern Nigeria, education had a late start. The first set of educated people in British Borgu were trained at Birnin Kebbi. Borgu had its first elementary school in 1924, led by a former student of the Birnin Kebbi school. Unlike the French system, the pupils were taught in Hausa, not English. English language was introduced only in 1947 after a change in British colonial education policy. The subjects were, therefore, *aikin gona* (Agriculture), *Lissafi* (arithmetic), *Karatu* (reading) and *Sana'a* (trade and craft). Northern colonial officials were originally against the teaching of English in colonial schools. Sir Percy

Girouard, the Governor of the Northern Nigeria Protectorate from 1907 to 1909, vehemently argued against it, believing that an English education would produce rebellious citizenry. The Resident at Sokoto, Major John Burden, during the same period was reported to have told the Governor that "natives should be educated through their hands, not through their heads." He warned that education could lead to the production of "contemptible pseudo-scholars and agitators" as it happened in Egypt and India, with serious implication for the colonial state (Tibenderana 2003, 33). Therefore, until the enactment of Education Ordinance in 1916, after extensive reviews and engagement with the Colonial Office in London, education in northern Nigeria was largely racist and purposely instituted to sustain the colonial hegemony. Even with that ordinance, right up to 1928, primary schools remained the only centres of education. In 1938, an additional elementary school was established in Bussa. The initial interest of the colonial authorities was only to train children of the aristocratic class and give them the necessary skills to support their future administrative responsibilities. Borgu didn't have a senior primary school until 1957 when one was established in Okuta. It had to temporarily relocate to Kaiama due to acute water scarcity. The school was eventually relocated to Wawa in 1958.

Up to the end of colonial rule in 1960, the highest institution of learning in Borgu was the senior primary school in Wawa. Students interested in further education went to Ilorin, Katsina, Birnin Kebbi, Keffi and other locations in northern Nigeria. It was, therefore, not surprising that the colonial authorities complained persistently about the shortage of human resource capacity for the Native Authority system. The Native Authority relied substantially on contract staff from other provinces and divisions across the north. The colonial system didn't support education beyond the need to staff colonial officialdom. Therefore, the level of education provided depended on the resources available and the functionality of the education to the colonial state. Unlike the neighbouring provinces in the south, missionary education was limited generally in northern Nigeria. Although there were missionary activities in central Nigerian area especially since the 1920s, the first missionary school in British Borgu was in Ilesha in 1930s and later Kaiama in 1945. All these schools quickly folded for want of patronage. Most of these missionary schools collapsed due to lack of patronage occasioned by poor mobilisation and community perception of missions as largely interested in winning converts to Christianity.

Water Crisis and Colonial Control

Water scarcity had been a historical issue in the region particularly in the southern parts of British Borgu. This was compounded by colonial rule and the institution of borders. Lack of water undermined administration and also contributed substantially to the depopulation of the region. In the entire region, water during dry season was a huge problem. Within a few days of the last rains, rivers and wells went dry. The rocky nature of the ground did not allow for deep wells that could last through the dry season. In 1934, it was reported that many people left Yashikira town because of insufficient water. All wells and soak holes dried up and water was being fetched from as far as three miles away. In 1934, eight hundred shillings was budgeted for wells in Kaiama but this was considered insignificant for the needs of the emirate. Kaiama town became free of guinea worm only in 1937 when wells were constructed. According to R. C. Wilson, the Director of Geological Survey in Nigeria, this persistent water scarcity was caused by the highly permeable sandstone bed of the region that doesn't retain water and the existence of many crystalline schists and gneisses. These rocks do not store water in quantity unless they are deeply decomposed or traversed by major joint planes or fault zones (NAK 1935).

Although people of this region have lived with these challenges for a long time with strong local adaptation capacity, the colonial system altered the adaptation and resilience measures of the people. In the pre-colonial period, movement and resettlement were frequent as people responded to their environmental vulnerabilities. Increasingly, settlements were managed by the Native Authority system and the earlier mobility of the people was sought to be curtailed. As more people settled in particular locations, they overstretched the water resources and this, combined with the environmental issues, tended to compound the challenge.

CHAPTER TEN

Colonialism, Identity Politics and Intergroup Relations

The colonial state was a divisive state. Its very structure was predicated on the logic of ethnic identification and ranking, dualism of spatial laws and associated territorial mapping. The ethnicity, or "tribe" as it was called, was a major group identity for colonial political organisation and administration. It was the most recognised group or basis for political engagement (Abdu 2010). Both the French and British administrations were structured along these lines. The colonial rendition of the history of the people that constituted the region was about tracing genealogies of tribes and communities for the purpose of administration and enhancing the surveillance capacities of the colonial state (Kuna 2005). In Nigeria, ethnic groups were ranked into the subordinate and super-ordinate. The process involved either a benign adoption of existing identities or a complete re-identification of people (Mamdani 1996). Ethnic groups with centralised pre-colonial political structures were rated higher than the acephalous ones. It was on this basis that provinces, districts and villages were carved out (Kuna 2005; Mamdani 1996, 2009). The process entailed several state policy formulations, geographical and ethnic definitions or re-definitions. The end result of this was the construction of divided and mostly conflicting societies.

Mamdani (1996) and Ekeh (1975) provide incisive expositions on how colonialism through this process instituted two publics. Ekeh argues that colonialism created two publics: an amoral civic public from which one expects benefit but which is not important in one's definition of citizenship, and a moral, primordial public defined in terms of one's ethnic group, in which relation is determined in terms of duties with strong moral and emotional attachment to such duties. In a related argument, Mamdani (1996, 62) examines how colonialism, through Indirect Rule, created two legal regimes (one civil and the other customary) and fostered what he called a "decentralised despotism" in the social construction of power. In this design, the seat of civic power expressed through civic law was the central state. Although the state claimed universal rights, these rights were the exclusive preserves of the people of metropolitan origin. Natives were placed under Native Authority whose power was expressed through a regime of customary law. The colonial state, therefore, created two distinct citizens: civic citizens and ethnic citizens or natives. The important implication of this was the fermenting of ethnic and religious identity which has continued to gain ascendance in post-colonial Africa.

Across the two Borgu colonies, differentiation and centralisation were two common mechanisms in administration and control. These defined the process of identification, separation and definition of geographical and cultural boundaries. While the British emphasised a paradoxical decentralised centralisation, the French *race policy* was centred on ethnic segregation and decentralisation. This informed the differential dynamics of intergroup relations in the two colonies. While French Borgu struggled with territorial borders such as cantons, *cercles* and villages, the hostilities and resistance was largely directed at the colonial authorities. In British Borgu, the decentralisation of power through the Native Authority system pitted the subjugated groups against the perceived undeserved beneficiaries of the colonial centralisation. The nature of control and resistance was often territorial and sometimes ethnic. This is not to hold colonialism solely responsible for the changing character of intergroup relations and conflict, but to identify the exacerbating influence of colonial control on the changes and how it provided the basis for some of the contemporary manifestations of same.

Colonial Cartography and Social Differentiation

Colonial political structures and mapping exercises had a significant impact on Borgu identity. As a partitioned region, the impact was both national and international. The territorial structure had strong legal and socio-political implications as it sought to either create new or obliterate old socio-cultural and political configurations. Through this, new identities and othering was created. The first of these was the division of Borgu between two colonial powers, thereby creating a new wedge within a single-culture group, disrupting the socio-ecosystem and building an artificial international frontier. The different traditions of political governance in the colonies and the process of managing their economies built new national identities and created two international bodies within a hitherto single socio-political entity. As much as the people tried to resist the international borders and continued their pre-colonial relationship, a new otherness had been created and had come to define Borgu's cultural relations.

The otherness was so pervasive that it affected cultural practices ranging from the culinary to the aesthetic in the two major languages as they both struggled to cope with the influence of, first, the languages of the colonial powers and second the political and economic ascendence of other dominant local/regional *lingua franca*, which may be there even before colonial rule. In British Borgu, the English and the Hausa languages[71] had a relatively strong political and economic influence in the north of Borgu while Yoruba had a similar influence in the south. In the French side, Dendi languages have continued to influence the Baatonu. While the influence of Dendi on Baatonu maybe there even before colonial rule, the privileged position of Dendi during colonial rule actually reinforced itspolitical expression.

---

[71] To a lesser extent, Yoruba has also been gaining influence in some Borgu communities particularly those in Kwara state.

Although cultural and economic relations continued across the frontier, the othering of the people was soon redefined and concretised. In the early period of colonial rule and even the post colonial period, a candidate for the throne of Nikki could emerge from any of the component segments in either of the countries as was seen in the case of Woru Yaru leaving Yashikira to eventually become the King of Nikki. This has been made relatively difficult, not by institutional design or restriction, but through subtle processes as the two nationalities consolidated and the local institutions became more structured to reflect a new citizenship structure, which excluded non-citizens of either nation.

Migration and settlement across the frontiers became more difficult with the new citizenship based on Westphalian sovereignty which was built on principles of international law that gave each nation-state exclusive control over its territory. This principle totally delegitimised pre-colonial Borgu and created new citizens of Borgu ancestry across two countries. The colonial imaginary wasn't an abstract construct; it was deeply rooted in colonial ideology and materially sustained through colonial schools, local laws and international maps, national flags and symbols, and in this process, two new communities and identities were framed. While there was seldom conflict between the two, the relationship became that of exclusion as one nation-state group tried to exclude the other from real or perceived benefits, particularly when competition for natural, economic or political resources is in involved.

Invented Identities: Emirates and Districts Identities in British Borgu

Territorial mapping and political structuring was a common phenomenon in the British colonial system. It was on this basis that Borgu was perpetually being restructured and placed under different political and geographical arrangements until the end of colonial rule. Sometimes, the restructuring was directed at finding the most convenient and cost-effective structure and, other times, it was to satisfy the ego, whims and caprices of British political officers. These territorial mappings and political structuring created new identities and redefined membership and belonging. While some of the structures coincided with pre-colonial formations, in some cases, historically conflicting or independent groups were placed together, thereby reopening old wounds and creating room for conflict. Prominent among these structures was the composition of emirates, districts and villages in the Native Authority system. As indicated in chapter 8, until 1954, Borgu was a two-emirate Province (and later Division) comprising Kaiama and Bussa emirates. Of the two, Kaiama was the most contentious as the Baatonu districts resented their subjection to the leadership of the Emir of Kaiama.

It has never been clear why Kaiama was made to enjoy paramountcy over the Baatonu principalities. The friendship of Mora Tasude with Lord Lugard is often cited as the major reason (Stewart 1993; Lafia 2006; Akinwumi 1995). Others have posited that it was a reward for Kaiama's collaboration with the colonialists to subjugate others in the region (Lafia 2004). While this may be correct or wrong, it is important to recognise that collaboration and resistance were two sides of the mode of engaging colonial domination. Bayart correctly observed that Africans related to the colonial situation in different ways, sometimes opposing and at other times joining it. It will, therefore, be "naïve to indulge in an anachronistic interpretation of these indigenous strategies in terms of 'nationalism' or 'collaboration' where in fact (the) consideration of local interest came into play, in a world which was indifferent to the national idea but which [was] subject to serious intra- and inter-societal tensions" (Bayart 2009, 24).

Surely, Lugard acknowledged and even cited his friendly relationship Mora Tasude in some of his documentations. He noted on his expedition to Borgu in 1894 thus:

> Whatever may have been his original designs, Kiama [Kaiama] and I became real friends. I was greatly struck with his [Tusude] fearless bearing and aristocratic carriage. He visited my camp alone and unarmed by night, and on more than one occasion I reciprocated his confidence by a midnight visit for a friendly and uninterrupted chat. Such a meeting occurred the night before I left, when he warned me that he had positive information that a robber chief with 600 warriors had planned to attack us by an ambush near one of the swollen streams we had to cross. He implored me to consider whether I was strong enough to go forward. Should I decide to do so, he heartily wished me success and victory; but if I judged it best to return, he

would see me safely out of Borgu. At the same time, with every evidence of sincerity, he warned me never to trust myself alone and unarmed at night in a Borgu village as I was now doing ... I wish I had time to tell you more of this chief, for whom I had conceived a real liking, and of our life during our week's stay in Kiama. We made a treaty together.... (Lugard 1895, 216 – 217)

However, despite this "real liking" for Tasude, Lugard took a unilateral decision to relocate the provincial capital of Borgu from Kaiama to Bussa in 1904. On his tour to Kaiama in 1904, in fact, without visiting Bussa, he decided that Bussa was better suited for the provincial capital. In his own words:

... Kaiama is ill-situated for the headquarters, which in a province nearly 200 miles long by only 65 broad, should be more nearly in the centre. Kaiama is only 30 miles from the south frontier, out of touch with the north and with the Niger navigation (being 50 miles from Fort Goldie), and is now of no political importance. It will be the station of an Assistant Resident, and the capital will be removed to Boussa [Bussa], which is central, so that the Resident can control the customs stations in the north, where the important kola caravans cross the province, and, being on the Niger, will be in touch with the enclave at Fort Goldie and the station of exit (for French flotillas) at Illo. The King of Boussa is, moreover, the most important chief in the province. I was unable to visit Boussa, but the Resident will select an experimental site and test its healthiness (Lugard 1904).

This relocation of provincial capital was later followed by the total abrogation of the Province and amalgamation with Kontagora Province. Imperialism did not operate on the basis of platonic friendships but more on the basis of economic and political interest. Of course, this doesn't vitiate Lugard's better familiarity with Kaiama and his widely acknowledged relationship with Mora Tasude. Lugard during this expedition visited four Borgu principalities and signed a protective treaty with three: Bussa, Kaiama and Nikki in that order. He also visited Ilesha but didn't sign any treaty because, "the local chief, who was, I understood, brother of the chief of Nikki, insisted strongly that he was entirely bound by the treaties I had already concluded [with Nikki]" (Lugard, 1895, 219).

Of the three treaty-signing principalities, Nikki was in French Borgu. It is, therefore, almost natural for the two in British Borgu to enjoy a level of importance. After the Anglo-French treaty, Lugard visited Kaiama twice. These visits were largely part of his tours of duty as he worked to consolidate on the region, first as a military-controlled region and later as a Province. To be sure, since the eighteenth century, the documented politics of Borgu revolved around Bussa, Nikki and Kaiama (Anene 1965).

It was probably this political importance that Lugard referred to in his 1904 report when he decided to relocate the provincial capital because Kaiama "is now of no political importance" in addition, of course, to other economic and strategic reasons (Lugard 1905). It, therefore, appears that the real or perceived "political importance" of Kaiama was a major determinant of his decision than mere friendship or acquaintance with Mora Tasude. This political importance might have been drawn from the treaty with Kaiama and the accounts of earlier European travellers to the region, particularly – Clapperton, the Lander Brothers, Barth and Lugard himself. Most colonial officials relied on these reports in navigating their ways in the new colonies.

It is not clear whether Lugard and Temple, the first Resident of Borgu, actually recognised the ethnic diversity of Borgu. Lugard's description of Borgu was naïve and typically based on Sudanic civilisation "... In the north (northern Borgu), the settlements of Fulani from Gando rear cattle, while the Baribas are agricultural. The whole of the south is now under Kaiama, the north under Boussa" (Lugard 1905, 75). Considering Kaiama's aristocratic link to Nikki, the early colonials appeared to think Kaiama and the other Baatonu territories were of the same ethnic background. Generally, the poor understanding of the geography, politics and cultural divisions might have made this decision easier. This can be seen from Lugard and Temple's reaction to the intransigence of Woru Yaru, then King of Yashikira. "Woro Yaru, the heir to the kingship at Nikki, had refused to acknowledge the French and settled in British Borgu, but he proved a feeble and useless person and he has now gone back to Nikki" (Lugard 1905, 75).

Woru was one of the first to protest his subjection to Kaiama and was dethroned. He left Yashikira in protest with almost half of the population of the town. However, his resistance was not only a resistance to supremacy of Kaiama; it was a combination of many things. It was, for example, a case of friendship going sour and transforming to enmity. Woru Yaru and Mora Tasude (then Yerima Bakaru) were believed to be friends and had carried out joint raids of caravans until the relationship collapsed during one of their expeditions, resulting in a violent confrontation and the beginning of their enmity. Woru Yaru was part of the leadership of the aborted coup against Tasude. It was only after the coup that he fled to Godebere, before moving to Yashikira where he became king, after a failed attempt at becoming the king of Nikki (Stewart 1993; Idris and Yaru 2008). This, however, does not in any way repudiate his or the general Baatonu people's legitimate resistance to their subordination to Kaiama.

The challenge was not just the mapping but the very nature of Native Authority administration and how it significantly differed from the pre-colonial system. Historically, political relations between polities, principalities and towns were largely based on historical ties, mutual cooperation, trust and protectionism. They weren't relationships of strong political domination. The pre-colonial political system of Borgu was opposed to the concentration of authority in the hands of one all-powerful individual since power was constantly contested by rivals and divided among an aristocratic class (Lombard 1970). This customary rivalry and the changing dynamics of politics and the economy of the region significantly eroded the authority of the kings in the period preceding colonial occupation. Colonialism changed this structure as specific polities and principalities were privileged over others and their leaders given powers and territorial control beyond what they used to have over the people. The districts and village structure were carved within this context, resulting in series of resistances and new identities, either based on the new political geography or an internal resistance to the new groupings and assertion of the old.

Domination and resistance was not only limited to Kaiama and the Baatonu districts as often portrayed, but pervasively spread across the entire Borgu and could be found in each of the districts. While the Kaiama situation provides a good example of how colonial political structuring and cartography created conflict, similar instances and dynamics of relationships were found across the emirates and districts of Borgu. As noted in 1936 Borgu Divisional Annual Report, even while the Baatonu districts resented the suzerainty of Kaiama, there were strong antiparties between the four Baatonu districts "Okuta and Gwanara have a long standing animosity; Gwanara and Okuta [Ilesha] are not on speaking terms, and all are jealous of Yashikira" (NAK 1936).

To be sure, all the districts of Borgu were a colonial contraption. Practically, none corresponded with the pre-colonial political and geographical structure. The districts were, therefore, as artificial as the emirates. Ethnic groups, villages and districts were arbitrarily and unjustly placed one above the other. As a result, almost all the districts were engulfed by one form of internal grievance or the other. What made the Kaiama situation peculiar was probably the ethnic difference between Kaiama which was Boko (of Bokobaru extraction) being placed over the four districts that were Baatonu. The Kaiama situation was more like a case of a minority ethnic group placed above the majority of ethnic groups (four districts)[72]. While they shared some historical and cultural affinity during the pre-colonial times, they were politically independent of each other.

The other driver was the colonial inspired authoritarian disposition of some of the emirs of Kaiama, particularly Tasude and later Ki-Yaru. Their strong political hold and repressive mien alienated the Baatonu communities, who, therefore, held the entire Kaiama community responsible for their behaviour, even if they were also victims of such oppression. This is not peculiar. Similar examples of this form of resistance can be seen in different forms in northern Nigeria where resistance to the emirate-style rule of the Hausa and Fulbe resulted in resistance to the entire Hausa and Fulbe communities, as seen in southern Kaduna, Bauchi, Jos, Adamawa and many other parts of northern Nigeria. The Borgu situation might not have escalated over the years beyond political bickering, largely because of historical relationships. Also, probably with the predominance of Islam across the two communities, there is, therefore, no major counter-popular or primordial identity that can be deployed

---

[72] Half of Yashikira district was in 1919 reported to be Boko-speaking – some of the villages including Gbasoro, Gbete, Karonzi and even Yashikira itself were recorded as Boko.

for differentiation. There is also limited competition for economic resources as most contestations are around local governance.

In Kaiama Emirate, Kenu was believed to be a major victim of colonial cartography. Despite the historical precedence of Kenu over most Baatonu principalities in British Borgu, it ended up as a village under the District Head Okuta. Gwanara, which was originally linked to Kenu, at a point, also ended up under Ilesha District and was later made a district capital. The territory of Gwanara included territory which previously belonged to Kenu. Kenu Town and Tebera, another independent territory, were placed under Okuta District and their leaders subordinated to the Head of Okuta in 1902 in a decision which Resident Kemble belatedly regretted but failed to reverse. He reported in 1904 that:

> The Sarkin Kenu [was] a dignified and obliging old man. If I had been able to visit this place before, I should have recommended him as a third class or even second class Chief, but something has always come in the way of my making rounds from Okuta through Tabira to Ilesha. [Chief of] Kenu says he was not under Okuta until "the Whiteman came." Okuta acknowledged this fact but says that the Whiteman who was at Okuta told him Kenu and other places south could be under him. I fancy the real fact of the matter is that Okuta was asked what towns were under him and he gave Kenu as one, and the officer said "all right" and wrote it down. No one went to Kenu to ask (NAK 1904).

To be sure, the Okuta District assessment of 1922 affirmed the "artificiality" of the Okuta District and stated that the "position which the Sarkin Okuta [King of Okuta] now enjoys is an innovation" and that Okuta before the colonial occupation was "nominally under Kenu" (NAK 1922, 88). This is not surprising considering the historical pre-eminence of Kenu over other Baatonu settlements in the south-western parts of Borgu. The relegation of Kenu was, therefore, a major source of contention in the region. It was reported that the King of Kenu, Komiterere II, emigrated to Nikki in 1902 in protest against his subordination to Okuta and Kaiama. All through the colonial period, successive heads of Kenu led a series of actions to ensure the reversal of the structure. These were often met with the combined repressive powers of the District Officer, the Ditsrict Head of Okuta and the Emir of Kaiama. Under Kperogi Toteri (1928 -1948) the relationship between Kenu and Okuta was better managed as he "respected" the Head of Kenu and allowed him access and enjoy some perquisite of his office. This changed drastically during the reign of Aliyu Kperogi who insisted on properly subjecting the Chief of Kenu to his control, a demand not agreeable to Woru Yerima, the then Chief of Kenu. They had a series of conflicts on the appointment of other lesser chiefs in the district, including the appointment of Head of Fulbe (*Mare Suno*) at Kenu in 1949. Kenu, under the leadership of Woru Yerima in the 1940s, didn't only resist Okuta and Kaiama; they made desperate efforts to elevate the political status of the village to a separate district. His protest and petition to the Emir of Ilorin did not go down well with the Emir of Kaiama, who on the issue had acted in solidarity with the District Head of Okuta. The situation of the Chief of Kenu degenerated in the 1950s when he aligned with two major opposition parties, the Northern Elements Progressive Union (NEPU), a radical and leading opposition group in northern Nigeria, and the Action Group (AG), a southern Nigerian political party.

The conflict resulted in the deposition of Woru Yerima in 1950 and his trial in the Kaiama Native Authority court where he was sentenced to six months imprisonment. On his release, he was not allowed to return to Kenu but told to settle in Mowa in Saki District. It was reported that seventy-four people from Kenu and two hundred and two people from Gwanara followed him in sympathy (Stewart 1993). The 1950 annual report described the situation as follows:

> The usually quiet[73] political scene of Kaiama Emirate was disturbed by the revolt of the Village Head of Kenu in Okuta District. Woru Yerima the Village Head defied the District Head and refused to obey the Emir's order to come into Kaiama. He was arrested, tried and convicted and a new Village Head has been appointed. Woru Yerima since his release from prison has settled down just over the boundary in Oyo Province and appears to be doing his utmost to stir up trouble in Okuta and Gwanara District (NAK 1950, 6).

---

[73] This may not be correct, as until the 1950s Kaiama Emirate was quite a turbulent Emirate, with series of contestations, difficulties in tax collection and internal conflicts.

In exile, with encouragement and support from Northern Elements Progressive Union (NEPU) and the Action Group (AG), Woru Yerima instituted a legal action against the Emir of Kaiama for wrongly arresting and convicting him, a case he not so surprisingly lost. With the abdication of Ki-Yaru in 1954, Woru Yerima petitioned the Divisional Officer. He chronicled his challenges with Okuta and the Emir of Kaiama and demanded that he be allowed to return to Kenu. The text is a poignant example of the despotic character of the Native Authority system and deserves an extensive quote:

> Due to a social misunderstanding between the former Emir of Kaiama and myself, I was discriminated and persecuted. The wish of my people was to have a separate (District) council of my town Kenu, independent of Okuta as formerly before the coming of the British people. I could not meet the need of my people unless it is approved by the Emirs of Kaiama and Ilorin. Therefore, I went to Ilorin to lay my prayers before the Emir's Council of Ilorin.
>
> During the time of my going to Ilorin, the Emir of Kaiama was at Kaduna to attend a meeting. Because my going was already discussed and approved by the Emir of Kaiama, I did not wait for his arrival from Kaduna again. At Ilorin, I forwarded my petition as directed by the Emir of Kaiama. The Emir of Ilorin told me to go and wait for his official approval after advising the Emir of Kaiama.
>
> ... Few days after the misunderstanding, the Emir of Kaiama came to my town, Kenu and called me in the public, then dismissed me from being the Village Head of Kenu. He assured the public that I was no more the Village Head of Kenu again. His reason was that I went to Ilorin without his knowledge.
>
> After my removal from office, I was called by the same Emir of Kaiama for punishment. I refused to attend the call. I waited for official summons if I might have a case to answer because there was no certificate of my office [sic]. Three days after, the Divisional Officer of Kaiama came to Kenu and invited me to meet him at Ilorin. I took my friend to Ilorin from where we were both arrested by the Native Authority Police of Kaiama, without a question. We arrived back in Kaiama in chains and we were kept in the Prison for seven days without a case. After seven days, we were called at Kaiama Native Authority Court where our sentence of six months each was confirmed.
>
> While I completed my term of the six month's imprisonment, I was discharged and told not to live within the northern boundary.

Thus I came to live in Mwa (Mowa), Saki Division, Oyo Province, Western Region.

I have my people's confidence; otherwise, thousands of them should not have followed me to my new place of domicile. And many villages had broken away to my new settlement. Those who opposed my dismissal from office like the village Heads of Kenu-Boko, Ayo, Yakereku, Ba, Makarakp and Bwe, were also dismissed from office. Four councillors like Umoru, Adullahi, Shero and the Liman [Imam] were fined £2 too.

Being the village Head of Kenu, I understand myself to be a public servant, and my duty was supposed to express the need of my people. That was why I devoted myself to the struggle for separation of Kenu from Okuta on account of my people's interest. For expressing the need of my people, I was persecuted and prosecuted. There was no other crime I committed. That was all for which I suffered the below inconveniences. (Cited in Stewart 1993, 381 - 383)

The petition was successful and he was allowed to return to Kenu. The next challenge was to determine whether he could be reinstated as the village head since a different person had been enthroned. His appeal for reinstatement was not determined until his death in 1956.

The partitioning of Kenu didn't only benefit Okuta; Gwanara took almost all the villages linked to Kenu. Although they both shared the same dynastic roots with Kenu being the base, the superiority of Gwanara over Kenu, even if not in the same district, was also a misnomer. It reversed the traditional relationship between the chief of Gwanara and that of Kenu, the latter being subordinated to the former. This created its own internal dynamics between the leaders of both polities as the Chief of Gwanara, Koto Kotogi, continued to assert his superiority over Kenu on some traditional rituals[74]. The conflict over Kenu and the resistance to the Emir of Kaiama resulted in the deposition of Koto Kotogi in 1913. The deposition of Koto Kotogi and the appointment of Shinabiya with the title of Suno Ali created another layer of conflict in the region as Gwanara was now subordinated to

---

[74] The ritual sacrifice of two bulls in Kenu was so important to the Chief of Gwanara that it almost resulted in a war as the Chief Kenu refused the then new Koto Kotogi access. In fact, he was reported to have threatened to kill him if he dared set foot in Kenu with the intention of carrying out the sacrifice.

Ilesha. Like the Kenu situation, this subordination was greatly resented by the Chief of Gwanara, particularly since until 1913 the Chief of Gwanara was a District Head.

Gwanara and Ilesha had a tortuous history of conflict and war in the immediate period before colonial rule. One of the most devastating wars of Borgu in the late nineteenth century was the war against Gwanara, largely instigated by Ilesha and Okuta, resulting in almost nine months of siege on Gwanara until their defence line was broken. The eventual invasion led to a near annihilation of Gwanara (Steward 1993). It was not until the advent of European occupation that Sina Kwera (Kpera?) returned to rebuild the town. He was to later become the King of Kenu and was succeeded in Gwanara by Sina Woru, with the title of Komiterere. Sina Woru was the king of Gwanara at the start of the British colonial occupation. At the start of British colonial rule, Sina Woru was a District Head. The reversal to Village Head status under Ilesha, against this history, was understandably devastating for Gwanara.

Under this situation, the relation between the Chief of Gwanara and that of Ilesha was shadowed by incessant disputes and inaction across the two communities. Decision-making became extremely difficult as taxes were not regularly collected, with several Gwanara communities insisting on non-allegiance to Ilesha. Shinaderu II, the Chief of Ilesha (1917 – 1925), with the support of the Emir of Kaiama, Yerima Kura (1916 – 21), made several incriminating allegations against the Chief of Gwanara, all intended to instigate the dethronement of his rival. This relationship of conflict continued until the two communities were separated and Gwanara regained its status as a District in 1922. However, even after this, several allegations were still made against the Chief of Gwanara, leading to his eventual deposition and trial in 1928. He committed suicide shortly after that (NAK 1928).

Yashikira District was also not free of these centrifugal tendencies. The district, for all intents and purposes, was also a creation of the British colonial authorities as it had no pre-colonial antecedent nor was Yashikira a major principality before colonial rule. It was, therefore, an amalgam of Baatonu and Boko/Bokobaru villages. Although the youngest of all the district capitals in terms of the history of its principal town of Yashikira and the pre-colonial political structure, it didn't have any clear political and territorial identity independent of Nikki before the colonial district mapping. Most of the areas in that axis were either under Nikki or Kaiama[75]. The British colonial mapping therefore created the district as a respect and support for Woru Yaru, who was at Bodebere at the start of colonial occupation and lost his claim to the throne of Nikki as a result of his support for the British forces against the French who were already occupying Nikki at the time the throne became vacant. He moved to Yashikira and became the first king, as a Lafiaru prince of Nikki. The colonial mapping exercise carved a number of Bokobaru settlements with historical alliance to Kaiama and placed them under Yashikira. Kaiama had occasionally made vexatious claims to these villages and even on the principal town of Yashikira, which it associated with its Bweru dynastic foundation. In inturn, Yashikira also have boundary grievances around these same settlements that Kaiama claims. Although, the situation hasn't resulted in any major conflict, its been source of occasional political contention.

A similar situation was also obtainable in Bussa Emirate. Bussa had probably since the seventeenth century suffered considerable political depression. It was arguably the smallest of all the principalities of Borgu, as its suzerain control was limited to the riverine communities largely made up of minority ethnic groups. Its control over Wawa, Babanna and even Agwara were a colonial creation. The Babanna axis was largely under Nikki during the pre-colonial period. Bussa's pre-colonial claim over Wawa was contentious. Wawa historically resisted its subjection to Bussa but Babanna, which was originally under Kaiama emirate at the start of colonial rule, didn't raise a major objection, even if it had always asserted its independence. This was understable as Nikki was in the other frontier and they shared ethnic and even political affinities with Bussa.

The challenges of intergroup relations were compounded by colonial administration and territorial boundary structure.Borgu, as examined in the earlier chapters, consisted of several independent polities with relatively strong political relations. The colonial mapping

---

[75] Kaiama and Yashikira have been embroiled in an unending border dispute since colonial times.

and the despotic Native Authority system served to exacerbate in a some cases existing tensions and contentions within these groupings. Although the Baatonu districts experienced internal resistance to subjugation, the role of Kaiama in instituting and supporting such domination only served to deepen its authoritarian hold and the narrative of domination and resentment.

Over the years, colonial mapping has also contributed to the invention of traditions as people orient into the new political structure and have built new rationalisations and narratives to sustain these structures. Colonial history has consequently become "the history." District and emirate identities have been constructed and the inequities and oppressive characteristics are ignored by the respective powers. Every community has developed a new narrative to sustain and even build historical authenticity around them.

An interesting dynamic that hasn't been unravelled is the contention between Kaiama and Bussa. Both were of the same ethnic Boko origin. Although there were some insignificant differences in dialect, such differences, outside of politics, could not warrant some of the developments in the colonial period. There is no evidence of a major conflict between Kaiama and Bussa during the pre-colonial period. We have earlier suggested a level of cooperation between the two entities, including the Gebe War. Kaiama's decision to seek protection from Nikki during its dynastic formative period appears to be a result of the political decline of Bussa. Available records indicate Kaiama's respect for Bussa as a probable progenitor of the Borgu aristocracy, even if this was later denied during the colonial period. The elevation of Kaiama as a provincial capital appears to have been the major point of departure in the relationship between Kaiama and Bussa. Bussa appeared to be averse to the colonial status of Kaiama, believing Kaiama should be placed under Bussa like Wawa or even Babanna. There are several records of fisticuffs between the entourage of the Emir of Kaiama and that of Bussa at several meetings. T. C. Newton, a Colonial Officer in Borgu, reported in 1909 that anytime the two met, it was almost certain that there would be an open fight between their respective followers (NAK 1911). The amalgamation of Kaiama and Bussa emirates exacerbated the situation as Kaiama saw it as a product of a conspiracy and the grand machination of Bussa and the Baatonu people. The new-found friendship between both and the isolation of Kaiama further deepened the frustration, distrust and angst against Bussa.

It was in reaction to this that Kaiama essentially severed its relationship with Bussa and built a desperate narrative to show its ethnogenetic/ethnographic difference with Bussa. They insisted on having Bokobaru as a distinct language in a colonial census. Otherwise, in Kaiama, the languages could easily have been subsumed into one. Insistence on linguistic difference was a protective measure designed to promote the political interests of both communities: Bussa tried to differentiate itself from Kaiama to possibly protect itself from being subsumed under Kaiama Emirate, considering the rapidity of structural changes in Borgu. Kaiama relished its super-ordinate status; its difference from Bussa would help to sustain its status. In fact, the Kaiama narrative of being of Nikki origin got strengthened during the period as it provided a strong ideological and political justification for the control of Baatonu districts that used to be provinces of Nikki. In this period, a new Kisra narrative was developed in Kaiama that tried to delegitimise Bussa and lay originative powers to Nikki. During this period, the Nikki origin of Kaiama, therefore, was not only that of the Kaiama aristocracy; it was often presented as if the entire community migrated from Nikki. Colonialism didn't only deepen differences across ethnicities; it invented new ones within single ethnic groups, polities and principalities.

Intergroup Relations in French Borgu

While the British paradoxically "decentralised" political powers by "centralising" authority in the hands of a few in the Native Authority system, the French decentralised power through the liberalisation and desegregation of authority. Therefore, the French, unlike the British who propped the traditional political system and strengthened it, accentuated the process of decline that had started even before the colonial occupation. The manner, in which this was carried out, through the new colonial political system, created new social groupings and impacted profoundly on intergroup relations. Lombard (1967, 1970), categorised these changes into "vertical and horizontal" changes.

On the vertical lane were the changes in the ethnic and political hierarchy of pre-colonial Borgu. The French "race policy", built on the doctrine that every status group constituted a tribe, disaggregated the Borgu political system and created chiefdoms for other ethnic groups, particularly the Fulbe and their Gando slaves. Each of these "tribes" were given autonomy to manage their affairs and relate with the colonial officials without the interlocution of the Borgu aristocracy. The complex relations of domination and subordination between the status or social groups was thus disrupted and each group (Wasangari, peasant Borgu, Fulbe pastoralists, Gando slaves, Dendi merchants) was directly subject to the colonial state. Curiously, the French didn't see the Baatonu and the Boko as different ethnic groups, despite the linguistic and historical differences. They were considered autochthones and collectively referred to as 'Bariba,' the name by which the Baatonu are known in Benin Republic's official records. It, thus, appears that French were more concerned about the power structure of Borgu than linguistic differences, as the Boko and Baatonu had built a complex web of power and were entwined in the Nikki aristocratic structure. The Gando, outside the slave system, were ethnically Baatonu people as indicated in a previous chapter. They could easily have been subsumed under the Wasangari.

In the new political structure, two or more different local authorities with similar functions in relation to their respective groups were created. According to Lombard (1970), such a measure was an important response to the practical necessity of ensuring separate census and taxation for each of the groups. It was also an important mechanism for meeting the French political and ideological commitment to "justice and liberalism", a doctrine it claimed defined its political presence in Africa. It is not clear whether the French decision to make the Fulbe independent of the political system in Borgu was racially driven, particularly since the Fulbe enjoyed strong political leverage in several French West African colonies. However, it was obvious that the Fulbe enjoyed a level of political patronage as a result of their economic resources, principally livestock. The colonial authorities, therefore, wanted to keep them within the Borgu territory as a cover for its relatively poor resource base. Although they paid higher taxes, they were exempted from labour and plantation work as they had better capacity to pay off for their labour days.

The colonial policy, therefore, meant the Borgu ruling aristocracy lost their economic base and control of the Fulbe. It also meant, for the Fulbe, the loss of the labour power of their Gando slaves who began to leave Fulbe farms in 1906, a process that spanned several generations. The Fulbe were thus obliged to engage in farming, an activity they had previously left to their slaves. In 1900, a political report from Kandi explains this policy. "The appointment of a chief for the Fulani area along with the Bariba chief would make the mutual independence of the two races more effective" (Bierschenck 1993, 226).

The creation of parallel chiefdoms for other social groups – Fulbe pastoralists, Dendi merchants and Gando slaves or lower caste groups – created a situation of territorial structure without effective ownership or control of land, since the land in Borgu was historically owned and controlled by the Baatonu/Boko people. Bierschenck (1993, 1994), who has done extensive work on the Fulbe in Borgu described it as "ethnification", particularly of the Fulbe who were considered not indigenous to Borgu. Bierschenck wrongly argues that to be an ethnic group in any particular formation, such a group must not only be culturally distinct, it must also have control over territory. Therefore, the ethnic group is not just a socio-cultural category, but also a geographical category. Since the Fulbe weren't considered "indigenous" to Borgu, the process of defining their chiefdom and providing territorial space amounted to "ethnification." In essence, the Fulbe were being transformed from an economic or occupational group to an ethnic group. This context is significantly different from the Fulbe aristocracy in northern Nigeria, whose political hegemony was based on political conquest and the institution of a Fulbe-led theocratic state, that is, the Caliphate of Sokoto, whose political system became profoundly important during the colonial occupation. It was also different from the representative system in British Borgu where the Fulbe were given an elective quota within the Native Authority system. In British Borgu, the Fulbe didn't have a parallel political institution and had no direct interface with the colonial authorities. Even when a head was appointed for the Fulbe in British Borgu, it was within the pre-colonial premise. The village or district heads did the appointment and the role was purely a representation of the Fulbe community and a conduit for the village or/and the district heads.

Therefore, in French Borgu, hitherto ethno-economic categories became important political groups with parallel and corresponding power to the Wasangari. In fact, they sometimes had more power than the Borgu groups, as the colonial authorities protected them as a result of their economic resource.

Associated with this was the increase in educated elites who constituted a threat to the native rulers, especially after the Second World War. Although these social categories were not necessarily different, as some of them could be found to have a dual responsibility, it is important to recognise their role in the changing dynamics of intergroup relations during the colonial period. Many of the politicians, post-1945, were prominent members of the aristocratic class. In addition to their ascribed privileged backgrounds, they occupied political offices and were important allies or opponents of other politicians (Bierschenck 1993).

Obviously, the emergence of this educated elite provided a counterbalance to both the chiefs and the colonial powers. A new political dynamic emerged. Although there were only a few of them in French Borgu, as compared to the other parts of Dahomey, it was clear to both the colonial authorities and the chiefs that a new social category had emerged that would have to either be supplanted, placated or penetrated.

In the horizontal lane was the territorial structure and mapping of the colonial authorities. The *cercles*, the subdivisions and villages broke down the few remaining links that Nikki had with its dependencies and provinces. Unlike the British who concentrated power on the emirate and districts through a Native Authority hierarchy, the French decentralised power and allowed for different direct levels of interface with the French colonial officers at all levels. The establishment of colonial administrative centres (*cercles*) in the major Dendi (Wangara) centres of Parakou and Kandi, while the ancient Borgu principalities like Nikki and Kaounde were left to rot as secondary administrative centres was a major blow to the Baatonu/Boko and their aristocratic class. Nikki became subordinate to its previous dependency and its nineteenth century enemy, while Kandi, its previous province, became the capital city of northern Borgu. With this, Nikki experienced a huge reversal of fortune as the king was administratively compelled to visit Parakou against the tradition of the Nikki aristocratic system. These administrative centres brought the Dendi Muslims closer to the colonial authorities. Their principal towns were classified as *chef-lieux de cercle* (Chief of Circle). The Dendi were considered by the French as the best mechanism for future economic development of the region (Lombard 1970). The French built schools and garrisons in these centres and encouraged Dendi children to enrol in school, creating a huge social distance between the Dendi and the Baatonu people.

This decentralisation of local political power by the colonial state was a profound change from the hitherto homogeneous and structured administrative leadership in what became French Borgu. Aside from the creation of a parallel chiefdom for the Fulbe, the French deliberately worked to undermine the powers of the Borgu chiefs. As the Gando were freed and the Fulbe given a different political authority, the Wasangari control over these social groups was lost, to the chagrin of the aristocracy, but the excitement of the "liberated" groups. This created deep resentment among the Wasangari group, exacerbated by the decision to create a paramount chief with an administrative status equivalent to those granted to the old sovereign Borgu, particularly in Parakou and Kandi. As a result, the Borgu aristocracy became isolated from these three groups (Fulbe, Gando and Dendi) and totally unable to assert its hitherto political control over them. Eventually, the whole political economy and power relations of the region was transformed. The loss of their slaves and their territorial rights over herds deprived the Wasangari of the economic base of their power.

While these changes occurred at the formal level, there were elements of resistance and coping mechanisms at the community level. The Borgu aristocracy still created informal mechanisms for extortion of the Fulbe, while the taboo against the Gando was strengthened. Although formal enslavement was prohibited as the Gando were liberated either by colonial policy or direct buy-off of freedom, people of Gando ancestry still suffered discrimination as they were regarded as lower caste.

SECTION THREE

POST-COLONIAL BORGU

CHAPTER ELEVEN

Continuity and Change in Post-Colonial Borgu

The post-colonial, in this context, is not defined as just the period after colonialism. It is a recognition of the interface of each phase of history and how one phase influences the others. It is, therefore, a deliberate periodisation, taking the colonial legacy, its political economy and impact, to be the problematic, as it shaped, defined and redefined, to a large extent, the contemporary realities of Borgu. The "post" in this regard is, therefore, not simply a conception of "after" colonialism, but more as an engagement (resistance and accommodation) with imperial control as defined by different complex dynamics (Webner and Ranger 1996). The post-colonial doesn't mean that the economy and politics has been decolonised or disentangled from its colonial legacy. It is rather a convenient periodisation of an important historical trajectory. As Achille Mbembe (1992; 3) has argued, in understanding post colonial power relations, it is important to look beyond what he called the "binary categories" – resistance against passivity, autonomy against subjection among others, but examine the immoral relations and tension between colonial and successor to colonial rule in all ramification.

Nevertheless, I recognise the tendency of major discourses on post-coloniality to wrongly define it as a mark or end of an era. Post-colonialism is both a continuity and change. This periodisation also comes with some expectations, for example, that the political independence from colonial subjugation would provide a major and decisive shift from the colonial condition to a better society. Also, that the historical domination will be transformed into a society of equity and social justice. Lamentably, the political independence of Africa didn't necessarily result in the freedom from imperial control or the reversal of the structures and processes instituted by the colonial state, even if people indigenous to the instituted nation-states took over the political leadership. The structure of the polities and the larger international political economy reinforced the imperial domination and control within the world capitalist system. Therefore, what is conceived as local to Borgu may, to some extent, be determined or structurally connected to the international political economy.

To be sure, the colonial political economy provided the material and institutional foundation for the development of the post-colonial Nigerian state. The transition from colonial to post-colonial economy and society led to changes in class relations with their attendant contradictions. Apart from the changes in leadership structure, the post-colonial state did not make any significant difference from the colonial state. The attainment of independence eliminated the colonial upper stratum of officialdom, thus opening up the top jobs, and all the attendant perquisites hitherto enjoyed by expatriate colonial administrators to well-placed indigenous people. Independence, to this class of Africans, meant access to the state and its resources.

This section examines the continuities and changes in the politics and society of Borgu in the post-independence era. The objective is to understand how the past has impacted on present-day Borgu. There is an increasing romanticisation of the past in a region that has long been cut off from the centre of political and economic activities and pushed to the margins of the two West African countries, Benin and Nigeria. Therefore, the feeling of "our past is better than our present" or "our people in the neighbouring country are doing better"[76] pervades the region

---

[76] Interview Discussions in Nikki June 2017

Partition and Post-colonial Borgu Identity

The major challenge with the partitioning of Borgu between two different West African countries is not just its arbitrariness, important as that is, but more the nature of the border itself, the shift from a history of flexible borders to a fixed border. Historically, Borgu, like most pre-colonial African societies, didn't have a fixed or hard territorial boundary. Borders were places of contact between different polities, rather than those of division. Ethnic and other identities were flexible and constantly changing as polities continually grew in influence, expanded and contracted. Borders were at once geographical, socio-political and cultural. The size of the polities changed in response to new economic and technological opportunities. For instance, the development in iron technology, cavalry and caravan trade significantly contributed to the expansion of Borgu territory, particularly west and southwards, up to the end of the eighteenth century. Depending on context, borders were, therefore, expanding and contracting.

As was the case with most pre-colonial African societies, boundaries were largely managed by what Herbst (2014) called "buffer mechanisms." Buffer states were instituted at distant frontiers or on the extremes of the political centre either as vassals, provinces or dependencies. That was the role places like Kenu, Gberegburu, Okuta, Kandi and others played for Nikki in the nineteenth century. Kaiama and Parakou played a similar role in the eighteenth century. The territorial boundaries of Borgu did not necessarily depend on the ethnic or cultural affinity of the people but more on military prowess and dynastic alliances. Ethnic attachment, as seen in the earlier chapters, was continually shifting.

Colonialism altered this formation and created fixed territorial boundaries with citizenship based on Westphalian principles. Against the expectations of post-independence boundary readjustments, the post-colonial African leaders unilaterally and, sometimes, collectively decided to retain the colonially defined nation-states as exclusive units of organisations and retained those boundaries. The Organisation of African Unity (OAU), at its first Ordinary Session of the Assembly of Head of States and Government in 1964, declared that "all member states pleased themselves to respect borders existing on their achievement of national independence" (Brownlie 1971). It also resolved to respect the sovereignty and territorial integrity of each state and for its inalienable right to independent existence. The colonial cartographic structure became the nucleus of the post-colonial state system, characterised by territorial sovereignty, populations attached to the territory and boundary lines that were closely guarded and controlled, even when they cut across people of the same socio-political and ecological system from just a few decades earlier. It was in this context that the Borgu boundary dividing Nigeria and Dahomey was retained with all the implications for the development and identity of the Borgu people in the two countries.

Despite the arbitrariness of the borders, over time, they became entrenched and deeply embedded in the communities, developing its own peculiar political economy. While borders are generally seen in their restrictive sense, the international border re-moulded Borgu identity and in some cases provided different corridors of opportunities for people dwelling at the frontiers (Fynn 1997). Once the border was consolidated, the initial resistance (largely through cross-migration) transformed into resignation and accommodation and exploration of opportunities associated with the borders.

While the arbitrariness of the border was quite unsettling for the people and to a large extent undermined the political, economic, social and natural eco-system, it is important to recognise that borders or borderlands, generally, around the world, are largely artificially partitioned cultural areas. Borgu is, therefore, just one example, but not necessarily peculiar (Asiwaju 1992). The immediate implication of this change is the transformation of Borgu from a relatively small socio-politically defined territory to a politically bounded territory within a larger and more complex social, economic and political context. This dissonance between ethnic groups and nation-state had significant implications for the identity and development of Borgu.

For the Borgu community, especially the Baatonu and Boko people, the split had a significant implication on community identity as they encountered other ethnicities within the new political configuration. They found themselves as constituting minorities, extreme minorities in Nigeria and a major ethnic group in Benin. This was surely a challenge in countries where ethnicity plays significant, obscurantist roles in politics. Thus, they were either pushed to the margin of development as in Nigeria or compelled to push back as was the case in Benin Republic. Counter-mobilisation of the Borgu identity to address the challenge of powerlessness and under-development has been insipid.

The partitioning, therefore, had a significant but contradictory impact on the region. While it might have significantly diminished Borgu identity and influence, especially in Nigeria, it conversely created an element of micro-nationalism directed at cultural preservation. That said, there is a significant difference between the experience of the rural peasantry and the educated elites of the two countries. The level of contact over the years between the educated elites of the region across the two countries has been minimal, compared to the peasants, particularly those living in the border towns and villages. Through formal education, new cultural values and class identity and networks have been built that could not find corresponding resonance across the countries. This is not only due to hard border lines and immigration procedures, but more a result of European linguistic barriers, which has become not only a second language but the language of the educated class.

As observed by Asiwaju:

> ... there have been parallel socialisation processes by which the obviously different languages and cultures of the two colonising powers have been adopted as the official language and culture of succeeding independent state. But the effects have been more deeply felt by Western-educated elites on either side than the non-literate majority of the local population who have remained attached to the indigenous culture and its traditions... (2005, 131)

The Borgu languages, unlike the Hausa and Yoruba languages in Nigeria which evolved in written Roman script, weren't languages of teaching. Thus they suffered from poor documentation and development. However, like the Hausa ethnic group in Niger and Nigeria as observed by Miles (1994), the national identity appears to have superseded Borgu identity. The common ancestry was not questioned and remains, in fact, strong. There is considerable pride in expressing it. But there is also a strong recognition of the difference in citizenship or national identity and a feeling of connection with the citizenship of either of the nation-states.

This appears different from the experience of the Yoruba in Benin Republic and Nigeria, where ethnic solidarity was believed to be accorded greater premium than national identity and solidarity (Kehinde 2010). Like the Sabe, as argued by Flynn (1997), the Borgu people across the borders connect the two national economic and political systems and redirect their marginal status to their own economic advantage and capitalised on the weak state system, have built informal networks and undermined the border through smuggling, or serving as brokers for smugglers, and human trafficking such as the recruitment of house helps and farmworkers. They asserted their rights to free movement within their Borgu "territorial space" irrespective of the international border by wedging themselves between the traditional institutions, traders and the state. The poor socio-economic condition of the people didn't necessarily erode the sense of national feelings or citizenship of these countries. They only tried to take advantage of this duality to maximise their gains by creatively, sometimes using kinship, to access economic and social opportunities across boundaries.

Despite the dominance of national identity, there is still a huge level of interaction and movement across the border. The division of borders is often ignored in most places except those with formal border posts. There are still common social, economic and religious activities. The Nikki Gaani Festival and other lesser ones attract people from both countries. The traditional religions of *bori* and *werengu* are still practised on the Benin side of Borgu and attract adherents from the Nigerian side. While the Borgu people are not big players in the large-scale cross-border trade, there is still a significant trade relationship between the two. This is possibly because of the historical significance of Nikki and the much larger size of Borgu in Benin. The Baatonu particularly associate their authenticity with Nikki; the languages and cultural practices of Borgu in Benin are deemed more authentic, even if they have been greatly influenced by French and other cultures on that side.

Dynamics of Post-Colonial Development

Post-colonial Africa has been largely preoccupied with the discourse and politics of development, with little or no significant result.

Different explanations have been offered for the crisis of development, which Ake summarises to include the colonial legacy, social pluralism and its fractious politics, corruption, poor labour discipline, lack of entrepreneurial skills, poor planning and execution, poor capital base, low levels of technical assistance, falling commodity prices, unfavourable terms of trade, and low levels of savings investment (Ake 1996). While all these are important and have had significant impact on development in Africa, the challenge, according to Ake (1996), is that development has never really been on the agenda because Africa has been "constituted to prevent the pursuit of development and the emergence of relevant and effective development paradigms and programs" (Ake 1996, 1).

Arguing along the same lines, Basil Davidson (1992) observes that the African development crisis is derived essentially from the construction of the African project on the basis of European models rather than on the basis of Africa's own rich and varied history and experience. Therefore, politics is recognised as the greatest impediment to development in Africa. These shaped the character of the state immensely and defined its attitudes, pattern, and essence in development processes, including its relationship with the society and the management and distribution of resources.

The independent states of Nigeria and Dahomey (later Benin) where Borgu is located inherited a diverse population that often became fractious as disparate groups competed for resources and identity. The difficulties in managing competition and national contention among these groups were a substantial strain on governance and development. This, coupled with the character of the state and economy, has created a huge development challenge, especially for marginal regions like Borgu in both countries. Colonialism bequeathed a weak economic and political foundation. The structure of the economy and state generated inequalities among different areas and segments of the countries. The challenge became even more daunting as the countries began to experience major political crisis within the first decade of independence. The states appeared incapable of regulating the factional competition for power, resources and opportunities within the ruling class because it was not independent of these factional groupings.

In Dahomey, for instance, limited opportunities occasioned by poor economic and political structure created huge tension and rivalry between major groups and members of the ruling class. The pre-independent coalition group, the *Parti Progress Dahoméen,* quickly collapsed as principal leaders representing the different regions of the north and south went their separate ways. As the political crisis deepened between 1960 when Benin secured its independence and 1970, leadership succession "swung like a pendulum" between the north and the south and, sometimes, between the zones of the south. Benin experienced its first military coup in 1963, barely three years after independence. Since then, the country has suffered five additional military coups and many constitutional changes aimed at reviving and sustaining its fledgeling democracy. It became entangled in a "tripartite ethno-regional political struggle, an equally divisive economic and social disparity between north and south, and a large surplus of repatriated workers who had staffed the French colonial states in West Africa" (Magnusson 2001, 218).

In 1972, the country fell into a full-fledged military rule led by Mathew Kerekou that eventually adopted a "nationalist Marxist-Leninist" ideology in 1974. Apart from nationalisation of businesses and schools and related institutions, the new ideology also provided a cover "to dismantle and re-centralise the three powerful regional patronage networks at the heart of the country's political paralysis and to increase employment through the creation of hundreds of state-owned enterprises" (Magnusson 2001, 218). The economic situation escalated as the state economic policy clashed with the foreign and domestic political, economic and political interest (Dossou-Yovo 1999). As part of responding to the deepening crisis, the government renamed Dahomey to People's Republic of Benin in 1975 and instituted a one-party state known as *Parti de la Révolution Popualaire du Bénin* (PRPB). In 1980, Kerekou transmuted from a military leader to a civilian president. Despite the deepening social, political and economic crisis, Benin remained under the authoritarian hold of a one-party state until 1985 when it reversed its authoritarian ideology to embrace neo-liberal economic reforms, with strong implications for the economy and society. The resultant escalation in civil and political crisis and the economic bankruptcy quickly compelled a political transition through a sovereign national conference in 1989/1990. Since then, Benin has remained an important example of liberal democracy, without significant changes in its economic profile and sustainable development.

****

Nigeria also had a similar trajectory. Like other African countries, it inherited a disarticulated economy built on primary communities with the political system revolving around the stronghold of three major ethno-regional groups divided across the north and south. Although each of the three major regions – north, west and east – had their own internal fissures, the major national contention was across north and south. The post-colonial leadership, after six years of political crisis, collapsed under the weight of a military coup and counter-coup which rapidly escalated into to three years of civil war (1967 -1970), with the attendant effect on the economy and politics of the country. Unequal competition for power and resources at the national level increased the instability in the system as successive compromises of the ruling class collapsed as quickly as they were patched up. Within this crisis and national confusion, according to Gavin (1976), "the ethics of business penetrated politics, the ethics of politics penetrated business, the ethics of gangsters penetrated both."

The end of the civil war didn't necessarily settle the question of national unity or what political scientists often referred to as the "national question" (Yahaya 1980; Mustapha 1986; Olukoshi and Osita 1996). Rather, it reopened a new vista even as the old remained unsettled. Some of the contradictions, as examined by Mustapha (1986), include: the contradictions between Nigeria and imperialism, the contradiction and contention among the three major ethnic groups, which defined the construct of the tripod of Nigerian politics, representing the three post-colonial regions; the minority questions – contradiction between the majority and minority ethnic groups across all the regions, whose fears and grievances had been articulated in the Willinks Commission report; the rivalry in multi-ethnic states, which constituted the component units of the federation – Kwara and Niger states, where Borgu communities are largely found in Nigeria, being important examples of this. Others include intra-ethnic contention and rivalries; inter-clan and community rivalries within a given district or local government – for instance, the tension and contention between the different districts and ethnic/sub-ethnic groups that constituted Borgu. These contradictions have become ingrained in the national political and economic development dynamics and have continued to define and redefine who gets what, when and how.

Development in Nigeria has, therefore, been mediated and influenced by what Olukoshi (2000) called "the context and pattern of the national question, the capitalist accumulation process has, in turn, shaped and reshaped the contradiction that underlies the question itself, sometimes giving them new meanings and context" (Olukoshi 2000, 78). He further argued that the contradiction has been compounded by uneven development, deepening inequalities and protracted military authoritarian rule. Even after the civil war, the country had to contend with more military coups and counter-coups all reflecting the power dynamics of the country. When the military initiated a transition to democracy, it eventually torpedoed the process through the annulment of the result of the presidential elections, plunging the country into another around of political brinksmanship, resulting in another military coup and then a full-blown dictatorship.

An important implication of protracted military rule in Nigeria was the increased concentration and centralisation of power and resources, as well as the erosion of federal values. This served to escalate the national political crisis and retard national development. The national response to the economic crisis was a Structural Adjustment Programme (SAP) in 1986 that further compounded the problem, escalating the economic crisis and consequently exacerbating the decomposition of the state.

This chronicle of development challenges may look broad and probably remote to the realities of a relatively small and marginal community like Borgu. They are, however, important national context that shaped and determined the relationship between the state, in both countries, and the Borgu communities. The important point here is that national and local development and politics were shaped, to a large extent, by these national realities. As a region located on the fringe of the two countries and minority ethnic groups, Borgu's capacity to engage at the national level was deeply constrained by the restrictive national space already occupied by bigger groups and interests. The influence of national politics and economy surely differed. While

Borgu in Benin has been a major player in the national and northern regional politics of Benin, the same has not been the case with Borgu in Nigeria. The difference may be a function of the size of the countries and the depth and breadth of diversity of each country. Benin is a relatively small country and Borgu has a wide geographical mass and population spread across four states within it. These are the Alibori, Atakora Donga and Borgou departments (states). Parakou, the capital city of Borgou department, is the second largest city in Benin and served as an important hub for other Borgu towns. To be sure, development in the region has not been equally distributed as there are strong outlays of excluded communities, sometimes with little or no state presence. The context in Nigeria is profoundly different. Nigeria is a very large country with over four hundred ethnic groups, of which the Borgu ethnicities are arguably some of the smallest. The capacity of the community to influence development within the larger politics of national diversity has always been deeply constrained.

Dilemmas of Development in Borgu

Borgu communities in Kebbi, Kwara and Niger states in Nigeria spread across five local government areas— Agwara, Baruten, parts of Bagudo, Borgu and Kaiama— are arguably some of the poorest communities in Nigeria in terms of both physical and human development. Despite the paucity of statistics to support this argument, major development indicators such as school enrolment, maternal mortality, infant mortality, literacy levels, poverty, unemployment and the exclusion of women, among others, are rated well below national, regional and state averages. For instance, Kaiama and Baruten in Kwara State are generally recognised as the least developed regions in the state, even if the two constitute about half the geographical landmass of the state. While some of these challenges are largely historical, as examined earlier, they have been deeply escalated by political, sociological, economic, geographical and demographic dilemmas as examined below.

Figure 1: Dilemma of development in Borgu

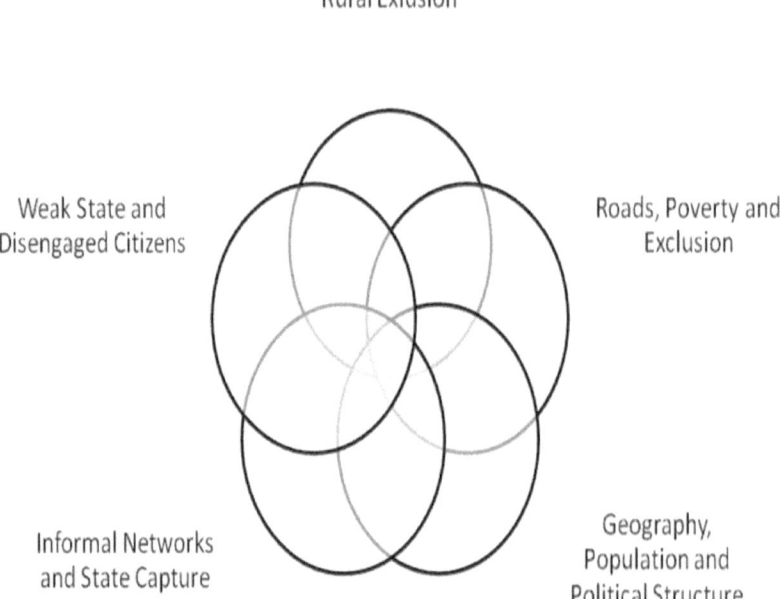

Dilemma of Urban Preference and Rural Exclusion

Urbanisation and urbanism have been largely promoted by the colonial and post-colonial state and are recognised as the face of development and modernity. The modernisation theory of development, which was the most influential in the immediate post-colonial period, regarded urbanisation as an important element of industrialisation and modernisation, while the rural represented traditional values and backwardness. Regardless, there were long established urban traditions in West Africa even before colonial occupation. Some principal towns and power centres were largely considered urban in the context of the development at that time. In Borgu, Bussa, Parakou, Nikki, Djougou, Illo and Kaiama were commercial centres on the caravan routes, protected by the machinery of centralised states and linking the coast to the major centres in the Central Sudan.

The colonial experience altered these formations, as already set out. According to Homes (1976), the alteration was influenced by three factors: the emergence of a rail system, colonial administrative structure and mineral exploitation. The rail system, built between 1896 and 1930 was introduced to meet the demands of the colonial economy. With this, trading routes across Borgu were diverted as a new transportation system with a new orientation was introduced. The system was to support the movement of raw materials of cotton and groundnuts from the northern region down to the coast in the south of Nigeria for onward shipping to Europe. Borgu towns, whose prosperity had depended on river and caravan trade were supplanted by the railway network. Instead, new railway labour camps emerged at Kafanchan, Makurdi and Minna, providing the nuclei for urban growth in the sparsely populated central Nigeria region (Home 1976, 59). As would be seen, the road network operated as an adjunct to the railways, not in competition with it (Gavin 1976). It, therefore, reinforced the exclusion of Borgu from major trading routes and consequently alienated it from the national economic mainstream.

The colonial administration created new towns and, in some cases, supplanted old political centres. Central administrative capitals enjoyed a privileged development interest. It is in this context that Parakou and, to some extent, Djougou, became more important than Nikki in colonial Dahomey. However, in Nigeria, none of the pre-colonial centres enjoyed that status. The province of Borgu, with capital in Kaiama (later Bussa), was abolished barely four years after effective colonial occupation. Borgu was, thereafter, placed under three different and distant provincial capitals at different times. The divisional capitals of Kaiama and Bussa were not only removed from their districts, but they were also extremely remote from the provincial capitals (Kontagora and later Ilorin).

Solid mineral exploration and exploitation was another driver of urbanisation, particularly tin mining around the Jos plateau and coal in the south. Borgu was not in the mining zone. Mining activities in Wawa District in the 1930s was discontinued even before it gained any prominence. Another important stimulant to urbanisation and urban networking was agriculture, particularly food and export commodities. While the French built on that through cotton production linked to Parakou, in Nigeria, Borgu was peripheral to the food production market and almost totally unconnected to the export market. As a result, the colonial economy in Nigeria didn't have any material link to any of the Borgu principal formations and they therefore, found themselves outside the urban network.

This was the structure inherited by the post-colonial-state. Borgu in Nigeria, in particular, was totally removed from the transportation network of the country, even as all the major roads that traversed the region are classified as "Trunk A" and deemed Federal Government roads. They were not in any way strategically linked to the national network or any urban centre. In fact, after almost six decades of independence, it is still not linked to any economic or political centre in the country. Borgu in Nigeria is, therefore, not only largely rural; it is literally and geographically on the fringe of the country.

The post-colonial state's approach to rural development is essentially a continuum from the colonial. Development is, therefore, ideologically skewed in favour of the urban areas, supported by large infrastructure, social services and industrial policies. Ake (1981) called it an "enclave development," a situation where development activities continued to be concentrated in a few urban areas to the detriment of the vast rural formations. Even when major development infrastructure was located in the region, like the Kainji Dam and the Borgu Game Reserve, it was principally done to serve the urban population, as would be seen. Rural development is often confused with agricultural development (Mabogunje 1981). Rural areas are specifically supported through development programmes that are attached to agriculture and the peasantry, particularly the provision of feeder roads, agricultural extension services, farm input and credit facilities to improve food production to feed the urban population. Some of the policies since independence include slogans like Operation Feed the Nation, Green Revolution and extensive World Bank-supported programmes like Agricultural Development Programmes (ADPs) of different phases or even the structural adjustment palliative like the Directorate for Food, Roads and Rural Infrastructure (DFFRI) and its political twin, the Better Life for Rural Women. Based on these development principles, Borgu is *ab initio* disadvantaged. Rural development programmes have been largely challenged by three dilemmas: the dilemma of design, which involves determining the best approach to rural development and schematic image as well as the dilemma of organisation, involving the appropriate structure for programme delivery. There is also the dilemma of implementation (Mabogunje 1981).

The ADP programme in Borgu Local Government of then Kwara State, centred in Kaiama in the 1980s, was a poignant example of the dilemma of these programmes. The programme invested hugely on physical structures, including offices and residential buildings for its staff, without corresponding impactful delivery on the programme. Years later, the structures remain in ruins at the end of the project, with buildings vandalised. As a result, despite the years of ostensible interest in agricultural development, the peasantry in a substantial part of Nigerian Borgu, to use the words of Goran Hyden (1980) have remained "uncaptured." They have not been fully integrated into the capitalist production relations and have remained victims of the urban market, at the receiving end of the agriculture value chain. The production system is still rain-fed, largely by small-holder farmers relying on hand tools and a huge labour, in some locations interspersed by a few wealthy peasants and "politico-farmers," politicians who hijack government's agricultural programmes for personal gain to the detriment of the poor peasants whom the programme was meant for. With poor infrastructure and social services, Borgu's integration into the national economic network has been minimal, despite being thought of as a "food basket." The major crops produced are food crops basically for subsistence and in the last few decades for the neighbouring local markets. The produce is largely corn, guinea corn, millet, a sprinkle of rice in the riverine areas and yams in Kaiama and Baruten local government areas. The yams in Kaiama and Baruten are locally processed (dried) into *Kikiyaa/Kinakunu* (in Boko and Baatonum) and mainly consumed as *elubo/amala* by Yoruba.

Dilemma of Geography, Population and Political Structure

The strong relationship between geography, politics and development has been long recognised (Mabogunje 1980; Herbst 2014). The extent of such influence has, however, been a subject of debate between political geographers and political economists. The nature and size of polities shape societal relationships with the state. While there is a general interest on the impact of government policies on development, there is no significant interest in how geography shapes development beyond works on political geography. To be sure, economists have always related economics of scale with size, even if such conversations are often associated with nation states or businesses, not territories within nations. Herbst (2014) did an extensive exposition on the geography and the broadcast of authority. He noted that until James Madison upturned the argument against small-size states, early conversations on state size had been in favour of small states. Classical political theory was observed to be in favour of small political units, ideally the city-state. Plato placed his ideal number of citizens to be 5,040, while Aristotle emphasised the need for a direct assembly and personal contact in an ideal state. Madison's intervention suggested that large states, apart from being democratic, are also able to manage factionalism (Herbst 2014). Subsequent traditions favoured large states and recognised it as critical to modernisation and development in the context of evolutionary growth from simple to familial to ethnic and beyond.

Borgu has been historically challenged by three dilemmas of geography—size, population and structure. These three significantly conspired with the post-colonial state to keep Borgu poor. Pre-colonial and colonial Borgu was a vast geographical territory typical of states in the savannah belt. As seen earlier, it has, since contact with colonial rule, never enjoyed any stability of political geography. It was first partitioned into two countries and within each of these countries, it has been severely balkanised and scattered into politically and economically weak entities. In Nigerian Borgu, it is scattered across five local governments in three different states (Kebbi, Kwara and Niger). In all the states, it constituted extreme minority groups in terms of population and remains located in the fringe of the states. This has not only denied them economic opportunity and basic infrastructure, but they also have in addition suffered political exclusion. Baruten and Kaiama local governments in Kwara, for instance, constitute more than half of the geographical mass of the state.

Table 9: Population Density of Borgu in Nigeria[77]

LGA	STATE	POPULATION	SIZE IN KM²	DENSITY
AGWARA	Niger	57,413	2,105	27
BARUTEN	Kwara	206,679	9,749	21
BORGU	Niger	172,835	11,782.5	15
KAIAMA	Kwara	124,015	6,917	18
TOTAL		560,942	30,607.5	18

Though a vast region, Borgu is arguably one of the more sparsely populated regions of Nigeria. Borgu covers more than 30,607 km². The region is larger than the entire south-east of Nigeria. Kaiama Local Government, one of the smallest in the region, is bigger than all the south-east states except Enugu State. Borgu Local Government in Niger state is larger than any state in south-west Nigeria except Oyo state. Only eleven of the thirty-six states of the Nigerian federation are larger in geographical mass than the combined size of the four main Borgu local governments. However, the geographical mass has no corresponding population. The population density of Nigerian Borgu, based on the 2006 population census, is barely eighteen persons per km², against the average of fifty-two and sixty-four per km² in Niger and Kwara states as a whole. The paucity of population is, even more, telling when compared to other regions of Nigeria. Ekiti State, one of the smallest in Nigeria, has a population density of three hundred and seventy-seven per km², while Abia, another small state, has a population density of four hundred and fifty per km².

With that level of population, Borgu communities constitute extreme minorities in the three states. Beyond the inability to raise adequate resources to finance development, as it was under colonial rule, it places the region under serious difficulties in its competition with other ethnic groups at the state and national levels for access to national resources and the attention of the state. The cost of providing basic services like roads, education, health facilities and even agricultural extension services is often higher, as such service points require large coverage. In a country where resources are shared based on population and political influence, Borgu is obviously disadvantaged. The inability to provide these services has created massive ungoverned spaces. Borgu, therefore, remains one of the

---

[77] This figures excludes Ilo in Kebbi state.

poorest regions in West Africa with limited state presence and development infrastructure.

The years of political structuring since the colonial times has not helped matters. The region has been structurally unstable even after independence. Borgu was a single local government, despite its size. It was later divided into local governments until 1991 when the Bussa Emirate segment of Borgu Local Government was excised and merged with Niger State. Before this period, Borgu Local Government covered more than 30,000 km^2, almost half the size of Kwara State but had only one local government. Baruten Local Government was created out of Borgu during the Second Republic, but the decision was quickly abrogated by the succeeding military government. Borgu, therefore, returned to its one local government regime until 1989 when Kaiama Local Government was created.

Borgu's ceding to Ilorin Province during the colonial period and later to Kwara State in 1967 didn't happen without protest. In 1967, the Borgu elite protested against being placed under Kwara State when it was created in 1967. The petition was believed to be successful when the Irikefe Panel advised that the local government be merged with the Northwestern State, which later metamorphosed to Niger State. Despite the subsequent state creations, this change never happened until 1991 when the emirate of Bussa (a political half of Borgu Local Government) was ceded to Niger State. By this period, Borgu was already split into three local governments, with one still bearing the original Borgu name. While the panel's recommendation was believed to be the basis for the merger of Bussa Emirate with Niger State, typical of military policy making, there was no adequate consultation across the old Borgu to allow for a collective decision on whether to move or not. Within the limted time for consultation, the Kaiama and Baruten elites, for some reasons, opted to remain in Kwara[78]. To be sure, Borgu was so divided across colonially invented identities that collective decisions might have been impossible as each of the three contending groups had its own local government and

---

[78] The political differences and district identities played an important role in this regards. The Kaiama and Baruten elites appeared more comfortable with the "devil they know than the angel they don't know". Summary of interviews with some Kaiama and Baruten politicians.

wouldn't trust the circumstances and politics behind the new and "suspicious" move[79].

As it is today, the Borgu region is not only on the fringes of two West African countries, it is, particularly in Nigeria, also on the fringes of three states without any direct link to any urban corridor. Located in the south-west of the defunct Northern Region, its relationship with the centres at different times in Zungeru, Lokoja, Kaduna, Lagos and Abuja was mediated by other lesser centres. Even in the contemporary federal structure, particularly in Kwara State, Kaiama and Baruten have no direct access to Ilorin, the capital city of the state. Approaching Ilorin has to be mediated from the north through Niger State and the south through Oyo State.

Dilemma of Roads, Poverty and Exclusion

A good road network is a very important infrastructure development everywhere, whether rural or urban. They define the extent of the broadcast of authority especially in developing societies, enhance market access and define the degree of citizens' participation in the governance processes. It is to this extent that roads have been very significant to both the pre-colonial and colonial authorities in most parts of Borgu. In fact, the colonial authorities were practically obsessed with roads and travelling. They spent most of their time travelling across the region to broadcast state authority to the people, ensure collection of taxes and open up places for state and market exploitation. Over 90% of passenger and freight in Borgu are dependent on road transportation and it has always been the most basic and primary means of communication.

The crisis of road infrastructure in Nigerian Borgu is particularly a historical one. During the colonial times, it was the most discussed by all European political and district officials and took most of their time. Since 1907, practically every colonial report had something to document about the challenges of communication in Borgu. District officials spent a substantial part of their time supporting road

---

[79] This is a summary of my interviews with different Borgu actors in Kaiama, Abuja, Bussa and Kaduna.

construction. It consumed a lot of community labour and Native Authority resources.

Road infrastructure constitutes a major development challenge in the region. In some parts, it is worse than what was bequeathed by the colonial authorities. In 1904, Lugard described the road from Kaiama to the River Niger as "perhaps the best we have seen (other than those of the Public Works Department), and the addition of a few culverts or ramps will render the road from the (River) Niger to Kaiama fit for carts, by which the shea and other produce can be conveyed to the river for export" (Lugard 1905, 76). This was not just an exaggeration; it was a reflection of the strategic nature of Borgu at this period to the economic interest of the then emerging colonial state. Since then, no other colonial official made any positive comment about the roads. While the colonial officials in the 1930s up to the 1940s complained persistently about the situation, no significant action was taken as the colonial government was not ready to invest resources to address the problem because the strategic relevance of the Borgu had dropped significantly over the years.

Joyce Cary, a British District Officer based in Kaiama (1917 – 1919), who later became an important novelist, has used roads and bridges as his major themes in his African fictional novels. Most of his writings depicted his lived experience in Borgu, particularly Kaiama. His novels, *Mister Johnson* (1962) and *Aissa Saved* (1940) and later his political writings, especially *The case for African Freedom* (1944) also depicted his experiences. These experiences were also reflected in a series of letters he wrote to his wife during his service in Borgu. Cary was transformed from his prejudiced impression of Borgu to a sympathizer. In *Mister Johnson*, Cary fictionally depicted Kaiama as Fada.

He invested a substantial part of his time initiating and supporting road construction across Kaiama Division until he left in 1919. He was particularly fond of his inventive foreman, Tasuki[80] who bears the same name in *Mister Johnson*. He described him in *Freedom for Africa* as "my bridge builder was a little pagan called Tasuki, about four feet high, and six stone weight, with a face and chin and beard,

---

[80] Tasuki lived to served several other European officers, and was often referred to Tasuki *Dotantan*, in apparent reference to his inventive culinary prowess.

very like the famous Kruger... Tasuki had invented all by himself and for this one job, the compound lever, the multiple pulleys, and several new devices never seen before and probably never used since ..." In a different letter, he called Tasuki "really a treasure ... he is the most precious of the discoveries, a man who can do a job with conscience" (Moody 1967, 148).

Cary completed the sixty-nine kilometre road from Kaiama to Wawa. It was the first time a seasonal road was constructed in that axis. He had planned to build the remaining twenty-three miles on to Bussa before he left Borgu (Moody 1967). The Kaiama-Wawa road was the first road to have been opened up beyond the caravan pathways. It was the first time any attempt would be made on roads in Borgu. The initial preoccupation was on roads leading to the colonial lodges in Kaiama and Bussa. Cary believed such roads would open up Borgu and increase trade, particularly after almost two decades of economic devastation occasioned by the diversion of the caravans and internationalisation of borders in Borgu.

Road infrastructure began to receive major attention only after the colonial government increased the Native Authority share of revenue to 70% in 1935. Before 1937, when the Kaiama – Ilorin road up to the boundary with Oyo and the Kaiama – Bussa road as far as River Oli was constructed, there was no single all-season road in Nigerian Borgu. However, on the French side, Borgu was already connected from the coast up to the colony of Niger in the north. The French were initially concerned about their landlocked colony of Niger. British Nigeria, being the historical outlet to the coast, they feared it could lead to the diversion of trade to the Nigerian side and, therefore, determinedly constructed a road network that passed through Borgu (Parakou – Kandi – Niger road) in northern Dahomey up to the coast. This was later supplemented by a railway. These provided an important and major road connection for French Borgu. The next was to concentrate on the arteries of roads into the interior to support cash crop production and promotion of trade. It appears the French appreciated the importance of roads to its economic interest and, therefor mobilised resources in support of the process.

The major challenge of road construction in British Borgu was the number of rivers that required to be bridged and the lack of capacity of the Native Authority to fund this complex construction. In 1939, there were six rivers that required bridging. These were the Oli River, which was the widest, then the Luda, Woko, Doro, Timo and Monai. Considering the expansive mass of Borgu, with a sparsely distributed population, roads had to extend longer distances to reach communities. Borgu was over 30,000 km^2, with a population of barely forty thousand people in 1940. In land mass, Borgu was 3.5 percent of the area and the ninth largest division in the Northern provinces.

Table 10: Kaiama NA Administration: Proposed Works Programme 1941 – 1946

Description	1941–42	1942–43	1943-44	1944–45	1945–46
Oyo Boundary – Kaiama (32 Miles)	-	50	50	50	50
Kaiama – Bussa 23 Miles (River Woro)	150	50	50	50	50
Kaiama – Yashikira (56 Miles)	50	50	50		
Oyo – Boundary – Ilesha – Okuta – Yashikira (78 Miles)	-	30	50	50	50
Ilesha – Gwanara (20 Miles)	-	20	20	10	10
Gwassoro – Shuya (27 Miles)				40	40
Total	200	200	200	200	200

Source: NAK 1941

In 1949, the government decided to establish a ferry at Bussa and made the New Bussa to Rofia road a Native Authority road. The road was expected to reach Shagunu at Mile 11 before the end of the 1950 financial year. Nevertheless, the help of the government of Northern Region was required to bridge the Swashi River; to make the road all-season. In the same year, the Kaiama – Gwassoro road was reported to have improved considerably and may have been motorable all season. A new road, some twenty miles in length, had been built from Gwassoro to Kosubosu on the Yashikira Road. The construction of Ilesha – Yashikira Trunk Road continued that year with a section from Yashikira to Chikanda on the frontier with Dahomey. The government had also decided to rebuild the Kaiama – Bussa Road as a Trunk B, an all season temporary bridge was constructed at Woro (NAK 1950).

No significant improvement was made on roads in most parts of Nigerian Borgu since independence. Apart from some of the bridges constructed, the condition has remained the same where it has not worsened. Although post-colonial Nigeria has been judged to have done well, relative to other African countries on the expansion of road networks (Herbst 2014), this effort has not impacted on Borgu in any significant way. Borgu did not benefit from the massive expansion of road networks during the oil boom period in the 1970s. Roads were largely concentrated around commercial and political centres. Rural areas with large geographical mass and low population were largely neglected.

Efficient transportation is, therefore, a significant missing link in the physical and human development in Borgu. According to Derwent Whittlesey, efficient transportation is important for political consolidation. This has been the case, whether in Roman Empire or the United States of America. Poor road network is generally a political weakness particularly in large territories (Herbst 2014). Poor road infrastructure and limited connectivity has isolated Borgu from the mainstream. It is far off from the political centre and excluded from major political activities. Its economy is poor because the peasants are not making enough from their labour and this affects agricultural productivity and the cycle continues. Health services and education are poorly accessed as qualified people are reluctant to stay in rural areas with limited transport access. It is, therefore, not surprising that the region has one of the lowest development indicators in their respective states.

The road crisis in Borgu is not just a function of the development model inherited from colonial rule. It is also a reflection of the deepening crisis of the Nigerian federal system, the increasing centralisation and concentration of power at the centre. Most of the major roads in Borgu are classified as federal roads. The origin of this classification is also colonial as defined by first generation road maps. With communities removed from the centres and not connected to any market, political and urban centre, the roads were hardly noticed; they are federal roads and also rural without any strategic link to any urban corridor, the state governments have been reluctant to do anything about them.

The idea of building a road network from Sokoto to Badagry that passes through mainland Borgu, with a new Niger bridge around Bussa was first mooted by the colonial government and later again in the 1970s, has been abandoned. Generally, whenever the state governments have decided to handle any roads for political reasons, it has often been badly constructed and used mostly to extract funds from the Federal Government as is the case with the Ilesha – Chikanda Road and Kishi – Kaiama Road in Baruten and Kaiama local governments respectively. Furthermore, these abandoned or neglected roads were sources of corruption for civil servant and politicians, as funds are budgeted for political patronage and work is never done as the case of Kaiama – Wawa Road since 2002[81] and the Kishi – Kaiama – Kosubosu Road since the 1980s. The Kaiama – Kosubosu segment of this road is practically lost. While roads have been a national challenge, the situation in Borgu appears to be peculiar as some of the roads in the region are arguably the only Federal roads that have never been paved. At the moment, apart from New Bussa and its neighbouring communities, no other part of Nigerian Borgu is easily accessible. Even the Bussa access is probably as a result of the Kainji Dam.

Dilemma of Informal Institutions, Networks and State Capture

The peculiarities of African politics, especially its widespread informal institutions and networks, have been extensively studied (Ekeh 1975; Lewis 1998; Sandbrook 1985 and 1998; Joseph 1987; Hyden 2006; Herbst 2014). These informal networks and relations are attached to the "economy of affection" which Hyden described as "personal investments in reciprocal relations with other individuals as a means of achieving goals that are seen as otherwise impossible to attain" (Hyden 2006, 73). These goals could be tangible or intangible and are considered sought-after and scarce. They could be electoral positions, appointments, prestige or status-related or even job opportunities, enlistment in government programmes or securing official documents. Engagement in the economy of affection could be incidental, one-off or regularised, but it involves largely working outside the formal institutional framework to achieve a certain objective. It is not necessarily "an expression of rationality or altruism.

---

[81] Information from the Ministry of Works and FERMA (Federal Roads Maintenance Agency) indicates that resources were budgeted for the rehabilitation of the road, but the work was never done. The Federal Executive Council re-awarded the contract for reconstructing the road in January 2019.

Nor does it have anything to do with romantic love. It is a practical and rational way of dealing with choices in the context of uncertainty and in situations where place, rather than distanciated (sic) space, dictates and influences people's preferences" (Hyden 2006, 74).

However, the structure of economy of affection cannot be explained outside the character of the state and economy of Africa, which are deeply rooted in history. States are inorganic, alien, unstable and removed, to a large extent, from the society. The relationship between the state (and its actors) and the society is, therefore, most times conflictual, sometimes exploitative and at other times, transactional. These processes of negotiation with the state and society are structured in different ways, depending on the issues involved and the context of the state and society. Principal modes in Borgu, as in most parts of Africa, are different expressions of patron-client, prebendalism and state capture.

The situation in Borgu was further compounded by its rurality, poverty, poor road networks and consequently poor market and even state access. The relationship with the state and participation in political affairs is often through the interlocution of some principal elements in the society such as traditional rulers, politicians (and their sometimes distant patrons), civil servants and other educated elite. To be sure, historically, the politics and social relations in Borgu were built around a patron-client structure. As seen in our discourse on pre-colonial Borgu, the relations between the Borgu aristocracy and the Fulbe ethno-economic groups was largely built around this structure. In exchange for protection, the Fulbe offered cattle and pastoral services to the aristocracy. Beyond this, the social structure revolved around the relationship between a patron (*dii* in Boko, *yinni* in Baatonu) and a client (*iba*). Most of the *dii* were drawn from the aristocratic class while the *iba* were of the common people. The *iba* provided services, including farm work, domestic assistance, and company for the *dii*, running errands, demonstrating the esteem of the patron, providing political support and sometimes sharing information on the activities of the patron's enemies. The *dii,* in return, offered economic benefits like gifts of cloth, protection from the authorities, and the sharing of social privilege (like horse riding). While the structure in relation to the Fulbe might have changed significantly since the colonial period, the *dii-iba* relationship is still relevant among Boko people, even if not prevalent. It has been simplified into a joking relationship (*yoboo*) between the two traditional social categories. Of course, the structured engagement and services have vanished with the changing dynamics of politics and economy and a new network has emerged within the prevailing context. However, the new structure is not fully an ascribed one; it is largely based on personal achievement and networks.

The post-colonial patron-client structure is extensive and the network goes beyond the immediate politics in Borgu. It could be part of a national network which in most cases Borgu had a limited or peripheral participation. Local patrons are also linked to other patrons outside Borgu. The nature and status of these patrons is shaped by the character of the government at the centre. The status of local patrons is not necessarily permanent. A patron in Borgu becomes a client at the state or national level. During military rule, the most influential local patrons were civil servants who may not have even been senior at the state or national level. In a political dispensation, the civil servants are somehow relegated in favour of active politicians, elected or appointed. The patrons at the local level (clients to those at the state and national level) are the vote dealers and brokers. They facilitate votes, either by mobilisation, manipulation or vote buying. In exchange, they grant patronage in form of cash, jobs, contracts, appointments and allocation of development projects which they have negotiated with their patrons at the higher level. Adapting this to Nigeria politics, Richard (1983) referred to it as "prebendal politics," a pattern of political behaviour that rationalises or justifies the "principle that offices of existing state may be competed for and then utilised for the personal benefit of the office-holders as well as that of their reference or support group" (Richard 1983, 54). The political office is, therefore, justifiably a reward and the resources therein can be used and dispensed as favours by the office holder as he wishes.

The nature of the structure is not uniform across Borgu. It is largely determined by the nature of politics in the state. For instance, the structure is loose, tentative and decentralised in Niger State. In Kwara, the political hierarchy is profound and essentially revolves around a family. Political analysts have often made reference to the Saraki dynasty. Olusola Saraki the patriarch of the dynasty, was a First Republic politician who became prominent in the Second Republic and eventually had an almost total control of the politics of Kwara State. He had determined the elected governors and other political officers in the state since 1979 and even got his son elected governor and daughter elected senator respectively at the same time, in 2003. His political structure had an ubiquitous influence in the politics of the state including the two local governments of Borgu, even if they do not share ethnic affinity with him. On his death, his son, Bukola Saraki, who later became the President of the Senate of the Federal Republic of Nigeria, took over the political structure from him and has continued to animate it[82].

Based on this, access to power and the exercise of authority is through personal patronage rather than the instrumentality of law. Positions are, therefore, occupied for personal gain, not public service. The distinction between the private and public interest became "purposely blurred" with time, in what Bratton (1988) called "neo-patrimonialism." Public resources became personal resources that could be distributed as personal favours in return for political support. Within this network in Borgu are full-time politicians, civil servants, the traditional rulers, youth groups and their leaders, occupational groups and traders. As depicted in Figure 2, the hierarchy is based on resource access, political appointment and proximity to the principal patron, who are in almost all the cases outside of Borgu.

Sandbrook (1988) described the patron-client relationship as a "dyadic [two persons] relationship characterised by unequal status, reciprocity, and personal contact." It is arranged in a hierarchical order with the patron at the top of hierarchy. This relationship could be part of a large series of networks linked to a central ego or a master patron, but a few individuals in the hierarchy have actual links with others at the same level or even the central ego. These networks are functions of poor integration and inadequate impersonal and formal guarantees of physical security, status, and wealth. Under such situations, people substitute formal structures and systems by attaching themselves to a "big man" capable of providing protection and even political and material advancement. It is a practical survivalist mechanism.

---

[82] The Saraki Dynasty lost its hold on the state after the 2019 General Elections. His party (the People's Democratic Party, PDP) lost all its positions in the contest to the All Progressives Congress (APC). The heir of the dynasty, Bukola Saraki also lost his senatorial position.

Figure 2: Patron-Client structure of Borgu

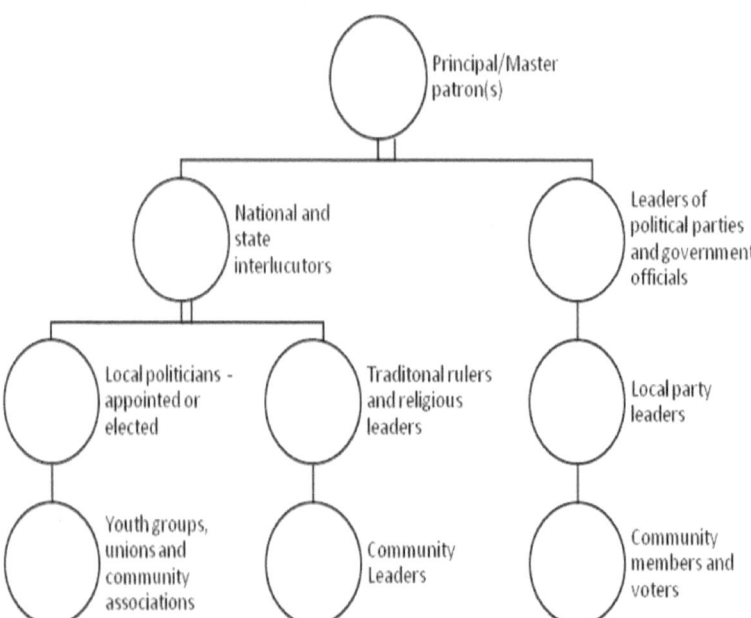

I agree with Hyden (2006) that these networks, although related or similar to others that have existed in the past, are not just remnant(s) of the past, but consciously created to enhance political privileges or social status in the society. They are a reflection of the structural realities of the state and economy. Nevertheless, while networks are realities of the society, what people do with the networks, their political access and control have an increasingly negative impact on development.

Clientelism, patronage system, prebendalism or patron-client relations, used both complementarily and interchangeably for the purpose of this work, is deeply entrenched in the contemporary politics in Borgu and have become important obstructions that continue to undermine the development of the region. It undermines development in two ways: first, likeblockages, it deprives Borgu of individual and collective opportunities from the state and federal governments because of weak players and the poor patron-client network. It also deprived the communities of quality representation at all levels because the patrons are interested only in clients who will really perform their roles as clients. Second, like a leakage, resources are siphoned for personal use instead of being invested for collective development. Because the poor people have realised that power or offices are for personal aggrandisement, they seek material favour as a matter of right. They demand immediate gratification. Every politician is, therefore, expected to be "generous" with resources and failure to do so is often punished with loss of political patronage, popularity and ultimately defeat. Performance or quality of representation is measured in the immediate, by the level of generosity demonstrated, not programme delivery or purposeful representation. Nevertheless, in the long run, people still question performance, but that is often only after the politician has lost his or her patronage power.

Voters now demand favours, including addressing immediate family or material needs. To meet these increasing demands, politicians continue to dip their hands into public resources, becoming even more corrupt and further undermining local development. The informal networks ultimately result in the elite capture of state and its institutions and reinforce the informal structure.

The state governments and the local government system have been practically captured by these elements, with the control and support of a/some master patrons at the higher levels. In ensuring effective capture, elections are manipulated, resources are selectively distributed and playable people are placed in strategic positions. Sometimes, the institutions of the state are deployed to ensure effective control. Politics is placed above development and nothing can be done in communities without the involvement of these patrons or their clients as the case may be. An attempt to circumvent them runs the risk of sabotage. If you engage them, the process is either slowed down or hijacked for their economic or political ends. In this context, the development challenge is a result of limited participation occasioned by limited access, and those who have access being more concerned with personal development and the development of those they favoured, not the community.

To sustain the network and its associated privileges, everything is fair in eliminating others who don't belong to the circle. Invented identities are, therefore, mobilised, including ward, district, local government or even locational identities. In Barutem Local Government area with four different districts and a deep contradictory influence between building a united local government area identity and inter district competition. Local government area, district or village/township associations are designed to strengthen local identities in competition with other groups[83]. Kaiama Local Government, also exhibits a comparable scenario, it is historically a single district, the villages around Kaiama mobilised through *Lakutu* (village) Development Associations to fence off the 'metropolitan' Kaiama against "occupying positions meant for them or to ensure their partaking in the share of spoils"[84]. Similarly, the people based in state or local government areas could gang up against those outside the state. The same way those based in the villages/ town mobilise those dwelling outside. These ingroup-outgroup structure is designed to delegitimise and eliminate others in the competition for power and resources.

There is, therefore, growing tension between those based in the states and those outside. Those at "home" have a feeling of authenticity and entitlement; they claim better understanding of the context and therefore reserve the right to occupy certain positions. Those outside challenge the competence, independence, capacity, network and social capital of those at home. Where these identities fail, they could question commitment and previous service to the community. Every person in a senior position is expected to serve his/her community by dispensing patronage – employment, contracts and related favours.

However, since the patron-client structure is highly dependent on external patrons, the decisions are taken in a manner that easily excludes those outside the state or community, because they cannot be trusted with power and cannot guarantee the sustenance of the structure as "outsiders".

---

[83] Character of Kerutere Desendant, Okuta, Weri Foundation Yashikira, Ilesha Bobo among others exhibites these tendancies.

[84] Interview in Kaiama, 10/09/2018

Dilemma of A Weak State and A Weak Society

Capabilities, weaknesses and social connections of the state in Africa have been a subject of discourse. This is based on the recognition of the state as a major driver of development. Its provisioning capacity and efficiency was believed to be important to the participation of citizens in the development processes. There is, however, a consensus among scholars that the post-colonial states in Africa have failed to meet the expectations of serving as the key to uncovering the societal trends and catalysing development. The nature of the post-colonial state in Nigeria exposes the intricate relationship between the state and its constituent groups and it has been a relationship of tension and contention which has significantly undermined the expectation that the state could help bridge the cultural divides and prepare the ground for development. To the contrary, the nature of economy and politics has served in breach of this process as they have engendered exclusion and competitive access to the state and its resources.

The state in Nigeria as represented by the federal, state, and local governments, has failed to gain the required spread, acceptance and broadcast of authority across Borgu, due to exclusion, geography, clientelism and poor service provision. To be sure, the relationship between the state and society has historically been tenuous in Borgu. The pre-colonial states didn't have a totalising presence and control. The central authority was mainly around the political centres. Formal political control of the hinterland was difficult and had to be earned through the building of loyalties and the use of force in most cases. Even with that, the society found means of avoiding the state through emigration and navigation of the large territory of the region. The colonial state attempted a totalistic hold within a confined border and the developing of institutions to ensure effective control of its territories. Nevertheless, the large geographical size of Borgu, its sparse population and physical inaccessibility allowed citizens to circumvent and disengage from the state. The post-colonial state has not made a fundamental shift from its origins and material essence. It is still perceived as intrusive, a threat and a nuisance to the society and should be avoided (Ake 1994). This historical evasion of the state has been further compounded by the failure of the state to provide, either for lack of access or ideological shifting of space in favour of the market, as we have seen since the embrace of economic liberalism.

The capacity of the Nigerian state was further weakened with the introduction of SAP in the 1980s. The effect of the implementation of SAP showed the inherent weakness of the Nigeria state. At several levels, the legitimacy of the state was directly or indirectly challenged either through open confrontation with the state or disengagement from the state. The deepening economic crisis undermined the capacity of the state to provide social services to the populace. The inability of the state to meet its previous obligations sharpened primordial cleavages and popular identities, resulting in the gradual decomposition of the state and a deepening exclusion of citizens. With shrinking resources, there has been increased exclusion of a segment of the elite in the distribution of the spoils of office and a heightened marginalisation of the minority groups from the benefits of development. As the state disengages from the critical, basic social provisioning, only the constituencies and clients of those who control state power actually continue to have access to the state resources through patronage.

This failure and lack of capacity of the state has been variously described as "failed", "weak", "decapitated", "fictitious" or "collapsed" state (Ake 1994 and 1996; Chazan 1994; Azarya 1994; Herbst 2014; Migdal 1988; and Zartman 1995). Irrespective of the appellation, the essence is to view the capacity of the state from service provision and broadcast of authority. It is more about the "capacity to design and implement policies, make credible commitments, run an efficient bureaucracy and provide constraints to opportunistic behavior" (Englebert 2000, 8). It is the failure to provide and sustain these responsibilities that result in a weak state.

Rice and Patrick (2008) defined a weak state from four service parameters: lack of capacity to foster a sustainable and equitable economic growth; maintenance of legitimate, transparent and accountable political institutions; good territorial control and securing the population from violent conflict; and lastly, the lack of capacity to meet the basic needs of its population. A weak state could also be associated with an inability to project state power and authority over and across its territories (Herbst 2014). A weak state is both a consequence of the nature of the society and a major characteristic of the post-colonial state. Despite the perceived omnipresence of the state in Nigeria, there are segments of the country where the state is never felt. Borgu is one of them. In substantial segments of the region, beyond the headquarters of the local government areas, districts and a few major villages, the state is practically absent in all material senses.

To cope with this failure, weakness or interferences of the state, citizens disengage from the state by "distancing themselves from it as a hedge against it instability and declining performance" (Azarya and Chazan, 112). In Borgu, people disengage from the state for three reasons. For some, especially in remote communities, it is part of the historical distrust and resistance to the interferences, demands and perceived totalising influence of the state. For others, it has to do with the failure of the state to provide the necessary political space, development and human security needs of the people. The third are those who capitalise on the weaknesses and decomposition of the state to undermine it for personal gains – the weaker the state, the better for them.

The first category is largely peasants, living deep in remote communities, with limited or no contact with the state. They are hardly involved in state activities and they may not have parallel political structures beyond the village or leadership of the farmstead. They are only linked to the state through market exploitation and community brokers. They have no access to education, health or any social service and hardly participate in political activities. The second category has had relationships with the state in the past and has been disappointed by its failures, corruption and abuse of power by political leaders. Some are retired civil servants, youth, and teachers. Their mode of disengagement includes avoidance of state activities except where immediate or delayed gratification is involved. The third category is largely politicians, business people and civil servants who benefit from the weakness of the state and serve to decompose it further. They engage in activities that undermine the efficiency and the capacity of the state such as corruption, vandalisation of state property and outright theft. Because the state has been weakened, these elements personalise the institutions and abuse power with impunity. Since the Borgu region is relatively inaccessible, they have no particular demand for public accountability. For this category, the state has been practically replaced by their patron-client network.

Citizens' disengagement in Borgu doesn't necessarily result in the establishment of parallel institutions, or even the strengthening of local institutions. In essence, the weakness of the state in Borgu is not a result of the strength of the civil society. It is more or less a case of weak state and weak society. There are few converging and inclusive civil societies or associational bodies. Alternative structures revolve around the traditional institutions and religious bodies. These institutions are very hierarchical and therefore undermine civic engagement or effective participation. The few associations - community, district, youth, students and in some cases women groupings - are in most cases opportunistic groups designed to maximise benefit from the state and not to counterbalance the state. They have, since the return to democracy in 1999, been overshadowed by partisan politics and have become linked to the patron-client networks. This weak associational base has deprived Borgu the necessarily social capital to contribute to its political and economic development. While there is still a strong element of trust among the people at the primordial realm of the society, the civic public, to use one of Ekeh's "two publics" (Ekeh 1975), enjoys massive distrust and the relations with public institutions has always been to undermine it. People appear to trust the non-formal, local institutions than any formal body or institutions associated with the government, where civil servants, politicians or the educated elite are in control.

The implication is the personalisation and capture of the state, particularly the local government authority, by a few individuals and social categories. The local governments cease to be an institution for the aggregation of local interest, community development and governance at the local level. It is now used to advance the political and economic interests of those who control it. Services provided are not regarded as public services as they are presented as personal services. Borgu, across the four local governments, is therefore littered with uncompleted, abandoned, out-of-service or vandalised interventions, including water points, schools, clinics, rural roads and even local government secretariats.

The appellation of being a "hard-to-reach" part of Kwara and Niger states serves a political and economic purpose as election results are manipulated and corruption and abuse of power without proper checks and accountability thrives. Federal and state government projects are located in these communities not for execution, but as a means of corruption - to pay out for jobs not done. The major roads in the region have been victims of this level of impunity. Because of the difficulties in physical access and assessment, projects are hardly inspected, services hardly supervised, researchers hardly visit, media and major civil society organisations hardly cover, leading to a black hole that serves well only the underhand who thrive in the dark. Most parts of the Borgu region have been removed from major networks of public accountability and thus impunity reigns. While this may not be peculiar to Borgu, it is a major development challenge in Nigeria and has been a main driver of the deepening poverty and exclusion in the region.

Conclusion

Reversing the Trend: Agenda for Development

This book demonstrates that the combined impact of imperial partitioning, colonialism and the character of post-colonial West Africa impoverished and excluded Borgu from the political and economic mainstream of West Africa. Reversing this trend will require responding to some of the key driving factors of the post-colonial situation and placing the region of Borgu on the path of sustainable development. This will involve a combination of strategic and policy level initiatives, regenerating civil society and strengthening local level cross-border relations. The sustainable development of the region should specifically be built on five important pillars: compensatory and strategic policy commitment, trans-frontier regional integration, strengthening of civil society, development of small towns and improved transport and communication infrastructure. This is not a typical rural development approach where rural areas are viewed simply from the perspective of agriculture and food production. As important as this is to agrarian societies like Borgu, development should be approached from a much broader perspective that could ultimately respond to the present social context with agriculture as an overarching economic fulcrum.

Compensatory and Strategic State Investment

To respond to the crisis of development in Borgu will require what Asiwaju (2005) called "compensatory action." Borgu should be compensated for over a century of abuse, mismanagement and neglect. The colonial authorities were the first to recognise this abuse and the need for remedial action. Governor-General Hugh Clifford referred to Bussa (Borgu) as one of the "ineptest pieces of mismanagement of native affairs ... in Nigeria" in 1924. He observed that "the sacrifices of native institutions, desires, tribal sentiments, tradition and customs to the mere administrative convenience of the Government and its officers can hardly ever have been carried out with more cynical indifference and ineptitude" (NAK 1915). In a similar vein, Hermon-Hodge, Colonial Resident of Ilorin in 1929, felt that "some reparation should be made to Bussa (and indeed the entire Borgu) for the suffering and sacrifices which have reduced a proud and comparatively populous race to a soured and sporadic handful" (cited in Crowder 1978, 172). The mismanagement did not end with colonial rule. It was actually accentuated in the post-colonial period with cynical viciousness.

Responding to the development challenges of Borgu will, therefore, require a level of historicity and strategic commitment to social justice. The state must recognise, at all levels that the dignity of the people has been grossly undermined and they have been historically denied social justice. In the words of Amartya Sen, (2009, vii) "what moves us, reasonably enough, is not the realisation that the world falls short of being completely just – which few of us expect – but that there are clearly remediable injustices around us which we want to eliminate." It is, therefore, important to accept that damage has been done to a whole region and work to remedy the situation. While this may sound naïve for a scholar, justice issues are historical issues. It may not resonate as injustice at the moment but could become a point of reference in future. The Nigerian State and that of Benin, as represented at the centres and sub-national levels, need to make a compensatory and strategic commitment to developing and improving the lives of people in Borgu.

Development is never attained by happenstance but through deliberate design, political commitment and resource investment. The compensatory action should be built into a national development framework supported by similar commitments at the state(s) and local government levels. The development crisis in Borgu should be seen as a national crisis and deliberate effort made to reverse the trend. While Borgu may not be the only region under a similar developmental crisis situation in these countries, it is arguably a compelling example of a region whose development has been reversed by years of colonial and post-colonial mismanagement.

In Nigeria for example, part of this deliberate compensatory engagement should include a special development plan for the region and a self-managed sub-national entity (Borgu State) to cover the entire pre-colonial Borgu in Nigeria. While I recognise that such demands are political and could be an elite plot for self-aggrandisement, a state for Borgu will pull all the scattered entities together and allow the people to autonomously engage the centre as done by other polities and nationalities. From the experience of other states, this may not solely or necessarily address the development challenges but it will importantly provide the necessary space and structure to support the development of the region in the long run. At the moment, Borgu is the only one of the four first-generation provinces of northern Nigeria that is yet to constitute a state in the federation of Nigeria, others being Bassa, Kabba and Kontagora. The first two have been merged to form Kogi State.

Transport and Communication Infrastructure

One of the major development challenges of Borgu is its total disconnect from the major political and economic centres, particularly in Nigeria. This is occasioned by a poor transport and communication network. Although mobile telephony has contributed significantly to bridging the communication gap, it has not done so in a strategic or development-inducing manner. As an agrarian community, the most important infrastructure is a proper transport network that will allow market access to support the agriculture value chain. As noted earlier, although Borgu in Nigeria has some of the earliest Federal Government roads, the Borgu sections of these roads have remained unmanaged and paved since inception. The challenge of the roads in Borgu is not dilapidation, they are largely a case of abandonment.

Access roads are the most important infrastructure needed in the region.

A good and efficient transport network will physically connect the agrarian communities and link them with non-agrarian economic services and centres. Experiences from other countries, especially in Asia, revealed that connectivity transforms rural livelihood and enhances development as it creates non-farm labour opportunities, which in turn stimulates positive socio-economic dynamics. Such an effort will require massive government investment. Transport infrastructure should be handled in three ways: providing effective linkages with major market centres; changing the orientation of roads to support the intra-Borgu network including its international borders,and investing in rail infrastructure to both complement and compete with roads.

Attention should be given to all the state and federal government roads in the Nigerian section of the region. Important are Bussa – Agwara, networking the regions of Borgu and Agwara Local Government, the Wawa – Kaiama – Kishi and the Kaiama- Kosubosu roads. Others are Ilesha to Chikanda; Ilesha to Gwanara. This road network will probably fare better if the government also revives the Sokoto – Badagry Road effort which predates colonial rule. It was a major pre-colonial caravan route linking Borgu to Oyo and the coast, putting the Atlantic in touch with the Sokoto Caliphate. The early European travellers to Borgu and Sokoto such as Clapperton, the Lander Brothers and Lugard traversed this road. The road connected major Borgu centres. The decision to develop the road was first initiated by the colonial authorities in the earlier phase of colonial rule, as way of diverting trade from the French's Niger and Dahomey to the Nigerian side. The French's swiftness in linking Niger to the coast through their slice of Borgu outsmarted and probably killed the British effort. The road then became a major road programme under the Second Development Plan. Obasanjo, then Federal Commissioner of Works, noted that in the post-Civil War development effort, "our major strategic policy was four north-to-south roads: Badagry-Kainji-Sokoto; Lagos-Ibadan-Jebba-Kaduna; Port-Harcourt-Aba-Enugu-Makurdi, and Calabar-Katsina-Ala-Maiduguri" (Obasanjo 2014, 234). While the last three have been completed, the first and the most important to Borgu has long been abandoned. If completed, the road will connect major towns in the northern side of the country to Lagos. In Borgu in particular, it will traverse Bussa, Wawa, Kaiama, and Ilesha among others. It will also link several villages and small towns to major urban centres and markets and boost agricultural production. It will facilitate easier inter-regional trade with Benin Republic. The road will shorten the distance between the north-western states of Sokoto, Zamfara and Kebbi with the coast and reduce the stress on Kaduna-Jebba-Ibadan-Lagos Road. It will increase food production and create market access that will ultimately contribute to reducing poverty in the region.

In addition to road, rail infrastructure will play an important role in developing the region. The rail network in the country is still structured in the colonial north-south orientation. A change in this orientation to include a west-east orientation will help capture some uncaptured markets in the country, which includes Borgu. Borgu can easily be linked to Mokwa with a three hundred to five hundred kilometre rail line. This will connect to Kainji Dam on the Niger and support the navigable parts of the Upper Niger in Niger and Kebbi states. Such an effort will create job opportunities and boost human development.

Related to transport is the need for other communication and information infrastructure. Most parts of Borgu, especially in Nigeria, have no access to national media, whether radio, television or newspapers. Not only is Borgu physically disconnected from the rest of the country, but it is also de-linked in terms of national issues and ideas. In some parts of Borgu, it is easier to access radio signals from Benin Republic than to access one from Nigeria. Although the issue of media coverage has been eased somewhat with satellite communication, it is still not adequate as Borgu issues are rarely reported in the national media. The reason for this is that just as geographically it is not physically accessible for trade or any other reason; it is also not accessible by the media. Lack of media access, in turn, reduces state broadcast of authority, undermines local languages and identity and reduces the mobilisation capacity of civil society.

Borgu needs to be linked through both conventional and new media. With the poor level of education in the region and a good radio culture, it particularly needs local or community radio stations to respond to the realities of the people. Local radio will help broadcast local issues and enhance community education, including cultural development, local entertainment and interface the entire region with the rest of the world. This could also support agricultural extension services through the local language and enhance market access.

Information and communication technology has an intrinsic capacity to break down boundaries. It has a tendency to eliminate distance and space. It will also help to soften barriers of hard borders and support the revival of a borderless region. With increasing trade and communication, borders could become less visible. As observed by Jackson, "The emergence of the interlinked economy brings with it an erosion of sovereignty as the powers of information technology directly touches local communities, academic, professional and social institutions; corporations; and individuals. It is this borderless world that gives participating economies the capacity for borderless prosperity" (Jackson 2005, 311). In the case of Borgu, information technology will help bridge the division in culture groups that have been created by colonialism.

Trans-frontier Regional Integration

Borgu people, even across the two countries of Nigeria and Benin, are culturally inseparable. Apart from culture, they share a number of natural resources including the eco-system of the region and huge and diverse economic and market potential. Although the people have tried to navigate the artificial borders and maintain strong cultural, economic and political relationships, most of these are done informally and the impact is not formally measureable. Trans-frontier integration is a citizens' approach to regional integration using both state and community structures. While national governments could support this effort, the process is largely driven by the people and their organisations for the benefit of local communities. It is a micro-level integration that could serve as a foundation for macro-level integration. It is what Duckacels referred to as "micro-diplomacy." It is a formalised relationship or cooperation among local authorities. Apart from responding to border issues of regional integration, it helps manage international cooperation and integration based on local geographical, cultural and historical realities. It is closer to the people and reflects their peculiarities. It could help support macro-diplomacy and international conventions and treaties. Because the border communities have suffered more from the obstructive effect of borders, they are in better position to appreciate the values of transboundary socio-economic planning and development (Asiwaju 1994).

The European Outline Convention, a product of local initiatives, is a prime example of this micro-diplomacy. Different European border regions instituted a mechanism for relationships across borders. Some of these initiatives include the *Regio Basiliensi,* created in 1963, the Eurogion launched in 1970 and the Conference of Upper Rhine Valley Planners which began in 1979. Others include the federal type Association of European Border Regions, based in Bonn, Germany, the Committee for the Promotion of Alpine Region Cooperation with headquarters in Turin, Italy, and several others inspired by trade and civil society (Asiwaju 1994, 2005).

This is more like a bottom-up approach to regional integration. In Borgu, this engagement can be led at different levels – civil society, traditional institutions and the local/sub-national states. To promote this effort, the region will need to establish a platform, possibly something like a *"Borgu Union."* It could be supported by other layers of associations that include trade groups, civil society, cultural and traditional institutions. The process could be led by the local authorities and state governments with strong feedback or debriefing mechanisms to the centre. Such integration will help weaken the border, enhance trade and reduce poverty.

Small Towns and Urban-Rural Connectivity

Increasingly, small towns are being recognised as important engines of urbanisation and rural development. The transformative character of these settlements is evidenced from developments in east and southern Africa in particular, Asia and Eastern Europe. These have to be built on the agriculture base of their regions to diversify the local economy and increase their share of service and industry (Tacoli and Vorley 2015). The importance of small towns in rural development is associated with their strategic and intermediation of major urban areas and the agrarian villages. Improving infrastructure and services in these areas often have corresponding impact on the urban market and rural development. Small towns have, therefore, become important in contemporary development planning. They are development stimulants and could easily catalyse improvement in the conditions of living in the rural areas. While the small towns harmonise rural economies, they also provide non-agrarian alternative livelihood.

The constitutive elements of small towns are generally context specific. However, they manifest the highest level of the rural area and at the lowest of the urban system (Vaisher, Stastna and Stonawka 2015). The definition of small towns is based on some important demographic and infrastructural variables including population size, settlement pattern, level of industrial development, occupational distribution and social infrastructures such as the road network and public services such as schools and healthcare.

Small towns are essential but often neglected settlements in development planning and the food system in West Africa. The simplistic binary of the urban-rural divide doesn't support a new sustainable development paradigm. Against an often linear understanding, the rural-urban relationship is a complex web of interlinkages, involving different expressions of rurality and urbanity (Tacoli and Agergaard 2017). In essence, there are different layers of settlements between the rural and the urban, each performing different development functions and connecting with each other at different levels.

Borgu across the two countries is deeply rural, with pockets of small towns. In Nigeria, the formative colonial district and village structure were expected to be lower-level political centres. Their economic significance was not recognised. The post-colonial state also appears to have continued with this arrangement. Even when local governments were created, their headquarters were largely conceived as political centres. Their economic significance was seldom recognised. The political development of most of these societies significantly depends on their economic growth. Investing in major towns like Agwara, Babanna, Bussa, Wawa, Kaiama, Ilesha, Gwanara, Okuta, Yashikira, Kosubosu, and even growing towns like Chikanda, Bani/Adena, Boriya, and Kemanji among others, could catalyse development in the region. They could become major market centres for agricultural produce from villages and a point of interface with urban producers and retailers and, therefore, create opportunities for non-agrarian economic activity, diversifying rural livelihood and providing off-season employment for rural dwellers. Already, these towns have developed a historical and close symbiotic relationship with surrounding villages.

The Federal Government will need to institute a Small Towns Development Policy and Programme to be complemented by state and local government commitments. The programme should commit to transforming small towns through adequate infrastructure and social services that will guarantee productivity and economic growth. Investment should include efficient and growth-driven town planning, titling of land, including farmlands, development of road infrastructure linking these towns with major urban centres and surrounding villages. The provision of basic social services, including education and health, is also essential. Considering the distance to major tertiary health facilities in Ilorin and Minna, the government should provide one tertiary facility in each of the two emirates of the old Borgu now spread across the two states. Other services should include water supply, housing, agro-processing and small-scale industry, effective agro-support mechanisms, including outgrowing, market and production specialisation.

Developing small towns and networking them with major urban centres and villages will also require managing population and settlement patterns. The current haphazard arrangement with pockets of miniature settlements across the region will need to be controlled without disrupting the livelihood and natural habitat of the people. Settlements should be clustered to allow for concentration of villages and access to social services like schools, water, health and extension services. As noted earlier, the vastness of Borgu and dispersed settlement pattern is a major development challenge within the context of the character of the state. The difficulties in accessing people and locations for census and related political and economic activities can be managed when people are encouraged to live in proximity to each other, which the provision of social services and markets will incentivise, instead of in the scattered little hamlets and family farm settlements that litter the region.

Small towns also need effective governance to grow. Apart from the traditional institutions and the local authorities, other governance structures around town management and social services will help ensure efficient service delivery and guarantee public accountability.

As economic activities in the region grow, the subsisting patron-client networks will be weakened by greater civil society activities, allowing for better public accountability. The development of small towns will also increase the diversity of the towns, not just in terms of social composition but also in political and economic opportunities.

Civil Society and Participatory Governance

The values of civil society as a major driver of change is increasingly being recognised in public policy. Their energy, innovation and ownership are important in delivering public services, identifying community needs and in driving a new development paradigm. Public policy benefits tremendously from community participation and citizen engagement. It is, therefore, always important to harness community ideas, energy, social capital and knowledge in addressing challenges and promoting inclusive development (Eversole 2011). This proposition is built on the theoretical assumption that communities, citizens or civil society, used interchangeably in this work, "possess *agency* in the sociological sense. That is, they have the ability to act and be agents of their own development" (Eversole 2011, 51).

With the growing recognition of the deficiencies of the traditional, centralised, bureaucratic, policy making process, there is an increasing interest by policy makers, academics and civil society, locally and internationally, on the roles of citizens and *locales* in policy initiation and administration. Towns, villages, local communities and citizens' associations are recognised as *agents* or *agencies* of policy-making and transformation. According to Eversole (2015, 52):

> The underlying discourse is thus very much about community agency. The argument is that place-based communities, with a bit of help and encouragement from enabling public policy, can create their own development trajectories. This interest in communities as a source of policy ideas and action echoes a broader trend in social theory that emphasises dispersed agency over centralised social structure.

However, this shift should be recognised and advanced with a deep appreciation of the diversity of rural areas and even of civil society.

These entities are not homogenous in any way. Differences in demography, class, occupation, gender, ethnicity, religion and even age can play a significant role in policy ownership and interest. This is particularly so with civil society. Therefore, its romanticisation should be treated with cautious optimism. This is not to question the tremendous capacity of civil society for public good; it is actually to recognise the "uncivil" elements in civil society in a plural context. As noted by Ikelegbe (2001, 1), in plural societies, civil society may become so "parochial, divisive, divergent and disarticulate that it actually undermines democracy." In essence, the agency of community and civil society are important, but it should be recognised that like many other social phenomena, their character can be influenced by the local and global political economy. Despite this possible challenge, focusing on rural communities and their associations makes a significant shift from a victim approach, where communities are seen as victims devoid of capacity to counteract and influence their conditions.

It is in this context that accountable governance and development in Borgu will require changing the character and dynamics of the communities and civil society to become important agencies of transformation. In doing this, it must be recognised that state institutions, as well as community institutions, have structural and cultural differences. They may, therefore, not necessarily work in harmony. Sometimes, or even most times, it is a relationship of conflict and contention. This has significant normative value as it promotes civic participation in the decision-making process and engenders responsive and responsible governance. These are important ingredients for an inclusive approach to development. An inclusive approach to governance conceives governance as "networked, participatory process involving communities and civil society." This form of governance promotes "innovation, negotiation and transformative partnership, with knowledge exchange, democratisation and decentralisation in decision making …" (Eversole 2015, 56). While centralisation creates opportunities for democratic innovation, it may also reinforce undemocratic political leaders and local power brokers as we've seen in most communities in Borgu.

Generally, good and accountable governance doesn't occur by fluke. It must be "nourished explicitly and consciously" (Rotberg

2007, 153). This is where citizen and state intervention becomes important. Borgu, like most parts of rural northern Nigeria, has a few civil associations that are mostly quite weak, most of them based on traditional structures and associational patterns. They are largely community-based and less formally organised. As a result, gender, religion, ethnicity and residency still play important roles (Walker 1999). While the communities are largely nonchalant to societal politics, the associational lives revolve around self-help groups, youth and students' associations, community associations and a few occupational associations largely led and controlled by people not indigenous to the communities. This renders them less effective in exploiting opportunities for enhanced contribution to democracy and development as they remain entangled in the patron-client structure of the society. Therefore, for these associations and communities to play significant roles in the local development of Borgu, they must be supported and their capacity expanded. A well-developed civil society will provide the necessary social capital including confidence, information, reciprocity, trust and cooperation essential for development.

The civil society in Borgu will require reinvention and orientation to engage more on governance issues and demand for public accountability from the local and state actors. The effort should be directed at strengthening society and creating room for popular participation. This will help reduce the patron-client system that permeates the region. As noted by Teles (2012, 29), "the reinvention of local governance ... requires a civil society reinvention, strengthening its capacity to create, engage and innovate. All dimensions of social capital – trust, social norms and voluntary works – should have a strong presence if governance is to work."

Conclusion

Borgu typifies exclusion, neglect and underdevelopment. It is an example of how colonial devastation and balkanisation have combined with post-colonial state failures and neglect, to produce one of the poorest regions in West Africa. Borgu has, in the last two hundred years, transformed from a politically strategic and economically vibrant region to one of the marginal regions in West Africa by most indices. As a major trading route, different trade orientations criss-crossed the region, creating one of the most diverse and economically active pre-colonial polities. Despite its sparse population and relatively small size, it stood up against some of the most powerful empires and polities in the area since the fifteenth century and had been influential in the politics of some of its neighbours. Reports of most of the nineteenth century European travellers indicate that centres like Nikki, Parakou, Djougou, Kaiama and Bussa were arguably urbanised based on the population, settlement pattern, diversity and market. The development of these centres was rudely interrupted by the character of the colonial and the post-colonial state, excluding probably Parakou and, to an extent, Bussa. Parakou is today the second largest city in Benin Republic. Bussa has also grown, especially since the construction of Kainji Dam in the 1970s.

The historical and political vibrancy of Borgu has been eclipsed by succeeding state policies starting from colonial times. It has remained divided into two countries with two linguistic orientations, Francophone Benin and Anglophone Nigeria. The sense of oneness of the people of the region has been further fractured within these countries through different territorial arrangements in both colonial and post-colonial periods. On the Nigerian side of the divide, against the pre-colonial integrity and structure of the region, Borgu was divided into two competing emirates, Kaiama and Bussa, with strong internal contradictions. In addition, through a series of territorial re-arrangements, Borgu was tossed around like a handball. For instance, in 1905, the bulk of Borgu Province was abrogated and merged with Kontagora Province, while sections of it comprising Illo, Kaoje, Lefaru and Gendenni in the north-east were merged with Gwandu Emirate as compensation to the Sokoto Caliphate for the loss of parts of its territory to the French in Niger. Although Agwara and Rofia were later restored to Borgu, Illo, Kaoje and Koenji remained in Gwandu Emirate and are now in Kebbi State. Borgu has not, since this period, enjoyed any territorial stability as it is currently spread across three states - Kwara, Niger and Kebbi - scattered across five local governments all in the margins of these states. Although French Borgu appears to be doing fairly better, it also went through similar structural instabilities. Apart from being balkanised into smaller administrative units for the convenience of colonial control, it was merged with different non-Borgu units. French Borgu is today spread across four divisions in Benin Republic.

The years of unstable political arrangements and division across the two countries have significantly impacted the development of the region as Borgu, especially the Nigerian Borgu and the border regions of Benin, remained on the periphery of the two countries. Borgu lost its strategic character as the political structure of the larger region and the trade orientation changed in response to the new dynamics of colonialism and the post-colonial state. While some other regions with lesser pre-colonial influence were urbanising, Borgu was reduced to a pitiable state. It is amongst the poorest by all major development indicators. It is politically marginal and economically disempowered. This level of crisis and underdevelopment is associated with the character of the colonial and post-colonial state in both countries.

Border regions are generally the least developed in Africa, unless where such regions coincide with industrial locations, urban areas or major political centres. They are often removed from the centres of urbanisation and development. The situation is Borgu is, therefore, not fundamentally different, except that it has been compounded by deliberate state neglect occasioned by exclusive economic and political doctrines and failing states in Nigeria and Benin Republic.

References

Introduction

Adekunle, O. Julius 2008. "The Wasangari: Politics and Identity in Borgu". *Anthropos*, Bd. 103, H 2. (2008), pp. 435 – 445.
Adekunle, O. Julius, 2004.*Politics and Society in Nigeria's Middle Belt: Borgu and the Emergence of a Political Identity*. Asmara, Africa World Press.
Akinwumi, Olayemi 1997. "Nigerian Borgu 1898 – 1989: A History of Intergroup Relations", PhD Dissertation, University of Ilorin.
Akinwumi, Olayemi 1998. "Oral Tradition in Changing Political Contexts: The Kisra Legend in Northern Borgu". *History in Africa*. Vol. 25, (1998), pp. 1 – 7.
Amselle, Jean-Loup 1998. *Mestizo Logics: Anthropology of Identity in Africa and Elsewhere*. Stanford, Stanford University Press.
Anene, J.C. 1965. "The Eclipse of the Borgawa".*Journal of Historical Society of Nigeria*, Vol. 3. No. 2 (December 1965). Pp. 211 – 220.
Anene, J.C. 1970. *The International Boundaries of Nigeria 1885 – 1960*, Harlow, Longman.
Asiwaju, A. I. 1979. "Dahomey, Yorubaland, Borgu and Benin in the nineteenth century". In Ade Ajayi (ed.) *General History of Africa, VI, Africa in the 18th Century until 1880s*, Heinemann and UNESCO.
Bayart, Jean-Francois, 2009.*The state in Africa: The Politics of the Belly*. Cambridge, Polity Press.

Bierschenck, Thomas 1993. "The Creation of a Tradition: Fulani Chiefs in Dahomey/Bénin from the Late 19th Century", *Paideuma: Mitteilungen zur Kulturkunde*, Bd. 39, pp. 217-244

Bierschenk, Thomas 1996. "Peuls et état Colonial dans le Borgou Français/Nord-Dahomey (1895 - 1940)". *Nomadic Peoples*, No. 38, Nomads and the State (1996), pp. 99-12.

Crowder, Michael 1978.*Colonial West Africa*, London, Frank Cass.

Crowder, Micheal 1973.*Revolt in Bussa*.London, Faber and Faber.

Davidson, Basil 1994. *The Search for Africa: A History in the Making*. Lomdon, James Currey.

Davidson, Basil. 1991. *African Civilisation Revisited.* Asmara, Africa World Press.

Duff, E.C. 1920. "Gazetteer of Kontagora Province", in Gazetteers of Northern Provinces of Nigeria, Vol 3, No. 25.

Fukuyama, Frances 1993. *End of History*

Hahonou, Éric Komlavi 2015. "The Quest for Honor and Citizenship in Post-Slavery Borgu (Benin)" The International Journal of African Historical Studies, Vol. 48, No. 2, pp. 325-344

Hallet, Robin,1974. Africa Since 1875: *A Modern History*. London, Heinemann.

Hellet, Robin 1965 (ed.) *The Niger Journal of Richard and John Lander*. London, Routledge and Kegan Paul.

Hermon-Hodge, H.B. 1921.*Gazetter of Ilorin Province*, pp. 115.

Hoskyns-Abrahall, T. 1925. "History of Bussa" 20/12/1925. National Archive, Kaduna.

Idris, Baba Musa 1973. "Political and Economic Relations in Bariba States". Uncompleted PhD Dissertation, University of Birmingham.

Idris, D. Mohammed and Yaru, I. Mohammed 2008. *Kaiama: From Great Trek to a Place to Rest.* Ilorin, Hyatee Press and Publishers.

Isichei, Elizabeth 1983. *A story of Nigeria*. London, Longman.

Kuba, Richard 1998. *Wasangari und Wangara. Borgu und Seine Nachbarn in Historischer Perspektive*, Lit, Hamburg.

Kuba, Richard and Akinwumi Olayemi, 2005. "Precolonial Borgu: Its History and Culture". In Akinwumi Ogundiran (ed.), *Precolonial Nigeria: Essays in Honor of Toyin Falola*. Asmara, Africa World Press.

Lafia, Hussaini 2006. *Borgu: The Endless Journey*. Ilorin, Haytee Press and Publishing Co.

Lewis, Peter (ed), 1998. *Africa: Dilemmas Development and Change*. Boulders, Westview Press.

Lombard, J. 1957. "Un Systéme Politique Tradition de Type Feodal: Les Bariba du Nord Dahomey.Apercu I'organisation Sociale et le Pouvoir Central", Bull, IFAN, xix. 464 – 506.

Lombard, J. 1960. "La vie Politique dans une Ancienne Societe de type Feodal: les Bariba du Dahomey", CEA, iii, pp. 5 – 45.

Lombard, J. 1965. *Structures de Type Feodal an Afrigue Noire: Etudes des Dynamismes Internes et de Relations Societe Chez les Bariba du Dahomey*, Paris.

Lombard, Joseph 1970. "Chieftaincy Among the Bariba of Dahomey, In Michael Crowder and O. Ikimi (eds.), *West African Chiefs: Their Changing Status under Colonial Rule and Independence*, Ile Ife, University of Ife Press.

Lovejoy 1974. "Inter-regional Monetary Flows in the Precolonial Trade of Nigeria", *Journal of African History*, XV (4), pp. 563 – 585.

Lovejoy, Paul E. 1971. "Long Distance Trade and Islam: The Case of the Nineteenth- Century Hausa kola Trade", *Journal of the Historical Society of Nigeria*, Vol. 5, No. 4, pp. 537 – 547.

Lovejoy, Paul E. 1978. "The Role of Wangara in the Economic Transformation of the Central Sudan in the Fifteenth and Sixteenth Centuries", *Journal of African History*, XIX, 2, pp. 173 – 193.

Lovejoy, Paul E. 1980. "Kola in the History of west Africa" (*La kola dans l'Afrique occidentale*), *Cashier d'Etudes Africaines*, Vol. 20, Cashier 77/78, pp. 97 – 134.

Lovejoy, Paul E. 1980. *Caravans of Kola: The Kola Trade 1700 1900*. Oxford. Oxford University Press.

Lovejoy, Paul E. 1983. *Transformation in Slavery*. Cambridge. Cambridge University Press.

Lovejoy, Paul E. and Baier Stephen 1975. "The Desert-Side Economy of the Central Sudan". *The International Journal of African Historical Studies*, Vol. 8, No. 4, pp. 551 – 581.

Lovejoy, Paul E. and Hogendorn, J.S. 1979. "Slave Marketting in West Africa" In Henry Gemery and Jan S. Hogendorn eds., *The Uncommon Market: Essays in the Economic History of the Atlantic Slave Trade*. New York, Academic Press. Pp. 214 – 235.

Mbembe, Achille 2001. *On the Post Colony*. Berkeley, University of California.

Meek, C.K. 1925. *The Northern Tribes of Nigeria*, London (pp 71 -72).

Mohammed, Yau Damisa and Nze, P. Nze 2009. *Borgu: Destined to Be*. Ilorin, Modern Impression.

NAK (1925) "Notes on Illo ", F. de F. Daniel, ILORPROF, 2907.

NAK (1926) "Anthropological and Historical Reports on Bussawa", A.B. Mathew, ILORPROF 3158/5

NAK (1926) "Anthropological report of Yaurawa", A.B. Mathew, K. 2099, SNP/MP No. 3923.

NAK (1936?) "History of Bussawa" M.T. Hoskyns-Abrahall K6, SNP.

NAK 1933. "Borgu – its Peoples History and Problems" Notes by M.M Grimwood, ILORPROF 3158.

Smith, Abdullahi 1987. *A Little New Light: Selected Historical Writings of Abdullahi Smith*. Zaria, the Abdullahi Smith Centre for Historical Research.

Stewart, H. Marjorie 1984. "Borgu People of Nigeria and Benin: The Disruptive Effects of Partition on Traditional Political and Economic Relations", *Journal of Historical Society of Nigeria*, Vol. 12, No. 3 – 4, pp. 95 – 120.

Stewart, H. Marjorie 1993. *Borgu and Its Kingdoms: A Reconstruction of a Western Sudanese Polity*. New York, the Edwin and Mellen Press.

Usman B.Y, 2006. *Beyond Fairy Tales: Selected Historical Writings of Yusufu Bala Usman*. Zaria, Abdullahi Smith Centre.

Usman, B.Y. 1981. *The Transformation of Katsina – 1400 – 1883*. Zaria, Ahmadu Bello University Press.

Welmer E. William, 1952. "Notes on the Structure of Bariba", *Languages*, Vol. 28, No.1 (Jan – Mar 1952), pp. 82 – 103.

Young Crawford, 1994. *The African Colonial State in Comparative Perspectives*. New Heaven, Yale University Press.

Chapter 1

Early States and Societies

Adekunle, O. Julius 1994. "Borgu and Economic Transformation 1700 - 1900: The Wangara Factor".*African Economic History*, No. 22, Pp. 1 – 18.

Adekunle, O. Julius 2004. *Politics and Society in Nigeria's Middle Belt: Borgu and the Emergence of a Political Identity*. Asmara, Africa World Press.

Adekunle, O. Julius 2008. "The Wasangari: Politics and Identity in Borgu". *Anthropos* Bd. 103, H. 2, pp. 435 – 445.

Akinwumi Olayemi and Raji Y. Adesina 1990. "The Wangara factor in the History of Nigerian Islam: The Example of Kano and Borgu". *Islamic Studies*, 29: 4, pp. 375 – 385.

Akinwumi, Duro Olayemi 1992. "The Oyo-Borgu Military Alliance of 1835: A Case Study in Pre-Colonial Military History".*Transafrican Journal of History*, Vol. 21, pp. 159 – 170.

Akinwumi, Olayemi 1998. "Oral Tradition in Changing Political Contexts: The Kisra Legend in Northern Borgu", *History in Africa*, Vol. 25, (1998), pp, 1 – 7.

Akinwumi, Olayemi 1998. "Oral Tradition in Changing Political Contexts: The Kisra Legend in Northern Borgu". *History in Africa*. Vol. 25, (1998), pp. 1 – 7.

Akinwumi, Olayemi, 1995. "Biologically-Based Warfare in the Pre-Colonial Borgu Society of Nigeria and Republic of Benin".*Transafrican Journal of History*, Vol. 24, Pp. 123 – 130.

Al-Hajj, A. Mohammed, 1968 "A Seventeenth Century Chronicle on the Origins and Missionary Activities of the Wangarawa", *Kano Studies* vol. 1 No. 4, 1968.

Amselle, Jean-Loup, 1998.*Mestizo Logic: Anthropology of Identity in Africa and Elsewhere*. Stanford, Stanford University Press.

Anene, J.C. 1965. "The Eclipse of the Borgawa".*Journal of Historical Society of Nigeria*, Vol. 3, No. 2, pp. 211 – 220.

Asiwaju, A. I. 1979. "Dahomey, Yorubaland, Borgu and Benin in the nineteenth century". In Ade Ajayi (ed.) *General History of Africa, VI, Africa in the 18th Century until 1880s*, Heinemann and UNESCO.

Bierschenk, Thomas 1993. "The Creation of a Tradition: Fulani Chiefs in Dahomey/Benin from the late 19th Century". *Paideuma: Mitteilungen zur Kulturkunde*, Ed. 39, pp 217 – 244.

Burnham Philip and Last, Murray 1994. "From Pastoralist to Politicians: The Problem of Fulbe "Aristocracy".*Cahiers d'Etudes Africaines*, Vol. 34.Cahier 133/135, *L'archpel peul*, pp. 313 – 357.

Burnham, Philp and Last, Murray. 1994. The Problem of Fulbe "Aristocracy".*Cahiers d'Estudes Africaines*, Vol. 34, Cahier 133/135, *L'archipel peul* (1994), pp. 313 -357.

Clapperton, Hugh 1829. *Journal of Second Expedition into the Interior of Africa*. London, John Murray.

Coast as recorded by Joseph Dupuis in Kumasi, 1820", *History in Africa*, Vol. 22, pp. 281 – 305.

Cohen, Abner 1969. *Custom and Politics in Urban Africa. A Study of Hausa Migrants in Yoruba Towns*, London.

Crowder, Michael 1973. *Revolt in Bussa: A Study of British 'Native Administration' in Nigerian Borgu, 1902 – 1935*. London, Faber and Faber.

Crowder, Micheal 1977.*West Africa: An Introduction to its History*. London, Longman.

Davidson, Basil 1994. *The Search for Africa: A History in the Making*. London, James Currey.

Davidson, Basil. 1991. *African Civilisation Revisited*. Asmara, Africa World Press.

Duff, E.C. 1920. "Gazetteer of Kontagora Province", in Gazetteers of Northern Provinces of Nigeria, Vol 3, No. 25.

Farais, Morea de Paulo Fernando, 1995. "Praise Splits the Subject of Speech: Construction of Kingship in the Manden and Borgu" In Graham Furniss and Liz Gunmer (eds), *Power, Marginality and African Oral Literature*. New York, Cambridge University Press.

Farias, De Moraes P.F. 1992. "A letter from Ki-Toro Mahamman Gaani, King of Busa (Borgu, Northern Nigeria) About the 'Kisra' Stories of Origin". *Sudanic Africa*, iii, 1992. 109 – 23.

Frobenius, Leo 1913. *The Voices of Africa*.Vol. 2 of 2.

Hahonou, Éric Komlavi 2015. "The Quest for Honor and Citizenship in Post-Slavery Borgu (Benin)" The International Journal of African Historical Studies, Vol. 48, No. 2, pp. 325-344.

Hall, S. Bruce 2011. *A History of Race in Muslim West Africa, 1600 – 1960*. New York, Cambridge University Press.

Hallam, W.K.R. 1966. "The Bayajida Legend in Hausa Folklore", *Journal of African History*, VII, 1. 47.

Heath, D.F. 1937. "Bussa Regalia". *Man*, Vol. 37 (May, 1937), pp. 77 – 80.

Hermon-Hodge, H.B. 1921.*Gazetteer of Ilorin Province*, pp. 115. Idris,Baba Musa 1973. "Political and Economic Relations in Bariba States". Uncompleted PhD Dissertation, University of Birmingham.

Idris, D. Mohammed and Yaru, I. Mohammed 2008.*Kaiama: From Great Trek to a Place to Rest.*Ilorin, Hyatee Press and Publishers.

Isichei, Elizabeth 1983. *A story of Nigeria*. London, Longman.

Kane, Oumar Ousmane 2016. *Beyond Timbuktu: An Intellectual History of Muslim West Africa*. Cambridge, Harvard University Press.

Kuba, Richard 1998. *Wasangari und Wangara. Borgu und Seine Nachbarn in Historischer Perspektive.*

Kuba, Richard and Akinwumi Olayemi, 2005. "Precolonial Borgu: Its History and Culture". In Akinwumi Ogundiran (ed.), *Precolonial Nigeria: Essays in Honor of Toyin Falola*. Asmara, Africa World Press.

Lafia, Hussaini 2004. *Gaani: The State Festival*. Ilroin, Haytee Press and Publsihers.

Lafia, Hussaini 2006. *Borgu: The Endless Journey*. Ilorin, Haytee Press and Publishing Co.

Lander, Richard and Lander John, 1932. *Journal of an Expedition to Explore the Course and Termination of the Niger etc*. London.

Lange, Dierk 2009. "An Assyrian Successor State in West Africa: The Ancestral Kings of Kebbi as Ancient Near Eastern Rulers".*Anthropos*, 104 (2009), pp. 359 – 382.

Laski, Harold 1931. *Introduction to Politics*. London, George Allen, London.

Law Robin 2009. "The 'Hamitic Hypothesis' in Indigenous West African Historical Thoughts".*History in Africa*. Vol. 36 (2009), pp. 293 – 314.

Hugh, Clapperton, 1829. *Journal of Second Expedition into the Interior of Africa*. London, John Murray.

Levzion, Nehemia 1968. *Muslim and the Chiefs in West Africa: A study of Islam in the Middle Volta Basin in the Pre-colonial Period*. Oxford, Oxford University Press.

Lombard, J. 1965. *Structures de Type Feodal an Afrigue Noire: Etudes des Dynamismes Internes et de Relations Societe Chez les Bariba du Dahomey*, Paris.

Lovejoy, E. Paul 1971. "Long-Distance Trade and Islam: The Case of Nineteenth Century Hausa Kola Trade".*Journal of Historical Society of Nigeria*, Vol. 5. No. 4, pp. 537 – 547.

Mamdani, Mahmood 2004. *Citizens and Subjects*: *Contemporary Africa and the Legacy of Late Colonialism*. Kampala, Fountain Publishers.

Maraes Farias, de Fernando Paulo 1995. "Praise Split the subject of Speech: Construction of Kinship in the Manden and Borgu".In Graham Furniss and Liz Gunmer (eds.), *Power, Marginality and African Oral Literature*. New York, Cambridge University Press.

Mbembe, Achille 2001. *On the Post Colony*. Berkeley, University of California.

McCall, F. Daniel, 1968. "Kisra, Chrosroes, Christ etc". Reviewed Work of *Africanobyzantine: Byzantine on Negro Sudanese Culture by Theodore Papadopoullos. Journal of Historical Societies*, Vol. 1 No. 2, pp 255 – 277.

Meek, C.K. 1925. *The Northern Tribes of Nigeria*, London (pp 71 -72).

Meyerowitz, L.R. Eva 1972. "The Origin of the "Sudanic" Civilisation". Anthropos, Bd. 67, H. 1/2, pp. 161 – 175.

NAK 1910. "Notes on Early History of Bussa". DOB/ASR/33

NAK 1926. "Anthropological and Historical Report on the Bussawa". Report by A.B. Mathew BORGUDISRT/SNP/17/2101.

O'Hear, Ann 2006. "Elite Slaves in Ilorin in the Nineteenth and Twentieth Centuries". *The International Journal of African Historical Studies,* Vol. 39, No. 2 (2006), pp. 247 – 273.

Oliver, Roland and Fage, J.D. 1995. *A short History of Africa* (6th Edition). London, Penguin Books.

Palmer, H. R. 1908. The Kano Chronicle, *The Journal of the Royal Anthropological Institute of Great Britain and Ireland*, Vol. 38, pp. 58-98

Palmer, H.R. 1914. "Bori Among Hausa". *Man,* Vol. 14 (1914), pp. 133 - 117.

Palmer, H.R. 1941. "Trident-Gods in Sahara and Western Sudan". *Man,* Vol 41 (May – June., 1941), pp. 60-62.

Palmer, R.H. 1928. *Sudanese Memoirs*, Lagos.

Robinson, David 2004. *Muslim Societies in African History*. New York, Cambridge University Press.

Salamone, Frank 1975. "Bori, a Friendly "Witchdoctor". *Journal of Religion in Africa*, Vol. 7 Fasc. 3 (1973), pp. 201 – 211.

Sanders, R. Edith 1969. "The Hamitic Hypothesis: Its Origin and Function in Time Perspective".*Journal of African History*, Vol. 10, No. 4, pp. 521 – 532.

Schottman, Wendy 2000. "Baat(unknown)nu Personal Names from Birth to Death". *Journal of the International African Institute*. Vol. 70, No. 1, pp. 79 – 106.

Smith, Abdullahi 1987. *A Little New Light: Selected Historical Writings of Abdullahi Smith*. Zaria, Abdullahi Smith Centre for Historical Research.

Stawart, Helen Marjorie, 1978. "Kingship and Succession to the Throne of Bussa".*Ethnology*, Vol. 17. No 2, pp. 169 – 182.

Stevens, Phillips. 1975. "The Kisra Legend and the Distortion of Historical Tradition".*The Journal of African History,* Vol. 16. No. 2 (1975), pp. 185 – 200.

Stewart Helen Marjorie, 1980. "The Kisra Legend as Oral History". *The International Journal of African Historical Studies*, Vol. 13. No. 1 (1980) pp. 51 – 70. Pp 119 – 137.

Stewart, H. Marjorie 1993. *Borgu and its Kingdoms: A Reconstruction of Western Sudanese Polity*. New York, the Edwin Mellen Press.

Stewart, H.M 1985. "The Borgu of Nigeria and Benin: The Disruptive Effect of Partition on Traditional Political and Economic Relations". *Journal of the Historical Society of Nigeria*, Vol. 12, No 3/4, pp. 95 -120.

Sudan". In Jack Goody (ed), *Literacy in Traditional Societies*, Cambridge. Pp. 162 - 195.

Temple, O. 1922. *Notes on the Tribes, Provinces, Emirates and States of Northern Nigeria*. Lagos, the CMS Bookshop, Lagos.

Usman B.Y, 2006. *Beyond Fairy Tales: Selected Historical Writings of Yusufu Bala Usman*. Zaria, Abdullahi Smith Centre.

Usman, B.Y. 1981. *The Transformation of Katsina – 1400 – 1883*. Zaria, Ahmadu Bello University Press.

Weise, Constanze 2013. "Governance and Ritual Sovereignty at the Niger – Benue Confluence: A Political and Cultural History of the Nigeria's Igala, Northern Yoruba and Nupoid-Speaking Peoples to the 1900 CE". A PhD History Dissertation, University of California, Los Angeles.

Wilks, Ivor 1968. "The Transmission of Islamic Learning in the Western Sudan". In Jack Goody (ed), *Literacy in Traditional Societies*, Cambridge. Pp. 162 - 195.

Wise, Christopher (ed.) 2011. *Ta'rikh al Fattash. The Timbuktu Chronicles 1493 – 1599* (English Translation), Trenton, Africa World Press.

Chapter 2

Political Centralisation and Dynastic Politics

Abdu, Hussaini 2010. *Clash of Identities: State, Society and Ethno-religious Conflicts in Northern Nigeria*. Kaduna, DevReach Publishers.

Adekunle O. Julius 2008. "The Wasangari: Politics and Identity in Borgu". *Anthropos,* Bd. 103, H. 2, pp. 435 – 445.

Adekunle, O. Julius 1994. "Borgu and Economic Transformation 1700 - 1900: The Wangara Factor".*African Economic History*, No. 22, pp 1 – 18.

Adekunle, O. Julius 2004. *Politics and Society in Nigeria's Middle Belt: Borgu and the Emergence of a Political Identity.* Asmara, Africa World Press.

Akinwumi, Duro Olayemi 1992. "The Oyo-Borgu Military Allaince of 1835: A Case Study in Pre-Colonial Military History".*Transafrican Journal of History*, Vol. 21, pp. 159 – 170.

Akinwumi, Olayemi 1998. "Oral Tradition in Changing Political Contexts: The Kisra Legend in Northern Borgu", *History in Africa*, Vol. 25, (1998), pp, 1 – 7.

Akinwumi, Olayemi, 1995. Biologically-Based Warfare in the Pre-Colonial Borgu Society of Nigeria and Republic of Benin".*Transafrican Journal of History*, Vol. 24, Pp. 123 – 130.

Al-Hajj, A. Mohammed, 1968 "A Seventeenth Century Chronicle on the Origins and Missionary Activities of the Wangarawa", *Kano Studies* vol. 1 No. 4, 1968.

Anene, J.C. 1965. "The Eclipse of the Borgawa".*Journal of Historical Society of Nigeria*, Vol. 3, No. 2, pp. 211 – 220.

Asiwaju, I. A. 1989. "Dahomey, Yorubaland, Borgu and Benin in the Nineteenth Century". In Ade Ajayi J.F. *General History of Africa Vol. VI*.Heinemann and UNESCO.

Bierschenk, Thomas 1993. "The Creation of a Tradition: Fulani Chiefs in Dahomey/Benin from the late 19th Century". *Paideuma: Mitteilungen zur Kulturkunde*, Ed. 39, pp 217 – 244.

Clapperton, Hugh 1829. *Journal of Second Expedition into the Interior of Africa*. London, John Murray.

Crowder, 1973. *Revolt in Bussa*. London, Faber and Faber.

Crowder, Michael 1978. *Colonial West Africa*. Frank Cass, London.

CSO/26/51245 "Assessment Report on Okuta District, Borgu Division, Kontagora Province" National Archive, Kaduna.

Falola, Toyin 1989. "Pre-Colonial Origins of the National Question in Nigeria: The Yoruba Identity as a Case Study". *Africa Revista do Centro de Estudes Africanos* USP, S. Paulo 12 – 13 (1), pp. 3- 24. 1989/1990.

Hallet, Robin ed. 1965. *The Journal of Richard and John Landers*. London, Routledge and Kegan Paul.

Hallet, Robin, 1974. *Africa Since 1875: A Modern History*. London, Heinemann.

Hermon-Hodge, H.B. 1921. *Gazetteer of Ilorin Province*, pp. 115.

Hoskyns-Abrahall, T. 1925. "History of Bussa" 20/12/1925. National Archive Kaduna.

Idris, Baba Musa 1973. "Political and Economic Relations in Bariba State". Unpublished PhD thesis, University of Birmingham.

Idris, D.M. and Yaru, I.M 2008. Kaiama: *From Great Trek to a Place to rest*. Ilorin, Haytee Press.

Jega, M.A. 2005. "Politics and Political Process in Northern Nigeria". In Yakubu, M.A., Jumare I.M. and Saeed, A.G. (eds.), *Northern Nigeria: A Century of Transformation, 1903 – 2003*. Kaduna, Arewa House.

Lafia, Hussaini 2004. *Gaani: The State Festival*. Ilorin, Haytee Press.

Lafia, Hussaini 2006. *Borgu: The Endless Journey*, Ilorin, Haytee Press.

Lander, Richard and Lander John, 1932. *Journal of an Expedition to Explore the Course and Termination of the Niger etc*. London

Lander, Richard, 1967. *Clapperton's Last Expedition to Africa*. London, Frank Cass.

Last, Murray 2005. "1903 Revisited". In Yakubu, M.A., Jumare I.M. and Saeed, A.G. (eds.) *Northern Nigeria: A Century of Transformation, 1903 – 2003*. Kaduna, Arewa House.

Lockhart, B.J. 2008. *A Sailor in the Sahara: The Life and Travels of Hugh Clapperton, Commander RN*. I.B. Tauris & Co. New York.

Lugard, F. D 1895. "An expedition to Borgu, on the Niger".*The Geographical Journal*, Vol. 6, No. 3, pp. 205 – 225.

Midgal, S. Joel 1988. *Strong State and Weak State: State-Society Relations and State Capabilities in the Third World*. Princeton, Princeton University Press.

Mockley-Ferryman, A.F. 1892. *Upland the Niger: Narrative of Major Claude Macdonald's Mission to the Niger and Benue*, London, George Philip and Son.

Mohammed, Yau Damisa and Nze, P. Nze 2009. *Borgu: Destined to Be*. Ilorin, Modern Impression.

Palmer, H. R. 1908. "The Kano Chronicle", *The Journal of the Royal Anthropological Institute of Great Britain and Ireland*, Vol. 38, pp. 58-98

Schottman, Wendy 2000. "Baat (unknown)nu Personal Names from Birth to Death". *Journal of the International African Institute*. Vol. 70, No. 1, pp. 79 – 106.

Stewart, H. M. 1981. "Anthropology and the Political Process". *Anthropos*, Bd. H. 3 / 4, pp. 441- 446.

Stewart, H.M 1985. "The Borgu of Nigeria and Benin: The Disruptive Effect of Partition on Traditional Political and Economic Relations". *Journal of the Historical Society of Nigeria*, Vol. 12, No 3/4, pp. 95 -120.

Stewart, H.M. 1978. "Kinship and Succession to the Throne of Bussa", *Ethnology*, Vol. 17, No. 2, pp. 169 – 182.

Stewart, H.M. 1980. "The Kisra Legend as Oral History". *The International Journal of African Historical Studies*, Vo. 13. No. 1, pp. 51 – 70.

Stewart, H.M. 1993. *Borgu and its Kingdoms: A Reconstruction of a Western Sudanese Polity*. Edwin Melles Press, New York.

Usman, Bala Yusufu 1981. *The Transformation of Katsina – 1400 – 1883*. Zaria, Ahmadu Bello University Press.

Yakubu, M.A., Jumare I.M. and Saeed, A.G. (eds.) 2005 .*Northern Nigeria: A Century of Transformation, 1903 – 2003*. Kaduna, Arewa House.

Chapter 3

Pre-colonial State and Economy

Adamu, Mahdi 1978. *The Hausa Factor in West African History*, Ibadan, Oxford University Press.

Adekunle, O. Julius 1994. "Borgu and Economic Transformation 1700 – 1900: The Wangara Factor", African Economic History, No 22, pp. 1 – 18.

Africanus, Leo 2010 (digital Edition). The History and Discription of Africa.Vol. 1.Cambridge, Cambridge University Press.

Ajayi, J.F.A. and Crowder, M. eds. 1974. *History of West Africa*, Vol. 1 New York, Columbia University Press.

Akinwumi, Olayemi and Raji, Y. Adesina 1990. "The Wangara Factor in the History of Nigerian Islam: The Example of Kano and Borgu". Islamic Studies (Islamabad), 29: 4. Pp. 375 - 385

Anene, J.C. 1965. "The Eclipse of the Borgawa". *Journal of the Historical Society of Nigeria*, Vol.3, No. 2, pp. 211 – 220.

Baier, Stephen 1977. "Trans-Saharan Trade and the Sahel: Damergu, 1870 – 1930, *Journal of African History*, XVIII, 1, pp. 37 – 60.

Baier, Stephen 1980. *An Economic History of Central Niger*, Oxford: Clarendon Press.

Beckles, M.D. Hilary 1985. "The Slave – Drivers' War: Bussa and the 1816 Barbados Slave Rebellion".*Boletin de Estudios Latinoamericanos y del Caribe*, No. 39, pp. 85 -110.

Crowder, 1973.*Revolt in Bussa*.London, Faber and Faber.

Dupuis, J. 1824. *Journal of a Residence in Ashantee*. London, Frank Cass.

Hellett, Robin 1965 (ed.) *The Niger Journal of Richard and John Lander*, London.

Hirshfield, Claire 1979. *The Diplomacy of Partition: Britain, France and the Creation of Nigeria 1890 – 1898.* Martinus Nijhoff, The Hague.

Idris, Baba Musa 1973. "Political and Economic Relations in Bariba State". Unpublished PhD thesis, University of Birmingham.

Johnson, Marion 1970. "The Cowrie Currencies of West Africa. Part I." *The Journal of African History*, vol. 11, no. 1, pp. 17–49.

Lander, Richard and Lander John, 1932. *Journal of an Expedition to Explore the Course and Termination of the Niger etc.* London.

Lander, Richard, 1967.*Clapperton's Last Expedition to Africa*. London, Frank Cass.

Law Robin and Lovejoy E. Paul 1999. "Borgu in the Atlantic Slave Trade", *African Economic History*, No 27, pp. 69 – 92.

Law, R. (1989). Slave-Raiders and Middlemen, Monopolists and Free-Traders: The Supply of Slaves for the Atlantic Trade in Dahomey c. 1715-1850. *The Journal of African History, 30*(1), 45-68.

Levtzion, N. and Hopkin J.F.P. 2000. *Corpus of Early Arabic Sources for West Africa*. Princeton, Markus Wiener Publishers.

Levtzion, Nehemia and Spaulding, Jay 2011. *Medieval West Africa: Views from Arab Scholars and Merchants.*Princeton, Markus Wiener Publishers.

Lovejoy 1974. "Inter-regional Monetary Flows in the Precolonial Trade of Nigeria", *Journal of African History*, XV (4), pp. 563 – 585.

Lovejoy, Paul E. 1971. "Long Distance Trade and Islam: The Case of the Nineteenth- Century Hausa kola Trade", *Journal of the Historical Society of Nigeria*, Vol. 5, No. 4, pp. 537 – 547.

Lovejoy, Paul E. 1978. "The Role of Wangara in the Economic Transformation of the Central Sudan in the Fifteenth and Sixteenth Centuries", *Journal of African History*, XIX, 2, pp. 173 – 193.

Lovejoy, Paul E. 1980. "Kola in the History of west Africa" (*La kola dans l'Afrique occidentale*), *Cashier d'Etudes Africaines*, Vol. 20, Cashier 77/78, pp. 97 – 134.

Lovejoy, Paul E. 1980. *Caravans of Kola: The Kola Trade 1700 1900.* Oxford. Oxford University Press.

Lovejoy, Paul E. 1983. *Transformation in Slavery*. Cambridge. Cambridge University Press.

Lovejoy, Paul E. and Baier Stephen 1975. The Desert-Side Economy of the Central Sudan". *The International Journal of African Historical Studies*, Vol. 8, No. 4, pp. 551 – 581.

Lovejoy, Paul E. and Hogendorn, J.S. 1979. "Slave Marketting in West Africa" In Henry Gemery and Jan S. Hogendorn eds., *The Uncommon Market: Essays in the Economic History of the Atlantic Slave Trade*. New York, Academic Press. Pp. 214 – 235.

Lugard, F.D. 1895. "An Expedition to Borgu, on the Niger".*The Geographical Journal*, Vol 6, No. 3, pp. 205 – 225.

Lugard, F.D. 1895. "*England and France on the Niger*". Nineteenth Century, 220. Pp. 903.

Mahadi, Abdullahi, 1990. "The Genesis of Kano's Economic Prosperity in the 19th Century: The Role of the State in Economic Development up to 1750, *Journal of Historical Society of Nigeria*, Vol. 12, No. 1/2, pp. 1 – 21.

Mohammed, Yau Damisa and Nze, P. Nze 2009. *Borgu: Destined to Be.* Ilorin, Modern Impression.

Moseley, K.P. 1992. "Caravel and Caravan: West Africa and the World-Economies, ca. 900 – 1900 AD", *Review (Fernand Braudel Centre),* Vol. 15, No. 3, Comparing World Systems, PP. 523 – 555.

Ogunremi, 'Deji 1975. "Human Porters in Nigeria in the Nineteenth Century – A Pillar in the Indigenous Economy".*Journal of the Historical Society of Nigeria*, Vol. 8, No. 1, pp. 37 – 59.

Patricia and Fredrick McKissack. 1994. *The Royal Kingdoms of Ghana, Mali and Songhai.* New York, Henry Holt and Company.

Robinson, David. 2004. *Muslim Society in African History*, New York, Cambridge University Press.

Stewart, H. Marjorie 1993. *Borgu and its Kingdoms: A Reconstruction of Western Sudanese Polity.* New York, the Edwin Mellen Press.

Stewart, M.H. 1979. "The Role of Manding in the Hinterland Trade of the Western Sudan", *Bulletin de l'IFAN, Series* B, 41 (2), pp. 281 – 302.

Chapter 4

Borgu and its Neighbours

Adekunle, O. Julius (2004).*Politics and Society in Nigeria's Middle Belt: Borgu and the Emergence of a Political Identity*, Asmara, Africa World Press.

Agiri B.A. (1975). "Early Oyo History Reconsidered". *History in Africa*, Vol.2, pp. 1 – 16.

Akinwumi, Duro Olayemi 1992. "The Oyo-Borgu Military Alliance of 1835: A Case Study in the Pre-Colonial Military History", *Transafrican Journal of History*, Vol. 21, pp. 159 – 170.

Asiwaju, A.I. 1973, "A Note on the History of Sabe", *Lagos Notes and Records*,Vol. 4, pp. 23 – 25.

Atanda, J.A. 1971. "The Fall of the Old Oyo Empire: A Re-construction of its Cause", *Journal of the Historical Society of Nigeria*, Vol. 5, No. 4 (June 1971), pp. 477 – 490.

Biobaku, S.O. (1956), *The Egba and their Neighbours*, London, Oxford University Press.

Biobaku, S.O. (ed.) 1973. Sources of Yoruba History. Oxford. Oxford Press.

Biobaku, S.O. 1955. *The Origin of the Yoruba*. London, Oxford University Press.

Bovill Edward William, 1995. *The Golden Trade of the Moors*. Markus Wiener Publishers, Princeton.

Clapperton, Hugh 1829. *Journal of Second Expedition into the Interior of Africa*. London, John Murray.

Constructions of Kingship in the Manden and Borgu", In Graham Furniss and Liz Gunner (eds.), New York, *Power, Marginality and African Literature*, Cambridge University Press.

Crowder, Michael 1973. *Revolt in Bussa*. London, Faber and Faber Limited.
Falola, T., & Genova, A. (Eds.).(2006). *Yorùbá Identity and Power Politics*. Boydell and Brewer.
Falola, T., & Usman, A. (Eds.). (2009). *Movements, Borders, and Identities in Africa*. Boydell and Brewer.
Gourley, K.A. 1982, "Long Trumpets of Northern Nigeria – In History and Today, *African Music*, Vol. 6, No.2, pp. 48 – 72.
Harris P.G. 1930. "Notes on Yauri (Sokoto Province), Nigeria", *The Journal of the Royal Anthropological Institute of Great Britain and Ireland*, Vol. 60, pp. 283 – 334.
Hodgkin, T. (1975). Nigerian Perspectives: An Historical Anthology, London.
Hunwick, J.O. 1971, "A Little-Known Diplomatic Episode in the History of Kebbi (c. 1594), *Journal of Historical Society of Nigeria*, Vol. 5. No. 4 (June 1971), pp. 575 – 581.
Idris, Baba Musa 1973. "Political and Economic Relations in Bariba State". Unpublished PhD thesis, University of Birmingham.
Jimada, Sha'aba Idris 2005.*The Nupe and the Origins and Evolution of the Yoruba c. 1275 – 1897*. The Abdullahi Smith Centre for Historical Research, Zaria.
Kuba, Richard and Akinwumi, Olayemi 2005. "Precolonial Borgu: Its History and Culture", In Akinwumi Ogundiran (ed), *Precolonial Nigeria: Essays in Honour of Toyin Falola*, Asmara, African World Press.
Lafia, Hussaini 2006. *Borgu the Endless Journey*, Ilorin, Heytee Press.
Lander, Richard and Lander John, 1932.*Journal of an Expedition to Explore the Course and Termination of the Niger etc*. London.
Lander, Richard, 1967.*Clapperton's Last Expedition to Africa*. London, Frank Cass.
Lange, Dierk 2009. "An Assyrian Successor State in West Africa: The Ancestral Kings of Kebbi as Ancient Near Eastern Rulers".*Anthropos*, No. 104, pp. 359 – 382.
Lange, Dierk 2011, "Origin of the Yoruba and the Lost Tribes of Isreal", *Anthropos*, No. 106, pp. 579 – 595.
Law, R. (1989). Slave-Raiders and Middlemen, Monopolists and Free-Traders: The Supply of Slaves for the Atlantic Trade in Dahomey c. 1715-1850. *The Journal of African History, 30*(1), 45-68.
Law, Robin 1970. "The Chronology of the Yoruba Wars of the Early Nineteenth Century: A Reconstruction", *Journal of the Historical Society of Nigeria*, Vol. 2, No. 6, (1970), pp. 215.
Law, Robin 1977. *The Oyo Empire, c. 1600 – c. 1836*, London, Oxford University Press, London.

Law, Robin 1985, "How Many Times Can History Repeat itself? Some Problems in the Traditional History of Oyo".*The Journal of African Historical Studies*, Vol. 18, No.1 pp. 33 – 51.

Law, Robin, (1995). "Central and Eastern Wangara": An Indigenous West African Perception of the Political and Economic Geography of the Slave Coast as recorded by Joseph Dupuis in Kumasi, 1820". *History in Africa*, Vol. 22, pp. 281 – 305.

Law, Robin, 1984. "How Truly Traditional is Our Traditional History? The Case of Samuel Johnson and the Recording of Yoruba Oral Tradition" *History in Africa*, Vol. XI pp.

Levtzion, N. and Hopkin J.F.P. 2000.*Corpus of Early Arabic Sources for West Africa*. Princeton, Markus Wiener Publishers.

Levtzion, Nehemia 1971. "Patterns of Islamization in West Africa", In Daniel F. McCall and Norman R. Bennet, *Aspect of West African Islam.*Boston University African Studies Centres, Vol. V.

Levtzion, Nehemia and Spaulding, Jay 2011.*Medieval West Africa: Views from Arab Scholars and Merchants*. Princeton, Markus Wiener Publishers.

Lovejoy, Paul E. 1971. "Long Distance Trade and Islam: The Case of the Nineteenth- Century Hausa Kola Trade", *Journal of the Historical Society of Nigeria*, Vol. 5, No. 4 (June 1971), pp. 537 – 547.

Lovejoy, Paul E. 1978. "The Role of Wangara in the Economic Transformation of the Central Sudan in the Fifteenth and Sixteenth Centuries", *Journal of African History*, XIX, 2, pp. 173 – 193.

Lovejoy, Paul E. 1980. *Caravans of Kola: The Kola Trade 1700 1900.* Oxford. Oxford University Press.

Mason, Michael 1970, "The Jihad in the South: An Outline of the Nineteenth Century Nupe Hegemony in North-eastern Yorubaland and Afenmai", *Journal of the Historical Society of Nigeria*, Vol. 5, No. 2 (June 1970), pp. 193 – 209.

Massing, W. Andreas 2000. "The Wangara, and Old Soninke Diaspora in West Africa?"*Cashiers d'estudes africaines,* 158. XL – 2, pp. 281 – 308.

McCall, F. Daniel and Bennet R. Norman 1971.*Aspect of West African Islam.* Boston University African Studies Centres, Vol. V.

Mora, Inuwa Mohammed 1994. *Mora Amali Dogo.* Zaria, Northern Nigeria Publishing Company.

Moraes Farias, de Paulo Fernando 1995. "Parise Splits the Subject of Speech:

Moreas Farais de P.F. 1974. "Silent Trade: Myth and Historical Evidence", *History in Africa*, Vol. 1 pp. 9 – 24.

Nadel, S.F. (1942) *A Black Byzantium: The Kingdoms of Nupe in Nigeria*, London, Oxford University Press.

NAK 1928. "History of Kaiama" Ilorin Gazateer, DOB/ASR/33/63.

Norrris, Graham Edward and Heine, Peter 1982. "Genealogical Manipulations and Social Identity in Sansanne Mango, Northern Togo: An "imam" – List and the Qasida of ar-Ra is Badis". *Bulletin of the School of Oriental and African Studies, University of London*, Vol. 45, No. 1 pp. 188 – 137.

O'Hear, Ann 2006. "Elite Slaves in Ilorin in the Nineteenth and Twentieth centuries", *The International Journal of African Historical Studies,* Vol. 39, No. 2 pp. 247 – 273.

Palmer, H.R. 1914. "Bori Among the Hausas", *Man*, Vol. 14 (1914), pp. 133 – 117.

Pardo, W. Anne 1971. "Songhay Empire Under Sonni Ali and Askia Muhammad: A Study in Comparisons and Contrasts", In Daniel F. McCall and Norman R. Bennet, *Aspect of West African Islam.* Boston University African Studies Centres, Vol. V.

Reichmuth, Stefan 1993, "Imam Umaru's Account of the Origin of the Ilorin Emirate: A Manuscript in the Heinz Solken Collection, Frankfurt", *Sudanic Africa*, Vol. 4, Special Issue on Kano, pp. 155 – 173.

Robinson, David. 2004. *Muslim Society in African History*, New York, Cambridge University Press.

Smith, R. (1965). "The Alafin in Exile: A Study of the Igboho Period in Oyo History". *The Journal of African History,* 6(1), 57-77.

Chapter 5

Scramble and Partitioning of Borgu

Anene, J. (1963). "The Nigeria-Dahomey Boundary". *Journal of the Historical Society of Nigeria, 2*(4), 479-485.

Anene, J.C 1965. "The Eclipse of Borgawa", *Journal of the Historical Society of Nigeria*, Vol. 3. No. 2.Pp. 211-220.

Anene, J.C. 1970. *The International Boundaries of Nigeria 1885 – 1960*. Longman, London.

Apata, Z.O. 1992. "Lugard and the Creation of Provincial Administration in Northern Nigeria", *Transafrican Journal of History*, Vo. 21 (1992), pp. 111– 123.

Boahen, Adu, A. 1987. *African Perspectives on Colonialism*. The Johns Hopkins University Press, Baltimore.

Crowder, Michael 1973. *Revolt in Bussa: A Study of British 'Native Administration' in Borgu 1902 – 1935.* Faber and Feber limited, London.

Crowder, Michael 1977. *West Africa: An Introduction to its History*. Longman, London.

Crowder, Michael 1978.*Colonial West Africa*. Frank Cass, London.

Davidson, Basil 1991. *African Civilisation Revisited*. Africa World Press, Asmara.

Davidson, Basil 1994. *The search for Africa.A History in the Making*. James Currey, Oxford.

Falola, Toyin and Heaton, M. Matthew, 2008. *A History of Nigeria*. Cambridge University Press, Cambridge.

Gavin, R.J. 1979. "Some Perspectives on Nigerian History", *Journal of the Historical Society of Nigeria,* Vol. 9, No. 4. (June 1979), pp. 15 – 38.

Guezo, A. 2012. "Abolition and West-African Societies: The Inconclusive Debate". *Journal of the Historical Society of Nigeria, 21*, pp. 1-20.

Hahn, H. 2012. "Heroism, Exoticism, and Violence: Representing the Self, "the Other," and Rival Empires in the English and French Illustrated

Press, 1880-1905". *Historical Reflections/ Réflexions Historiques, 38*(3), 62-83.

Harris, Dwight Norman, 1911. "French Colonial Expansion in West Africa, the Sudan and the Sahara", *The American Political Science Review*, Vol. 5, No. 3 (Aug. 1911), pp. 353 – 373.

Henry, Froidevaux 1904. "M. Froidevaux's Letter", *Bulletin of the American Geographical Society*, Vol. 36, No. 5 (1904), pp. 288 – 291.

Hirshfield, Claire 1979. *The Diplomacy of Partition: Britain, France and the Creation of Nigeria 1890 – 1898.* Martinus Nijhoff, The Hague.

Hogben, S.J. 1930. *The Mohammedan Emirates of Nigeria.* Oxford.

Hopkins, A.G. 1973. *An Economic History of West Africa.* New York

Lugard, F.D. 1895. "An Expedition to Borgu on the Niger", *The Geographical Journal*, Vol. 6, No. 3 (Sep. 1895), pp. 2015 – 225.

Mockley-Ferryman, A.F. 1892.*Upland the Niger: Narrative of Major Claude Macdonald's Mission to the Niger and Benue*, London, George Philip and Son.

Oliver, Roland and Fage J.D. 1962.*A short History of Africa*. Penguin Books, London.

Ukpabi, C. Sam 1987. *Mercantile Soldiers in Nigerian History*. Gaskiya Corporation Limited, Zaria.

Ukpabi, S. (1966). "The Origins 0f The West African Frontier Force". *Journal of the Historical Society of Nigeria,3*(3), 485-501.

Ukpabi, S. (1971). "The Anglo-French Rivalry in Borgu: A Study of Military Imperialism". *African Studies Review, 14*(3), 447-461.

Watts, J. M. 1983. *Silent Violence: Food, Famine and Peasantry in Northern Nigeria*. Athens and London, University of Georgia Press.

Chapter 6

Borgu under Colonial Rule

Ake, C. 1981. *A political Economy of Africa.* Essex, Longman.
ANB (National Achieve of Benin). 2. *Résident du Borgou au Gouverneur,* 18.9.1899.
ANB 1990. 44 *Cercle du Monye* Niger, RP 5/1900.
ANB 22.*Garde indigene. Postt de Nikki,* RP 25.2.1900 and *cercle du Borgou,* RP 3/1900.
ANB 28, Cercle du Moyen Niger, RP 1934 and 1935.
ANB 29, Notes des chefs du Borgou, 1930.
Ayo, Bamidele 1986. "Traditional Rulers and the Operations of Local Administration in the Republic of Benin", Verfassung und Recht in ubersee/Law and Politics in Africa, Asia and Latin America, Vol. 19, No. 2 pp. 139 – 147.
Bierschenck, Thomas 1993. "The Creation of Tradition: Fulani Chiefs in Dahomey/Benin from the Late 19th Century", *Paidama: Mitteilungen zur Kulturkunde,* Bd. 39, pp. 217 – 224.
Boahen, A, Adu 1987.*African Perspectives on Colonialism.* Baltimore, the John Hopkins University Press.
Crowder, Michael 1973.*The Revolt in Bussa: A Study of 'Native Administration' in Nigerian Borgu 1902 – 1935.*London, Faber and Faber.
Crowder, Michael 1975. "The 1916 -1917 Revolt Against the French in Dahomeyan Borgu", *Journal of the Historical Society of Nigeria,* Vol. 8, No. 1, pp. 99 – 115.
Crowder, Michael 1978. *Colonial West Africa.* London, Frank Cass.
Ekekwe E. 1986. *Class and State in Nigeria.*London, Longman.
Ezenekwe, C. Jonathan, 1953. "West Africa".*Journal of International Affairs.*Vol, 7, No. 2, pp. 168 – 176.
Fyfe, Christopher 1963. "The Colonial Situation in "MISTER JOHNSON". *Modern Fiction Studies, Vol. 9, 3 JOYCE CARY*: Special Number.

Harris, Dwight Norman 1911. "French Colonial Expansion in West Africa, The Sudan, and Sahara". *The American Political Science Review*. Vol. 5, No. 3, pp. 353 – 373.

Herbst, Jeffrey, 2014. *States and Power in Africa: Comparative Lessons in Authority and Control (New Edition)*. Princeton and Oxford, Princeton University Press.

Huillery, Elise 2009. "History Matters: The Long-Term Impact of the Colonial Public Investment in French West Africa", *American Economic Journal: Applied Economics*, Vol. 1 No. 2, pp, pp.176 – 215.

Jega, M. Attahiru 2005. "Politics and Political Process in Northern Nigeria". In A.M. Yakubu, et.al. (eds.) Northern Nigeria: A Century of Transformation 1903 – 2003. Kaduna, Arewa House, Ahmadu Bello University.

Lombard, J. 1970. "Chieftaincy Among the Bariba of Dahomey". In Michael Crowder and Obaro Ikimi eds. *West African Chiefs*.Ile-Ife, University of Ife Press.

Mamdani, Mahmood 2004. *Citizens and Subjects: Contemporary Africa and the Legacy of Late Colonialism*.Kampala, Fountain Publishers.

NAK 1915. SNP/42/ (Crowder)

NAK 1919."Kaiama District Assessment Report". BORG DIST/DOB/ASR/10

NAK 1924."History of Borgu". DOB/HIS/38

NAK 1925 "History of Bussawa by MT. Hoskyns-Abrahall, SNP, 17.

NAK 1926 "Agwara – Rofia Boundary".DOB/BOU/18. File 606, BORG DIV.

NAK 1926."Bussa Territory – Possible Restoration".DOU/BOU/17. BORGU DIST.

NAK 1928. "History of Kaiama". Ilorin Gazetteer, DOB/ASR/33

NAK 1928. "Ilorin Gazeteer". DOB/ASR/33

NAK 1934. Native Administration Policy: Pagan Administration.

NAK 1935. "Kenu Village, Okuta District Assessment Report"- DJ Health (DO), DOB/ASR/17.

NAK 1936 "Gazetteer of Aliyara District".DOB/ASR/28.

NAK 1940. Bussa Native Authority Tax 1940 – 1941. DOB/BOU/1

NAK 1941. "General Tax and Jangali – 1939 – 1940". DOU/BOU/1

NAK 1953."Notes on Borgu Divisional Procedure". Borgu Divisional Note Book containing History notes on Etymology, History, Organisation and Procedure".ILOR PROF 3158.

NAK 1955. "General Tax 1954 -1955". DOB/ASR/12

NAK 1957 "Report on Sokoto-Ilorin Provincial Boundary Dispute concerning Tungan Abarshi and Adjacent Hamlets". DOB/BOU/20.

NAK 3158B "Bussa Emirate Note Book: Notes on Organisation and Procedure".ILOR PROF.

NAK 3813 "Borgu – Its Peoples History and Problems".ILORPROF.

NAK Memorandum from the Secretary of Northern Provinces to the Resident of Province.DOB/HIS/59.

Turaki, Yusuf 1993. *The British Colonial Legacy in Northern Nigeria: A Social Ethical Analysis of the Colonial and Post-Colonial Society and Politics in Nigeria*. Jos, Challenge Press.

Watts, J. M. 1983. *Silent Violence: Food, Famine and Peasantry in Northern Nigeria*. Berkeley, University of California Press.

William, Gavin 1976. "Nigeria; A Political Economy". In Gavin Williams (ed.) *Nigeria: Economy and Society*. Rex Collings, London. pp. 11 – 54.

Yahaya A.D. 1980. *The Native Authority System in Northern Nigeria 1950 – 1970*. Ahmadu Bello University Press, Zaria.

Yahaya, A.D. 2005. "Traditional Leadership and Institutions: The Colonial Transformation of the Emirate System".In A.M. Yakubu, et.al. (eds.) *Northern Nigeria: A Century of Transformation 1903 – 2003*. Kaduna, Arewa House, Ahmadu Bello University.

Chapter 7

Anticolonial Revolts in Borgu

Bio Bigou, Léon Bani 1983.*L'opposition des Bariba du Borgou à la pénétration et à l'occupation coloniales [i.e. coloniale] de 1888 à 1916: le cas de Bio Guera:* contribution à l'étude de l'histoire des Baatombu Bariba. Cotonou.

Bio Bigou, Léon Bani 1995. *Les origines du peuple Baatonu (Bariba)*. Flamboyant, Cotonou.

Crowder, Michael 1975. "The 1916 -1917 Revolt Against the French in Dahomeyan Borgu", *Journal of the Historical Society of Nigeria,* Vol. 8, No. 1, pp. 99 – 115.

Crowder, Michael 1978. *Colonial West Africa*. Frank Cass, London.

Crowder, Michal 1973. *The Revolt in Bussa: A Study of 'Native Administration' in Nigerian Borgu 1902 – 1935.* Faber and Faber, London.

Debourou, Mama Djibril 2012. "La Société Baatonnu du Nord-Bénin: son passé, son Dynamisme, ses Conflits et ses Innovations". Paris, Études Africaines, Hamttan.

Debourou, Mama Djibril 2013. *La guerre Coloniale au Nord du Dahomey: Bio Guéra, entre Mythe et Réalité: Le Sens de son combat pour la Liberté (1915-1917).* Paris, *Études Africaines*, Hamttan.

Debourou, Mama Djibril, 2015. La résistance des Baatombu à la pénétration Française dans le Haut-Dahomey (1895-1915): Saka Yerima ou l'injuste oubli. *Études Africaines*, Histoire Series, Paris.

Grätz, T. (2000). "La rébellion de Kaba (1916-1917) dans l'imaginaire politique au Bénin (Kaba's rebellion (1916-1917)" in Benin's Political Imagery). *Cahiers D'Études Africaines*, 40(160), 675-703.

Idris Baba Musa 1973. "Political and Economic Relations in Bariba State". Unpublished PhD thesis, University of Birmingham.

Mahmood, M. M. 1964. *Joyce Cary's Africa*.Methuen and Co. London.

Mamdani, Mahmood 1999. "Historicising Power and Responses to Power: Indirect Rule and its Reform", *Social Research*, Vol. 66, No. 3, Prospect for Democracy, pp. 859 -886.

NAK 1914, BORGDIV/DOB/AR/5

NAK 1915. SNP/10/331p/ 21 June 1915.

NAK 1915."Bussa Disturbances of 1915". SNP/331/

NAK 1916, SNP/10/364p/1961

NAK 1923. BORGDIV/DOB/AR17 – Annual report 1923; Revolt in Bussa pp. 176 – 177.

NAK 1924/1925, /SNP/18/CR 47 Hoskyns-Abrahall on Kitoro Gani

NAK 1925. BORGDIST/DOB/AR/20

NAK 1925.BORGDIST/DOB/BOU/17.

NAK 1926. BORGDIST/DOB/BOU/17, Diggle, D.O. Borgu to Resident Kontagora.

NAK/BORDIST 1925. BORGDIST/5 Political Officer's Dairy: Entry by Walter Nash 29/4/1925.

NAK/SPN/18/CR.47 "Annual Report on Chiefs. Ilorin Province.

Chapter 8

Amalgamation of Bussa and Kaiama Emirates

Crowder, Michael 1973.*Revolt in Bussa*. London, Frank Cass.
Crowder, Michael 1978.*Colonial West Africa*. London, Frank Cass.
Mahmood, M. M. 1964. *Joyce Cary's Africa*. London, Methuen and Co. Lafia, Hussaini 2006.*Borgu the Endless Journey*, Ilorin, Heytee Press.
NAI/CSO.26/2/ File No. 33625, Vol. II.
NAK 1914, BORGDIV/DOB/AR/5
NAK 1915. SNP/10/331p/ 21 June 1915.
NAK 1915."Bussa Disturbances of 1915". SNP/331/
NAK 1916, SNP/10/364p/1961
NAK 1923. BORGDIV/DOB/AR17 – Annual report 1923; Revolt in Bussa pp. 176 – 177.
NAK 1924/1925, /SNP/18/CR 47 Hoskyns-Abrahall on Kitoro Gani
NAK 1925. BORGDIST/DOB/AR/20
NAK 1925. BORGDIST/DOB/BOU/17.
NAK 1926. BORGDIST/DOB/BOU/17, Diggle, D.O. Borgu to Resident Kontagora.
NAK 1954 "Retirement of Haliru Kiyaru, Emir of Kaiama". DOB/HIS/31.
NAK 1956. "*Kayan Sarautar Sarakunan Kaiama*", No.66, Vol, 111/427.
NAK/BORDIST 1925. BORGDIST/5 Political Officer's Dairy: Entry by Walter Nash 29/4/1925.
NAK/SPN/18/CR.47 "Annual Report on Chiefs. Ilorin Province.
Yakubu, A. M. 2006. *Emirs and Politicians: Reforms, Reaction and Recrimination in Northern Nigeria 1950 – 1966.*Kaduna, Baraka Press.

Chapter 9
Politics and Underdevelopment under Colonial Rule

Adejunmobi, S. 1976. Problems of Education in Dahomey-A Nigerian View. *The Journal of Negro Education, 45*(3), 275-283.

Bierschenk, Thomas 1993. "The Creation of a Tradition: Fulani Chiefs in Dahomey/Benin from the late 19th Century", *Paideuma: Mitteilungen zur Kulturkunde*, Bd. 39, pp. 217 – 244.

Boahen, A. Adu 1987. *African Perspectives on Colonialism*. Baltimore, the Johns Hopkins University Press.

Bunche, R. 1934. French Educational Policy in Togo and Dahomey. *The Journal of Negro Education*, 3(1), 69-97.

Clapperton, H. 1829. *Journal of Second Expedition into the Interior of Africa.* London, John Murray.

Cooper, Frederick 2010. "Writing the History of Development", *Journal of Modern European History*, Vol. 8, No.1 pp. 2 – 23.

Crowder, Michael 1964. "Colonial Rule in West Africa – Factor for Division or Unity", *Civilisations*, Vol. 14, No. 3, pp. 167 – 182.

Firmin-Sellers, Kathryn 2000. "Institutions, Context and Outcomes: Explaining French and British Rule in West Africa. *Comparative Politics*, Vol. 32, No. 3 pp. 253 – 272.

Fitzgerald, E. 1992. "Economic Constraints on the Continuation of Colonial Rule in French Colonial Africa: The Problem of Recurrent Costs. Proceedings of the Meeting of the French Colonial Historical Society, 16, 115-125.

Huillery, Elise 2009. "History Matters: The Long-Term Impact of Colonial Public Investment in French West Africa".*American Economic Journal: Applied Economics*, Vol. 1, No. 2, pp. 176 – 215.

K. E. R. 1950. Economic Development in French West Africa.*The World Today*, 6(12), 535-544

Kirk-Greene, A.H.M. 1972. *Gazetteers of the Northern Provinces of Nigeria*. Vol III. London, Frank Cass.

Kwanashie, A. George 2002. *The Making of the North in Nigeria 1900 – 1965.* Kaduna, Arewa House, Ahmadu Bello University.

Lockhart, Bruce Jamie 2008.*A Sailor in the Sahara: The Life and Travels in Africa of Hugh Clapperton, Commander,* London, RN. I.B. Tauris and Co.

Lombard, J. 1970. "Chieftaincy Among the Bariba of Dahomey". In Michael Crowder and Obaro Ikime eds. *West African Chiefs: Their Changing Status under Colonial Rule and Independence.* Ile Ife, University of Ife Press.

Lugard, F. 1905. "Annual Colonial Report: Northern Nigeria – 1904". No. 476.

Mahood, M.M. 1964. *Joyce Cary's Africa.* London, Metheuen and Co.

Mamdani, Mahmood 1999. "Historicizing Power and Responses to Power: Indirect Rule and its Reform", *Social Research,* Vol. 66, No. 3 pp. 859 – 886.

Moody, P.R. 1967. "Road and Bridge in Joyce Cary's African Novels".*TheBulletin of the Rocky Mountain Modern Language Association,* Vol. 21, No. 4, pp. 145 – 149.

NAK 1917, "Foge Island Jangali", DOB/BOU/4

NAK 1919. "Gazetteer of Kaiama District", DOB/ASR/26

NAK 1925, "Assessment of Taxation – Capitation", DOB/ASR/12

NAK 1934 see Stewart on geological survey.

NAK 1935 "Borgu Division Development of". Ilorin Province 24042.

NAK 1935.Development of Borgu Division, No. 24042. Memo submitted by R.C. Wilson,

NAK 1936.Borgu Division Annual Report. G.G. Grimwood. DOB/AR/31

NAK 1937."Annual Report of Education. DOB/HIS/75

NAK 1937a.Ilorin Province – Annual Report. 3444/1

NAK 1937b. Blue Book: Annual Report and Blue Book returns. DOB/HIS/77.

NAK 1938. "Annual Report on Social and Economic Progress of the People – Borgu Division".DOB/HIS/76. Pp. 79

NAK 1939. "Borgu – Its People, History and Problems", ILORPROF, File No. 3813.

NAK 1939.Quarterly Report – Borgu Division, DOB/QHR/55.

NAK 1950.Annual Report, Borgu Division – Part I and II. Ilorin Province, File No. 5474/S.1

NAK 1950.Annual Report, Ilorin Province 5474.

NAK 1919a."Kaiama District Assessment Report". BORRDIST/DOB/ASR/10

Qlọruntimẹhin, B. 1972. "Theories and Realities in The Administration of Colonial French West Africa from 1890 To The First World War". *Journal of the Historical Society of Nigeria*, 6(3), 289-312.

Osoba, O. S. 1969. "The Phenomenon of Labour Migration in the Era of British Colonial Rule: A Neglected Aspect of Nigerian Social History", *Journal of the Historical Society of Nigeria*, Vol. 4, No. 4 pp. 515 – 538.

Tibenderana, K. Peter 2003. *Education and Cultural Change in Northern Nigeria 1906 – 1966*. Fountain Publishers, Kampala.

Varva, Ayati Toryina 2008. "The Impact of the Colonial Economy on Yam production in Tiv Land 1900 – 1960", *Journal of the Historical society of Nigeria*, Vol. 17 pp. 16 – 27.

Woodson, C.G. 1950. "French West Africa", *Negro History Bulletin*, Vo. 13, No. 5, pp. 108 -116.

Yakubu, A. M. 2006. *Emirs and Politicians: Reforms, Reaction and Recrimination in Northern Nigeria 1950 – 1966*.Kaduna, Baraka Press.

Young, Crowford, 1994. *The African Colonial State in Comparative Prespective*. New Heaven and London, Yale University Press.

Zelaza, Tiyambe 1985. "The Political Economy of British Colonial Development and Welfare in Africa".*Transafrican Journal of History*, Vol 14, pp. 139 – 161.

Chapter 10

Colonialism, Identities and Intergroup Relations

Abdu, Hussaini 2010. *Clash of Identities: State, Society and Ethno-Religious Conflicts in Northern Nigeria*.Kaduna, DevReach Publishers.

Adekunle, O. Julius 2004.*Politics and Society in Nigerian Middle Belt: Borgu and the Emergence of a Political Identity*. Asmara, Africa World Press.

Akinwumi, Olayemi (undated). "Colonial Administrative Structure and the Impact on Inter-Group Relations in Borgu". In Aliyu A. Idrees and Yakubu A. Ochefu eds. *Studies in the History of Central Nigeria Area*, Volume 1. Abuja, CSS Limited.

Akinwuni, Olayemi 1995. "British Colonial Policy and the Accentuation of Inter-Group Crisis in Southern Borgu, Nigeria – 1900 – 1954", Nigerian Journal of Inter-Group relations vo. 1.

Anene, J.C. 1965. "The Eclipse of Borgawa".*Journal of the Historical Society of Nigeria*. Vol. 3. No. 2 pp. 211 – 220.

Anene, J.C. 1970. *The International Boundaries of Nigeria; 1885 – 1960*. Ibadan, Longman.

Asiwaju, I. Anthony 2005. "Trans-frontier Regionalism: The European Union Perspectives on Post-Colonial Africa with Special Reference to Borgu. In Nicole, N. Heather and Townsend-Gault, Ian (eds.) *Holding the Line: Borders in a Global World*. Vancouver, UBC Press.

Bayart, Jean-Francois, 2009. *The State in Africa: The Politics of the Belly*. Cambridge, Polity Press.

Bierschenck, Thomas 1993. "The Creation of a Tradition: Fulani Chiefs in Dahomey/Bénin from the Late 19th Century", *Paideuma: Mitteilungen zur Kulturkunde*, Bd. 39 (1993), pp. 217-244

Bierschenk, Thomas 1996. "Peuls et état Colonial dans le Borgou Français/Nord-Dahomey (1895 - 1940)". *Nomadic Peoples*, No. 38, Nomads and the State (1996), pp. 99-12.

Blanton, Robert, Mason, T. David and Athow, Brian 2001. "Colonial Style and Post-Colonial Ethnic Conflict in Africa". *Journal of Peace Research*, Vol. 38, No. 4 (Jul., 2001), pp. 473-491

Burnham, Philip and Last, Murray 1994. "From Pastoralist to Politician: The Problem of a Fulbe "Aristocracy" (Des pasteurs auxdignitaires: la question de l'aristocratie fulɓe)", *Cahiers d'Études Africaines*, Vol. 34, Cahier 133/135, L'archipel peul, pp. 313-357

Crowder, Michael 1964. "Colonial Rule in West Africa: Factors for Division or Unity". *Civilizations,* Vol. 14, No. 3, pp. 167 -182.

Crowder, Michael 1993.*Revolt in Bussa: A Study of British 'Native Administration' in Nigerian Borgu, 1902 – 1935*. Faber and Faber, London.

Crowder, Michael, 1978. *Colonial West Africa*. London, Frank Cass.

Ekeh, P. Peter 1975. "Colonialism and the two Publics in Africa: A Theoretical Statement".*Comparative Studies in Society and History*, Vol. 17, No. 1 pp. 91 – 112.

Idris D. Mohammed and Yaru I. Mohammed, 2008. .*Kaiama: From Great Trek to a Place to Rest*. Ilorin, Haytee Press.

Kuna, J. Mohammad 2005. "Coloniality and the Geography of Conflicts: A Typology. In A.M. Yakubu, I.M. Jumare and A.G. Saeed, (eds.), *Northern Nigeria: A Century of Transformation, 1903 – 2003*, Kaduna, Baraka Press.

Lafia, Hussaini 2006. *Borgu: The Endless Journey*. Ilorin, Haytee Press.

Lombard J. 1967. "Autorités Traditoionelles et Pouvoirs Européens en Afrique Noire-Declin d'ure Aristocratie le Régime Colonial".*Coll. De la Foundation Nationale des Science Politique Cahier* No. 152.

Lombard, J. 1970. "Chieftaincy among the Bariba and Dahomey. In Michael Crowder and Obaro Ikimi eds. *West African Chiefs: Their Changing Status under Colonial Rule and Independence*, Ile-Ife, University of Ife Press.

Lombard, Jacques 1965, *"Structures de type " féodal " en Afrique Noire. Études des dynamiques internes et des relations sociales chez les Bariba du Dahomey"*, Paris, Mouton-EPHE.

Lugard, F. 1905. "Annual Colonial Report: Northern Nigeria – 1904". No. 476.

Mahood, M.M. 1964. *Joyce Cary's Africa*. London, Metheuen and Co.

Mamdani, Mahmood 1999. "Historicising Power and Response to Power: Indirect Rule and its Reform".*Social Research*, Vol. 66. No. 3, 859 – 886.

Mamdani, Mahmood 2001. *When Victims Become Killers: Colonialism, Nativism and the Genocide in Rwanda*. New Jersey, Princeton University Press.

Mamdani, Mahmood, 1996. *Citizens and Subject: Contemporary Africa and the Legacy of Late Colonialism*, Kampala, Fountain Publishers.

NAK (1937) Gazetteer of Gwanara District. DOB/ASR/30

NAK 1911. Report on Chiefs. BORGDIV/DOB/HIS/3

NAK 1920.Gazetteer of Yashikira District, Kaiama Emirate, DOB/ASR/22.

NAK 1922.Okuta District General; Assessment Report.DOB/ASR/15.

NAK 1928.Quarterly Report, Borgu Division, DOB/QHR/34.

NAK 1950. Annual Report Ilorin Province by R.H. Maddox, Resident; File No. 5474.

NAK 1936. Borgu Division Annual Report. G.G. Grimwood. DOB/AR/31

Nicole, N. Heather and Townsend-Gault, Ian (eds.) 2005.*Holding the Line: Borders in a Global World.* Vancouver, UBC Press.

Stewart M.H. 1978. "Tradition and a Changing Political Order: A Dispute Affecting the Chieftaincies of Kaiama and Kenu in Nigeria".*Géneva Afrique*, Vol. 17. No. 1.

Stewart, M.H. 1985. "The Borgu People of Nigeria and Benin: The Disruptive Effect of Partition on Traditional and Economic Relations.*Journal of Historical Society of Nigeria*, Vol. XII No. 3/4, pp. 345

Stewart, M.H. 1993. *Borgu and Its Kingdoms: A Reconstruction of a Western Sudanese Polity*. Lewiston, The Edwin Mellen Press.

Wallenstein, I. 1960. "Ethnicity and National Integration in West Africa".*Cahier d'Estudes Africanines*, Vol. 1, Cahier 3, pp. 129 – 139.

Widstrand, Gosta Carl 1969. *African Boundary Problems*. Uppsala, The Scandinavian Institute of African Studies.

Young, Crowford 1994. *The African Colonial States in Comparative Prespective*. New Heaven and London, Yale University Press.

Chapter 11

Continuity and Change in Post-Colonial Borgu

Adejumobi, Said 2000. "Negotiating Space for Rural Communities? Market Orthodoxy and Changing Concept of Welfare Services in Africa. *African Journal of Political Science*, Vol.5, No. 1, pp. 29 – 45.

Ake, Claude 1981. *A Political Economy of Africa*. Essex, Longman.

Ake, Claude 1994. *Democratisation and Disempowerment in Africa*. Lagos, Malthouse Press.

Ake, Claude 1996. *Democracy and Development in Africa*. Ibadan, Spectrum Books.

Asiwaju, A. I. (ed.) 1984. *Partitioned Africans: Ethnic Relations Across Africa's International Boundaries 1884 – 1984*. Lagos, University of Lagos Press.

Asiwaju, A.I. 2001. *West African Transformation: Comparative Impacts of French and British Colonialism*. Lagos, Malthouse Press.

Asiwaju, A.I. 2005. "Transfrontier Regionalism: The European Union Perspective on Postcolonial Africa, with Special Reference to Borgu". In Nicol N. Heather and Townsend-Gault Ian, *Holding the Line: Borders in a Global World,* Vancouver, UBC Press.

Azarya, Victor 1994. "Civil Society and Disengagement in Africa". In John Haberson, Donald Rothchild and Naomi Chazan (eds.), *Civil Society and the State in Africa, Boulder and London*, Lynne Rienner Publishers.

Azarya, Victor and Chazan Naomi 1998. "Disengagement from the state in Africa. Reflections on the Experiences of Ghana and Guinea. In Peter

Lewis (ed) *Dilemmas of Development and Change*. Oxford, Westview Press.

Bayart, Jean-Francois, Ellis, Stephen and Hibou, Beatrice 1999.*The Criminalisation of the state in Africa*. Oxford. James Currey.

Bierschenk, Thomas 2002. "The Local Appropriation of Democracy: An Analysis of the Municipal Elections in Parakou, Republic of Benin".*The Journal of Modern African Studies*, Vol. 44, No. 4. Pp. 543 – 571.

Bierschenk, Thomas and Oliver de Sardan, Jean-Pierre 2003. "Powers in the Village: Rural Benin Between Democratisation and Decentralisation. *Journal of the International African Institute*, Vol. 73, No. 2, pp. 145 – 173.

Bratton, Michael and Van de Walle, Nicolas 1998. Neo-patrimonial Regimes and Political Transitions in Africa. In Peter Lewis (ed) *Dilemmas of Development and Change*. Oxford, Westview Press.

Browlie, Ian (ed.), 1971. *Basic Documents on African Affairs*. Oxford, Clarendon Press.

Cary, Joyce 1944. *The Case for African Freedom*. London.

Cary, Joyce 1947. *Britain and West Africa*. London.

Cary, Joyce 1962, *Mister Johnson*. London, New York, Time Incorporated.

Cary, Joyce, *Aissa Saved* 1940. London, Thistle Publishers (2016 Edition).

Chabal, Patrick 1978. *Africa: The Politics of Suffering and Smiling*. London, Zed Books.

Clapham, Christopher 1982. "Clientelism and the State", in C. Clapham, ed., *Private Patronage and Public Power: Political Clientelism in the Modern State*, New York, St Martin's Press.

Davidson Basil, 1992. *The Black Man's Burden*. James Currey, London.

Dossou-Yovo, Noel 1999."The experience of Benin".*International Journal on World Peace*, Vol. 16, No. 3, pp. 59 – 74.

Ekeh, P. Peter 1975. "Colonialism and the two Publics in Africa: A Theoretical Statement".*Comparative Studies in Society and History*, Vol. 17, No. 1 pp. 91 – 112.

Englebert, Pierre 2000. "Pre-colonial Institutions, Post-Colonial State and Economic Development in Tropical Africa", *Political research Quarterly*, Vol. 53, No. 1, pp. 7 – 36.

Flynn, K. Donna 1997. "We are the Border": Identity, Exchange and the State along the Benin-Nigeria Border". *American Ethnologist*. Vol. 24, No. 2, pp. 311 – 330.

Fukuyama, Francis 1995. Trust: *The Social Virtues of the Creation of Prosperity*, New York, Free press.

Herbst, Jeffrey, 2014. *States and Power in Africa: Comparative Lessons in Authority and Control (New Edition)*. Princeton and Oxford, Princeton University Press.

Home, R.K. 1976. "Urban Growth and Urban Government: Contradiction in Colonial Political Economy". In Williams, Gavin (ed.) *Nigeria: Economy and Society*, London, Rex Collings.
Hyden, Goran 1980. *Beyond Ujamaa in Tanzania: Underdevelopment and the Uncaptured Peasantry*. Berkeley, University of the California Press.
Hyden, Goran 2006.*African Politics in Comparative Perspectives*. Cambridge, Cambridge University Press.
Hyden, Goran and Bratton Micheal, eds., 1992.*Governance and Politics in Africa*. Boulder, Lynee Rienner.
Jega Attahiru (ed.) 2000. *Identity Transformation and Identity Politics under Structural Adjustment in Nigeria*. Uppsala, Nordiska Afrikainstitutet.
Jega, Attahiru 2000. "The state and Identity Transformation under Structural Adjustment in Nigeria". In Jega, Attahiru (ed.) *Identity Transformation and Identity Politics under Structural Adjustment in Nigeria*. Uppsala, Nordiska Afrikainstitutet.
Joseph, A. Richard 1987. D*emocracy and Prebendal Politics in Nigeria: The Rise and Fall of the Second Republic.* Ibadan, Spectrum Books.
Kehinde, M. Olujimi 2010. "Implications of Colonially Determined Boundaries in (West) Africa: The Yoruba of Nigeria and Benin in Perspective". Durham Theses, Durham university. http:/etheses.dur.ac.uk/496.
Kitchelt, Herbert and Wilkinson, I. Steven (eds) 2007. *Patrons, Clients and Policies: Patterns of Democratic Accountability and Political Competition*. Cambridge, Cambridge University Press.
Laakso, Liisa and Olukoshi, O. Adebayo (eds.) 1996.*Challenges to the Nation-State in Africa*. Uppsala, Nordiska Afrikainstitutet.
Lewis, Peter (ed.) 1998. *Africa: Dilemmas of Development and Change*. Oxford, Westview Press.
Lugard, F. 1905. "Annual Colonial Report: Northern Nigeria – 1904". No. 476.
Mabojunje, I Akin 1981. "Geography and the Dilemma of Rural Development in Africa.*Geografiska. Series B, Human Geography*, Vol. 63, No. 2 (1981), pp. 73 -86.
Magnusson, A. Bruce 2001. "Democratisation and Domestic Insecurity: Navigating the Transition in Benin".*Comparative Politics*, Vol. 33, No. 2, pp. 211 – 230.
Mahood, M.M. 1964. *Joyce Cary's Africa*. London, Metheuen and Co.
Mbembe, Achille 2001.*On the Post colony*. Berkeley, University of California Press.
Mbembe, Achille, 1992a. "Provisional Notes on the Post Colony", *Africa* 62 (1), pp. 3 – 37.

Mbembe, Achille, 1992b. "The Banality of Power and Aesthetics of Vulgarity in the Post Colony". *Public Culture* vol. 4 (2), pp. 1 – 30.

Mbembe, Achille, 2005. "On Post Colony: A Brief Response to Critics". *Qui Parle*, Vol. 15, No. 2, pp. 1 – 49.

Migdal, S. Joel 1988. *Strong Societies and Weak States: State-Society Relations and State Capabilities in the Third World*. Princeton, Princeton University Press.

Miles, William 1994. *Hausaland Divided: Colonialism and Independence in Nigeria and Niger*. New York and London, Cornell University Press.

Mohan, Giles and Zack-Willan, T. (eds.) 2004.*The Politics of Transition in Africa*, Oxford, James Currey and Asmara, Africa World Press.

Moody, P.R. 1967. "Road and Bridge in Joyce Cary's African Novels".*The Bulletin of the Rocky Mountain Modern Language Association*, Vol. 21, No. 4, pp. 145 – 149.

Moss, J. Todd and Resnick, Danielle 2018.*African Development: Making Sense of the Issues and Actors*. Boulder, Lynne Reinner Publishers.

Mustapha, Abdul Raufu 1986. "The National Question and Radical Politics in Nigeria". *Review of African Political Economy*, No.37, December.

NAK 1937. Ilorin Province – Annual Report. 3444/1

NAK 1950. Annual Report, Borgu Division – Part I and II. Ilorin Province, File No. 5474/S.1

Olukoshi, O. Adebayo and, Osita Agbu 1996. "The Deepening Crisis of Nigerian Federalism and the Future of Nation-State". In Olukoshi O.A. and Laakso, Liisa (eds), *Challenges of to the Nation-State in Africa*. Uppsala, Nordiska Afrikainstitutet.

Rodney, Walter 1972. *How Europe Underdeveloped Africa*. Washington, DC. Howard University Press.

Sandbrook, Richard 1985. *The Politics of Africa's Economic Stagnation*. Cambridge, Cambridge University Press.

Sandbrook, Richard 1998. "Patron-Client and Factions: New Dimensions of Conflict Analysis in Africa". In Peter Lewis (ed), *Dilemmas of Development in Africa*. Oxford, Westview Press.

Van de Walle, Nicolas 2007. "Meet the Boss, Same as the old Boss? The Evolution of Political Clientelism in Africa". In Kitchelt, Herbert and Wilkinson, I. Steven (eds). *Patrons, Clients and Policies: Patterns of Democratic Accountability and Political Competition*. Cambridge, Cambridge University Press.

Werbner, Richard, and Ranger, Terence (eds.), 1996. *Post-Colonial Identities in Africa*. London, Zed Books.

Williams, Gavin (ed.) 1976. *Nigeria: Economy and Society*, London, Rex Collings.

Yahaya, A.D. 1982. "Introduction".In Dudley, B.J. *An Introduction to Nigerian Government and Politics*, London, Macmillan.
Young Crawford, 1994.*The African Colonial State in Comparative Perspectives*. New Heaven, Yale University Press.
Zartman, I. William (ed), 1970. *The Political Economy of Nigeria*. New York, Praeger.
Zartman, I. William ed. 1995. *Collapsed States: The Disintegration and Restoration of Legitimate Authority*.Boulder, Lynne Rienner Publishers.

Conclusion

Reversing the Trend: Agenda for Development

Asiwaju, I. A. (ed.) 2018. *Border Regions in Africa: History of Political Marginalization and Infrastructural Deprivation in Ogun State of South West Nigeria.* Ibadan University Press.

Asiwaju, I.A. 1994. "Borders and Borderlands as Linchpins for Regional Integration in Africa. Lessons of the European Experience", *Africa Development/Afrique et Developpement*, vol. 17, No. 2, pp. 45 – 63.

Asiwaju, I.A. 2005. "Transfrontier Regionalism: The European Union Perspective on Post-Colonial Africa, With Special Reference to Borgu", In Nicol, N. Heather and Townsend-Gault, Ian (eds.), *Holding the Line: Borders in a Global Word.* Vancouver, UBC Press.

Bayart, Francois Jean 1986. "Civil Society in Africa". In Chabal, Patrick, Political Domination in Africa (ed), Cambridge, Cambridge University Press.

Bratton, Michael 1989. "Beyond the State: Civil Society and Associational Life in Africa, *World Politics*, Vol. 41, No. 3, pp. 407 – 430.

Chukwura, O. A. 2018. "Border Communities and the Right to Development". In Asiwaju I. A. (ed.) *Border Regions in Africa: History of Political Marginalization and Infrastructural Deprivation in Ogun State of South West Nigeria.* Ibadan University Press.

Duckacels, D. Ivo. 1986. "International Competence of Sub-Regional: Borderlands and Beyond". In O.J. Martinez ed. *Across Boundaries: Transborder Interaction in Comparative Perspective*, Elpaso, Western Taxes Press.

Eversole, Robyn 2011. "Community Agency and Community Engagement: Re-theorising Participation in Governance", *Journal of Public Policy*, vol. 31, No. 1, pp. 51 – 71.

Hyden, Goran 1989. "Local Governance and Economic – Demographic Transition in Rural Africa, *Population and Development Review*, vol. 15, pp. 193 – 211.

Hyden, Goran 1998. "Building Civil Society at the Turn of the Millennium", In Burdidge, J. (ed.), *Beyond the Prince and Merchant: Citizens Participation and the Rise of Civil society*, Brussels, International Institute of Cultural Affairs.

Ikelegbe, Augustine 2001. "The Perverse Manifestation of Civil Society: Evidence from Nigeria".*The Journal of Modern African Studies*, Vol. 39, No. 1, pp. 1 – 24.

Jackson, Steven 2005. "Technopoles and Development in Borderless World; Boundaries Erased and Boundaries Constructed", In Nicol, N. Heather and Townsend-Gault, Ian (eds.), *Holding the Line: Borders in a Global Word*. Vancouver, UBC Press.

Mabogunje, A. 2018. "Tending the Meadow as the Margin".In Asiwaju I. A.(ed.) *Border Regions in Africa: History of Political Marginalization and Infrastructural Deprivation in Ogun State of South West Nigeria*. Ibadan University Press.

Moss, J. Todd and Danielle Resnick 2018. *Africa Development: Making Sense of the Issues and Actors*. Boulder, Lynne Rienner Publishers.

Nicol, N. Heather and Townsend-Gault, Ian (eds.) 2005, *Holding the Line: Borders in a Global Word*. Vancouver, UBC Press.

Obadare, Ebenezer 2004. "The Alternative Genealogy of Civil Society and Its Implication for Africa. Notes for Further Research", *Africa Development/Afrique et Developpement*, Vol. 29, No. 4, pp. 1 – 18.

Obasanjo, Olusegun 2014. *My Watch: Early Life and Military (Vol. 1)*. Lagos, Prestige Publishers.

Orvis, Stephen 2003. "Kenyan Civil Society: Bridging the Urban-Rural Divide? *The Journal of Modern African Studies*, Vol. 41, No. 2, pp. 247 -268.

Petel, Satish 2009. "Reinventing Local Governments: People's Participation and Empowerment. *The Indian Journal of Political Science*, Vol. 70, No. 2, Pp. 381 – 386.

Rezvani, reza Mohammed, Shakoor Ali et.al. 2009. "The Role and Function of Small Towns in Rural Development using Network Analysis Method: Case of Roniz Rural District (Estahban City, Province of Fars, Iran", *Journal of Goegraphy and Regional Planning* Vol. 2(9).

Rotberg, I. Robert 2007. "On Improving Nation-State Governance, *Daedalus*, Vol. 136, No. 1, pp. 152 -155.

Selee, D. Andrew 2002. "Democracy Close to Home: Citizen Participation and Local Governance", *Georgetown Journal of International Affairs*, Vol. 3, No. 1, Special:9/11, pp. 95 – 102.

Sen, Amartya 2009.*The Idea of Justice*.London, Allen Lane.

Steel, Griet and Lindert van Paul 2017. "Mobility and Connectivity: Driving Rural Livelihood Transformation in Africa".*Briefing*, IIED, March 2017.

Teles, Filipe 2012. "Local Governance, Identity and Social Capital: A Framework for Administrative Reform", *Theoretical and Empirical Researches in Urban Management*, Vo. 7, No. 4, pp. 20 – 34.

Tocoli, Cecilia and Vorley, Bill 2015. "Reframing the Debate on Urbanisation, Rural Transformation and Food Security.*Briefing*, IIED, February 2015.

Vaishar, Antonin, Stastna, Milada and Stonawska Katerina 2015. "Small Towns – Engines of Rural Development in South-Monrovian Region (Czechia): An Analysis of the Demographic Development. ACTA Universitatis Agriculturae et Silviculturae Mendeliane Brunensis, Vol. 63, No. 153, pp. 1395 – 1404.

Waghmore, Suryakant 2002. "Rural Development: Role of the State", *Economic and Political Weekly*, Vol. 37, No. 29, pp. 3001 – 3003.

Walker, Judith-Ann 1999. "Civil Society, the Challenge to the Authoritarian State and the Consolidation of Democracy in Nigeria", *Journal of Opinion*, Vol. 27, No. 1, pp. 54 – 48.

Index

A

Abeokuta, 267
Action Group, x, 258, 287, 288
Adamu, Mahdi, xiii, 30, 82, 363
Addis Ababa, xvii
African Borderlands Research Network (ABORNE), xvii
African frontier, xviii
African Regional Institute, Imeko, Ogun State, southwestern Nigeria, xix
African Union Border Programme, xvii, xix
Ago Oja, 163, 164
Agricultural Development Programmes, 314
Agwara, 39, 197, 201, 205, 207, 213, 225, 229, 232, 253, 269, 291, 311, 317, 340, 344, 349, 374
Agwara Local Government, 340
Agwarra, 39
Ake, Claude, 204, 307, 314, 331, 332, 373, 385
Alaafin Onigbogi, 157
Alemika, Etannibi, xiii
Ali, Richard, xiv, 94, 163, 214
Alibori, 36, 37, 311
Aliyara District, 202, 229, 374
Alkali court, 202
Alpine Region Cooperation, 343
Amalgamation, 87, 196, 212, 213, 225, 243, 244, 245, 253, 292
Americans, xv
Anglo-Egyptian Condominium, xix
Anglo-French 'Steeple Chase to Nikki', xix
Anglo-French Convention of 1898, 186
Anglo-French scramble for Borgu, 172
Anglo-French treaty, 223, 283
Anthropology, xv, xvii, 351, 356, 362
Arabian world, 52
Arabs, 50

Argungu Emirate, 39, 232
Aristotle, 316
Asante, 82, 83, 111, 135, 137
Ashafa, Abdullahi, xiii
Asia, xvi, 102, 340, 343, 373
Asiwaju, Anthony, xiii, xx, 30, 86, 89, 158, 304, 305, 338, 343, 351, 356, 361, 366, 382, 385, 390, 391
Askia Dynasty, 151
Assimilation, 191, 215, 217
Association of Borderlands Scholars, xv
Atakora Mountains, 32, 37, 103, 107
Atlantic markets, 121
Atlantic slave trades, 129
Autochthonous communities, 72, 86, 90, 92, 96

B

Baatombu, 34, 35, 36, 47, 63, 64, 72, 85, 376
Baatonu, 29, 34, 35, 36, 37, 38, 45, 47, 53, 63, 64, 72, 74, 76, 82, 88, 90, 99, 100, 109, 114, 115, 129, 132, 138, 149, 150, 155, 156, 186, 194, 209, 211, 220, 244, 246, 248, 249, 250, 255, 258, 267, 269, 274, 279, 281, 283, 284, 285, 286, 290, 292, 293, 294, 295, 296, 304, 306, 325, 376

Baatonum, 33, 36, 37, 38, 47, 59, 66, 67, 69, 73, 78, 79, 96, 111, 125, 128, 143, 149, 155, 162, 186, 315
Baatonum dialects, 37
Babanna, 33, 37, 38, 39, 46, 54, 79, 100, 183, 201, 225, 291, 292, 344
Bakpari, Gunu, 116
Balewa, Tafawa, 244, 249
Bamaribere, 113
Bana-Wure, 74
Banduku, 126
Bank for Reconstruction and Development, x, 263
Baquaqua, Mahommah Gardo, 132, 133
Bariba, 34, 36, 59, 66, 82, 103, 131, 132, 158, 180, 294, 295, 352, 353, 354, 357, 361, 363, 367, 374, 376, 377, 380, 383
Barutem Local Government, 330
Ba-Sabi, Ali, 237
Basorun, 159
Bassa, 339
Bate, 39, 75
Baumann, Hermann, 49
Bayajida, 50, 357
Ba-Yaru, Sabi, 213, 258
Benin Republic, 23, 28, 36, 38, 294, 305, 306, 341, 349, 350
Benue, 39, 51, 174, 359, 362, 372
Benue-Congo languages, 39
Berba, 37
Berbers, 50
Beresoni, 113
Better Life for Rural Women, 314
Bight of Benin, 131, 174
Bio-Wure, 74
Birmingham University, UK, xiii
Birnin Kebbi, 274
Bissakwera, 212
Bissan, 37, 38
Black Africa, 50

Boko, 29, 33, 34, 35, 36, 37, 38, 39, 45, 47, 53, 56, 57, 58, 59, 63, 64, 66, 67, 69, 72, 73, 74, 76, 77, 78, 79, 80, 82, 84, 85, 86, 87, 88, 90, 91, 94, 95, 96, 99, 104, 109, 111, 113, 114, 115, 117, 120, 125, 128, 132, 138, 143, 148, 150, 155, 156, 164, 187, 209, 218, 235, 236, 241, 285, 289, 290, 292, 294, 295, 296, 304, 315, 325
Bokobaru, 37, 38, 40, 94, 285, 290, 293
Bonda, 39
Bonikpara dialect, 37
Boo, 37, 38
Borderlands Studies, xv, xvii, xix
Borea, 183
Borgu aristocrats, 82
Borgu Game Reserve, 314
Bori, 79, 358, 369
Boriya, 95, 185, 186, 246, 271, 344
Borno, 33, 50, 58, 59, 126, 132, 134, 135, 137, 138, 147, 150, 180
Bouba, 37
Bouka, 38
Bouy, 183
BREXIT, xvi
British Colonial Development and Welfare Act, 262
British Colonial Secretary, 182
British Foreign Office, 172
British Government, 119
British Political Officers, 198, 216
Buhari, Mohammadu, 163
Burden, John, 275
Burkina Faso, 37
Bussa, vi, viii, 29, 31, 32, 33, 37, 38, 39, 46, 47, 52, 53, 54, 55, 56, 58, 59, 63, 64, 65, 66, 75, 78, 79, 81, 86, 87, 88, 90, 91, 94, 95, 96, 97, 98, 103, 104, 105, 106, 107, 108, 109, 112, 113, 114, 115, 116, 117,

119, 123, 124, 126, 128, 129, 133, 135, 136, 140, 141, 146, 151, 152, 153, 154, 156, 157, 161, 162, 165, 169, 172, 173, 174, 175, 176, 177, 178, 179, 180, 181, 182, 183, 186, 188, 194, 195, 196, 197, 199, 200, 201, 202, 203, 204, 205, 207, 210, 212, 213, 214, 215, 225, 226, 227, 228, 229, 230, 231, 232, 233, 235, 243, 244, 245, 246, 251, 252, 253, 254, 256, 257, 265, 266, 269, 270, 275, 281, 282, 283, 291, 292, 293, 312, 313, 318, 319, 321, 322, 323, 338, 340, 344, 349, 352, 356, 357, 358, 359, 361, 362, 363, 367, 371, 373, 374, 375, 376, 377, 378, 383
Bussawa, 38, 353, 358, 374
Busu-deno, 90, 91
Bweru, 54, 95, 99, 291

C

Calabar, 174, 340
Campbell, M. J., 245, 248, 250, 251, 252
Cape Coast, 169
Caravan tolls, 205
Caravans, 70, 88, 96, 99, 102, 115, 118, 136, 137, 138, 141, 143, 146, 195, 229, 282, 284, 321
Carthaginians, 59
Cary, Joyce, 212, 233, 320, 386
Catholic missionaries, 272
Census Book, 206
Chachra, Sandeep, xiii
Chamberlain, Joseph, 182, 185
Chessboard Policy, 182, 185
Chief Chamberlain, 94
Chikanda, 66, 229, 322, 324, 344
Chosroes, Sassanian, 55
Christian Missionaries, 261
Chukwuma, Innocent, xiii

Civilisation, 50, 157, 184, 192, 261, 283
Clifford, Hugh, 230, 265, 338
Colonial financial memoranda, 203
Colonial historiography, 49
Colonial legacy, 27, 301, 307
Colonial Office, 181, 192, 275
Colonialism, vi, 170, 193, 261, 284, 293, 303, 307, 358, 371, 373, 374, 379, 382, 383, 384, 385, 386, 388
Commonwealth, 263
Conference of Upper Rhine Valley Planners, 343
Cowry shells, 126
Cross-Border Initiatives Programme, xix
Cross-border relations, 30, 337
Crowder, Michael, 24, 25, 30, 31, 34, 53, 62, 86, 87, 89, 97, 98, 102, 106, 107, 109, 119, 141, 143, 153, 155, 172, 174, 198, 211, 214, 215, 216, 217, 218, 221, 224, 227, 228, 229, 230, 231, 232, 233, 234, 235, 236, 237, 238, 239, 240, 242, 244, 254, 265, 338, 352, 353, 356, 361, 363, 367, 371, 373, 374, 376, 378, 379, 380, 383

D

Dado, 74
Dagomba, 147
Dahomey, 23, 82, 102, 106, 111, 130, 131, 132, 134, 140, 141, 148, 173, 175, 177, 178, 180, 181, 200, 210, 216, 217, 220, 228, 234, 235, 238, 265, 270, 272, 274, 296, 304, 307, 308, 313, 321, 322, 340, 351, 352, 353, 356, 357, 361, 364, 367, 371, 373, 374, 376, 379, 380, 382, 383
Dakarekareland, 52
Dallo Boso, 148
dan Fodio, Usman, 163

Daura, 132
de Gironcourt, G. R, 56
de Santarem, Joao, 169
Deema, 47, 63
Dekana, 38
Dendawa, 82
Dendi, 35, 40, 63, 68, 70, 71, 79, 82, 83, 93, 110, 131, 134, 135, 140, 150, 151, 181, 214, 273, 274, 279, 294, 295, 296, 297
Dhazi shrine, 80
Directorate for Food, Roads and Rural Infrastructure (DFFRI), 314
District Administrators, 216
District Cash Book, 206
District Courts, 202, 203
District Heads, 199, 202, 204, 205, 206, 227, 229, 245, 246, 250, 253, 255
District Officer, x, 200, 203, 206, 212, 220, 230, 231, 232, 233, 244, 245, 246, 247, 248, 250, 252, 254, 256, 257, 268, 286, 320
District Register, 206
Djougou, 81, 82, 83, 84, 117, 124, 125, 126, 128, 135, 136, 137, 141, 142, 146, 160, 217, 241, 267, 312, 313, 349
Dogo, Mora Amali, 98, 108, 117, 144, 183
Dompago, 125
Donkeys, 126, 127, 137, 139, 141, 144
Dosso, 36
Dunkasa, 120, 125, 184
Dunkassa, 38
Duplicate Assessment Note, 206
Dyula, 70, 134

E

Earth Priests, 46, 64, 66, 79, 81, 86, 89, 90, 91, 159

Ebo, Adedeji, xiii
Economic Community of Central African States, xix
Economics, xv, 374, 379
Edinburgh, xvii
Egwu, Sam, xiii
Egypt, 49, 51, 182, 275
Ekiti State, 317
Eleduwe, 108, 157, 160
Elementary schools, 273
Elukumi, 156
Emirate Court, 202, 203
English language, 274
Enugu State, 317
Environmental Engineering, xv
Ethno-economic groups, 35, 325
Europe, xv, xvi, 89, 129, 137, 169, 171, 172, 192, 234, 261, 262, 263, 313, 343, 388
European Outline Convention, 343
European Science Foundation, xvii

F

Facticity, 61
Fage, John, 49, 50, 51, 53, 358, 372
Falatas, 59
Farias, Moreas, xiii, 56, 57, 149, 150, 151, 356, 358, 368
First World War, 223, 234, 267, 274, 381
Foge Island, 46, 380
France, xviii, 24, 171, 172, 173, 174, 175, 176, 178, 179, 180, 181, 182, 183, 215, 234, 262, 263, 363, 364, 372
French colonial policies, 234
French Dahomey, xvii
French Parliament, 215, 263, 274
Frobenius, Leo, 52, 53, 56, 356
Fukuyama, Francis, 26, 352, 386
Fulanin Adamawa, 41

Fulbe, 35, 40, 41, 57, 58, 59, 66, 67, 69, 70, 76, 77, 82, 83, 84, 94, 97, 98, 101, 102, 107, 108, 116, 118, 123, 128, 129, 130, 140, 152, 153, 154, 157, 160, 161, 162, 163, 164, 194, 198, 203, 208, 215, 219, 220, 221, 234, 253, 254, 270, 285, 287, 294, 295, 297, 325, 356, 383
Fulbe-Borgu, 40, 118, 161

G

Gaani, Kitoro, 56, 75, 95, 100, 102, 110, 111, 114, 118, 143, 149, 219, 231, 306, 356, 357, 361
Gando, 34, 35, 67, 76, 77, 80, 94, 128, 129, 219, 220, 221, 234, 283, 294, 295, 297
Ganouru, 117
Gao, 126, 135
Garafini, 226, 228
Gbaagizi Settlement, 95
Gbajibo, 32, 178, 179, 186, 257
Gbasorro, 65
Gbasso, 38, 75, 99, 100, 115, 241
Gbegazi, 65
Gbegbazi, 94
Gbekou, 235, 236, 237, 240, 242
Gbemgbereke, 117, 235, 236
Gbere, 47, 63, 64, 65, 98, 157
Gberia deities, 96
Gbewalla, 54
Gbodo, 163
Gebe War, 292
Gejere, 116, 118
German Togoland, 179
Germany, 171, 172, 173, 179, 180, 343
Gerontocratic administrations, 63
Gesere, 83
Ghana, xvii, 51, 170, 365, 385
Girouard, Percy, 275
Gold Coast, 182

Goldie, George, 172, 174, 179, 182, 183, 185, 188, 195, 282
Gomji, 80
Gonja, 82, 88, 135, 136, 137, 141, 147, 170, 221
Gourma, 77, 151
Governor-General, 216, 218, 219, 220, 228, 232, 235, 238, 247, 272, 338
Green Revolution, 314
Guinea Savannah, 32, 33, 103
Guinea savannah vegetation, 123
Guiso, Sanni, 241
Gummi, 138
Gungawa, 39, 79, 153
Gurai, 33
Gurma, 37, 129, 175, 181
Gwanara, 36, 100, 108, 140, 146, 162, 163, 187, 194, 197, 201, 205, 208, 214, 215, 225, 244, 246, 253, 254, 269, 285, 286, 287, 289, 290, 322, 340, 344, 384
Gwandu, 84, 107, 118, 153, 154, 162, 176, 179, 196, 198, 268, 349
Gwangwazo, xii
Gwari, 153
Gwaria,, 74
Gwariland, 52
Gwasoro, 185

H

Hamites, 49
Hamitic Hypothesis, 49, 51, 61, 357, 358
Harmattan trade wind, 33
Hausa, v, 23, 32, 33, 34, 35, 38, 50, 54, 56, 70, 71, 78, 79, 81, 82, 83, 86, 88, 106, 111, 118, 123, 126, 128, 129, 130, 131, 134, 135, 136, 137, 138, 140, 141, 144, 146, 147, 148, 150, 152, 153, 154, 155, 162, 170, 200, 252, 255, 266, 267, 274,

279, 285, 305,353, 356, 357, 358, 363, 364, 368
Hidarou, 38
Hyden, Goran, 315, 324, 325, 328, 387, 391

I

Ibadan, x, xiii, 29, 257, 267, 270, 340, 363, 382, 385, 387, 390, 391
Ibbi, 174
Ibrahim, Jibrin, xiii, 163
Igbuzor, Otive, xiii
Ilesha, 36, 66, 100, 108, 140, 144, 146, 160, 162, 163, 164, 177, 186, 188, 194, 201, 206, 208, 214, 215, 225, 244, 246, 253, 254, 269, 275, 282, 285, 286, 290, 322, 324, 330, 340, 344
Illo, 32, 37, 39, 40, 46, 47, 53, 54, 63, 70, 75, 81, 84, 86, 87, 88, 89, 90, 94, 97, 105, 107, 109, 112, 118, 123, 124, 135, 136, 141, 151, 152, 154, 163, 176, 186, 188, 195, 196, 198, 282, 312, 349, 353
Ilorin, x, 80, 84, 107, 108, 116, 132, 141, 154, 156, 157, 160, 161, 162, 163, 164, 181, 198, 203, 230, 243, 244, 247, 251, 252, 256, 258, 265, 267, 270, 275, 287, 288, 313, 318, 319, 321, 338, 345, 351, 352, 353, 357, 358, 361, 362, 365, 367, 369, 374, 377, 378, 380, 383, 384, 388
Immigrants, 269
Indirect Rule, 191, 192, 221, 278, 377, 380, 383
International African Association, 173
International Law, xvi
Irikefe Panel, 318
Islam, 51, 52, 53, 56, 68, 71, 77, 81, 82, 83, 91, 110, 114, 118, 135, 137, 138, 148, 149, 150, 155, 273,
285, 353, 355, 357, 358, 363, 364, 368, 369
Islamic jihads, 84, 121
Islamisation in Hausaland, 70
Italy, 171, 343
Ivory Coast, 36, 238

J

Jahun,, 41
Jannah, 141
Jega, Attahiru, xiii, 136, 138, 361, 374, 387
Jerou, 38
Jihad from the Kabawa, 102
Judicial Council, 202, 232

K

Kaama, 33, 38, 65, 94
Kabaru, 33, 64, 65, 96, 114
Kabba, 141, 339
Kabbawa, 50
Kabe, 38, 163, 202
Kabigera, 38
Kaduna, x, xiii, xviii, 29, 233, 251, 252, 256, 267, 270, 285, 288, 319, 340, 352, 360, 361, 362, 374, 375, 378, 380, 381, 382, 383
Kagogi, 38, 47, 65, 80
Kaiama, vi, viii, xii, 29, 33, 37, 38, 40, 54, 55, 59, 65, 67, 71, 73, 74, 75, 76, 77, 78, 79, 80, 81, 88, 94, 95, 96, 97, 100, 101, 102, 103, 104, 105, 106, 107, 108, 109, 111, 112, 114, 115, 117, 119, 120, 121, 123, 124, 125, 126, 128, 129, 132, 136, 137, 140,141, 144, 146, 153, 154, 157, 159, 160, 161, 162, 163, 164, 176, 177, 178, 179, 180, 182, 183, 184, 185, 186, 188, 194, 195, 196, 197, 199, 200, 201, 202, 203, 204, 205, 206, 208, 209, 210, 211,

212, 213, 214, 215, 218, 225, 227, 228, 229, 231, 232, 243, 244, 245, 246, 247, 248, 249, 250, 251, 252, 253, 254, 255, 256, 257, 258, 266, 268, 269, 270, 271, 275, 276, 281, 282, 283, 284, 285, 286, 287, 288, 289, 290, 291, 292, 293, 303, 311, 312, 313, 315, 316, 317, 318, 319, 320, 321, 322, 324, 330, 340, 344, 349, 352, 357, 361, 369, 374, 378, 380, 383, 384
Kainji Dam, 33, 314, 324, 341, 349
Kainji Lake, 46
Kambari, 38, 39, 47, 58, 63, 65, 68, 79, 107, 152, 153, 154, 269
Kambari people, 39
Kambarin Beriberi, 39, 71, 82, 98, 138
Kandi, 36, 37, 82, 88, 93, 94, 100, 117, 124, 135, 136, 142, 150, 160, 183, 217, 218, 219, 229, 235, 239, 240, 267, 272, 274, 295, 296, 297, 303, 321
Kanem-Borno, 58, 59
Kanem-Bornu, 210
Kanibe, 38, 39, 47, 64, 65
Kanikoko, 185
Kano, xii, 83, 127, 132, 135, 136, 137, 138, 199, 267, 270, 355, 358, 360, 362, 363, 365, 369
Kanuri, 35, 59, 96, 138
Karabonde, 47, 64, 91, 97, 200, 203
Karimama, 32, 135
Karishi, 52
Kassati, 39, 40
Katsina, 128, 132, 136, 138, 155, 267, 275, 340, 354, 359, 362
Katsinawa, 59, 138
Katunga, 164
Kebbawa, 32, 153

Kebbi, 28, 39, 52, 57, 153, 228, 274, 275, 311, 316, 317, 341, 349, 357, 367
Kemanji, 74, 80, 96, 114, 159, 185, 344
Kerekou, Mathew, 308
Ketu, 158
Kibegra, 47
Ki-neno, 74, 90
King Gezo of Dahomey, 130
King Kora, 52
King Leopold, 173
King Majiya II, 161
Kingdom of Dendi, 40
kingdom of Kenu, 33
Kingmakers' Council, 113
Kisra, iv, ix, 50, 51, 52, 53, 54, 55, 56, 57, 58, 59, 60, 62, 74, 75, 81, 86, 87, 88, 94, 105, 109, 110, 149, 156, 293, 351, 355, 356, 358, 359, 360, 362
Kogi State, 339
Kolanuts,, 71, 134, 135, 137, 149
Kombiya, Baa, 145
Konko, 33, 104
Konko Shrine, 65
Kontagora, 39, 152, 153, 196, 197, 211, 212, 213, 215, 227, 230, 232, 243, 267, 268, 282, 313, 339, 349, 352, 356, 361, 377, 378
Kontagora Emirate, 39
Kontangora, 52
Konwosso, 38
Kouande, 37, 94, 100, 117, 137, 142, 150, 162, 272
Kounde, 100, 136, 183, 217
Kpera, Sero, 84, 116, 117, 120, 157, 161, 162, 163, 164, 194, 219, 290
Kperogi, Farooq, xiii
Kubkli, 33
Kubli, 46, 66
Kunji, 197, 229, 232

Kura (Akuto), Sulaiman Yerima, xii
Kuro-Boko, 33
Kwara, 28, 36, 98, 183, 214, 215, 241, 249, 279, 309, 311, 315, 316, 317, 318, 319, 326, 334, 349
Kwara State, 311, 318, 327
Kwassoro, 39

L

Lagos, xiii, xx, 59, 130, 132, 181, 182, 184, 186, 229, 233, 247, 319, 340, 358, 359, 366, 385, 391
Lake Chad, xx, 59, 174
Lake Chad Basin, xx
Lake Chad region, 59
Lander Brothers, 24, 31, 98, 103, 139, 155, 158, 169, 283, 340
Lander, John, 59, 357, 361, 363, 364, 367
Laru, 37, 38, 39, 47, 63, 65, 80
Lashibe, 39, 65, 95
Lasibe, 47
Lekumi, 156
Libations, 79
Lieutenant-Governors, 216
Local governance, 193, 250, 286, 348
Lokoja, 174, 267, 319
Lord Salisbury, 172, 174
Lugard, Frederick, 24, 29, 31, 102, 105, 106, 109, 127, 139, 143, 144, 169, 170, 177, 178, 180, 185, 188, 192, 194, 195, 196, 211, 229, 261, 264, 266, 281, 282, 283, 320, 340, 361, 364, 371, 372, 380, 383, 387
Lugardian structure, 250
Lukman, Salihu, xiii
Lumma, 39, 65

M

Madeguru, 52
Madison, James, 316

Magiro, 79, 96
Mahdi-type rebellion, 273
Maikano, Fatima Abdullahi, xi, xii
Mainstream academia, xv
Makata, 39
Mako, Bio Adamou, xiii
Makurdi, 313, 340
Malale., 227
Malam, Magajin, 153
Malanville, 32, 218
Mali, 26, 38, 40, 47, 56, 58, 62, 86, 126, 148, 150, 234, 365
Mali Empire, 26, 38, 47, 56
Malinke, 47, 70, 149
Manchester cottons, 141
Mande, 37, 38, 47, 56, 58, 70, 71, 83, 86, 89, 129, 134, 148, 149, 150
Marami, 38
Maratem, 64
Martius, Albrecht, 52
McNeil, William H, 109
Metallurgical works, 46
Mewi, 65, 67, 94
Micro-diplomacy, 342, 343
Middle Niger, 175, 181
Minna, 313, 345
Mokole, 37, 160
Mole-Dagbane language, 70
Monai., 47, 322
Morai, 145
Mushirri, 39
Muslim, 56, 60, 70, 71, 72, 82, 83, 84, 93, 96, 102, 129, 130, 131, 132, 134, 149, 150, 154, 177, 199, 255, 273, 274, 357, 358, 365, 369
Muslim world view, 60

N

Nago, 131, 156
Nagwamatse, Umaru, 39, 153
Nari, 72, 74
National Archives, Kaduna, xiii

Nationalism, 171, 281, 305
Native Authority system, 191, 193, 201, 209, 210, 224, 249, 250, 275, 276, 278, 281, 288, 292, 293, 295
Native Courts, 202
Native Treasury, 198, 203, 206
Negazi, 38
Newton, T. C., 292
Niger, xvii, xix, xx, 28, 32, 39, 45, 46, 47, 51, 52, 53, 54, 58, 64, 70, 79, 102, 107, 124, 126, 127, 130, 136, 141, 142, 152, 154, 161, 171, 172, 173, 174, 175, 176, 177, 178, 179, 180, 181, 182, 185, 186, 188, 195, 197, 214, 217, 218, 227, 231, 239, 240, 242, 257, 264, 265, 282, 305, 309, 311, 316, 317, 318, 319, 320, 321, 323, 326, 334, 340, 341, 349, 352, 357, 359, 361, 362, 363, 364, 367, 372, 373, 388
Niger Bend, 174, 175, 180, 181, 182
Niger District Protectorate, 174
Niger State, 318
Niger Valley, 46
Niger-Congo conglomerate, 58
Nigerian Army, 24
Nigerian National Boundary Commission, xvi
Nikki, viii, ix, xix, 29, 32, 33, 36, 37, 47, 52, 53, 54, 55, 63, 64, 67, 68, 71, 75, 78, 81, 82, 83, 84, 86, 87, 88, 89, 90, 91, 92, 93, 94, 95, 96, 97, 98, 99, 100, 101, 104, 105, 106, 107, 108, 109, 111, 112, 113, 114, 115, 116, 117, 119, 125, 126, 127, 129,132, 136, 137, 140, 141, 143, 144, 145, 146, 150, 153, 155, 157, 161, 162, 163, 164, 176, 177, 178, 179, 180, 181, 182, 183, 184, 186, 189, 194, 210, 212, 215, 217, 218, 234, 235, 237, 240, 241, 242, 249, 251, 254, 271, 280, 282, 283, 284, 286, 291, 292, 293, 294, 296, 302, 303, 306, 312, 313, 349, 373
Nile Valley, 49, 58, 182
Nok Culture, 46
Northern Elements Progressive Union, 287, 288
Northern Nigeria, ix, 188, 194, 195, 196, 198, 204, 224, 228, 244, 248, 253, 275, 356, 360, 361, 362, 367, 368, 371, 374, 375, 378, 380, 381, 382, 383, 387
Northern Peoples' Congress, 258
Northern Province, 199
Nugent, Paul, xvii
Nupe, 23, 32, 37, 38, 47, 59, 65, 102, 107, 111, 120, 126, 130, 131, 140, 141, 148, 149, 152, 153, 154, 155, 156, 157, 158, 160, 161, 162, 170, 181, 197, 266, 367, 368
Nyantruku people, 160
Nyfee (Nupe), 111

O

Obasanjo, Olusegun, 340, 391
Oduduwa, 50, 156, 157
Ogbomosho, 158, 163
Okuta, 33, 36, 66, 100, 108, 115, 140, 145, 146, 162, 163, 186, 188, 194, 197, 201, 205, 206, 207, 208, 214, 215, 225, 244, 245, 246, 248, 252, 253, 254, 269, 271, 275, 285, 286, 287, 288, 289, 290, 303, 322, 330, 344, 361, 374, 384
Old Oyo, 156, 157
Olive shells, 126
Oliver, Roland, 49, 50, 51, 358, 372, 386
Operation Feed the Nation, 314
Oranyan, 156, 157, 159
Oranyan Dynasty, 156
Organisation of African Unity, x, 303
Otefo, 163

Ottoman Empire, 173
Ouassa, 136
Ouorou, Sounour, 241
Oyo, v, 23, 30, 32, 77, 80, 102, 107, 108, 116, 130, 131, 132, 148, 155, 156, 157, 158, 159, 160, 161, 162, 163, 164, 170, 177, 266, 268, 269, 287, 289, 317, 319, 321, 322, 340, 355, 360, 366, 367, 368, 369
Oziya, 33, 96

P

Pagans, 199
Palestine, 51
Parakou, 29, 36, 37, 77, 81, 82, 83, 88, 93, 94, 100, 117, 136, 140, 141, 146, 159, 162, 217, 218, 235, 239, 241, 267, 274, 296, 297, 303, 311, 312, 313, 321, 349, 386
Pastoralism, 69
Patrilinealism, 118
Patron-client structure., 325
Patronymics, 70, 71, 72, 138, 150
Pila-Pila, 37, 238
Pilla-Pilla, 125
Pissa, 202
Pleistocene, 45, 87
Political Science, xv, 372, 374, 385, 391
Political structuring, 280, 284, 318
Porto Novo, 229, 238
Prebendalism, 325, 328
Primitivity, 261, 264
Prophet Muhammad, 51, 52, 96, 110
Public Health, xv
Public Works Department, 320
Puissa, 33, 37, 38, 47, 80, 94, 99, 100
Purukaru, Sabi, 218, 241, 242

Q

Quidah, 131, 132

Quranic schools, 216

R

Red Sea, 50
Republic of Benin, xvii, xviii, 28, 308, 355, 360, 373, 386
Republic of Sudan, xix
River Alibori, 32
River Niger, 24, 32, 33, 36, 37, 39, 40, 45, 55, 59, 70, 91, 95, 103, 107, 124, 151, 152, 154, 157, 165, 169, 170, 172, 175, 176, 207, 264, 320
River Oli, 32, 39, 321
River Soto, 32
Royal Niger Company, 173, 175, 178, 182
Royal West African Frontier Force, x, 24, 185

S

Sabi-Kpai, 74
Sabukki, 226
Sahara, 49, 52, 103, 121, 129, 134, 140, 358, 361, 372, 374, 380
Saint Domingue, 131
Salaga, 125, 126, 127, 137, 142, 162
Sango, 149, 159
Sansanni, 39
Sao Tome, 131
Saraki, Olusola, 327
Sardauna, 252, 253
Sarraut, Albert, 261
Sarsako, 33
Say-Barruwa line, 175
Second Development Plan, 340
Second Republic, 318, 326, 387
Second World War, 199, 234, 238, 250, 263, 296
Segbana, 38, 47, 141
Seligman, C. G., 49

Sen, Amartya, 338, 392
Senegal, 40, 50, 217
Seru Kperu, 33, 66
Sha, Dung Pam, xiii
Shagunu, 39, 46, 65, 80, 201, 226, 228, 229, 322
Shaki, 108, 158, 164, 270
Shea butter, 125, 170
Shereno, 39
Shifting cultivation, 46
Shori, 183
Sijilmasa, 126
Simpson, Ward, 196
Sinade, 235
Slave labour, 128
Small Towns Development Policy, 345
Smith, Abdullahi, 25, 51, 147, 156, 157, 160, 354, 359, 367, 369
Sokoto, 23, 59, 83, 126, 131, 135, 136, 137, 138, 148, 152, 153, 156, 161, 163, 176, 182, 196, 198, 199, 210, 224, 232, 255, 270, 275, 295, 323, 340, 349, 367, 374
Sokoto Caliphate, 23, 83, 126, 131, 137, 148, 152, 153, 156, 161, 199, 210, 224, 255, 340, 349
Somba, 37, 238
Somborgu, 37
Songhai, v, 23, 26, 30, 32, 34, 51, 56, 57, 62, 63, 74, 82, 83, 86, 94, 95, 102, 110, 148, 149, 150, 151, 152, 155, 156, 157, 365
Songhay Empire, 40, 70, 135, 152, 369
Soninke, 47, 83, 149, 150, 368
Sorou, Sero, 116
Sorubu, 37
South America, xvi
Southern Rhodesia, 50
St. Philip, 133
State Counsel, 93
Sub-Native Authority Council, 246
Sudan, 30, 33, 36, 38, 40, 41, 50, 51, 58, 129, 135, 136, 150, 179, 312, 353, 358, 359, 364, 365, 368, 372, 374
Sudanic Civilisation, 49, 50
Suku-Suku, Woru, 227, 228
Sultan of Niki, 58
Suma'ila, Mohammed, 248
Suno, Bagou, 63, 64, 88, 90, 91, 92, 93, 99, 155, 194, 212, 214, 215, 220, 246, 256, 287, 289
Suzerainty, 47, 180, 204, 244, 285

T

Tabera, 66, 146, 194
Taberu, 66, 108, 185, 186
Taneka, 37
Tapa, 131
Tasude, Mora, 95, 109, 144, 177, 180, 183, 194, 197, 211, 212, 213, 214, 227, 243, 257, 281, 282, 283, 284, 285
Taxation, 198, 204, 205, 380
Temple, C. L., 53, 54, 283, 359
Territorial mapping, 280
Tienga, 37, 46, 47, 64, 65
Timbuktu, 40, 50, 56, 128, 129, 135, 151, 156, 169, 180, 357, 359
Tiv, 59, 381
Togo-Ghana borderlands, xvii
Tomtaro, 63, 64, 92
Toro, Dan, 41, 154, 155, 183
Toronkawa, 41
Town Council, 200, 201
Traore, Karim, ii
Turaki, 197, 225, 226, 227, 229, 230, 231, 244, 375

U

Ubandoma, 200, 204, 245, 248, 253

Ulakami Island, 197
Umoru, Ajia, 227, 289
United States of America, 173, 323
Upper Black Volta River, 70
Upper Volta, 234
Usani, Nkechi, xiv
US-Mexico border, xv

V

Village Heads, 198, 202, 205, 206, 246, 253
Village Household Sheets, 206
Voltaic language group, 36
Von Pawlikowski, Herr, 179

W

Wangara, 30, 35, 40, 56, 69, 70, 71, 81, 82, 83, 84, 93, 116, 118, 123, 125, 128, 131, 134, 135, 137, 138, 140, 141, 146, 147, 148, 150, 153, 155, 161, 170, 214, 220, 267, 296, 352, 353, 355, 357, 360, 363, 364, 368
Wasangari, 34, 35, 62, 64, 71, 74, 76, 77, 82, 84, 85, 86, 87, 88, 89, 91, 98, 103, 104, 111, 128, 140, 142, 144, 145, 149, 150, 152, 155, 219, 220, 222, 234, 294, 296, 297, 351, 352, 355, 357, 360
Wawa, 37, 38, 39, 46, 59, 64, 65, 66, 68, 79, 88, 94, 95, 97, 98, 102, 103, 106, 107, 108, 109, 119, 124, 125, 128, 129, 130, 141, 146, 153, 161, 162, 163, 176, 183, 197, 201, 202, 203, 207, 213, 227, 246, 253, 258, 266, 269, 275, 291, 292, 313, 321, 324, 340, 344
Waziri, 54, 200, 203, 204
Wehene, Yon, 120
Wenususu, 47
Weregu, 79

West Africa, xvii, 23, 24, 32, 33, 40, 51, 62, 82, 124, 126, 129, 131, 132, 134, 149, 156, 162, 169, 171, 174, 175, 176, 182, 215, 217, 218, 220, 221, 231, 234, 266, 271, 272, 273, 308, 312, 318, 337, 344, 348, 352, 356, 357, 361, 363, 364, 365, 367, 368, 371, 372, 373, 374, 376, 378, 379, 381, 383, 384, 386
West African Islamic historiography, 50
Western Plateau, 39
Western Region, 268, 289
Western Sudan, 151
Whittlesey, Derwent, 323
Wilson, R. C, 276, 380
Witchcraft, 67, 81, 105, 114, 120
Witwatersrand, Johannesburg, South Africa, xvii
Woaba, 37
World Bank, x, 314
Wozibe, 64, 65, 66, 80, 96, 114

Y

Yakubu, Mahmood, xiii, 248, 250, 257, 361, 362, 374, 375, 378, 381, 382, 383
Yamma, Aliu Sarkin, 213
Yaru, Woru, 184, 212, 244, 251, 255, 256, 283, 291, 352, 357, 361
Yashikira, 36, 65, 100, 144, 145, 150, 186, 188, 194, 197, 201, 202, 205, 208, 212, 213, 214, 244, 246, 249, 253, 254, 269, 276, 280, 283, 285, 290, 291, 322, 330, 344, 384
Yashikira Trunk Road, 322
Yaurawa, 32, 353
Yauri, 30, 39, 59, 107, 111, 128, 130, 136, 141, 152, 153, 154, 196, 197, 207, 212, 213, 225, 228, 229, 232, 244, 251, 268, 269, 367

Yelwa, 32, 153, 197, 213, 227, 229, 232, 244, 267
Yemen, 51
Yerima (Baa Giya Kpandu), Musa Zume, xii
Yerima, Sabi, 96, 107, 184, 235, 287
Yoabu, 37, 38
Yola, 180, 248
Yoobu, 76
Yoruba, v, 23, 32, 34, 36, 50, 80, 106, 111, 125, 129, 131, 132, 134, 140, 141, 149, 155, 156, 157, 158, 159, 162, 163, 164, 200, 279, 305, 306, 315, 356, 359, 361, 366, 367, 368, 387
Yorubaphone, 37

Z

Zabarma, 37, 212
Zaberma, 135
Zakana, 33, 73, 91, 95
Zakari, Tanimudari, xiii
Zali, 65, 226, 227
Zamfara State, xx, 79
Zanzibar, 126, 174
Zaputa, 79
Zaria, 136, 138, 155, 270, 354, 359, 362, 367, 368, 372, 375
Zarma, 149
Zarmaganda, 148
Zekana shrine, 64
Zoughou, 133
Zungeru, 227, 267, 319
Zuru, 228
Zzono, 76, 77

www.ingramcontent.com/pod-product-compliance
Lightning Source LLC
Chambersburg PA
CBHW021815300426
44114CB00009BA/181